2D Apple Games by Tutorials

By the raywenderlich.com Tutorial Team

Caroline Begbie, Mike Berg, Michael Briscoe, Ali Hafizji,
Marin Todorov and Ray Wenderlich

2D Apple Games by Tutorials

Caroline Begbie, Mike Berg, Michael Briscoe, Ali Hafizji, Marin Todorov and Ray Wenderlich

Copyright ©2016 Razeware LLC.

ISBN: 978-1-942878-28-5

Dedications

"For my mum, who frequently challenges and always inspires me; also for Muffin, my patient and loyal puppy."

— *Caroline Begbie*

"To my wonderful wife and family, who make it possible to do what I do."

— *Mike Berg*

"To my father who ignited my love of computers. To my daughters Meghan and Brynne, and all six of my grandchildren. And to Lindsay for all the love and support."

— *Michael Briscoe*

"To my wife for always being supportive and to our bun in the oven, your parents await your arrival."

— *Kauserali Hafizji (a.k.a. Ali)*

"To my father."

— *Marin Todorov*

"To the authors, editors and leads at raywenderlich.com. Teamwork lets you dream bigger!"

— *Ray Wenderlich*

About the authors

Caroline Begbie is living the dream as an indie iOS developer, educator and explorer. She loves the graphics and animation side of iOS and watches Disney movies "for research."

Mike Berg is a full time game artist who is fortunate enough to work with many different indie game developers from all over the world. When he's not manipulating pixel colors, he loves to eat good food, spend time with his family, play games and be happy.

Michael Briscoe is an independent software developer with over 30 years of programming experience. Learning BASIC on a Commodore 64 way back in 1984, he's been hooked on coding ever since. He enjoys creating simulations and games for all Apple platforms. You can visit his website at skyrocketsoftware.wordpress.com.

Kauserali Hafizji (a.k.a. Ali) is a freelance software developer. He is fortunate to have worked on several large projects. He loves creating software that people use everyday whether it's on the web, watch, phone or tv. A good read, cool dip in the pool and a hot cheesy meal would be the perfect end to his weekend. You can find out more about Ali on his website at: alihafizji.com.

Marin Todorov is a part of Realm and raywenderlich.com. He's also the author of books and apps. You can find out more at www.underplot.com.

Ray Wenderlich is part of a great team — the raywenderlich.com team, a group of over 100 developers and editors from across the world. He and the rest of the team are passionate both about making apps and teaching others the techniques to make them. When Ray's not programming, he's probably playing video games, role playing games, or board games.

About the editors

Kyle Gorlick is the tech editor of this book. Kyle is a software developer currently focused on mobile apps and games. When not developing, he likes to watch basketball and play volleyball. You can learn more about him and what he's working on at kylegorlick.com.

Chris Belanger is the editor of this book. Chris is the Book Team Lead and Lead Editor for raywenderlich.com. If there are words to wrangle or a paragraph to ponder, he's on the case. When he kicks back, you can usually find Chris with guitar in hand, looking for the nearest beach, or exploring the lakes and rivers in his part of the world in a canoe.

Tammy Coron is the final pass editor of this book. Tammy is an independent creative professional and the host of two podcasts — Roundabout: Creative Chaos and Invisible Red. She's also the founder of Just Write Code, a small independent production company based in West Tennessee. Find out more at tammycoron.com.

About the artists

Mike Berg created the artwork for most of the games in this book. Mike is a full time game artist who is fortunate enough to work with many different indie game developers from all over the world. When he's not manipulating pixel colors, he loves to eat good food, spend time with his family, play games and be happy.

Vinnie Prabhu created all the music and sounds for the games in this book. Vinnie is a music composer/software engineer from Northern Virginia who has created music and sound work for concerts, plays and video games. He's also a staff member on OverClocked ReMix, an online community for music and video game fans. You can find Vinnie on Twitter as @palpablevt.

Vicki Wenderlich created many of the illustrations in this book and the artwork for Drop Charge. Vicki is Ray's wife and business partner. She is a digital artist who creates illustrations, game art and a lot of other art or design work for the tutorials and books on raywenderlich.com. She also runs gameartguppy.com, which is a website where she creates free and inexpensive art assets for game developers to use in their games. When she's not making art, she loves hiking, a good glass of wine and attempting to create the perfect cheese plate.

Table of Contents:

Introduction

In this book, you'll learn how to make 2D games for iOS, macOS, tvOS and even watchOS. You'll do this using Swift and Apple's built-in 2D game framework: SpriteKit. However, this raises a number of questions:

- **Why SpriteKit?** SpriteKit is Apple's built-in framework for making 2D games. It's easy to learn, especially if you already have some Swift or iOS experience.

- **Why iOS?** For a game developer, there's no better platform. The development tools are well-designed and easy to learn. Plus, the App Store makes it incredibly simple to distribute your game to a massive audience — and get paid for it!

- **Why macOS, tvOS and watchOS?** One of the great things about SpriteKit is that it works on iOS, macOS, tvOS and watchOS. If you get your game running on iOS, it's incredibly easy to get it working on the other platforms too.

- **Why Swift?** Swift is an easy language to learn, especially if you're new to programming.

- **Why 2D?** As impressive as 3D games may be, 2D games are a lot easier to make. The artwork is far less complicated, and programming is faster and doesn't require as much math. All of this allows you, as a developer, to focus on creating killer gameplay.

If you're a beginner, making 2D games is definitely the best way to get started.

If you're an advanced developer, making a 2D game is still much faster than making a 3D game. Since it's not necessarily the case that you earn more money with 3D games, why not go for the easier win? Plus, some people prefer 2D games anyway!

So rest easy — with 2D games and SpriteKit, you're making great choices!

History of this book

Three years ago, we wrote a book named *iOS Games by Tutorials*, covering how to make 2D games with SpriteKit. One year later, we released a second edition fully ported to Swift, as a free update for existing customers. One year after that, we completely revamped it, renamed it and released it as *2D iOS & tvOS Games by Tutorials*. This year, we're doing it again with *2D Apple Games by Tutorials*.

At WWDC 2016, Apple announced a lot of cool new features to both SpriteKit and Xcode, including built-in tile map support and the ability to run SpriteKit on watchOS. Yes, you read that correctly!

These changes were so significant that we decided it would be better to completely revamp the book (again!) — we even included new games!

If you already read *2D iOS & tvOS Games by Tutorials* and you're wondering what's new in this book, here are the highlights:

- **Zombie Conga**: Chapters 1-6 are mostly the same, with some minor updates to support Swift 3 and iOS 10. We also removed the chapter showing how to port the game to tvOS; that's because we added a brand new section, "Section V: Other Platforms", which covers this topic — and more — in greater detail.

- **Cat Nap**: These chapters also remain the same, with some minor updates to support Swift 3 and iOS 10. Just like we did with Zombie Conga, we removed the chapter showing how to port the game to tvOS.

- **Pest Control**: First introduced in *iOS Games by Tutorials*, this new and improved version shows you how to use the new tile maps features in SpriteKit (Chapters 12-13), as well as how to save and load game data (Chapter 14).

- **Drop Charge**: In these chapters, you'll review previous material in the book and learn about simple state machines, particle systems and juice, all updated for Swift 3 and iOS 10. Because Apple released so many new features for GameplayKit this year, we decided it would be too much to properly cover in this book. As such, the chapters dealing with GameplayKit have been removed, and will be covered elsewhere.

- **Zombie Piranhas**: These new chapters introduce you to a new game specifically designed to teach you how to work with other Apple platforms like macOS, tvOS and watchOS (Chapters 18-20).

- **CircuitRacer**: These chapters were also updated for Swift 3 and iOS 10. However, since Apple has abandoned iAd, we removed the chapter which covered that topic.

As you can see, it's somewhat of a major overhaul. If you read the book before, but want to read it again and have limited time, the best thing to do is focus on the new games, or the chapters that interest you most.

About this book

This book is something special to us. Our goal at raywenderlich.com is for this to be the best book on 2D game programming you've ever read.

There are a lot of game programming books out there, and many of them are quite good, so this might be a lofty goal. But here's what we've done to try to accomplish it:

- **Learn by making games**: Other books teach the high-level concepts and show code snippets, but many leave you on your own to put together a complete, functioning game. In this book, you'll learn by making six games in a variety of genres — games that are actually fun. Our hope is that you can and will reuse techniques or code from these games to make your own games.

- **Learn by challenges**: Every chapter in this book includes some challenges at the end that are designed to help you practice what you've learned. Following a tutorial is one thing, but applying it yourself is quite another. The challenges in this book take off the training wheels and push you to solidify your knowledge by grappling with a problem on your own. Because we're not mean, we also provide the solutions to our challenges. But try not to look soon, or you might spoil the fun. =]

- **Focus on polish**: The key to making a hit game is polish — adding loads of well-considered details that set your game apart. Because of this, we've put our money where our mouths are and invested in a top-notch artist and sound designer to create resources for the games in this book. We've also included a chapter all about polishing your game with special effects — otherwise known as adding "Juice" — which we think you'll love.

- **High-quality tutorials**: Our site is known for its high-quality programming tutorials, and we've put a lot of time and care into the tutorials in this book to make them equally valuable, if not more so. Each chapter has been put through a rigorous multi-stage editing process — resulting in some chapters being rewritten several times! We've strived to ensure that each chapter contains great technical content while also being fun and easy to follow.

After you finish reading this book, please let us know if you think we were successful in meeting these goals. You can email Ray anytime at ray@raywenderlich.com.

We hope you enjoy the book — we can't wait to see what games you make on your own!

iOS game development: a history

As you'll see, it's easy to make games with SpriteKit — but it wasn't always so. In the early days of iOS, your only option was to make your game with OpenGL ES, which (along with Metal) is the lowest-level graphics API available on the platform. OpenGL ES is notoriously difficult to learn, and it was a big barrier to entry for many beginning game developers.

After a while, third-party developers released some game frameworks on top of OpenGL, the most popular of which was called Cocos2D — in fact, several of us wrote a book on the subject! Many of the games at the top of the App Store charts were made with Cocos2D, and many developers can say that Cocos2D was their entry point into the world of game development.

Cocos2D was a great framework, but it wasn't written or supported by Apple. Because of this, there were often problems when new versions of iOS were released, or with integrating other Apple APIs into the system.

To resolve this, with iOS 7 Apple released a new framework for making 2D games: SpriteKit. Its API is very similar to Cocos2D, with similar types for the sprites, actions and scenes that Cocos2D developers know and love, so fans of the older framework will have no trouble getting up to speed. SpriteKit also has a few extra bells and whistles, like support for playing videos, making shapes and applying special image effects.

The SpriteKit API is well-designed and easy to use, especially for beginners. Best of all, you can use it knowing that it's fully supported by Apple and heavily optimized to make 2D games on iOS — and now with support for macOS, tvOS and watchOS, it makes it the clear choice for Apple 2D game development.

From here on out, if you want to make a 2D game on iOS, macOS, tvOS and watchOS, we definitely recommend using SpriteKit rather than other game frameworks. There's one big exception: if you want to make a cross platform game (i.e. for Android, Windows, etc). SpriteKit is an Apple-only API so it will be more challenging to port your game from SpriteKit to other platforms than using other options such as Unity. If you're interested in learning Unity, please check out our newly released book, *Unity Games by Tutorials*, which you can order here: https://www.raywenderlich.com/store/unity-games-by-tutorials.

If you just want to make something simple for Apple platforms only, SpriteKit is the way to go. So let's get you up to speed with SpriteKit!

What you need

To follow along with the tutorials in this book, you need the following:

- **A Mac running OS X El Capitan or later.** This is so you can install the latest version of the required development tool: Xcode.

- **Xcode 8.0 or later.** Xcode is the main development tool for Apple platforms. You need to use Xcode 8.0 or later in this book. You can download the latest version of Xcode for free from the Apple developer site: https://developer.apple.com/xcode/download/

- **An iPhone or iPad running iOS 10 or later, and a paid membership to the iOS development program [optional].** For most of the chapters in the book, you can run your code on the iOS 10 Simulator that comes with Xcode. However, there are a few chapters later in the book that require a device for testing. Also note that SpriteKit performs better on physical devices than it does in the Simulator, so your frame rates will appear lower than expected when running your game in the Simulator.

- **An Apple TV [optional]:** You do not need an Apple TV since you can work with the Apple TV simulator, but it's definitely handy to test with a physical remote — plus awesome to see your games on the big screen!

- **An Apple Watch [optional]:** Just like you do not need an Apple TV, you also do not need an Apple Watch; using the simulator is perfectly acceptable.

If you don't have the latest version of Xcode installed, be sure to do that before continuing with the book.

Who this book is for

This book is for beginning to advanced iOS developers. Wherever you fall on that spectrum, you'll learn a lot from this book!

This book does require some basic knowledge of Swift. If you do not know Swift, you can still follow along with the book because all of the instructions are in step-by-step format. However, there will likely be parts that are confusing due to gaps in your knowledge. Before beginning this book, you might want to go through our Swift Apprentice series, which covers the basics of Swift development:

- www.raywenderlich.com/store

How to use this book

There are two ways to use this book, depending on whether you are a complete beginner to Apple game development or an advanced developer with knowledge of other 2D game frameworks.

If you are a complete beginner

If you're a complete beginner to Apple game development, the best way to read this book is from cover to cover. We have arranged the chapters to introduce the material in the most logical manner to build up your skills one layer at a time.

If you are an advanced developer

If you're an advanced developer with knowledge of other 2D game frameworks, you'll have an easier time adapting to SpriteKit, as the core concepts and syntax will look very familiar.

Our suggestion is to skim through the early chapters and focus more on the later, more advanced chapters, or where you have a particular interest.

Don't worry — you can jump right into any chapter in the book, because we'll always have a starter project waiting for you!

What's ahead: an overview

2D Apple Games by Tutorials is split into six sections, moving from beginning to advanced topics. In each section, you'll create a complete mini-game, from scratch! The book also includes a bonus chapter at the end that we think you'll enjoy.

Take a look at what's ahead!

Section I: Getting started

This section covers the basics of making 2D games with SpriteKit. These are the most important techniques, the ones you'll use in almost every game you make. By the time you reach the end of this section, you'll be ready to make your own simple game.

Throughout this section, you'll create an action game named Zombie Conga, where you take the role of a happy-go-lucky zombie who just wants to party!

There are six chapters in this section; they are:

1. **Chapter 1, Sprites**: Get started by adding your first sprites to the game: the background and the zombie.

2. **Chapter 2, Manual Movement**: You'll make the zombie follow your touches around the screen and get a crash-course in basic 2D vector math.

3. **Chapter 3, Actions**: You'll add cats and crazy cat ladies to the game, as well as basic collision detection and gameplay.

4. **Chapter 4, Scenes**: You'll add a main menu to the game, as well as win and lose scenes.

5. **Chapter 5, Camera**: You'll make the game scroll from left to right, and finally, add the conga line itself.

6. **Chapter 6, Labels**: You'll add a label to show the zombie's lives and the number of cats in his conga line.

Section II: Physics and nodes

In this section, you'll learn how to use the built-in 2D physics engine included with SpriteKit. You'll also learn how to use special types of nodes that allow you to play videos and create shapes in your game.

In the process, you'll create a physics puzzle game named Cat Nap, where you take the role of a cat who has had a long day and just wants to go to bed.

7. **Chapter 7, Scene Editor**: You'll begin by creating the first level of the game. You'll gain a better understanding of Xcode's level designer, better known as the scene editor.

8. **Chapter 8, Beginning Physics**: In this chapter, you're going to take a little detour in order to learn the basics of creating physics simulations for your games. As a bonus, you'll learn how to prototype games inside an Xcode playground.

9. **Chapter 9, Intermediate Physics**: You'll learn about physics-based collision detection and create custom classes for your SpriteKit nodes.

10. **Chapter 10, Advanced Physics**: You'll add two more levels to the game as you learn about interactive bodies, joints between bodies, composed bodies and more.

11. **Chapter 11, Crop, Video and Shape Nodes**: You'll add special new blocks to Cat Nap while learning about additional types of nodes that allow you to do amazing things, like play videos, crop images and create dynamic shapes.

Section III: Tile Maps

In this section, you'll learn about tile maps in SpriteKit and how to save and load game data.

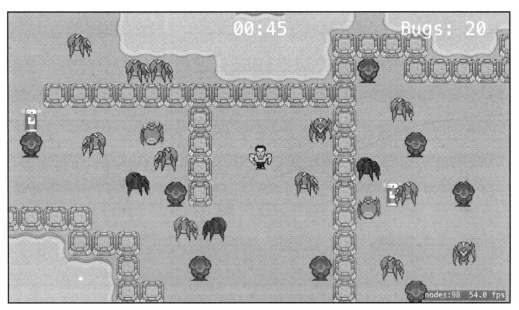

In the process, you'll create a game named Pest Control, where you take control of a vigorous, impossibly ripped he-man named Arnie. Your job is to lead Arnie to bug-fighting victory by squishing all those pesky bugs.

There are three chapters in this section; they are:

12. **Chapter 12, Beginning Tile Maps**: You'll learn the basics about tile maps in SpriteKit by creating a tile set and a background tile map.

13. **Chapter 13, Intermediate Tile Maps**: You'll take things a step further by learning how to access tile maps in code and how to create a tile map with randomly placed tiles.

14. **Chapter 14, Saving and Loading Games**: You'll finish up by adding a winning end state and a heads-up display. You'll also learn how to automatically save the game when you leave it and then reload it from where you left off.

Section IV: Juice

In this section, you'll learn how to take a good game and make it great by adding a ton of special effects and excitement — also known as "juice."

In the process, you'll create a game named Drop Charge, where you're a space hero with a mission to blow up an alien space ship — and escape with your life before it explodes. To do this, you must jump from platform to platform, collecting special boosts along the way. Just be careful not to fall into the red hot lava!

There are three chapters in this section; they are:

15. **Chapter 15, Making Drop Charge**: You'll put together the basic gameplay using the scene editor and code, flexing the SpriteKit muscles you've developed working through previous chapters.

16. **Chapter 16, Particle Systems**: You'll learn how to use particle systems to create amazing special effects.

17. **Chapter 17, Juice Up Your Game**: You'll trick out your game with music, sound, animation, more particles and other special effects, experiencing for yourself the benefits of mastering the details.

Section V: Other Platforms

In this section, you'll learn how to leverage your iOS knowledge to build games for the other Apple Platforms: macOS, tvOS and watchOS.

In the process, you'll create a game named Zombie Piranhas. In this game, your goal is to catch as many fish as possible without hooking a zombie — because we all know what happens when zombies are around.

There are three chapters in this section; they are:

18. **Chapter 18, macOS Games**: You'll take a complete iOS game and add a target for macOS. Along the way, you'll learn some of the differences between the platforms, such as windows and mouse and keyboard events.

19. **Chapter 19, tvOS Games**: Building from Chapter 18, you'll add another target for tvOS. You'll learn concepts such as Focus and parallax icons, Top Shelf and working with the Apple TV Remote.

20. **Chapter 20, watchOS Games**: Lastly, you'll add a target for watchOS, and you'll learn about gestures, the Digital Crown and Haptic Feedback. You'll also discover some of the design considerations when working with a small device.

Section VI: Advanced Topics

In this section, you'll learn some APIs other than SpriteKit that are good to know when making games for the Apple platforms. In particular, you'll learn how to add Game Center leaderboards and achievements into your game. You'll also learn how to use the ReplayKit API.

In the process, you'll integrate these APIs into a top-down racing game named Circuit Racer, where you take the role of an elite race car driver out to set a world record — which wouldn't be a problem if all this debris wasn't on the track!

21. **Chapter 21, Game Center Achievements**: Enable Game Center for your game and award the user achievements for accomplishing certain feats.

22. **Chapter 22, Game Center Leaderboards**: Set up various leaderboards for your game and track and report the player's scores.

23. **Chapter 27, ReplayKit**: You'll learn how to allow players to record and share videos of their games with ReplayKit.

Section VI: Bonus chapter

And that's not all — on top of the above, we included a bonus chapter about making your own game art:

29. **Chapter 29, Making Art for Programmers**: If you liked the art in these mini-games and want to learn how to either hire an artist or make some art of your own, look no further than this chapter! This chapter guides you through drawing a cute cat in the style of this book with Illustrator.

Book source code and forums

You can get the source code for the book here:

www.raywenderlich.com/store/2d-ios-tvos-games-by-tutorials/source-code

You'll find all the code from the chapters, as well as solutions to the challenges for your reference.

We've also set up an official forum for the book at www.raywenderlich.com/forums. This is a great place to ask any questions you have about the book, or to submit any errors you might find.

PDF Version

We also have a PDF version of this book available, which can be handy if you want a soft copy to take with you, or you want to quickly search for a specific term within the book.

Buying the PDF version of the book also has a few extra benefits: free PDF updates each time we update the book, access to older PDF versions of the book, and you can download the PDF from anywhere, at anytime.

Visit the book store page here: raywenderlich.com/store/2d-ios-tvos-games-by-tutorials.

License

By purchasing 2D Apple Games by Tutorials, you acquire the following license:

- You are allowed to use and/or modify the source code provided with 2D Apple Games by Tutorials in as many games as you want, with no attribution required.

- You are allowed to use and/or modify all art, music and sound effects that are included with 2D Apple Games by Tutorials in as many games as you want, but must include this attribution line somewhere inside your game: "Artwork/sounds: from 2D Apple Games by Tutorials book, available at http://www.raywenderlich.com."

- The source code included in 2D Apple Games by Tutorials is for your personal use only. You are NOT allowed to distribute or sell the source code in 2D Apple Games by Tutorials without prior authorization.

- This book is for your personal use only. You are NOT allowed to sell this book without prior authorization, or distribute it to friends, co-workers or students — they would need to purchase their own copy.

All materials provided with this book are provided on an "as-is" basis, without warranty of any kind, express or implied, including but not limited to the warranties of merchantability, fitness for a particular purpose and non-infringement. In no event shall the authors or copyright holders be liable for any claim, damages or other liability, whether in an action of contract, tort or otherwise, arising from, out of or in connection with the software or the use or other dealings in the software.

All trademarks and registered trademarks appearing in this guide are the property of their respective owners.

Acknowledgements

We would like to thank many people for their assistance in making this book possible:

- **Our families**: For bearing with us during this hectic time as we worked all hours of the night to get this book ready for publication!

- **Everyone at Apple**: For developing an amazing 2D game framework and other helpful APIs for games, for constantly inspiring us to improve our apps and skills, and for making it possible for many developers to have their dream jobs! Special thanks for the Apple TV dev kits as well. :]

- **Ricardo Quesada**: Ricardo is the lead developer of Cocos2D, which got many of us into making games. SpriteKit seems to draw quite a bit of inspiration from Cocos2D, so Ricardo deserves "mad props" for that as well.

- And most importantly, **the readers of raywenderlich.com and you**! Thank you so much for reading our site and purchasing this book. Your continued readership and support is what makes this all possible!

Section I: Getting Started

This section covers the basics of making 2D games with SpriteKit. These are the most important techniques, the ones you'll use in almost every game you make. By the time you reach the end of this section, you'll be ready to make your own simple game.

Throughout this section, you'll create an action game named Zombie Conga, where you take the role of a happy-go-lucky zombie who just wants to party!

Chapter 1: Sprites

By Ray Wenderlich

Now that you know what SpriteKit is and why you should use it, it's time to try it out for yourself!

The first minigame you'll build in this book is named Zombie Conga. Here's what it will look like when you're finished:

In Zombie Conga, you take the role of a happy-go-lucky zombie who wants to party!

Luckily, the beach town you occupy has an overly abundant cat population. You simply need to bite them and they'll join your zombie conga line.

But watch out for crazy cat ladies! These wizened warriors in red dresses won't take kindly to anyone stealing their beloved cats and will do their best to make the zombie rest in peace — permanently.

You will build this game across the next six chapters, in stages:

1. **Chapter 1, Sprites**: You are here! Get started by adding your first sprites to the game: the background and the zombie.

2. **Chapter 2, Manual Movement**: You'll make the zombie follow your touches around the screen and get a crash course in basic 2D vector math.

3. **Chapter 3, Actions**: You'll add cats and crazy cat ladies to the game, as well as basic collision detection and gameplay.

4. **Chapter 4, Scenes**: You'll add a main menu to the game, as well as win and lose scenes.

5. **Chapter 5, Camera**: You'll make the game scroll from left to right, and finally, add the conga line itself.

6. **Chapter 6, Labels**: You'll add labels to show the zombie's number of lives and the number of cats in his conga line.

Time to get this conga started!

Getting started

Start Xcode and select **File > New > Project...** from the main menu. Select the **iOS/Application/Game** template and click **Next**.

Enter **ZombieConga** for the Product Name, choose **Swift** for Language, **SpriteKit** for Game Technology, **Universal** for Devices and click **Next**.

Select somewhere on your hard drive to save your project and click **Create**. At this point, Xcode will generate a simple SpriteKit starter project for you.

Take a look at what SpriteKit made. In Xcode's toolbar, select the iPhone 7 Plus and click **Play**.

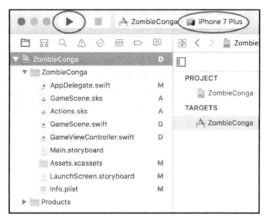

After a brief splash screen, you'll see a single label that says, "Hello, World!". When you drag your mouse across the screen, the text will bounce and some spinning rounded rectangles will appear.

In SpriteKit, a single object called a **scene** controls each "screen" of your app. Scenes are represented by SpriteKit's `SKScene` class.

Right now, this app just has a single scene: `GameScene`. Open **GameScene.swift** and you'll see the code that displays the label and the spinning rounded rectangles.

It's not important to understand this code quite yet — you're going to remove it all and build your game one step at a time.

For now, delete everything in **GameScene.swift** and replace it with the following:

```swift
import SpriteKit

class GameScene: SKScene {
  override func didMove(to view: SKView) {
    backgroundColor = SKColor.black
  }
}
```

Note that `GameScene` is a subclass of `SKScene`. SpriteKit calls the method `didMove(to:)` before it presents your scene in a view; it's a good place to do some initial setup of your scene's contents. Here, you simply set the background color to black.

Zombie Conga is designed to run in landscape mode, so you need configure the app for this. Select the **ZombieConga** project in the project navigator and then select the **ZombieConga** target. Go to the **General** tab and make sure only **Landscape Left** and **Landscape Right** are checked.

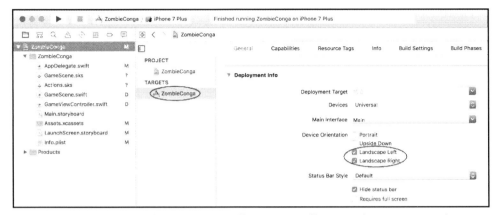

The SpriteKit project template automatically creates a file named **GameScene.sks**. You can edit this file with Xcode's built-in scene editor to lay out your game scene visually. Think of the scene editor as a simple Interface Builder for SpriteKit.

You'll learn all about the scene editor in Chapter 7, "Scene Editor", but you won't be using it for Zombie Conga as it will be easier and more instructive to create the sprites programmatically instead.

Control-click **GameScene.sks**, select **Delete** and then select **Move to Trash**. While you're at it, also delete **Actions.sks**, another file you won't need for this game.

Since you're no longer using these files, you'll have to modify the template code appropriately.

Open **GameViewController.swift** and replace the contents with the following:

```swift
import UIKit
import SpriteKit

class GameViewController: UIViewController {
  override func viewDidLoad() {
    super.viewDidLoad()
    let scene =
      GameScene(size:CGSize(width: 2048, height: 1536))
    let skView = self.view as! SKView
    skView.showsFPS = true
    skView.showsNodeCount = true
    skView.ignoresSiblingOrder = true
    scene.scaleMode = .aspectFill
    skView.presentScene(scene)
  }

  override var prefersStatusBarHidden: Bool {
    return true
  }
}
```

Previously, the view controller loaded the scene from **GameScene.sks**, but now it creates the scene by calling an initializer on GameScene instead.

Notice that when you create the scene, you pass in a hard-coded size of **2048x1536** and set the scale mode to aspectFill.

This is a good time for a quick discussion about how this game is designed to work as a universal app.

Universal app support

> **Note:** This section is optional and for those who are especially curious. If you're eager to get coding as soon as possible, feel free to skip to the next section, "Adding the art".

We've designed all the games in this book as universal apps, which means they will work on the iPhone and the iPad. The scenes for the games in this book have been designed with a base size of 2048x1536, or reversed for portrait orientation, with the scale mode set to aspect fill.

Aspect fill instructs SpriteKit to scale the scene's content to fill the entire screen, even if SpriteKit needs to cut off some of the content to do so. This results in your scene appearing as-is on the iPad Retina (excluding the 12.9-inch iPad Pro), which has a resolution of 2048x1536, but as scaled/cropped on the iPhone to fit the phone's smaller size and different aspect ratio.

Here are a few examples of how the games in this book will look in landscape orientation on different devices, moving from smallest to largest aspect ratio:

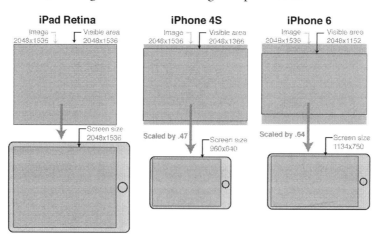

- **iPad Retina [4:3 or 1.33]**: Displayed as-is to fit the 2048x1536 screen size.

- **12.9-inch iPad Pro [4:3 or 1.33]**: Aspect fill will scale the 2048x1536 visible area by 1.33 to fit the 2732x2048 screen.

- **iPad non-Retina [4:3 or 1.33]**: Aspect fill will scale a 2048x1536 visible area by 0.5 to fit the 1024x768 screen.

- **iPhone 4s [3:2 or 1.5]**: Aspect fill will scale a 2048x1366 visible area by 0.47 to fit the 960x640 screen.

- **iPhone 5 [16:9 or 1.77]**: Aspect fill will scale a 2048x1152 visible area by 0.56 to fit the 1136x640 screen.

- **iPhone 6/7 [16:9 or 1.77]**: Aspect fill will scale a 2048x1152 visible area by 0.64 to fit the 1334x750 screen.

- **iPhone 6/7 Plus [16:9 or 1.77]**: Aspect fill will scale a 2048x1152 visible area by 0.93 to fit the 1920x1080 screen.

Since aspect fill will crop the scene on the top and bottom for iPhones, we've designed the games in this book to have a main "playable area" that is guaranteed to be visible on all devices. Basically, the games will have a 192-point margin on the top/bottom in landscape and the left/right in portrait, in which you should avoid putting essential content. We'll show you how to visualize this later in the book.

Note that you'll only use one set of art in this book: the art to fit the base size of 2048x1536. The art will be displayed as-is on iPad Retina, upscaled on the 12.9-inch iPad Pro and downscaled on other devices.

> **Note:** The downside of this approach is that the art will be bigger than necessary for some devices, such as the iPhone 4s, thereby wasting texture memory and space. The pro of this approach is that the game stays nice and simple and works well on all devices.
>
> An alternate approach would be to add different images as needed for each device and scale factor (i.e. iPad@1x, iPad@2x, iPhone@2x, iPhone@3x), leveraging the power of Xcode's asset catalogs. However, that would require generating a large set of images, so we will keep things simple for now.

Adding the art

Next, you need to add the game art to the project. In Xcode, open **Assets.xcassets**, select the **Spaceship** entry and press the Delete key to remove it — unfortunately, this is not a game about space zombies! :] At this point, only **AppIcon** will remain.

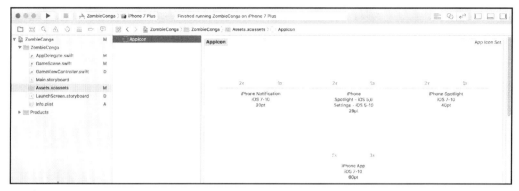

With **AppIcon** selected, drag the appropriate icon from **starter/resources/icons** into each slot:

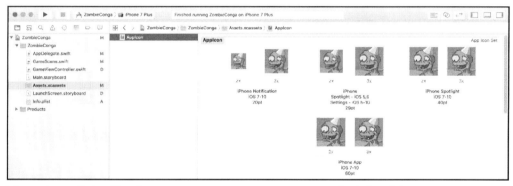

Then, drag all the files from **starter/resources/images** into the left sidebar:

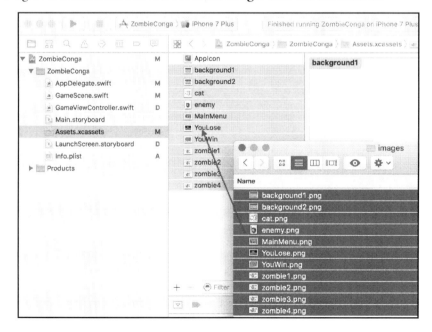

By including your images in the asset catalog, Xcode will automatically build **texture atlases** containing these images and use them in your game, which will automatically increase performance.

Launch screen

> **Note:** This is another optional section, as it won't have any impact on gameplay; it simply adds a "nice-to-have" feature that you'd typically want in a game. If you'd rather get straight to coding, feel free to skip to the next section, "Displaying a sprite".

There's one last thing you should do to get this game started on the right foot: configure the launch screen.

The launch screen is what iOS displays when your app is first loading, which usually takes a few seconds. Your app actually has a launch screen already. When you launched your app earlier, you may have noticed the brief, blank white screen. That was it!

A launch screen should give the player the impression that your app is starting quickly — the default white screen, needless to say, does not. For Zombie Conga, you'll show a splash screen with the name of the game.

In iOS, apps have a special **launch screen** file; this is basically a storyboard, **LaunchScreen.storyboard** in this project, that you can configure to present something onscreen while your app is loading. The advantage of this over the old method of just displaying an image is that you can use Auto Layout for finer control of the appearance of the screen on different devices.

Time to try this out. Open **LaunchScreen.storyboard**. You'll see the following:

From the Object Library in the Utilites Area, drag an **Image View** into the view and resize it to fill the entire area:

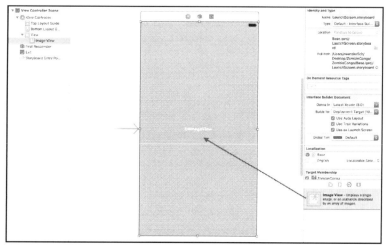

Next, you need to set the image view so that it always has the same width and height as its containing view. To do this, make sure the image view is selected and then click the **Pin** button in the lower right — it looks like a TIE fighter from Star Wars. In the Add New Constraints screen, click the four light-red lines so that the image view is pinned to each edge. Make sure that **Constrain to margins** isn't checked and that all values are set to 0, then click **Add 4 Constraints**.

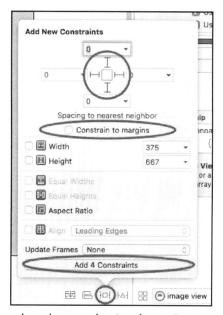

With the image view selected, make sure the Attributes Inspector — the fourth tab on the right — is showing. Set Image to **MainMenu** and set Content Mode to **Aspect Fill**.

Build and run your app again, and if necessary, rotate your simulator to the right with **Hardware > Rotate Right**. This time, you'll see a brief Zombie Conga splash screen:

Which will be quickly followed by a (mostly) blank, black screen:

This may not look like much, but you now have a starting point upon which to build your first SpriteKit game.

Move on to the next task, which also happens to be one of the most important and common when making games: displaying an image on the screen.

Displaying a sprite

When making a 2D game, you usually put images on the screen representing your game's various elements: the hero, enemies, bullets and so on. Each of these images is called a **sprite**.

Sprites

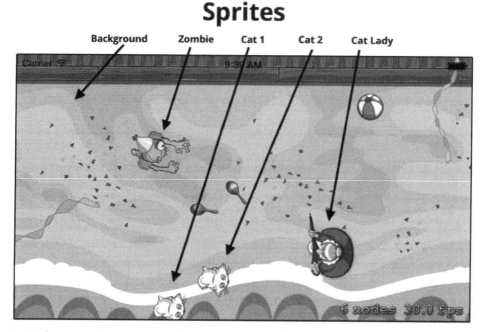

SpriteKit has a special class named SKSpriteNode that makes it easy to create and work with sprites. This is what you'll use to add all your sprites to the game.

Creating a sprite

Open **GameScene.swift** and add this line to didMove(to:), right after you set the background color:

```
let background = SKSpriteNode(imageNamed: "background1")
```

You don't need to pass the image's extension; SpriteKit will automatically determine that for you.

Build and run, ignoring the warning for now. Hmm, you still see a blank screen — what gives?

Adding a sprite to the scene

You haven't done anything wrong — it's just that a sprite won't show up onscreen until you add it as a child of the scene, or as one of the scene's descendant **nodes**.

To do this, add this line of code right after the previous line you added:

```
addChild(background)
```

You'll learn about nodes and scenes later. For now, build and run again, and you'll see part of the background appear in the bottom left of the screen:

Obviously, that's not quite what you want. To get the background in the correct spot, you have to set its position.

Positioning a sprite

By default, SpriteKit positions sprites so they are centered at (0, 0), which in SpriteKit represents the bottom left. Note that this is different from the UIKit coordinate system in iOS, where (0, 0) represents the top left.

Try positioning the background somewhere else by setting the position property. Add this line of code right before calling `addChild(background)`:

```
background.position = CGPoint(x: size.width/2, y: size.height/2)
```

Here, you position the background to the center of the scene. Even though this is a single line of code, there are four important things to understand:

1. The type of the `position` property is `CGPoint`, which is a simple structure that has x and y components:

```
public struct CGPoint {
    public var x: CGFloat
    public var y: CGFloat
    // ...
}
```

2. You can easily create a new `CGPoint` with the initializer shown above.

3. Since you're writing this code in an `SKScene` subclass, you can access the size of the scene at any time with the `size` property. The `size` property's type is `CGSize`, which is a simple structure like `CGPoint` that has width and height components.

```
public struct CGSize {
    public var width: CGFloat
```

```
    public var height: CGFloat
    // ...
}
```

4. A sprite's position is within the coordinate space of its parent node, which in this case is the scene itself. You'll learn more about this in Chapter 5, "Camera".

Build and run, and your background will be fully visible:

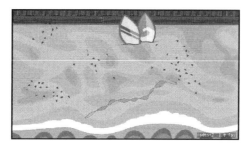

> **Note:** You may notice you can't see the entire background on iPhone devices — parts of it overlap on the top and bottom. This is by design, so the game will work on both the iPad and the iPhone, as discussed in the "Universal app support" section earlier in this chapter.

Setting a sprite's anchor point

Setting the position of the background sprite means setting the *center* of the sprite to that position.

This explains why you could only see the upper-right portion of the sprite earlier. Before you set the position, the position defaulted to (0, 0), which placed the center of the sprite in the lower-left corner of the screen.

You can change this behavior by setting a sprite's anchor point. Think of the anchor point as "the spot within a sprite that you pin to a particular position". Here's an illustration showing a sprite positioned at the center of the screen, but with different anchor points:

To see how this works, find the line that sets the background's position to the center of the scene and replace it with the following:

```
background.anchorPoint = CGPoint.zero
background.position = CGPoint.zero
```

CGPoint.zero is a handy shortcut for (0, 0). Here, you set the anchor point of the sprite to (0, 0) to pin the lower-left corner of the sprite to whatever position you set — in this case, also (0, 0).

Build and run, and the image is still in the right spot:

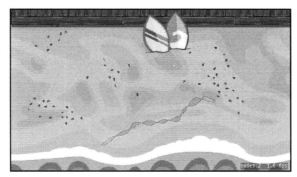

This works because now you're pinning the lower-left corner of the background image to the lower-left corner of the scene.

Here, you changed the anchor point of the background for learning purposes. However, usually you can leave the anchor point at its default of (0.5, 0.5), unless you have a specific need to rotate the sprite around a particular point — an example of which is described in the next section.

So, in short: when you set the position of a sprite, by default you are positioning the center of the sprite.

Rotating a sprite

To rotate a sprite, you simply set its zRotation property. Try it out on the background sprite by adding this line right before the call to addChild(_:):

```
background.zRotation = CGFloat(M_PI) / 8
```

Rotation values are in radians, which are units used to measure angles. This example rotates the sprite π / 8 radians, which is equal to 22.5 degrees. Also notice that you convert M_PI, which is a Double, into a CGFloat. You do this because zRotation requires a CGFloat and Swift doesn't automatically convert between types like some other languages do.

> **Note:** I don't know about you, but I find it easier to think about rotations in degrees rather than in radians. Later in the book, you'll create helper routines to convert between degrees and radians.

Build and run, and check out your rotated background sprite:

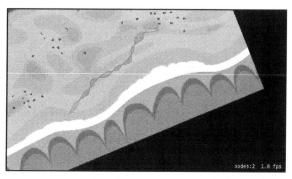

This demonstrates an important point: Sprites are rotated about their anchor points. Since you set this sprite's anchor point to (0, 0), it rotates around its bottom-left corner.

> **Note:** Remember that on the iPhone, the bottom-left of this image is actually offscreen! If you're not sure why this is, refer back to the "Universal app support" section earlier in this chapter.

Try rotating the sprite around the center instead. Replace the lines that set the anchor point and position with these:

```
background.anchorPoint = CGPoint(x: 0.5, y: 0.5) // default
background.position = CGPoint(x: size.width/2, y: size.height/2)
```

Build and run, and this time the background sprite will have rotated about the center:

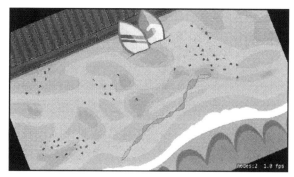

This is all good to know! But for Zombie Conga, you don't want a rotated background, so comment out that line:

```
// background.zRotation = CGFloat(M_PI) / 8
```

If you're wondering when you might want to change the anchor point in a game, imagine you're creating a character's body out of different sprites, one each for the head, torso, left arm, right arm, left leg and right leg:

If you wanted to rotate these body parts at their joints, you'd have to modify the anchor point for each sprite, as shown in the diagram above.

But again, usually you should leave the anchor point at default unless you have a specific need, like the one shown here.

Getting the size of a sprite

Sometimes when you're working with a sprite, you want to know how big it is. A sprite's size defaults to the size of the image. In SpriteKit, the class representing this image is called a texture.

Add these lines after the call to `addChild(_:)` to get the size of the background and log it to the console:

```
let mySize = background.size
print("Size: \(mySize)")
```

Build and run, and in your console output, you'll see something like this:

```
Size: (2048.0, 1536.0)
```

Sometimes it's useful to get the size of a sprite programmatically, as you do above, instead of hard-coding numbers. Your code will be much more robust and adaptable.

Sprites and nodes

Earlier, you learned that to make a sprite appear onscreen you need to add it as a child of the scene, or as one of the scene's descendant **nodes**. This section will delve more deeply into the concept of nodes.

Everything that appears on the screen in SpriteKit derives from a class named SKNode. Both the scene class (SKScene) and the sprite class (SKSpriteNode) derive from SKNode.

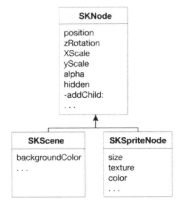

SKSpriteNode inherits a lot of its capabilities from SKNode. It turns out that the position and rotation properties are derived from SKNode rather than being particular to SKSpriteNode. This means that just as you can set the position or rotation of a sprite, you can do the same thing with the scene itself or with anything else that derives from SKNode.

You can think of everything that appears on the screen together as a graph of nodes, often referred to as a **scene graph**. Here's an example of what such a graph might look like for Zombie Conga if there were one zombie, two cats and one crazy cat lady in the game:

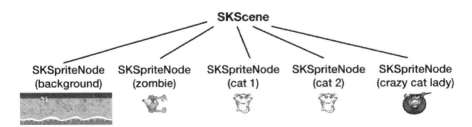

You'll learn more about nodes and the neat things you can do with them in Chapter 5, "Camera". For now, you'll add your sprites as direct children of the scene.

Nodes and z-position

Every node has a property you can set named `zPosition`, which defaults to 0. Each node draws its child nodes in the order of their z-position, from lowest to highest.

Earlier in this chapter, you added the following line to **GameViewController.swift**:

```
skView.ignoresSiblingOrder = true
```

- If **ignoresSiblingOrder** is **true**, SpriteKit makes no guarantee as to the order in which a node draws its child nodes that share the same `zPosition`.

- If **ignoresSiblingOrder** is **false**, a node will draw its child nodes that share the same `zPosition` in the order in which they were added to their parent.

In general, it's good to set this property to `true`, because it allows SpriteKit to perform optimizations under the hood to make your game run faster.

However, setting this property to `true` can cause problems if you're not careful. For example, if you were to add a zombie to this scene at the same `zPosition` as the background — which would happen if you left them at the default z-position of 0 — SpriteKit might draw the background on top of the zombie, covering the zombie from the player's view. And if zombies are scary, just imagine invisible ones!

To avoid this, you'll set the background's `zPosition` to −1. This way, SpriteKit will draw it before anything else you add to the scene, which will default to a `zPosition` of 0.

In **GameScene.swift**, add this line right before the call to `addChild(_:)`:

```
background.zPosition = -1
```

Phew! No invisible zombies.

Finishing touches

That's it for this chapter! As you can see, adding a sprite to a scene takes only three or four lines of code:

1. Create the sprite.

2. Position the sprite.

3. Optionally set the sprite's z-position.

4. Add the sprite to the scene graph.

Now it's time for you to test your newfound knowledge by adding the zombie to the scene.

Challenges

It's important for you to practice what you've learned on your own, so most chapters in this book have at least one challenge.

I highly recommend giving all the challenges a try, because while following a step-by-step tutorial is educational, you'll learn a lot more by solving a problem by yourself. In addition, each chapter will continue where the previous chapter's challenges left off, so you'll want to stay in the loop!

If you get stuck, you can find solutions in the resources for this chapter — but to get the most from this book, give these your best shot before you look!

Challenge 1: Adding the zombie

Right now, your game has a nice background, but it's missing the star of the show. As your first challenge, give your zombie a grand entrance.

Here are a few hints:

- Inside **GameScene.swift**, add a constant property named `zombie` of type `SKSpriteNode`. Initialize it with the image named **zombie1**.

- Inside `didMove(to:)`, position the zombie sprite at (**400, 400**).

- Also inside `didMove(to:)`, add the zombie to the scene.

If you've got it right, you'll see the zombie appear onscreen like so:

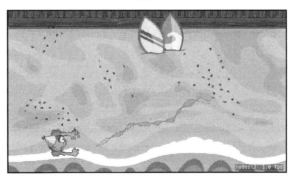

Run your game on the iPad Retina simulator to prove it works there as well — just with a bigger viewable area!

Challenge 2: Further documentation

This chapter covers everything you need to know about sprites and nodes to keep working on the game.

However, it's good to know where to find more information in case you ever have questions or get stuck. I highly recommend you check out Apple's *SKNode Class Reference* and *SKSpriteNode Class Reference*, as these cover the two classes you'll use most often in SpriteKit, and it's good to have a basic familiarity with the properties and methods they contain.

You can find the references in Xcode by selecting **Help > Documentation and API Reference** from the main menu and searching for SKNode or SKSpriteNode.

And now for your second challenge: Use the information in these docs to double (scale to 2x) the zombie's size. Answer this question: Did you use a method of SKSpriteNode or SKNode to do this?

Chapter 2: Manual Movement

By Ray Wenderlich

If you completed the challenges from the previous chapter, you now have a rather large zombie on the screen:

> **Note:** If you were unable to complete the challenges or skipped ahead from the previous chapter, don't worry — simply open the starter project from this chapter to pick up where the previous chapter left off.

Of course, you want the sprite to move around, not just stand there — this zombie's got an itch to boogie!

There are two ways to make a sprite move in SpriteKit:

1. As you might have noticed in the previous chapter from the template code provided by Apple, you can make a sprite move using a concept called **actions**. You'll learn more about actions in the next chapter.

2. You can make a sprite move in a more "conventional" way — and that's to set the position manually over time. It's important you learn this method first as it affords more control and will help you understand what actions will do for you.

However, to set a sprite's position over time, you need a method that the game calls periodically as it runs. This introduces a new topic: the SpriteKit game loop.

The SpriteKit game loop

A game works like a flipbook animation. You draw a successive sequence of images, and when you flip through them fast enough, it gives the illusion of movement.

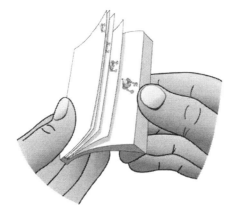

Each individual picture that you draw is called a **frame**. Games typically try to draw frames at either 30 or 60 times per second and try to keep that rate consistent so the animations feel smooth. This rate of drawing is called the **frame rate**, or specifically **frames per second (FPS)**. By default, SpriteKit displays this in the bottom-right corner of your game:

Note: It's handy of SpriteKit to show your frames per second onscreen by default because you want to keep an eye on the FPS as you develop your game to make sure your game is performing well. Ideally, you want at least 30 FPS.

You should only pay attention to the FPS display on an actual device, though, as you'll get very different performance on the simulator.

In particular, your Mac has a faster CPU and way more memory than an iPhone or iPad, but abysmally slow simulated rendering, so you can't count on any accurate performance measurements from your Mac — again, always test performance on a device!

Besides the FPS, SpriteKit also displays the count of nodes that it rendered in the last pass.

You can remove the FPS and node count from the screen by going into **GameViewController.swift** and setting both `skView.showsFPS` and `skView.showsNodeCount` to `false`.

Behind the scenes, SpriteKit runs an endless loop, often referred to as the **game loop**, which looks like this:

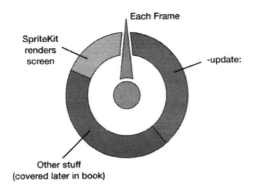

In each frame, SpriteKit does the following:

1. **Calls a method on your scene named `update(_:)`.** This is where you can put code that you want to run every frame — making it the perfect spot for code that updates the position or rotation of your sprites.

2. **Does some other stuff.** You'll revisit the game loop in other chapters, filling in your understanding of the rest of this diagram as you go.

3. **Renders the scene.** SpriteKit then draws all of the objects that are in your scene graph, issuing OpenGL draw commands for you behind the scenes.

SpriteKit tries to draw frames as fast as possible, up to 60 FPS. However, if update(_:) takes too long, or if SpriteKit has to draw more sprites than the hardware can handle at one time, the frame rate might decrease.

Here are two tips to keep your game running fast:

1. **Keep update(_:) fast**. For example, you want to avoid slow algorithms in this method since it's called each frame.

2. **Keep your node count as low as possible**. For example, it's good to remove nodes from the scene graph when they're offscreen and you no longer need them.

Now you know that update(_:) is called each frame and is a good spot to update the positions of your sprites — so it's time to make this zombie move!

Moving the zombie

You're going to implement the zombie movement code in five phases. This is so you can see some common beginner mistakes and solutions, and in the end, understand how each phase works.

Before you begin, open **GameScene.swift** and comment out the line in didMove(to:) that sets the zombie to double its size:

```
// zombie.setScale(2) // SKNode method
```

This line was just a test, so you don't need it anymore. Zombies are scary enough at normal size! :]

Phase one: A fixed distance per frame

To start, you'll implement a simple but less-than-ideal method: moving the zombie a fixed amount per frame.

Inside **GameScene.swift**, add the following method:

```
override func update(_ currentTime: TimeInterval) {
  zombie.position = CGPoint(x: zombie.position.x + 8,
                            y: zombie.position.y)
}
```

Here, you update the position of the zombie to be eight points further along the x-axis than last time, and to keep the same position along the y-axis. This makes the zombie move from left to right.

Build and run, and you'll see the zombie move across the screen:

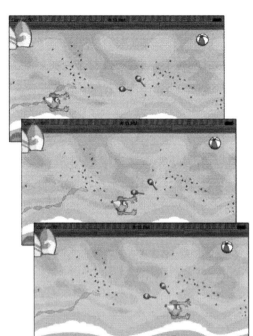

This is great stuff, but the movement feels a bit jagged and irregular. To see why, take a look back at the SpriteKit game loop.

Remember, SpriteKit tries to draw frames as quickly as possible. However, there will usually be some variance in the amount of time it takes to draw each frame: sometimes a bit slower, sometimes a bit quicker.

This means the amount of time between calls to your update(_:) loop can vary. To see this yourself, add some code to print out the time elapsed since the last update. Add these variables to the GameScene property section, right after the zombie property:

```
var lastUpdateTime: TimeInterval = 0
var dt: TimeInterval = 0
```

Here, you create properties to keep track of the last time SpriteKit called update(_:) and the delta time since the last update, often abbreviated as dt.

Then, add the following lines to the beginning of update(_:):

```
if lastUpdateTime > 0 {
  dt = currentTime - lastUpdateTime
} else {
  dt = 0
```

```
}
lastUpdateTime = currentTime
print("\(dt*1000) milliseconds since last update")
```

Here, you calculate the time since the last call to update(_:), store that value in dt, then log the time in milliseconds (1 second = 1000 milliseconds).

Build and run, and you'll see something like this in the console:

```
33.4451289963908 milliseconds since last update
16.3537669868674 milliseconds since last update
34.1878019971773 milliseconds since last update
15.6998310121708 milliseconds since last update
33.9883069973439 milliseconds since last update
33.5779220040422 milliseconds since last update
```

As you can see, the amount of time between calls to update(_:) always varies slightly.

> **Note:** SpriteKit tries to call your update method 60 times per second (roughly every 16 milliseconds).
>
> However, if it takes too long to update and render a frame of your game, SpriteKit may call your update method less frequently, and the FPS will drop.
>
> You can see that here — some frames are taking over 30 milliseconds. You're seeing such a low FPS because you're running on the simulator.
>
> As mentioned earlier, you can't count on the simulator for accurate performance measurements. If you try running this code on a device, you should see a much higher FPS.
>
> Note that even if your game runs at a smooth 60 FPS, there will always be some small variance in how often SpriteKit calls your update method. Therefore, you need to take the delta time into account in your calculations — and you'll learn how to do that next!

Since you're updating the position of the zombie a fixed amount per frame, rather than taking this time variance into consideration, you're likely to wind up with movement that looks jagged or irregular.

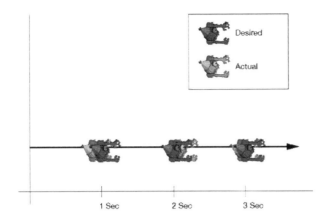

The correct solution is to figure out how far you want the zombie to move per second and then multiply this by the fraction of a second since the last update. Give that a shot.

Phase two: Using delta time for smooth velocity

Begin by adding the following property to the top of GameScene, right after dt:

```
let zombieMovePointsPerSec: CGFloat = 480.0
```

You're saying that in one second, the zombie should move 480 points, about 1/4th of the scene's width. You set the type to CGFloat because you'll be using this value in calculations with other CGFloat values inside a CGPoint.

Right after that line, add one more property:

```
var velocity = CGPoint.zero
```

So far, you've used CGPoints to represent positions. However, it's also quite common and handy to use CGPoints to represent **2D vectors**.

A 2D vector represents a **direction** and a **length**:

$$(480.0, 0)$$

points per sec

The diagram above shows an example of a 2D vector you might use to represent the zombie's movement. You can see that the orientation of the arrow shows the **direction** in which the zombie should move, while the arrow's **length** indicates how far the zombie should move in a second. The direction and length together represent the zombie's **velocity** — you can think of it as how far, and in what direction, the zombie should move in 1 second.

However, note that the velocity has no set position. After all, you should be able to make the zombie move in that direction, at that speed, no matter where the zombie starts.

Try this out by adding the following new method:

```
func move(sprite: SKSpriteNode, velocity: CGPoint) {
  // 1
  let amountToMove = CGPoint(x: velocity.x * CGFloat(dt),
                             y: velocity.y * CGFloat(dt))
  print("Amount to move: \(amountToMove)")
  // 2
  sprite.position = CGPoint(
    x: sprite.position.x + amountToMove.x,
    y: sprite.position.y + amountToMove.y)
}
```

You've refactored the code into a reusable method that accepts the sprite to be moved and a velocity vector by which to move it. Taking it line-by-line:

1. Velocity is in points per second, and you need to figure out how many points to move the zombie in this frame. To determine that, this section multiplies the points per second by the fraction of seconds since the last update. You now have a point representing the zombie's position, which you can also think of as a vector from the origin to the zombie's position, as well as a vector representing the distance and direction to move the zombie in this frame:

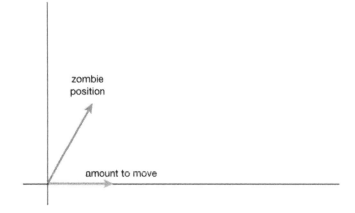

2. To determine the zombie's new position, simply add the vector to the point:

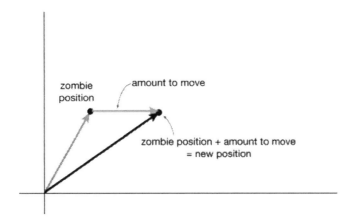

You can visualize this with the diagram above, but in code you simply add the x- and y-components of the point and the vector together.

> **Note:** To learn more about vectors, check out this great guide: http://www.mathsisfun.com/algebra/.

Finally, inside `update(_:)`, replace the line that sets the zombie's position with the following:

```
move(sprite: zombie,
  velocity: CGPoint(x: zombieMovePointsPerSec, y: 0))
```

Build and run, and now the zombie moves much more smoothly across the screen. Look at the console log, and you'll also see that the zombie is now moving a different number of points each frame, based on how much time has elapsed.

```
0.0 milliseconds since last update
Amount to move: (0.0, 0.0)
47.8530780237634 milliseconds since last update
Amount to move: (11.4847387257032, 0.0)
33.3498929976486 milliseconds since last update
Amount to move: (8.00397431943566, 0.0)
34.2196339915972 milliseconds since last update
Amount to move: (8.21271215798333, 0.0)
```

If your zombie's movement still looks jittery, be sure to try it on a device instead of on the simulator, which has different performance characteristics.

Phase three: Moving toward touches

So far, so good, but now you want to make the zombie move toward whatever spot the player touches. After all, everyone knows zombies are attracted to noise!

Your goal is for the zombie to move toward the point the player taps and keep moving even after passing the tap location until the player taps another location to draw his attention. There are four steps to make this work.

Step 1: Finding the offset vector of the tap

First, you need to figure out the offset between the location of the player's tap and the location of the zombie. You can get this by simply subtracting the zombie's position from the tap position.

Subtracting points and vectors is similar to adding them, but instead of adding the x- and y-components, you — that's right — subtract them! :]

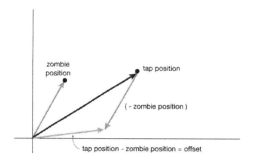

This diagram illustrates that if you subtract the zombie position from the tap position, you get a vector showing the offset amount. You can see this even more clearly if you move the offset vector so it begins from the zombie's position:

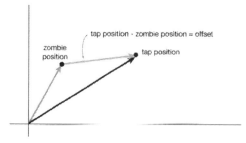

By subtracting these two positions, you get something with a direction and a length. Call this the offset vector.

Try it out by adding the following method:

```
func moveZombieToward(location: CGPoint) {
    let offset = CGPoint(x: location.x - zombie.position.x,
                         y: location.y - zombie.position.y)
}
```

You're not done writing this method; this is only the beginning!

Step 2: Calculating the offset vector length

Now you need to figure out the length of the offset vector.

Think of the offset vector as the hypotenuse of a right triangle, where the lengths of the other two sides of the triangle are defined by the x- and y- components of the vector:

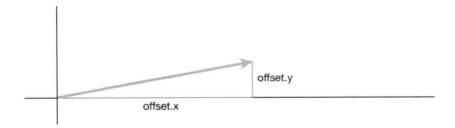

You want to find the length of the hypotenuse. To do this, you can use the Pythagorean theorem. You may remember this simple formula from geometry — it says that the length of the hypotenuse is equal to the square root of the sum of the squares of the two sides.

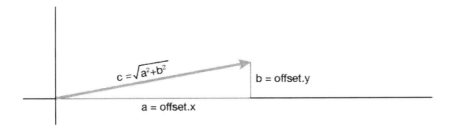

Put this theory into practice. Add the following line to the bottom of moveZombieToward(location:):

```
let length = sqrt(
    Double(offset.x * offset.x + offset.y * offset.y))
```

Currently, you have an offset vector where:

• The **direction** points where the zombie should go.

• The **length** is the length of the line between the zombie's current position and the tap location.

What you want is a velocity vector where:

• The **direction** points where the zombie should go.

• The **length** is `zombieMovePointsPerSec`, the constant you defined earlier as 480 points per second.

So you're halfway there — your vector points in the right direction, but isn't the right length. How do you make a vector pointing in the same direction as the offset vector, but of a certain length?

Step 3: Reducing to the unit vector

The first step is to convert the offset vector into a **unit vector**, which means a vector of length 1. According to geometry, you can do this by simply dividing the offset vector's x- and y- components by the offset vector's length.

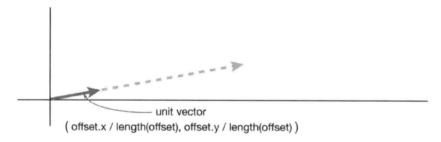

unit vector
(offset.x / length(offset), offset.y / length(offset))

This process of converting a vector into a unit vector is called **normalizing** a vector.

Once you have this unit vector, which you know is of length 1, it's easy to multiply it by `zombieMovePointsPerSec` to make it the exact length you want.

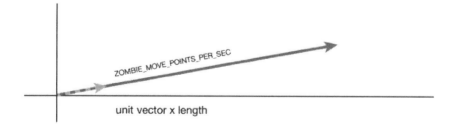

unit vector x length

Give it a try. Add the following lines to the bottom of moveZombieToward():

```
let direction = CGPoint(x: offset.x / CGFloat(length),
                        y: offset.y / CGFloat(length))
velocity = CGPoint(x: direction.x * zombieMovePointsPerSec,
                   y: direction.y * zombieMovePointsPerSec)
```

Now you've got a velocity vector with the correct direction and length. There's only one step left!

Step 4: Hooking up to touch events

In SpriteKit, to get notifications of touch events on a node, you simply need to set that node's isUserInteractionEnabled property to true and then override that node's touchesBegan(withEvent:), touchesMoved(withEvent:) and/or touchesEnded(withEvent:) methods. Unlike other SKNode subclasses, SKScene's isUserInteractionEnabled property is set to true by default.

To see this in action, implement these touch handling methods for GameScene:

```
func sceneTouched(touchLocation:CGPoint) {
  moveZombieToward(location: touchLocation)
}

override func touchesBegan(_ touches: Set<UITouch>,
    with event: UIEvent?) {
  guard let touch = touches.first else {
    return
  }
  let touchLocation = touch.location(in: self)
  sceneTouched(touchLocation: touchLocation)
}

override func touchesMoved(_ touches: Set<UITouch>,
    with event: UIEvent?) {
  guard let touch = touches.first else {
    return
  }
  let touchLocation = touch.location(in: self)
  sceneTouched(touchLocation: touchLocation)
}
```

This will update the zombie's velocity direction so that it points wherever the user taps the screen.

Finally, inside update(_:), edit the call to move(sprite:velocity:) so it passes in velocity (updated based on the touch) instead of the preset amount:

```
move(sprite: zombie, velocity: velocity)
```

That's it! Build and run, and now the zombie will chase your taps. Just don't get too close — he's hungry!

> **Note:** You can also use gesture recognizers with SpriteKit. These can be especially handy if you're trying to implement complicated gestures, such as pinches or rotations.
>
> You can add the gesture recognizer to the scene's view in `didMove(to:)`, and you can use `SKScene`'s `convertPoint(fromView:)` and `SKNode`'s `convert(_:to:)` methods to get the touch in the coordinate space you need.
>
> For a demonstration of this, see the sample code for this chapter, which includes a commented-out demonstration of gesture recognizers for you. Since it does the same thing as the touch handlers you implemented, comment out your touch handlers when you run with the gesture recognizers if you want to be sure the gestures are working.

Phase four: Bounds checking

As you play the latest version of the game, you might notice that the zombie happily runs straight off the screen if you let him. While you have to admire his enthusiasm, in Zombie Conga you'd like him to stay on the screen at all times, bouncing off an edge if he hits one.

To do this, you need to check if the newly calculated position is beyond any of the screen edges and make the zombie bounce away, if so. Add this new method:

```
func boundsCheckZombie() {
  let bottomLeft = CGPoint.zero
  let topRight = CGPoint(x: size.width, y: size.height)

  if zombie.position.x <= bottomLeft.x {
    zombie.position.x = bottomLeft.x
```

```
      velocity.x = -velocity.x
    }
  if zombie.position.x >= topRight.x {
    zombie.position.x = topRight.x
    velocity.x = -velocity.x
  }
  if zombie.position.y <= bottomLeft.y {
    zombie.position.y = bottomLeft.y
    velocity.y = -velocity.y
  }
  if zombie.position.y >= topRight.y {
    zombie.position.y = topRight.y
    velocity.y = -velocity.y
  }
}
```

First, you make constants for the bottom-left and top-right coordinates of the scene.

Then, you check the zombie's position to see if it's beyond or on any of the screen edges. If it is, you clamp the position and reverse the appropriate velocity component to make the zombie bounce in the opposite direction.

Now, call your new method at the end of update(_:):

```
boundsCheckZombie()
```

Build and run, and you have a zombie bouncing around the screen. I told you he was ready to party!

Phase five: Limiting the playable area

Run the game on your iPhone 7 simulator and move your zombie toward the top of the screen. Notice that your zombie moves offscreen before he bounces back!

Run the game on the iPad simulator, and you'll see the game works as expected. Does this give you a clue as to what's going on?

Recall from the "Universal app support" section in Chapter 1 that Zombie Conga has been designed with a 4:3 aspect ratio (2048x1536). However, you want to support up to a 16:9 aspect ratio, which is what the iPhone 5, 6/7, and 6/7 Plus use (1136x640, 1334x750 and 1920x1080, respectively).

Take a look at what happens with a 16:9 device. Since you've configured the scene to use aspect fill, SpriteKit first calculates the largest 16:9 rectangle that fits within the 2048x1536 space: that's 2048x1152. It then centers that rectangle and scales it to fit the actual screen size; for example, the iPhone 7's 1334x750 screen requires scaling by ~0.65.

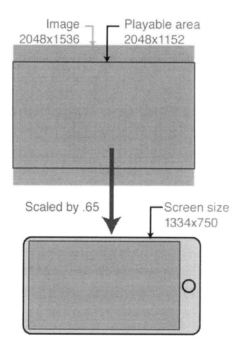

This means that on 16:9 devices, there are 192-point gaps at the top and bottom of the scene that won't be visible (1536 - 1152 = 384. 384 / 2 = 192). Hence, you should avoid critical gameplay in those areas — such as letting the zombie move in those gaps.

First, add a new property to `GameScene` to store the playable rectangle:

```
let playableRect: CGRect
```

Then, add the following initializer to set the value appropriately:

```
override init(size: CGSize) {
  let maxAspectRatio:CGFloat = 16.0/9.0 // 1
  let playableHeight = size.width / maxAspectRatio // 2
  let playableMargin = (size.height-playableHeight)/2.0 // 3
  playableRect = CGRect(x: 0, y: playableMargin,
                        width: size.width,
                        height: playableHeight) // 4
  super.init(size: size) // 5
}

required init(coder aDecoder: NSCoder) {
  fatalError("init(coder:) has not been implemented") // 6
}
```

Line by line, here's what this code does:

1. Zombie Conga supports aspect ratios from 3:2 (1.33) to 16:9 (1.77). Here, you make a constant for the maximum aspect ratio supported, 16:9 (1.77).

2. With aspect fill and a scene that is 2048x1536, the playable width will always be equal to the scene width, regardless of aspect ratio. To calculate the playable height, you divide the scene width by the maximum aspect ratio.

3. You want to center the playable rectangle on the screen, so you determine the margin on the top and bottom by subtracting the playable height from the scene height and dividing the result by 2.

4. You put it all together to make a rectangle with the maximum aspect ratio, centered on the screen.

5. You call the initializer of the superclass.

6. Whenever you override the default initializer of a SpriteKit node, you must also override the `required NSCoder` initializer, which is used when you're loading a scene from the scene editor. Since you're not using the scene editor in this game, you simply add a placeholder implementation that logs an error.

To visualize this, add a helper method to draw this playable rectangle to the screen:

```
func debugDrawPlayableArea() {
  let shape = SKShapeNode()
  let path = CGMutablePath()
  path.addRect(playableRect)
  shape.path = path
  shape.strokeColor = SKColor.red
  shape.lineWidth = 4.0
  addChild(shape)
}
```

For the moment, don't worry about how this works; you'll learn all about SKShapeNodes in Chapter 11, "Crop, Video and Shape Nodes". For now, consider this a black box that draws the debug rectangle to the screen.

Next, call this method at the end of didMove(to:):

```
debugDrawPlayableArea()
```

And finally, modify the first two lines in boundsCheckZombie() to take into consideration the y-values in playableRect:

```
let bottomLeft = CGPoint(x: 0, y: playableRect.minY)
let topRight = CGPoint(x: size.width, y: playableRect.maxY)
```

Build and run, and you'll see the zombie now bounces correctly according to the playable rectangle, drawn in red and matched to the corners of the screen:

Then, build and run on an iPad simulator, and you'll see the zombie bounces correctly there, as well, according to the playable rectangle:

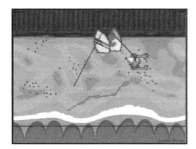

The playable area outlined in red is exactly what you see on the iPhone device, which has the largest supported aspect ratio, 16:9.

Now that you have a playable rectangle, you simply need to make sure the rest of the gameplay takes place in this box — and your zombie can party everywhere!

> **Note:** An alternate method would be to restrict the zombie's movement based on the visible area of the current device. In other words, you could let the zombie move all the way to the edges of the iPad, rather than restricting him to the minimum playable area.
>
> However, this would make the game easier on the iPad, as there'd be more space to avoid enemies. For Zombie Conga, we think it's more important to have the same difficulty across all devices, so we're keeping the core gameplay in the guaranteed playable area.

Rotating the zombie

The zombie is moving nicely, but he always faces the same direction. Granted, he's undead, but this zombie is on the curious side and would like to turn to see where he's going!

You already have a vector that includes the direction the zombie is facing: velocity. You just need to find the rotation angle to get the zombie facing in that direction.

Once again, think of the direction vector as the hypotenuse of a right triangle. You want to find the angle:

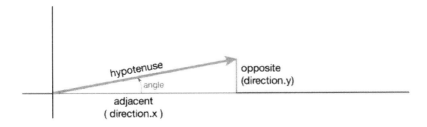

You may remember from trigonometry the mnemonic *SOH CAH TOA*, where the last part stands for:

```
tan(angle) = opposite / adjacent
```

Since you have the lengths of the opposite and adjacent sides, you can rewrite the above formula as follows to get the angle of rotation:

```
angle = arctan(opposite / adjacent)
```

If none of this trigonometry rings any bells, don't worry. Just think of it as a formula that you type in to get the angle — that's all you need to know.

Give this formula a try by adding the following new method:

```
func rotate(sprite: SKSpriteNode, direction: CGPoint) {
  sprite.zRotation = CGFloat(
    atan2(Double(direction.y), Double(direction.x)))
}
```

This uses the equation from above. It includes a bunch of casting because `CGFloat` is defined as a `Double` on 64-bit machines and as a `Float` on 32-bit machines.

This works because the zombie image faces to the right — which is an angle of 0 degrees or radians. If the zombie image were instead facing the top of the screen, you'd have to add an additional rotation to compensate.

Now call this new method at the end of `update`:

```
rotate(sprite: zombie, direction: velocity)
```

Build and run, and the zombie rotates to face the direction in which he's moving:

Congratulations, you've given your zombie life! The sprite moves smoothly, bounces off the edges of the screen and rotates on both the iPhone and the iPad — a great start to a game.

It's time to try some of this on your own to make sure you've got it down.

Challenges

This chapter has three challenges, and they're particularly important ones. They'll give you useful practice with vector math and introduce new math utilities you'll use throughout the rest of the book.

As always, if you get stuck, you can find solutions in the resources for this chapter — but give it your best shot first!

Challenge 1: Math utilities

As you've no doubt noticed while working on this game, you frequently have to perform calculations on points and vectors: adding and subtracting points, finding lengths and so on. You've also been doing a lot of casting between `CGFloat` and `Double`.

So far in this chapter, you've done all of this yourself inline. That's a common way of doing things, but it can get tedious and repetitive in practice. It's also error-prone.

Create a new file with the **iOS/Source/Swift File** template and name it **MyUtils.swift**. Then replace the contents of **MyUtils.swift** with the following:

```swift
import Foundation
import CoreGraphics

func + (left: CGPoint, right: CGPoint) -> CGPoint {
  return CGPoint(x: left.x + right.x, y: left.y + right.y)
}

func += (left: inout CGPoint, right: CGPoint) {
  left = left + right
}
```

In Swift, you can make operators like +, −, ∗ and / work on any type you want. Here, you make them work on `CGPoint`.

Now you can add points like the ones below — but don't add this anywhere; it's just an example:

```swift
let testPoint1 = CGPoint(x: 100, y: 100)
let testPoint2 = CGPoint(x: 50, y: 50)
let testPoint3 = testPoint1 + testPoint2
```

OK! Time to override the operators for subtraction, multiplication and division on `CGPoints`. Add this code to the end of **MyUtils.swift**:

```swift
func - (left: CGPoint, right: CGPoint) -> CGPoint {
  return CGPoint(x: left.x - right.x, y: left.y - right.y)
```

```
  }

  func -= (left: inout CGPoint, right: CGPoint) {
    left = left - right
  }

  func * (left: CGPoint, right: CGPoint) -> CGPoint {
    return CGPoint(x: left.x * right.x, y: left.y * right.y)
  }

  func *= (left: inout CGPoint, right: CGPoint) {
    left = left * right
  }

  func * (point: CGPoint, scalar: CGFloat) -> CGPoint {
    return CGPoint(x: point.x * scalar, y: point.y * scalar)
  }

  func *= (point: inout CGPoint, scalar: CGFloat) {
    point = point * scalar
  }

  func / (left: CGPoint, right: CGPoint) -> CGPoint {
    return CGPoint(x: left.x / right.x, y: left.y / right.y)
  }

  func /= ( left: inout CGPoint, right: CGPoint) {
    left = left / right
  }

  func / (point: CGPoint, scalar: CGFloat) -> CGPoint {
    return CGPoint(x: point.x / scalar, y: point.y / scalar)
  }

  func /= (point: inout CGPoint, scalar: CGFloat) {
    point = point / scalar
  }
```

Now you can subtract, multiply or divide a CGPoint by another CGPoint. You can also multiply and divide points by scalar CGFloat values, as below — again, don't add this anywhere; it's just an example:

```
let testPoint5 = testPoint1 * 2
let testPoint6 = testPoint1 / 10
```

Finally, add a class extension on CGPoint with a few helper methods:

```
#if !(arch(x86_64) || arch(arm64))
func atan2(y: CGFloat, x: CGFloat) -> CGFloat {
  return CGFloat(atan2f(Float(y), Float(x)))
}
```

```
func sqrt(a: CGFloat) -> CGFloat {
  return CGFloat(sqrtf(Float(a)))
}
#endif

extension CGPoint {

  func length() -> CGFloat {
    return sqrt(x*x + y*y)
  }

  func normalized() -> CGPoint {
    return self / length()
  }

  var angle: CGFloat {
    return atan2(y, x)
  }
}
```

The #if/#endif block is true when the app is running on 32-bit architecture. In this case, CGFloat is the same size as Float, so this code makes versions of atan2 and sqrt that accept CGFloat/Float values rather than the default of Double, allowing you to use atan2 and sqrt with CGFloats, regardless of the device's architecture.

Next, the class extension adds some handy methods to get the length of the point, return a normalized version of the point (i.e., length 1) and get the angle of the point.

Using these helper functions will make your code a lot more concise and clean. For example, look at move(sprite:velocity:):

```
func move(sprite: SKSpriteNode, velocity: CGPoint) {
  let amountToMove = CGPoint(x: velocity.x * CGFloat(dt),
                             y: velocity.y * CGFloat(dt))
  print("Amount to move: \(amountToMove)")
  sprite.position = CGPoint(
    x: sprite.position.x + amountToMove.x,
    y: sprite.position.y + amountToMove.y)
}
```

Simplify the first line by multiplying velocity and dt using the * operator. Also, simplify the final line by adding the sprite's position and amount to move using the += operator. Your end result should look like this:

```
func move(sprite: SKSpriteNode, velocity: CGPoint) {
  let amountToMove = velocity * CGFloat(dt)
  print("Amount to move: \(amountToMove)")
  sprite.position += amountToMove
}
```

Your challenge is to modify the rest of Zombie Conga to use this new helper code, and verify that the game still works as expected. When you're done, you should have the following calls, including the two mentioned already:

- += operator: 1 call

- − operator: 1 call

- * operator: 2 calls

- `normalized()`: 1 call

- `angle`: 1 call

When you're done, you'll notice your code is a lot cleaner and easier to understand. In future chapters, you'll use a math library we made that's very similar to the one you created here.

Challenge 2: Stop that zombie!

When you tap the screen, the zombie moves toward the tap point — but continues beyond it.

That's fine for Zombie Conga, but in another game you might want the zombie to stop where you tap. Your challenge is to modify the game to do this.

Here are a few hints for one possible implementation:

- Create an optional property called `lastTouchLocation` and update it whenever the player touches the scene.

- Inside `update(_:)`, check the distance between the last touch location and the zombie's position. If that remaining distance is less than or equal to the amount the zombie will move this frame (`zombieMovePointsPerSec * dt`), then set the zombie's position to the last touch location and the velocity to zero. Otherwise, call `move(sprite:velocity:)` and `rotate(sprite:direction:)` like normal. `boundsCheckZombie()` should always occur.

- To do this, use the − operator once and call `length()` once using the helper code from the previous challenge.

Challenge 3: Smooth moves

Currently, the zombie immediately rotates to face the tap location. This can be a bit jarring — it would be nicer if the zombie rotated smoothly over time to face the new direction.

To do this, you need two new helper routines. Add these to the bottom of **MyUtils.swift** (to type π, use Option-P):

```swift
let π = CGFloat.pi

func shortestAngleBetween(angle1: CGFloat,
                          angle2: CGFloat) -> CGFloat {
  let twoπ = π * 2.0
  var angle = (angle2 - angle1)
    .truncatingRemainder(dividingBy: twoπ)
  if angle >= π {
    angle = angle - twoπ
  }
  if angle <= -π {
    angle = angle + twoπ
  }
  return angle
}

extension CGFloat {
  func sign() -> CGFloat {
    return self >= 0.0 ? 1.0 : -1.0
  }
}
```

`sign()` returns **1** if the `CGFloat` is greater than or equal to **0**; otherwise it returns **-1**.

`shortestAngleBetween(angle1:angle2:)` returns the shortest angle between two angles. It's not as simple as subtracting the two angles, for two reasons:

1. Angles "wrap around" after 360 degrees (2 * π). In other words, 30 degrees and 390 degrees represent the same angle.

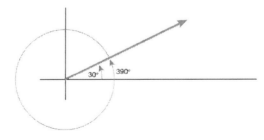

2. Sometimes the shortest way to rotate between two angles is to go left, and other times to go right. For example, if you start at 0 degrees and want to turn to 270 degrees, it's shorter to turn -90 degrees than to turn 270 degrees. You don't want your zombie turning the long way around — he may be undead, but he's not stupid!

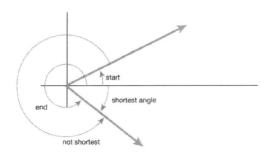

So this routine finds the difference between the two angles, chops off any amount greater than 360 degrees and then decides if it's faster to go right or left.

Your challenge is to modify rotate(sprite:direction:) to take and use a new parameter: the number of radians the zombie should rotate per second.

Define the constant as follows:

```
let zombieRotateRadiansPerSec:CGFloat = 4.0 * π
```

And modify the method signature as follows:

```
func rotate(sprite: SKSpriteNode, direction: CGPoint,
            rotateRadiansPerSec: CGFloat) {
  // Your code here!
}
```

Here are a few hints for implementing this method:

- Use shortestAngleBetween(angle1:angle2:) to find the distance between the current angle and the target angle. Call this shortest.

- Figure out the amount to rotate this frame based on rotateRadiansPerSec and dt. Call this amountToRotate.

- If the absolute value of shortest is less than the amountToRotate, use that instead.

- Add amountToRotate to the sprite's zRotation — but multiply it by sign() first, so that you rotate in the correct direction.

- Don't forget to update the call to rotate the sprite in update(_:) so that it uses the new parameter.

If you completed all three of these challenges, great work! You really understand moving and rotating sprites using the "classic" approach of updating values yourself over time.

Ah, but the classic, while essential to understand, always gives way to the modern. In the next chapter, you'll learn how SpriteKit can make some of these common tasks much easier, through the magic of actions!

Chapter 3: Actions

By Ray Wenderlich

So far, you've learned how to move and rotate SpriteKit nodes — a node being anything that appears onscreen — by manually setting their positions and rotations over time.

This do-it-yourself approach works and is quite powerful, but SpriteKit provides an easier way to move sprites incrementally: **actions**.

Actions allow you to do things like rotate, scale or change a sprite's position over time — with only a single line of code! You can also chain actions together to create movement combinations quite easily.

In this chapter, you'll learn all about SpriteKit actions as you add enemies, collectibles and basic gameplay logic to your game.

You'll see how actions can simplify your game-coding life, and by the time you've finished this chapter, Zombie Conga will be action-packed!

> **Note:** This chapter begins where the previous chapter's Challenge 3 left off. If you were unable to complete the challenges or skipped ahead from an earlier chapter, don't worry — simply open the starter project from this chapter to pick up where the previous chapter left off.

Move action

Right now, your zombie's "life" is a bit too carefree. Let's add action to this game by introducing enemies to dodge: crazy cat ladies!

Open **GameScene.swift** and create the start of a new method to spawn an enemy:

```
func spawnEnemy() {
  let enemy = SKSpriteNode(imageNamed: "enemy")
  enemy.position = CGPoint(x: size.width + enemy.size.width/2,
                           y: size.height/2)
  addChild(enemy)
}
```

This code is a review from the previous two chapters: You create a sprite and position it at the vertical center of the screen, just out of view to the right.

Now you'd like to move the enemy from the right of the screen to the left. If you were to do this manually, you might update the enemy's position each frame according to a velocity.

No need to trouble yourself with that this time! Simply add these two lines of code to the bottom of spawnEnemy():

```
let actionMove = SKAction.move(
  to: CGPoint(x: −enemy.size.width/2, y: enemy.position.y),
  duration: 2.0)
enemy.run(actionMove)
```

To create an action in SpriteKit, you call one of several static constructors on the SKAction class, such as the one you see here, move(to:duration:). This particular constructor returns an action that moves a sprite to a specified position over a specified duration (in seconds).

Here, you set up the action to move the enemy along the x-axis at whatever speed is necessary to take it from its current position to just off the left side of the screen in two seconds.

Once you've created an action, you need to run it. You can run an action on any `SKNode` by calling `run(_:)`, as you did in the above code.

Give it a try! For now, call this method inside `didMove(to:)`, right after calling `addChild(zombie)`:

```
spawnEnemy()
```

Build and run, and you'll see the crazy cat lady race across the screen:

Not bad for only two lines of code, eh? You could have even done it with a single line of code, if you hadn't needed to use the `actionMove` constant for anything else.

Here, you saw an example of `move(to:duration:)`, but there are a few other move action variants:

- **moveTo(x:duration:)** and **moveTo(y:duration:)**. These let you specify a change in only the x- or y-position; the other is assumed to remain the same. You could have used `moveTo(x:duration:)` in the example above to save a bit of typing.

- **moveBy(x:y:duration:)**. The "move to" actions move the sprite to a particular point, but sometimes it's convenient to move a sprite by an offset from its current position, wherever that may be. You could've used `moveBy(x:y:duration:)` in the example above, passing `-(size.width + enemy.size.width)` for x and `0` for y.

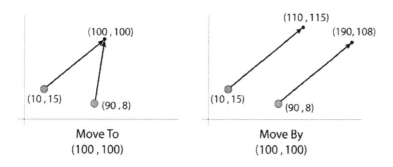

You'll see this pattern of "[action] to" and "[action] by" variants for other action types, as well. In general, you can use whichever of these is more convenient for you — but keep in mind, if either works, the "[action] by" actions are preferable because they're reversible. For more on this topic, keep reading.

Sequence action

The real power of actions lies in how easily you can chain them together. For example, say you want the cat lady to move in a "V" — down toward the bottom of the screen, then up to the goal position.

To do this, replace the lines that create and run the move action in spawnEnemy() with the following:

```
// 1
let actionMidMove = SKAction.move(
   to: CGPoint(x: size.width/2,
               y: playableRect.minY + enemy.size.height/2),
   duration: 1.0)
// 2
let actionMove = SKAction.move(
   to: CGPoint(x: -enemy.size.width/2, y: enemy.position.y),
   duration: 1.0)
// 3
let sequence = SKAction.sequence([actionMidMove, actionMove])
// 4
enemy.run(sequence)
```

Take a look at this line-by-line:

1. Here, you create a new move action, just like you did before, except this time it represents the "mid-point" of the action — the bottom middle of the playable rectangle.

2. This is the same move action as before, except you've decreased the duration to 1.0, since it will now represent moving only half the distance: from the bottom of the "V", to the left side of the screen.

3. Here's the new sequence action! As you can see, it's incredibly simple — you use the sequence(_:) constructor and pass in an Array of actions. The sequence action will run one action after another.

4. You call run(_:) in the same way as before, but pass in the sequence action this time.

That's it! Build and run, and you'll see the crazy cat lady "bounce" off the bottom of the playable rectangle:

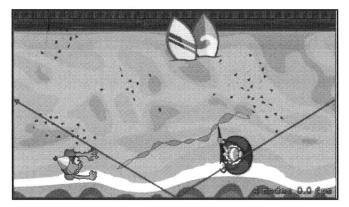

The sequence action is one of the most useful and commonly used actions — chaining actions together is just so powerful! You'll use the sequence action many times in this chapter and throughout the rest of this book.

Wait-for-duration action

The wait-for-duration action does exactly what you'd expect: It makes the sprite wait for a period of time, during which the sprite does nothing.

"What's the point of that?" you may be wondering. Well, wait-for-duration actions only truly become interesting when combined with a sequence action.

For example, you'll make the cat lady briefly pause when she reaches the bottom of the "V" shape. To do this, replace the line in spawnEnemy() that creates a sequence with the following lines:

```
let wait = SKAction.wait(forDuration: 0.25)
let sequence = SKAction.sequence(
  [actionMidMove, wait, actionMove])
```

To create a wait-for-duration action, call wait(forDuration:) with the amount of time to wait in seconds. Then, simply insert it into the sequence of actions where you want the delay to occur.

Build and run, and now the cat lady will briefly pause at the bottom of the "V":

Run-block action

At times, you'll want to run your own block of code in a sequence of actions. For example, let's say you want to log a message when the cat lady reaches the bottom of the "V".

To do this, replace the line in spawnEnemy() that creates a sequence with the following:

```
let logMessage = SKAction.run() {
  print("Reached bottom!")
}
let sequence = SKAction.sequence(
  [actionMidMove, logMessage, wait, actionMove])
```

To create a run-block action, simply call run(_ block:) and pass in a block of code to execute.

Build and run, and when the cat lady reaches the bottom of the "V", you'll see the following in the console:

```
Reached bottom!
```

> **Note:** If your project still includes the print statements from earlier chapters, now would be a great time to remove them. Otherwise, you'll have to search your console for the above log statement — it's doubtful you'll notice it within the sea of messages scrolling by.
>
> While you're at it, you should remove any comments as well, to keep your project nice and clean.

Of course, you can do far more than log a message here — since it's an arbitrary code block, you can do anything you want!

You should be aware of one more action related to running blocks of code:

- **run(_:queue:)** lets you run the block of code on an arbitrary dispatch queue instead of in the main SpriteKit event loop.

Reversing actions

Let's say you want to make the cat lady go back the way she came. After she moves in a "V" to the left, she should move in a "V" back to the right.

Here's one way to do this. After she goes offscreen to the left, make her run the existing `actionMidMove` action to go back to the middle, and creating a new `moveTo(duration:)` action to send her back to the start position.

But SpriteKit gives you a better option. You can reverse certain actions in SpriteKit simply by calling `reversed()` on them, resulting in a new action that is the opposite of the original action.

For example, if you run a `moveBy(x:y:duration:)` action, you can run the reverse of that action to go back the other way:

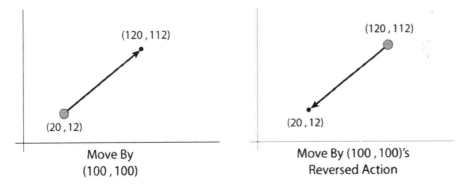

Not all actions are reversible — for example, `move(to:duration:)` is not. To find out if an action is reversible, look it up in the `SKAction` class reference, which indicates it clearly.

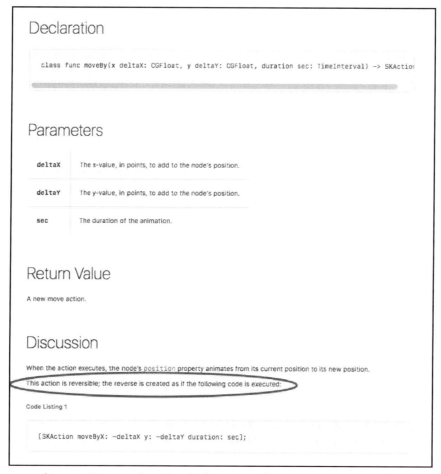

Time to try this out. First, replace the declarations of `actionMidMove` and `actionMove` in `spawnEnemy()` with the following code:

```
let actionMidMove = SKAction.moveBy(
  x: -size.width/2-enemy.size.width/2,
  y: -playableRect.height/2 + enemy.size.height/2,
  duration: 1.0)
let actionMove = SKAction.moveBy(
  x: -size.width/2-enemy.size.width/2,
  y: playableRect.height/2 - enemy.size.height/2,
  duration: 1.0)
```

Here, you switch the `move(to:duration:)` actions to the related `moveBy(x:y:duration:)` variant, since that is reversible.

Now, replace the line in spawnEnemy() that creates sequence with the following lines:

```
let reverseMid = actionMidMove.reversed()
let reverseMove = actionMove.reversed()
let sequence = SKAction.sequence([
  actionMidMove, logMessage, wait, actionMove,
  reverseMove, logMessage, wait, reverseMid
])
```

Here, you create the reverse of the actionMidMove and actionMove actions by calling reversed() on each, and insert them into the sequence.

Build and run, and now the cat lady will go one way, then back the other way:

> **Note:** If you try to reverse an action that isn't reversible, then reversed() will return an action with the same duration that doesn't change anything.

Because sequence actions are also reversible, you can simplify the above code as follows. **Remove** the lines where you create the reversed actions and replace the sequence creation with the following lines:

```
let halfSequence = SKAction.sequence(
  [actionMidMove, logMessage, wait, actionMove])
let sequence = SKAction.sequence(
  [halfSequence, halfSequence.reversed()])
```

This simply creates a sequence of actions that moves the sprite one way, and then reverses the sequence to go back the other way.

Astute observers may have noticed that the first half of the sequence logs a message as soon as the sprite reaches the bottom of the screen, but on the way back, the message isn't logged until after the sprite has waited at the bottom for one second.

This is because the reversed sequence is the exact opposite of the original, unlike your first implementation of the reversal. Later in this chapter, you'll read about the group action, which you could use to fix this behavior.

Repeating actions

So far, so good, but what if you want the cat lady to repeat this sequence multiple times? Of course — there's an action for that!

You can repeat an action a certain number of times using `repeat(_:count:)`, or an endless number of times using `repeatForever(_:)`.

For the cat lady's movement, you'll go with the endless variant. Replace the line that runs your action in `spawnEnemy()` with the following two lines:

```
let repeatAction = SKAction.repeatForever(sequence)
enemy.run(repeatAction)
```

Here, you create an action that repeats the sequence of other actions endlessly, and run that repeat action on the enemy.

Build and run, and now your cat lady will continuously bounce back and forth. I told you — she's crazy!

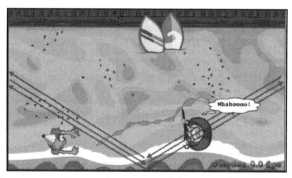

Congratulations! You now understand many useful types of actions:

- Move actions

- Sequence actions

- Wait-for-duration actions

- Run-block actions

- Reversing actions

- Repeating actions

Next, you're going to put all of these together in a new and interesting way to make cat ladies spawn periodically, so your zombie can never get too comfortable.

Periodic spawning

Right now, the game spawns a single cat lady at launch. To prepare for periodic spawning, you'll revert the `spawnEnemy()` code to the original version that simply moves the cat lady from right to left. You'll also introduce random variance so the cat lady doesn't always spawn at the same y-position.

First things first. You need a helper method to generate a random number within a range of values. Add this new method to **MyUtils.swift**, alongside the other math utilities you added in the Challenges section of the previous chapter:

```swift
extension CGFloat {
  static func random() -> CGFloat {
    return CGFloat(Float(arc4random()) / Float(UInt32.max))
  }

  static func random(min: CGFloat, max: CGFloat) -> CGFloat {
    assert(min < max)
    return CGFloat.random() * (max - min) + min
  }
}
```

This extends `CGFloat` to add two new methods. The first gives a random number between 0 and 1, and the second gives a random number between specified minimum and maximum values.

It's not important for you to understand these methods beyond that. But if you're really curious, you can read the following note:

> **Note:** `random()` calls `arc4random()`, which gives you a random integer between 0 and the largest value possible to store with an unsigned 32-bit integer, represented by `UInt32.max`. If you divide that number by `UInt32.max`, you get a float between 0 and 1.
>
> Here's how `random(min:max:)` works. If you multiply the result of `random()` — remember, that's a float between 0 and 1 — by the range of values (`max...min`), you'll get a float between 0 and the range. If you add to that the `min` value, you'll get a float between `min` and `max`.
>
> This is a very simple way of generating a random number. If you need more advanced control, check out the randomization APIs in GameplayKit.

Voilà, job done!

Next, head back to **GameScene.swift** and replace the current version of spawnEnemy()
with the following:

```
func spawnEnemy() {
  let enemy = SKSpriteNode(imageNamed: "enemy")
  enemy.position = CGPoint(
    x: size.width + enemy.size.width/2,
    y: CGFloat.random(
      min: playableRect.minY + enemy.size.height/2,
      max: playableRect.maxY - enemy.size.height/2))
  addChild(enemy)

  let actionMove =
    SKAction.moveTo(x: -enemy.size.width/2, duration: 2.0)
  enemy.run(actionMove)
}
```

You've modified the fixed y-position to be a random value between the bottom and top
of the playable rectangle, and you've reverted the movement back to the original
implementation — well, the moveTo(x:duration:) variant of the original
implementation, anyway.

Now it's time for some action. Inside didMove(to:), replace the call to spawnEnemy()
with the following:

```
run(SKAction.repeatForever(
  SKAction.sequence([SKAction.run() { [weak self] in
                     self?.spawnEnemy()
                   },
                   SKAction.wait(forDuration: 2.0)])))
```

This is an example of chaining actions together inline instead of creating separate
variables for each. You create a sequence of calling spawnEnemy() and waiting two
seconds, and repeat this sequence forever.

Note that you're having the scene itself run the action. This works because the scene is a
node, and any node can run actions.

> **Note:** You are using a weak reference to self here. Otherwise the closure passed
> to run(_ block:) will create a strong reference cycle and result in a memory
> leak.

Build and run, and the crazy cat ladies will spawn endlessly, at varying positions.

Remove-from-parent action

If you keep the game running for a while, an invisible problem will start to take shape.

You can't see it, but there are a big army of cat ladies offscreen to the left. This is because you never remove the cat ladies from the scene after they've finished moving.

A never-ending list of nodes in a game is never good. This node army will eventually consume all the memory on the device, and at that point, the OS will automatically terminate your app, which from a user's perspective will look like your app crashed.

To keep your game running smoothly, a good rule of thumb is "If you don't need it anymore, remove it." And as you may have guessed, there's an action for that, too! When you no longer need a node and want to remove it from the scene, you can either call `removeFromParent()` directly or use the remove-from-parent action.

Give this a try. Replace the call to `run(_:)` inside `spawnEnemy()` with the following:

```
let actionRemove = SKAction.removeFromParent()
enemy.run(SKAction.sequence([actionMove, actionRemove]))
```

Build and run, and now your nodes will clean up properly. Ah — much better!

> **Note:** `SKAction.removeFromParent()` removes the node that runs the action from its parent. This raises a question: What happens to actions after you run them? Calling `run(_:)` stores a strong reference to the action you give it, so won't that slowly eat up your memory?
>
> The answer is no. SpriteKit nodes do you the favor of automatically removing their references to actions when the actions finish running. So you can tell a node to run an action and then forget about it, feeling confident that you haven't leaked any memory.

> However, there is an exception. Actions that use a closure such as run(_ block:) can result in a strong reference cycle. As with any closure, use weak or unowned as needed to prevent a memory leak, such as you did earlier in this chapter.

Animation action

This one is super useful, because animations add a lot of polish and fun to your game.

To run an animation action, you first need to gather a list of images called **textures** that make up the frames of the animation. A sprite has a texture assigned to it, but you can always swap out the texture with a different one at runtime by setting the texture property on the sprite.

In fact, this is what animations do for you: automatically swap out your sprite's textures over time, with a slight delay between each.

Zombie Conga already includes some animation frames for the zombie. As you can see below, you have four textures to use as frames to show the zombie walking:

zombie1.png   zombie2.png   zombie3.png   zombie4.png

You want to play the frames in this order:

1   2   3   4   3   2

You can then repeat this endlessly for a continuous walk animation.

Give it a shot. First, create a property for the zombie animation action:

```
let zombieAnimation: SKAction
```

Then, add the following code to `init(size:)`, right before the call to `super.init(size:)`:

```
// 1
var textures:[SKTexture] = []
// 2
for i in 1...4 {
  textures.append(SKTexture(imageNamed: "zombie\(i)"))
}
// 3
textures.append(textures[2])
textures.append(textures[1])

// 4
zombieAnimation = SKAction.animate(with: textures,
  timePerFrame: 0.1)
```

Take a look at this one section at a time:

1. You create an array that will store all of the textures to run in the animation.

2. The animation frames are named **zombie1.png**, **zombie2.png**, **zombie3.png** and **zombie4.png**. This makes it easy to fashion a loop that creates a string for each image name and then makes a texture object from each name using the `SKTexture(imageNamed:)` initializer. The first `for` loop adds frames 1 to 4, which is most of the "forward walk".

3. This adds frames 3 and 2 to the list — remember, the textures array is 0-based. In total, the textures array now contains the frames in this order: 1, 2, 3, 4, 3, 2. The idea is to loop this for a continuous animation.

4. Once you have the array of textures, running the animation is easy — you simply create and run an action with `animate(with:timePerFrame:)`.

Finally, add this line to `didMove(to:)`, just after calling `addChild(zombie)`:

```
zombie.run(SKAction.repeatForever(zombieAnimation))
```

This runs the action wrapped in a repeat-forever action, which will seamlessly cycle through the frames 1,2,3,4,3,2,1,2,3,4,3,2,1,2....

Build and run, and now your zombie will strut in style!

Stopping action

Your zombie's off to a good start, but there's one annoying thing: When the zombie stops moving, his animation keeps running. Ideally, you'd like to stop the animation when the zombie stops moving.

In SpriteKit, whenever you run an action, you can give the action a key by using a variant of run(_:), named run(_:withKey:). This is handy because it allows you to stop the action by calling removeAction(forKey:).

Give it a shot by adding these two new methods:

```
func startZombieAnimation() {
  if zombie.action(forKey: "animation") == nil {
    zombie.run(
      SKAction.repeatForever(zombieAnimation),
      withKey: "animation")
  }
}

func stopZombieAnimation() {
  zombie.removeAction(forKey: "animation")
}
```

The first method starts the zombie animation. It runs the animation as before, but tags it with a key named "animation".

Also note, the method first uses action(forKey:) to make sure there isn't already an action running with the key "animation"; if there is, the method doesn't bother running another one.

The second method stops the zombie animation by removing the action with the key "animation".

Now, go to `didMove(to:)` and comment out the line that runs the action there:

```
// zombie.run(SKAction.repeatForever(zombieAnimation))
```

Call `startZombieAnimation()` at the beginning of `moveZombieToward(location:)`:

```
startZombieAnimation()
```

And call `stopZombieAnimation()` inside `update(_:)`, right after the line of code that sets `velocity = CGPoint.zero`:

```
stopZombieAnimation()
```

Build and run, and now your zombie will only move when he should!

Scale action

You have an animated zombie and some crazy cat ladies, but the game is missing one very important element: cats! Remember, the player's goal is to gather as many cats as she can into the zombie's conga line.

In Zombie Conga, the cats won't move from right to left like the cat ladies do. Instead, they'll appear at random locations on the screen and remain stationary. Rather than have the cats appear instantly, which would be jarring, you'll start them at a scale of 0 and grow to a scale of 1 over time. This will make the cats appear to "pop" into the game.

To implement this, add the following new method:

```
func spawnCat() {
  // 1
  let cat = SKSpriteNode(imageNamed: "cat")
  cat.position = CGPoint(
    x: CGFloat.random(min: playableRect.minX,
                      max: playableRect.maxX),
    y: CGFloat.random(min: playableRect.minY,
                      max: playableRect.maxY))
  cat.setScale(0)
  addChild(cat)
  // 2
  let appear = SKAction.scale(to: 1.0, duration: 0.5)
  let wait = SKAction.wait(forDuration: 10.0)
  let disappear = SKAction.scale(to: 0, duration: 0.5)
  let removeFromParent = SKAction.removeFromParent()
  let actions = [appear, wait, disappear, removeFromParent]
  cat.run(SKAction.sequence(actions))
}
```

Reviewing each section:

1. You create a cat at a random spot inside the playable rectangle. You set the cat's scale to 0, which makes the cat effectively invisible.

2. You create an action to scale the cat up to normal size by calling `scale(to:duration:)`. This action isn't reversible, so you also create a similar action to scale the cat back down to 0. In sequence, the cat appears, waits for a bit, disappears and is then removed from the parent.

You want the cats to spawn continuously from the start of the game, so add the following inside `didMove(to:)`, just after the line that spawns the enemies:

```
run(SKAction.repeatForever(
  SKAction.sequence([SKAction.run() { [weak self] in
              self?.spawnCat()
            },
            SKAction.wait(forDuration: 1.0)])))
```

This is very similar to the way you spawned the enemies. You run a sequence that calls `spawnCat()`, waits for one second and then repeats.

Build and run, and you'll see cats pop in and out of the game:

You should be aware of a few variants of the scale action:

- **scaleX(to:duration:)**, **scaleY(to:duration:)** and **scaleX(to:y:duration:)**: These allow you to scale the x-axis or the y-axis of a node independently, which you can use to stretch or squash a node.

- **scale(by:duration:)**: The "by" variant of scaling, which multiples the passed-in scale by the current node's scale. For example, if the current scale of a node is 1.0 and you scale it by 2.0, it is now at 2x. If you scale it by 2.0 again, it is now at 4x. Note that you couldn't use `scaleBy(duration:)` in the previous example, because anything multiplied by 0 is still 0!

- **scaleX(by:y:duration:)**: Another "by" variant, but this one allows you to scale x and y independently.

Rotate action

The cats in this game should be appealing enough that the player wants to pick them up, but right now they're just sitting motionless.

You'll give them some charm by making them wiggle back and forth while they sit.

To do this, you need the rotate action. To use it, you call the `rotate(byAngle:duration:)` constructor, passing in the angle (in radians) by which to rotate.

Replace the declaration of the `wait` action in `spawnCat()` with the following:

```
cat.zRotation = -π / 16.0
let leftWiggle = SKAction.rotate(byAngle: π/8.0, duration: 0.5)
let rightWiggle = leftWiggle.reversed()
let fullWiggle = SKAction.sequence([leftWiggle, rightWiggle])
let wiggleWait = SKAction.repeat(fullWiggle, count: 10)
```

Then, inside the declaration of the `actions` array, replace the `wait` action with `wiggleWait`, as shown below:

```
let actions = [appear, wiggleWait, disappear, removeFromParent]
```

Rotations go counterclockwise in SpriteKit, so negative rotations go clockwise. First, you rotate the cat clockwise by 1/16 of π (11.25 degrees) by setting its `zRotation` to −π/16.0.

Next, you create `leftWiggle`, which rotates counterclockwise by 22.5 degrees over a period of 0.5 seconds. Since the cat starts out rotated clockwise by 11.25 degrees, this results in the cat being rotated counterclockwise by 11.25 degrees.

Because this is a "by" variant, it's reversible, so you use `reversed()` to create `rightWiggle`, which simply rotates back the other way to where the cat started.

You create a `fullWiggle` by rotating left and then right. Now the cat has completed its wiggle and is back to its start position. This "full wiggle" takes a total of one second, so in `wiggleWait`, you repeat this 10 times to have a 10-second wiggle duration.

Build and run, and now your cats look like they've had some catnip!

Group action

So far, you know how to run actions one after another in sequence, but what if you want to run two actions at exactly the same time? For example, in Zombie Conga, you want to make the cats scale up and down slightly as they're wiggling.

For this sort of multitasking, you can use what's called the group action. It works in a similar way as the sequence action, where you pass in a list of actions. However, instead of running them one at a time, a group action runs them all at once.

Time to try this out. Replace the declaration of the `wiggleWait` action in `spawnCat()` with the following:

```
let scaleUp = SKAction.scale(by: 1.2, duration: 0.25)
let scaleDown = scaleUp.reversed()
let fullScale = SKAction.sequence(
  [scaleUp, scaleDown, scaleUp, scaleDown])
let group = SKAction.group([fullScale, fullWiggle])
let groupWait = SKAction.repeat(group, count: 10)
```

This code creates a sequence similar to that of the wiggle sequence, except it scales up and down instead of wiggling left and right.

It then sets up a group action to run the wiggling and scaling at the same time. To use a group action, you simply provide it with the list of actions that should run simultaneously.

Now replace `wiggleWait` with `groupWait` inside the declaration of the actions array, as shown below:

```
let actions = [appear, groupWait, disappear, removeFromParent]
```

Build and run, and your cats will bounce with excitement:

> **Note:** The duration of a group action is equal to the longest duration of any of the actions it contains. So if you include an action that takes one second and another that takes 10 seconds, both actions will begin to run at the same time, and after one second, the first action will be complete. The group action will continue to execute for nine more seconds until the other action is complete.

Collision detection

You've got a zombie, you've got cats, you've even got crazy cat ladies — but you don't have a way to detect when things collide.

There are multiple ways to detect collisions in SpriteKit, including using the built-in physics engine, as you'll learn in Chapter 9, "Intermediate Physics". In this chapter, you'll take the simplest and easiest approach: bounding-box collision detection.

There are three basic ideas you'll use to implement this:

1. You need a way of getting all of the cats and cat ladies in a scene into lists, so that you can check for collisions one by one. An easy solution is to give nodes a name when you create them, allowing you to use `enumerateChildNodes(withName:using:)` on the scene to find all the nodes with a certain name.

2. Once you have the lists of cats and cat ladies, you can loop through them to check for collisions. Each node has a `frame` property that gives you a rectangle representing the node's location onscreen.

3. If you have the frame for either a cat or a cat lady, and the frame for the zombie, you can use `CGRect`'s `intersects(_:)` method to see if they collide.

Time to give this a shot. First, set the name for each node. Inside `spawnEnemy()`, right after creating the enemy sprite, add this line:

```
enemy.name = "enemy"
```

Similarly, inside `spawnCat()`, right after creating the cat sprite, add this line:

```
cat.name = "cat"
```

Then, add these new methods to the file:

```
func zombieHit(cat: SKSpriteNode) {
  cat.removeFromParent()
}

func zombieHit(enemy: SKSpriteNode) {
  enemy.removeFromParent()
}

func checkCollisions() {
  var hitCats: [SKSpriteNode] = []
  enumerateChildNodes(withName: "cat") { node, _ in
    let cat = node as! SKSpriteNode
    if cat.frame.intersects(self.zombie.frame) {
      hitCats.append(cat)
    }
  }
  for cat in hitCats {
    zombieHit(cat: cat)
  }

  var hitEnemies: [SKSpriteNode] = []
  enumerateChildNodes(withName: "enemy") { node, _ in
    let enemy = node as! SKSpriteNode
    if node.frame.insetBy(dx: 20, dy: 20).intersects(
      self.zombie.frame) {
      hitEnemies.append(enemy)
    }
  }
  for enemy in hitEnemies {
    zombieHit(enemy: enemy)
  }
}
```

Here, you enumerate through any child of the scene that has the name "cat" or "enemy" and cast it to an `SKSpriteNode`, since you know it's a sprite node if it has that name.

You then check if the frame of the cat or enemy intersects with the frame of the zombie. If there is an intersection, you simply add the cat or enemy to an array to keep track of it. After you finish enumerating the nodes, you loop through the `hitCats` and `hitEnemies` arrays and call a method that removes the cat or enemy from the scene.

Notice that you don't remove the nodes from within the enumeration. It's unsafe to remove a node while enumerating over a list of them, and doing so can crash your app.

Also, notice that you do a little trick for the cat lady. Remember that the frame of a sprite is the sprite's entire image, including transparent space:

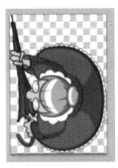

That means if the zombie went into the area of transparent space at the top of the cat lady image, it would "count" as a hit. Totally unfair!

To resolve this, you shrink the bounding box a little by using `CGRect`'s `insetBy(dx:dy:)` method. It's not a perfect solution, but it's a start. You'll learn a better way to do this in Chapter 10, "Advanced Physics".

Add the following call of your collision detection method at the end of `update(_:)`:

```
checkCollisions()
```

Build and run, and now when you collide with a cat or enemy, it disappears from the scene. It's your first small step toward the zombie apocalypse!

The SpriteKit game loop, round 2

There's a slight problem with the way you're detecting collisions, and it's related to SpriteKit's game loop.

Earlier, you learned that during SpriteKit's game loop, first update(_:) gets called, then some "other stuff" occurs, and finally SpriteKit renders the screen:

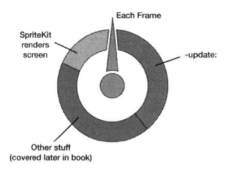

One of the things in the "other stuff" section is the evaluation of the actions you've been learning about in this chapter:

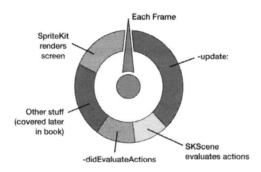

Herein lies the problem with your current collision detection method. You check for collisions at the end of the update(_:) loop, but SpriteKit doesn't evaluate the actions until *after* this update(_:) loop. Therefore, your collision detection code is always one frame behind!

As you can see in your new event loop diagram, it would be much better to perform collision detection after SpriteKit evaluates the actions and all the sprites are in their new spots. So comment out the call at the end of update(_:):

```
// checkCollisions()
```

And implement `didEvaluateActions()` as follows:

```
override func didEvaluateActions() {
   checkCollisions()
}
```

You probably won't notice much of a difference in this case — because the frame rate is so fast, it's hard to tell it was behind. But it could be quite noticeable in other games, so it's best to do things properly.

Sound action

The last type of action you'll learn about in this chapter also happens to be one of the most fun — it's the action that plays sound effects!

Using the `playSoundFileNamed(_:waitForCompletion:)` action, it takes just one line of code to play a sound effect with SpriteKit. The node on which you run this action doesn't matter, so typically you'll run it as an action on the scene itself.

First, you need to add sounds to your project. In the resources for this chapter, find the folder named **Sounds** and drag it into your project. Make sure that **Copy items if needed**, **Create groups** and the **ZombieConga** target are all selected, and click **Finish**.

Now for the code. Add this line to the end of `zombieHit(cat:)`:

```
run(SKAction.playSoundFileNamed("hitCat.wav",
   waitForCompletion: false))
```

Then, add this line to the end of `zombieHit(enemy:)`:

```
run(SKAction.playSoundFileNamed("hitCatLady.wav",
   waitForCompletion: false))
```

Here, you play the appropriate sound action for each type of collision. Build and run, move the zombie around and enjoy the sounds of the smash-up!

Sharing actions

In the previous section, you may noticed a slight pause the first time the sound plays. This can occur whenever the sound system loads a sound file for the first time. The solution to this problem also demonstrates one of the most powerful features of SpriteKit's actions: sharing.

The SKAction object doesn't itself maintain any state, and that allows you to do something cool: reuse actions on any number of nodes simultaneously! For example, the action you create to move the cat ladies across the screen looks something like this:

```
let actionMove =
  SKAction.moveTo(x: -enemy.size.width/2, duration: 2.0)
```

But you're creating this action for every cat lady. Instead, you could create an SKAction property, store this action in it and then use that property wherever you're currently using actionMove.

> **Note:** In fact, you could modify Zombie Conga so it reuses most of the actions you've created so far. This would reduce the amount of memory your system uses, but that's a performance improvement you probably don't need to make in such a simple game.

But how does this relate to the sound delay?

The application is loading the sound the first time you create an action that uses it. So to prevent the sound delay, you can create the actions in advance and then use them when necessary.

Create the following properties:

```
let catCollisionSound: SKAction = SKAction.playSoundFileNamed(
  "hitCat.wav", waitForCompletion: false)
let enemyCollisionSound: SKAction = SKAction.playSoundFileNamed(
  "hitCatLady.wav", waitForCompletion: false)
```

These properties hold shared instances of the sound actions you want to run.

Finally, replace the line that plays the sound in zombieHit(cat:) with the following:

```
run(catCollisionSound)
```

And replace the line that plays the sound in zombieHit(enemy:) with the following:

```
run(enemyCollisionSound)
```

Now you're reusing the same sound actions for all collisions rather than creating a new one for each collision.

Build and run again. You'll no longer experience any pauses before the sound effects play.

As for music, stay tuned (no pun intended!) — you'll learn about that in the next chapter, where you'll wrap up the core gameplay by adding a win/lose scene to the game.

But before you move on, be sure to get some practice with actions by working through the challenges for this chapter!

Challenges

This chapter has three challenges, and as usual, they progress from easiest to hardest.

Be sure to do these challenges. As a SpriteKit developer, you'll be using actions all the time, so it's important to practice with them before moving further.

As always, if you get stuck, you can find solutions in the resources for this chapter — but give it your best shot first!

Challenge 1: The ActionsCatalog demo

This chapter covers the most important actions in SpriteKit, but it doesn't cover all of them. To help you get a solid understanding of all the actions available to you, I've created a little demo named ActionsCatalog, which you can find in the resources for this challenge.

Open the project in Xcode and build and run. You'll see something like the following:

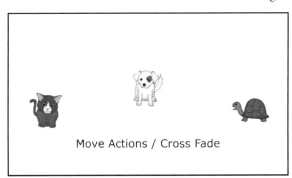

Each scene in the app demonstrates a particular set of actions, shown as the part of the label before the backslash. This first example demonstrates the various move actions.

Each time you tap the screen, you'll see a new set of actions. As the scenes transition, you'll also see different transition effects, shown as the part of the label after the backslash.

Your challenge is to flip through each of these demos, then take a look at the code to answer the following questions:

1. What action constructor would you use to make a sprite follow a certain pre-defined path?

2. What action constructor would you use to make a sprite 50% transparent, regardless of what its current transparency settings are?

3. What are "custom actions" and how do they work at a high level?

You can check your answers in the comment at the top of GameScene.swift in the solution project for this chapter.

Challenge 2: An invincible zombie

Currently, when an enemy hits the zombie, it destroys the enemy. This is a sneaky way of avoiding the problematic scenario of the enemy colliding with the zombie multiple times in a row as it moves through the zombie, which would result in the squish sound effect playing just as many times in rapid succession.

Usually in a video game, you'd resolve this problem by making the player sprite invincible for a few seconds after it gets hit, so the player has time to get his or her bearings.

Your challenge is to modify the game to do just that. When the zombie collides with a cat lady, he should become temporarily invincible instead of destroying the cat lady.

While the zombie is invincible, he should blink. To do this, you can use the custom blink action that's included in ActionsCatalog. Here's the code for your convenience:

```
let blinkTimes = 10.0
let duration = 3.0
let blinkAction = SKAction.customAction(
    withDuration: duration) { node, elapsedTime in
  let slice = duration / blinkTimes
  let remainder = Double(elapsedTime).truncatingRemainder(
    dividingBy: slice)
  node.isHidden = remainder > slice / 2
}
```

If you'd like a detailed explanation of this method, see the comment in the solution for the previous challenge. Here are some hints for solving this challenge:

• You should create a variable property to track whether or not the zombie is invincible.

• If the zombie is invincible, you shouldn't bother enumerating the scene's cat ladies.

• If the zombie collides with a cat lady, don't remove the cat lady from the scene.

Instead, set the zombie as invincible. Next, run a sequence of actions that first makes the zombie blink 10 times over three seconds, then runs the block of code described below.

- The block of code should set `isHidden` to `false` on the zombie, making sure he's visible at the end no matter what, and set the zombie as no longer invincible.

Challenge 3: The conga train

This game is called Zombie Conga, but there's no conga line to be seen just yet!

Your challenge is to fix that. You'll modify the game so that when the zombie collides with a cat, instead of disappearing, the cat joins your conga line!

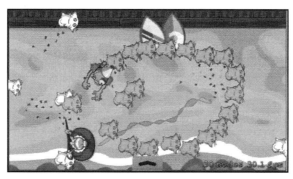

In the process of doing this, you'll get more practice with actions, and you'll also review the vector math material you learned in the last chapter. Yes, that stuff still comes in handy when working with actions!

First, when the zombie collides with a cat, don't remove the cat from the scene. Instead, do the following:

1. Set the cat's name to "train" instead of "cat".

2. Stop all actions currently running on the cat by calling `removeAllActions()`.

3. Set the scale of the cat to `1` and its rotation to `0`.

4. Run an action to make the cat turn green over `0.2` seconds. If you're not sure what action to use for this, check out `ActionsCatalog`.

After this, there are three more things you have to do:

1. Create a constant `CGFloat` property to keep track of the cat's move points per second. Set it to `480.0`.

2. Set the zombie's `zPosition` to `100`, which will make the zombie appear on top of the other sprites. Larger z values are "out of the screen", smaller values are "into the screen" and the default value is `0`.

3. Make a new method named `moveTrain()`. The basic idea for this method is that every so often, you make each cat move toward the current position of the previous cat. This creates a conga line effect!

Use the following template:

```
func moveTrain() {
  var targetPosition = zombie.position

  enumerateChildNodes(withName: "train") { node, stop in
    if !node.hasActions() {
      let actionDuration = 0.3
      let offset = // a
      let direction = // b
      let amountToMovePerSec = // c
      let amountToMove = // d
      let moveAction = // e
      node.run(moveAction)
    }
    targetPosition = node.position
  }
}
```

You need to fill in a through d by using the `CGPoint` operator overloads and utility functions you created last chapter, and e by creating the appropriate action. Here are some hints:

1. You need to figure out the offset between the cat's current position and the target position.

2. You need to figure out a unit vector pointing in the direction of the offset.

3. You need to get a vector pointing in the direction of the offset, but with a length of the cat's move points per second. This represents the amount and direction the cat should move in a second.

4. You need to get a fraction of the `amountToMovePerSec` vector, based on the `actionDuration`. This represents the offset the cat should move over the next `actionDuration` seconds. Note that you'll need to cast `actionDuration` to a `CGFloat`.

5. You should move the cat a relative amount based on the `amountToMove`.

Finally, don't forget to call `moveTrain()` at the end of `update(_:)`.

And that's it — who said you couldn't herd cats? If you got this working, you've truly made this game live up to its name: Zombie Conga!

Chapter 4: Scenes

By Ray Wenderlich

Zombie Conga is beginning to look like a real game. It has character movement, enemies, sounds, animation, collision detection — and if you finished the challenges from the last chapter, even its namesake: a conga line!

However, right now all the action takes place in a single **scene** of the game: the default GameScene created for you by the SpriteKit project template.

In SpriteKit, you don't have to place everything within the same scene. Instead, you can create multiple unique scenes, one for each "screen" of the app, much like how view controllers work in iOS development.

In this short chapter, you'll add two new scenes: one for when the player wins or loses the game and another for the main menu. You'll also learn a bit about using the cool transitions you saw in the ActionsCatalog demo from last chapter's Challenge 1.

But first, you need to wrap up some gameplay logic so you can detect when the player should win or lose the game. Time to get to work!

> **Note:** This chapter begins where the previous chapter's Challenge 3 left off. If you were unable to complete the challenges or skipped ahead from an earlier chapter, don't worry — simply open the starter project from this chapter to pick up where the previous chapter left off.

Win and lose conditions

Here's how the player will win or lose Zombie Conga:

- **Win Condition**: If the player creates a conga line of 15 or more cats, the player wins!

- **Lose Condition**: The player will start with five lives. If the player spends all of his or her lives, the player loses.

Right now, when a crazy cat lady collides with the zombie, nothing bad happens — there's only a sound. To make this game challenging, you'll change this so collisions with a cat lady result in the following effects:

1. The zombie loses a life.

2. The zombie loses two cats from his conga line.

Time to make it so. Inside **GameScene.swift**, add a new property to keep track of the zombie's lives and another to keep track of whether the game is over:

```
var lives = 5
var gameOver = false
```

Next, add this new helper method to make the zombie lose two cats from his conga line:

```
func loseCats() {
  // 1
  var loseCount = 0
  enumerateChildNodes(withName: "train") { node, stop in
    // 2
    var randomSpot = node.position
    randomSpot.x += CGFloat.random(min: -100, max: 100)
    randomSpot.y += CGFloat.random(min: -100, max: 100)
    // 3
    node.name = ""
    node.run(
      SKAction.sequence([
        SKAction.group([
          SKAction.rotate(byAngle: π*4, duration: 1.0),
          SKAction.move(to: randomSpot, duration: 1.0),
          SKAction.scale(to: 0, duration: 1.0)
```

```
        ]),
      SKAction.removeFromParent()
    ]))
    // 4
    loseCount += 1
    if loseCount >= 2 {
      stop[0] = true
    }
  }
}
```

Looking at this section by section:

1. Here, you set up a variable to track the number of cats you've removed from the conga line, then you enumerate through the conga line.

2. You find a random offset from the cat's current position.

3. You run a little animation to make the cat move toward the random spot, spinning around and scaling to 0 along the way. Finally, the animation removes the cat from the scene. You also set the cat's name to an empty string so it's no longer considered a normal cat or a cat in the conga line.

4. You update the variable that's tracking the number of cats you've removed from the conga line. Once you've removed two or more, you set the stop Boolean to true, which causes SpriteKit to stop enumerating the conga line.

Now that you have this helper method, call it in zombieHit(enemy:), right after playing the enemy collision sound, and add a line to subtract 1 from the lives counter:

```
loseCats()
lives -= 1
```

You're ready to add the code that checks if the player should win or lose. Begin with the lose condition. Add this to the end of update(_:):

```
if lives <= 0 && !gameOver {
  gameOver = true
  print("You lose!")
}
```

Here, you check if the number of remaining lives is 0 or less, and you make sure the game isn't already over. If both of these conditions are met, you set the game to be over and log out a message.

To check for the win condition, you'll make a few modifications to moveTrain().

First, add this variable at the beginning of the method:

```
var trainCount = 0
```

You'll use `trainCount` to keep track of the number of cats in the train. Increment this counter with the following line inside the `enumerateChildNodes(withName:using:)` block, before the call to `hasActions()`:

```
trainCount += 1
```

Finally, add this code at the end of `moveTrain()`:

```
if trainCount >= 15 && !gameOver {
  gameOver = true
  print("You win!")
}
```

Here, you check if there are more than 15 cats in the train, and you make sure the game isn't over already. If both of these conditions are met, you set the game to be over and log out a message.

Build and run, and see if you can collect 15 cats.

When you do, you'll see the following message in the console:

```
You win!
```

That's great, but when the player wins the game, you want something a bit more dramatic to happen. A proper "game over" scene should do the trick!

Creating a new scene

To create a new scene, you simply create a new class that derives from SKScene. You can then implement init(size:), update(_:), touchesBegan(_:with:) or any of the other methods you overrode in GameScene to implement the behavior you want.

For now, you're going to keep things simple with a bare-bones new scene. In Xcode's main menu, select **File > New > File...**, select the **iOS/Source/Swift File** template and click **Next**.

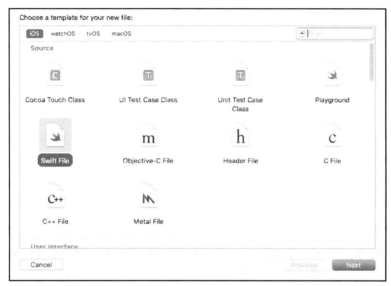

Enter **GameOverScene.swift** for Save As, make sure the **ZombieConga** target is checked and click **Create**.

Open **GameOverScene.swift** and replace its contents with some bare-bones code for the new class:

```
import Foundation
import SpriteKit

class GameOverScene: SKScene {
}
```

With this, you've created an empty class, derived from SKScene, which defaults to a blank screen when presented. Later in this chapter, you'll return to this scene to add artwork and logic.

Now, how do you get to this new scene from your original scene?

Transitioning to a scene

There are three steps to transition from one scene to another:

1. **Create the new scene:** First, you create an instance of the new scene itself. Typically, you'd use the default `init(size:)` initializer, although you can always choose to create your own custom initializer if you want to be able to pass in extra parameters. Later in this chapter, you'll do just that.

2. **Create a transition object:** Next, you create a transition object to specify the type of animation you'd like to use to display the new scene. For example, there are crossfade transitions, flip transitions, door-opening transitions and many more.

3. **Call the SKView's presentScene(_:transition:) method:** In iOS, `SKView` is the `UIView` that displays SpriteKit content on the screen. You can get access to this via a property on the scene: `view`. You can then call `presentScene(_:transition:)` to animate to the passed-in scene (created in step 1) with the passed-in transition (created in step 2).

It's time to give this a try.

Open **GameScene.swift** and add the following lines in `moveTrain()`, right after the code that logs "You win!" to the console (within the `if` statement):

```
// 1
let gameOverScene = GameOverScene(size: size)
gameOverScene.scaleMode = scaleMode
// 2
let reveal = SKTransition.flipHorizontal(withDuration: 0.5)
// 3
view?.presentScene(gameOverScene, transition: reveal)
```

These three lines correspond exactly to the three steps above.

Notice that after creating the game over scene, you set its scale mode to the same as the current scene's scale mode to make sure the new scene behaves the same way across different devices.

Also notice that to create a transition, there are various constructors on `SKTransition`, just as there are various constructors for actions on `SKAction`. Here, you choose a flip horizontal animation, which flips up the scene into view from the bottom of the screen. For a demo of all the transitions, refer to ActionsCatalog, as discussed in the previous chapter's challenges.

Now, add the exact same lines as above to update(_:), right after the code that logs "You lose!" to the console (again, within the if statement):

```
// 1
let gameOverScene = GameOverScene(size: size)
gameOverScene.scaleMode = scaleMode
// 2
let reveal = SKTransition.flipHorizontal(withDuration: 0.5)
// 3
view?.presentScene(gameOverScene, transition: reveal)
```

Build and run, and either win or lose the game. Feel free to cheat and change the number of cats to win to less than 15 — after all, you're the developer!

Whether you win or lose, when you do, you'll see the scene transition to a new blank scene:

That's really all there is to scene transitions! Now that you have a new scene, you can do whatever you like in it, just as you did in GameScene.

For Zombie Conga, you'll modify this new scene to show either a "You Win" or a "You Lose" background. To make this possible, you will create a custom scene initializer to pass in either the win or lose condition.

Creating a custom scene initializer

Open **GameOverScene.swift** and modify GameOverScene as follows:

```
class GameOverScene: SKScene {
  let won:Bool

  init(size: CGSize, won: Bool) {
    self.won = won
    super.init(size: size)
  }
```

```
  required init(coder aDecoder: NSCoder) {
    fatalError("init(coder:) has not been implemented")
  }
}
```

Here, you add a custom initializer that takes just one extra parameter: a Boolean that should be `true` if the player won and `false` if the player lost. You store this value in a property named `won`.

Next, implement `didMove(to:)` to configure the scene when it's added to the view hierarchy:

```
override func didMove(to view: SKView) {
  var background: SKSpriteNode
  if (won) {
    background = SKSpriteNode(imageNamed: "YouWin")
    run(SKAction.playSoundFileNamed("win.wav",
        waitForCompletion: false))
  } else {
    background = SKSpriteNode(imageNamed: "YouLose")
    run(SKAction.playSoundFileNamed("lose.wav",
        waitForCompletion: false))
  }

  background.position =
    CGPoint(x: size.width/2, y: size.height/2)
  self.addChild(background)

  // More here...
}
```

This looks at the `won` Boolean and chooses the proper background image to set and the sound effect to play.

In Zombie Conga, you want to display the game over scene for a few seconds and then automatically transition back to the main scene. To do this, add these lines of code right after the "More here..." comment:

```
let wait = SKAction.wait(forDuration: 3.0)
let block = SKAction.run {
  let myScene = GameScene(size: self.size)
  myScene.scaleMode = self.scaleMode
  let reveal = SKTransition.flipHorizontal(withDuration: 0.5)
  self.view?.presentScene(myScene, transition: reveal)
}
self.run(SKAction.sequence([wait, block]))
```

By now, this is all review for you. The code runs a sequence of actions on the scene, first waiting for three seconds and then calling a block of code. The block of code creates a new instance of GameScene and transitions to that with a flip animation.

One last step: You need to modify your code in GameScene to use this new custom initializer. Open **GameScene.swift** and inside update(_:), change the line that creates the GameOverScene to indicate that this is the lose condition:

```
let gameOverScene = GameOverScene(size: size, won: false)
```

Inside moveTrain(), change the same line, but indicate that this is the win condition:

```
let gameOverScene = GameOverScene(size: size, won: true)
```

Build and run, and play until you win the game. When you do, you'll see the win scene, which will then flip back to a new game after a few seconds:

Now that your game is close to done, it's a good time to turn off the debug drawing for the playable rectangle. Comment out this line in didMove(to:):

```
// debugDrawPlayableArea()
```

Background music

You almost have a complete game, but you're missing one thing: awesome background music!

Luckily, we've got you covered. Open **MyUtils.swift** and add the following to the bottom of the file:

```
import AVFoundation

var backgroundMusicPlayer: AVAudioPlayer!
```

```
func playBackgroundMusic(filename: String) {
  let resourceUrl = Bundle.main.url(forResource:
    filename, withExtension: nil)
  guard let url = resourceUrl else {
    print("Could not find file: \(filename)")
    return
  }

  do {
    try backgroundMusicPlayer =
      AVAudioPlayer(contentsOf: url)
    backgroundMusicPlayer.numberOfLoops = -1
    backgroundMusicPlayer.prepareToPlay()
    backgroundMusicPlayer.play()
  } catch {
    print("Could not create audio player!")
    return
  }
}
```

SpriteKit has no built-in way to play background music, so you'll have to fall back on other iOS APIs to do it. One easy way to play music in iOS is to use the `AVAudioPlayer` class inside the AVFoundation framework. The above helper code uses an `AVAudioPlayer` to play some background music in an endless loop.

Back in **GameScene.swift**, try it out by adding this line to the top of `didMove(to:)`:

```
playBackgroundMusic(filename: "backgroundMusic.mp3")
```

Here, you make the game play the background music when the scene first loads.

Finally, you need to stop the background music when the player switches scenes, so they can hear the "you win" or "you lose" sound effects. To do this, add this line right after the "You win!" log line in `moveTrain()`:

```
backgroundMusicPlayer.stop()
```

Also add that same line right after the "You lose!" log line in `update(_:)`:

```
backgroundMusicPlayer.stop()
```

Build and run, and enjoy your groovy tunes!

Challenges

This was a short and sweet chapter, and the challenges will be equally so. With only one challenge for this chapter, it's time to add a main menu scene to the game.

As always, if you get stuck, you can find the solution in the resources for this chapter — but give it your best shot first!

Challenge 1: Main menu scene

Often, it's best to start a game with an opening or main menu scene, rather than throw the player right into the action. The main menu often includes options to start a new game, continue a game, access game options and so on.

Zombie Conga's main menu scene will be simple. It will show an image and let the player tap to continue straight to a new game. This will effectively be the same as the splash screen, except it will allow the player more time to get her bearings.

Your challenge is to implement a main menu scene that shows the **MainMenu.png** image as a background and upon a screen tap, uses a "doorway" transition over 1.5 seconds to transition to the main action scene.

Here are a few hints for how to accomplish this:

1. Create a new class that derives from `SKScene` named `MainMenuScene`.

2. Implement `didMove(to:)` on `MainMenuScene` to display **MainMenu.png** in the center of the scene.

3. Inside **GameViewController.swift**, edit `viewDidLoad()` to make it start with `MainMenuScene` instead of `GameScene`.

4. Build and run, and make sure the main menu image appears. So far, so good!

5. Finally, implement `touchesBegan(_:with:)` in `MainMenuScene` to call a helper method, `sceneTapped()`. `sceneTapped()` should transition to `GameScene` using a "doorway" transition over 1.5 seconds.

If you've gotten this working, congratulations! You now have a firm understanding of how to create and transition between multiple scenes in SpriteKit.

Chapter 5: Camera

By Ray Wenderlich

So far, Zombie Conga's background has been stationary. In contrast, many games have large scrolling worlds, like the original *Super Mario Bros.*:

The red box shows what you can see on the screen, but the level continues beyond to the right. As the player moves Mario to the right, you can think of the background as moving to the left:

There are two ways to accomplish this kind of scrolling in SpriteKit:

1. **Move the background**. Make the player, enemies and power-ups children of the "background layer." Then, to scroll the game, you can simply move the background layer from right to left, and its children will move with it.

2. **Move the camera**. Alternatively, you can use SpriteKit's built in SKCameraNode class, which makes creating scrolling games even easier. You simply add a camera node to the scene, and the camera node's position represents the center of the current view.

In this chapter, you're going to use SKCameraNode to scroll the game, since this is the easiest method and likely what developers will use the most, now that it's available. It's time to get scrolling!

> Note: This chapter begins where the previous chapter's Challenge 1 left off. If you were unable to complete the challenges or skipped ahead from an earlier chapter, don't worry — simply open the starter project from this chapter to pick up where the previous chapter left off.

Lights, camera, action!

Working with SKCameraNode is a cinch. You simply:

1. Create an instance SKCameraNode.

2. Add it to the scene and set the scene's camera property to the camera node.

3. Set the camera node's position, which will represent the center of the screen.

Give this a try. Open **GameScene.swift** and add the following new property for the camera node:

```
let cameraNode = SKCameraNode()
```

This completes step 1. Next, add these lines to the end of didMove(to:):

```
addChild(cameraNode)
camera = cameraNode
cameraNode.position = CGPoint(x: size.width/2, y: size.height/2)
```

This completes steps 2 and 3, centering the view in the middle of the scene.

Build and run, and you'll see the following:

The game works as before, except now you're using a camera node. To see the benefit of this, make the camera follow the zombie by adding this line of code to the end of `update(_:)`:

```
cameraNode.position = zombie.position
```

Build and run, and you'll see that the camera now follows the zombie:

That was easy! But right now, the background is only sized to match the visible area. You don't want your zombie walking through the void, so comment out that line for now.

```
// cameraNode.position = zombie.position
```

A scrolling background

As you may remember from Chapter 2, you're using a background named **background1** that's the same size as the scene itself. Your project contains a second background named **background2** that's designed to be placed to the right of background1, like so:

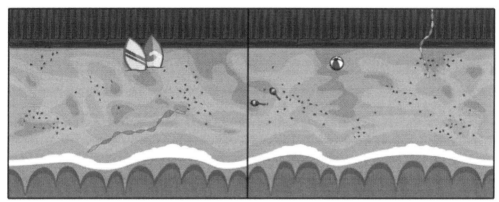

background1   **background2**

Your first task is simple: combine these two background images into a single node so you can easily scroll them both at the same time.

Add this new method to `GameScene`:

```
func backgroundNode() -> SKSpriteNode {
  // 1
  let backgroundNode = SKSpriteNode()
  backgroundNode.anchorPoint = CGPoint.zero
  backgroundNode.name = "background"

  // 2
  let background1 = SKSpriteNode(imageNamed: "background1")
  background1.anchorPoint = CGPoint.zero
  background1.position = CGPoint(x: 0, y: 0)
  backgroundNode.addChild(background1)

  // 3
  let background2 = SKSpriteNode(imageNamed: "background2")
  background2.anchorPoint = CGPoint.zero
  background2.position =
    CGPoint(x: background1.size.width, y: 0)
  backgroundNode.addChild(background2)

  // 4
  backgroundNode.size = CGSize(
    width: background1.size.width + background2.size.width,
    height: background1.size.height)
```

```
      return backgroundNode
  }
```

Take a look at this section by section:

1. You create a new SKNode to contain both background sprites as children. In this case, instead of using SKNode directly, you use an SKSpriteNode with no texture. This is so you can conveniently set the size property on the SKSpriteNode to the combined size of the background images.

2. You create an SKSpriteNode for the first background image and pin the bottom-left of the sprite to the bottom-left of backgroundNode.

3. You create an SKSpriteNode for the second background image and pin the bottom-left of the sprite to the bottom-right of background1 inside backgroundNode.

4. You set the size of the backgroundNode based on the size of the two background images.

Next, replace the code that creates the background sprite in didMove(to:) with the following:

```
let background = backgroundNode()
background.anchorPoint = CGPoint.zero
background.position = CGPoint.zero
background.name = "background"
addChild(background)
```

This simply creates the background using your new helper method rather than basing it on a single background image.

Also note that before, you had the background centered onscreen. Here, you pin the lower-left corner to the lower-left of the scene, instead.

Changing the anchor point to the lower-left like this will make it easier to calculate positions when the time comes. You also name the background, "background", so you can readily find it.

Your goal is to make this camera scroll from left to right. To do this, add a property for the camera's scrolling speed:

```
let cameraMovePointsPerSec: CGFloat = 200.0
```

Next, add this helper method to move the camera:

```
func moveCamera() {
  let backgroundVelocity =
    CGPoint(x: cameraMovePointsPerSec, y: 0)
```

```
    let amountToMove = backgroundVelocity * CGFloat(dt)
    cameraNode.position += amountToMove
}
```

This calculates the amount the camera should move this frame, and updates the camera's position accordingly.

Finally, call this new method inside update(_:), right after the call to moveTrain():

```
moveCamera()
```

Build and run, and now you have a scrolling background:

But as the screen scrolls, the zombie disappears offscreen, the cats stop spawning — and eventually, you see the void:

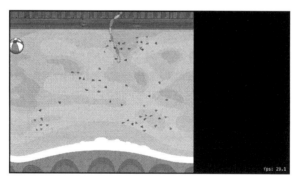

Don't worry. It's not the end of the world yet; it's only a minor zombie apocalypse! Nonetheless, it's time to fix these problems — starting by endlessly scrolling the background.

An endlessly scrolling background

The most efficient way to continuously scroll your background is to make two background nodes instead of one and lay them side by side:

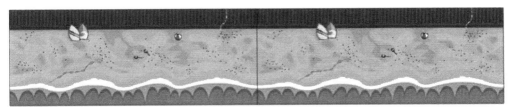

Then, as you scroll both images from right to left, as soon as one of the images goes offscreen, you simply reposition it to the right:

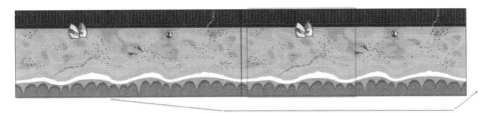

To do this, replace the code that creates the background node in `didMove(to:)` with the following:

```
for i in 0...1 {
  let background = backgroundNode()
  background.anchorPoint = CGPoint.zero
  background.position =
    CGPoint(x: CGFloat(i)*background.size.width, y: 0)
  background.name = "background"
  addChild(background)
}
```

Also, if you still have the lines that get and log the background's size, comment them out.

The above wraps the code in a `for` loop that creates two copies of the background and then sets their positions, so the second copy begins after the first ends.

Next, add this computed property:

```
var cameraRect : CGRect {
  let x = cameraNode.position.x - size.width/2
      + (size.width - playableRect.width)/2
  let y = cameraNode.position.y - size.height/2
      + (size.height - playableRect.height)/2
```

```
    return CGRect(
      x: x,
      y: y,
      width: playableRect.width,
      height: playableRect.height)
  }
```

This is a helper method that calculates the current "visible playable area". You'll be using this for calculations throughout the rest of the chapter.

Next, add the following code to the bottom of `moveCamera()`:

```
enumerateChildNodes(withName: "background") { node, _ in
  let background = node as! SKSpriteNode
  if background.position.x + background.size.width <
      self.cameraRect.origin.x {
    background.position = CGPoint(
      x: background.position.x + background.size.width*2,
      y: background.position.y)
  }
}
```

For each of the two background nodes, you check to see if the right-hand side of the background is less than the left-hand side of the current visible playable area — in other words, if it's offscreen. Remember, you set the anchor point of the background to its bottom-left.

If the background is completely offscreen, you simply move the background node to the right by double the width of the background. Since there are two background nodes, this places the offscreen node immediately to the right of the other, onscreen node.

Build and run, and now you have a continuously scrolling background! You saved the world from ending — even if it still has zombies.

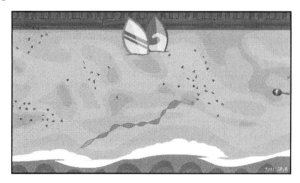

Fixing the gameplay

You've fixed the background, but the gameplay is still wonky. Nothing appears to stay on the screen!

WHAT IZ   HAPPEN...?

Start by reining in the zombie. In **GameScene.swift**, review boundsCheckZombie() and see if you can spot the problem:

```
let bottomLeft = CGPoint(x: 0, y: playableRect.minY)
let topRight = CGPoint(x: size.width, y: playableRect.maxY)
```

This code assumes that the visible portion of the scene never changes from its original position. To correct that assumption, change the lines above so they look like this:

```
let bottomLeft = CGPoint(x: cameraRect.minX, y: cameraRect.minY)
let topRight = CGPoint(x: cameraRect.maxX, y: cameraRect.maxY)
```

Here you grab the coordinates from the visible playable area, rather than hardcoding a fixed position.

Looking at the same method, update the zombie.position.x <= bottomLeft.x branch as follows:

```
if zombie.position.x <= bottomLeft.x {
  zombie.position.x = bottomLeft.x
  velocity.x = abs(velocity.x)
}
```

Since the visible playable area is moving now, it's possible for the zombie to bump into the left boundary even if his x-velocity is positive. This code will ensure that whenever the zombie reaches the left boundary, his x-velocity will stay pointed toward the right.

The cats have a problem as well. Inside `spawnCat()`, change the lines that set the cat's position to the following:

```
cat.position = CGPoint(
  x: CGFloat.random(min: cameraRect.minX,
                    max: cameraRect.maxX),
  y: CGFloat.random(min: cameraRect.minY,
                    max: cameraRect.maxY))
cat.zPosition = 50
```

This updates the cat so it spawns within the visible playable area rather than a fixed area. You also update the cat's `zPosition` to make sure it stays on top of the background, but below the zombie.

There's one last thing. Since the background is continuously scrolling, your gameplay will be a lot more dynamic if you disable the code that stops the zombie once he reaches the target point. This way, the zombie will always keep running. Remember, this was the zombie's original behavior before your second challenge in Chapter 2.

To let your zombie loose, comment out the relevant code in `update(_:)`, as shown below:

```
/*
if let lastTouchLocation = lastTouchLocation {
  let diff = lastTouchLocation - zombie.position
  if diff.length() <= zombieMovePointsPerSec * CGFloat(dt) {
    zombie.position = lastTouchLocation
    velocity = CGPoint.zero
    stopZombieAnimation()
  } else {
  */
    move(sprite: zombie, velocity: velocity)
    rotate(sprite: zombie, direction: velocity,
      rotateRadiansPerSec: zombieRotateRadiansPerSec)
  /*}
}*/
```

Build and run, and now most of the gameplay works smoothly:

w00t, you're almost done — the only thing left to fix are the enemies! And that challenge is left to you. :]

Challenges

There's only one challenge this time: fixing the gameplay for the enemies.

As always, if you get stuck, you can find the solutions in the resources for this chapter — but give it your best shot first!

Challenge 1: Fixing the enemies

After a while, the crazy cat ladies stop spawning and in some cases appear behind the background.

Look at `spawnEnemy()` and you'll see this is because you're still creating the spawn point assuming the camera never moves, rather than using the currently visible playable area.

Your challenge is to modify this method to instead spawn enemies right outside of the currently visible playable area. Also, be sure to set the enemies' `zPosition` to match that of the cat so they don't appear behind the background.

After you do this, you'll notice that as the level goes on, the enemies spawn faster and faster. Find out why this is and fix it.

> **Hint:** It has something to do with `actionMove` — is there an alternative action type you can use instead?

If you got this working, congratulations — you now have a complete scrolling game! There's just one bit of polish to wrap things up before we move on to another game: adding some labels to Zombie Conga.

Chapter 6: Labels

By Ray Wenderlich

Text is an important element in games; it's one of the few ways you have to communicate details about the game state to the player. For example, currently in Zombie Conga, there's no indication of how many lives you have remaining — which can be quite frustrating if you run out unexpectedly!

In this chapter, you'll learn how to display fonts and text within your game. Specifically, you'll add two labels to Zombie Conga: one to display your current lives and one to display your count of cats.

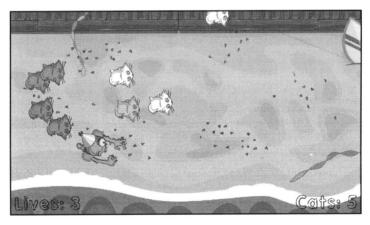

Note: This chapter begins where the previous chapter's Challenge 1 left off. If you were unable to complete the challenge or skipped ahead from an earlier chapter, don't worry — simply open the starter project from this chapter to pick up where the previous chapter left off.

Built-in fonts and font families

In iOS, fonts are broken into sets named "families". A font "family" consists of variants of the same font — such as lighter or heavier versions of the font — which may be useful in different situations.

For example, the "Thonburi" font family consists of three fonts:

1. **Thonburi-Light**: A thin/light version of the font.

2. **Thonburi**: A standard version of the font.

3. **Thonburi-Bold**: A bold version of the font.

Some font families have even more variants; the "Avenir" family has 12!

iOS ships with a number of built-in font families and fonts, so before you start using labels, you need to know what's available to you. To find out, you'll create a simple SpriteKit project that lets you see these different fonts at a glance.

Create a new project in Xcode by selecting **File > New > Project...** from the main menu. Select the **iOS/Application/Game** template and click **Next**.

Enter **AvailableFonts** for the Product Name, select **Swift** as the Language, **SpriteKit** as the Game Technology, **Universal** for Devices and then click **Next**.

Select a location on your hard drive to store the project and click **Create**. You now have a simple SpriteKit project open in Xcode that you'll use to list the font families and fonts available in iOS.

You want this app to run in portrait mode, so select **AvailableFonts** in the project navigator and then select the **AvailableFonts** target. Go to the General tab, check **Portrait** and uncheck all other orientations.

Just like in Zombie Conga, you'll create this scene programmatically rather than using the scene editor. To do this, select **GameScene.sks** and **Actions.sks** and delete them from your project. Then open **GameViewController.swift** and replace the contents with:

```swift
import UIKit
import SpriteKit

class GameViewController: UIViewController {
  override func viewDidLoad() {
    super.viewDidLoad()
    let scene =
      GameScene(size:CGSize(width: 2048, height: 1536))
    let skView = self.view as! SKView
    skView.showsFPS = false
    skView.showsNodeCount = false
```

```
      skView.ignoresSiblingOrder = true
      scene.scaleMode = .aspectFill
      skView.presentScene(scene)
    }

    override var prefersStatusBarHidden: Bool {
      return true
    }
  }
}
```

This is similar to the code you used in Zombie Conga; it simply creates and presents GameScene to the screen.

Next, open **GameScene.swift** and replace its contents with the following:

```
import SpriteKit

class GameScene: SKScene {

  var familyIndex: Int = -1

  required init?(coder aDecoder: NSCoder) {
    super.init(coder: aDecoder)
  }

  override init(size: CGSize) {
    super.init(size: size)
    showNextFamily()
  }

  func showCurrentFamily() -> Bool {
    // TODO: Coming soon...
    return true
  }

  override func touchesBegan(_ touches: Set<UITouch>,
                             with event: UIEvent?) {
    showNextFamily()
  }

  func showNextFamily() {
    var familyShown = false
    repeat {
      familyIndex += 1
      if familyIndex >= UIFont.familyNames.count {
        familyIndex = 0
      }
      familyShown = showCurrentFamily()
    } while !familyShown
  }
}
```

You begin by displaying the first available font family. Every time the user taps, you advance to display the next font family that is successfully shown. In iOS, you can get a list of the built-in font family names by calling `UIFont.familyNames`.

The code to display the fonts in the current font family will be in `showCurrentFamily()`, so implement that now by replacing that method's contents with the following:

```
// 1
removeAllChildren()

// 2
let familyName = UIFont.familyNames[familyIndex]

// 3
let fontNames = UIFont.fontNames(forFamilyName: familyName)
if fontNames.count == 0 {
  return false
}
print("Family: \(familyName)")

// 4
for (idx, fontName) in fontNames.enumerated() {
  let label = SKLabelNode(fontNamed: fontName)
  label.text = fontName
  label.position = CGPoint(
    x: size.width / 2,
    y: (size.height * (CGFloat(idx+1))) /
      (CGFloat(fontNames.count)+1))
  label.fontSize = 50
  label.verticalAlignmentMode = .center
  addChild(label)
}
return true
```

Taking this code section by section:

1. You remove all of the children from the scene so that you start with a blank slate.

2. You get the current family name based on the `familyIndex` that you increment with each tap.

3. `UIFont` has another helper method to get the names of the fonts within a family, named `fontNames(forFamilyName:)`. You call this here and store the results. If the results array is empty, do not show this font family. You also log out the family name, in case you're curious about it.

4. You then loop through `fontNames` and create a label using each font; the text of each label displays the name of the corresponding font. Since labels are the subject of this chapter, you'll review them in more detail next.

Creating a label

Creating a label is easy. You simply call `SKLabelNode(fontNamed:)` and pass in the name of the font:

```
let label = SKLabelNode(fontNamed: fontName)
```

The most important property to set is the text, because this is what you want the font to display.

```
label.text = fontName
```

You also usually want to set the font size (unless you want the default of 32 points).

```
label.fontSize = 50
```

Finally, just as with any other node, you position it and add it as a child of another node — in this case, the scene itself:

```
label.position = yourPosition
addChild(label)
```

For now, don't worry too much about the math you're using to position the labels. Also, don't worry about your use of `verticalAlignmentMode` — that's simply a little code magic to space the labels evenly up and down the screen. You'll learn more about alignment later in this chapter.

Build and run. Now, every time you tap the screen, you'll see a different built-in font family:

Tap through to get an idea of what's available. Try to find the font named "Chalkduster" — you'll be using that shortly in Zombie Conga.

This app will be a handy reference in the future when you're wondering which font would be the perfect match for your game.

> **Note:** Available fonts may vary across iOS version and device, so be sure to account for all of your app's supported versions and devices when choosing fonts.

Adding a label to Zombie Conga

Now that you know a little more about the available fonts, it's time to use what you've learned to add a label to Zombie Conga. You'll start with a simple label to show the player's remaining lives.

Open your Zombie Conga project, using either your post-challenge project file from the previous chapter or the starter project for this chapter.

With the appropriate project loaded in Xcode, open **GameScene.swift** and add this line to the bottom of the list of properties:

```
let livesLabel = SKLabelNode(fontNamed: "Chalkduster")
```

Here, you create an SKLabelNode, passing in the "Chalkduster" font you discovered in AvailableFonts earlier.

Next, add these lines to the bottom of `didMove(to:)`:

```
livesLabel.text = "Lives: X"
livesLabel.fontColor = SKColor.black
livesLabel.fontSize = 100
livesLabel.zPosition = 150
livesLabel.position = CGPoint(x: size.width/2, y: size.height/2)
addChild(livesLabel)
```

Here, you do the same sorts of things you already learned about: set the text to a placeholder, set the position to the center of the screen, set the font size and then add the node as a child of the scene. You also set a new property, `fontColor`, to set the color of the text.

Build and run, and you'll see the label. But wait! It scrolls off the screen as the camera moves!

It's because you added the label as a child of the scene; as you move the camera, it "looks at" different parts of the scene.

What you really want is for the label to stay in the same position relative to the camera node. You can do this by adding the label as a child of the camera node instead.

Change the last two lines to the following:

```
livesLabel.position = CGPoint.zero
cameraNode.addChild(livesLabel)
```

Remember, a node's position is relative to the position of its parent, so `CGPoint.zero` means the center of the camera.

Build and run, and you'll see the label is now in a fixed position near the center of the screen:

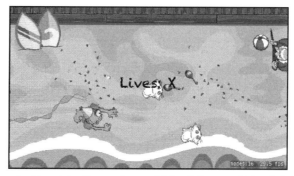

This looks good, but in Zombie Conga it would look better if this label were aligned to the bottom-left of the playable area. For you to understand how to do this, I'd like to introduce you to the concept of **alignment modes**.

Alignment modes

So far, you know you can place a label by setting its position, but how can you control the placement of the text in relation to the position?

Unlike SKSpriteNode, SKLabelNode doesn't have an anchorPoint property. In its place, you can use the verticalAlignmentMode and horizontalAlignmentMode properties.

The verticalAlignmentMode controls the text's vertical placement in relation to the label's position, and the horizontalAlignmentMode controls the text's horizontal placement. You can see this visually in the following diagram:

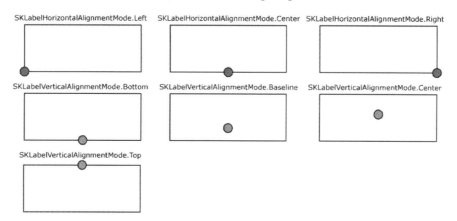

The red and blue points in the diagram show, for the different alignment modes, where each label's bounding box will be rendered in relation to the label's position. There are two things worth noting here:

- The default alignment modes of `SKLabelNode` are `center` for horizontal and `baseline` for vertical.

- `baseline` uses the actual font's baseline, which you can think of as the "line" on which you would draw a font if you were writing on ruled paper. For example, the tails of letters such as "g" and "y" will hang below the baseline — and thus, the defined position.

To align the lives label to the bottom-left of the screen, you want to set the alignment modes to `left` for horizontal and `bottom` for vertical. This way, you can simply set the position to the bottom-left of the playable area.

It's time to try this out. Delete the line that sets the label's position and replace it with the following:

```
livesLabel.horizontalAlignmentMode = .left
livesLabel.verticalAlignmentMode = .bottom
livesLabel.position = CGPoint(
  x: -playableRect.size.width/2 + CGFloat(20),
  y: -playableRect.size.height/2 + CGFloat(20))
```

Here you set the alignment modes as discussed, and then set the position to the bottom-left of the playable area. Here's a diagram to help you visualize this:

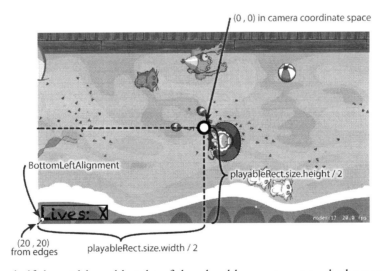

You subtract half the width and height of the playable area to get to the bottom-left corner, then add a 20-point margin to provide some space between the label and edges.

Build and run, and now you'll see the label correctly positioned in the bottom-left of the playable area.

Loading custom fonts

While the list of built-in fonts is large, there will be times you want to use fonts that aren't included by default.

For example, in Zombie Conga, it would be nice to switch to a font that's less intrusive in the game, but none of the fonts included by default are going to meet your needs. Luckily, Apple has made it super simple to use a **True Type Font** (TTF) in your project.

First, you need to find the font you want to use. One excellent source of fonts is http://www.dafont.com. Open your browser of choice and go to that URL; you'll see there's a large selection of categories from which to choose, including one named **Fancy\Cartoon**.

Click on that category, and you'll see a huge list of fonts with example text. Some people could spend hours looking through these fonts just for fun, so take as much time as you like to see what's available.

Now that you're back, the font you're going to use is named **Glimstick** by Uddi Uddi. Type that name into the search bar on the dafont.com website. A font preview will appear:

This fun cartoony font is a perfect fit for the minigame you're creating. Click the **Download** button. Once the download is complete, unzip the package and find the file named **GLIMSTIC.TTF**. The resources for this chapter also include a copy of this font, in case you have trouble downloading it.

> **Note:** It's important to check the license for any fonts you want to use in your project. Some fonts require permission or a license before you can use them, so checking now could save a lot of headache and cost later.
>
> You can see just above the download button that the Glimstick font you're using is marked as **Free**, but to be sure, always check the license information included in the downloaded zip file.

Now that you have your font, drag **GLIMSTIC.TTF** into your Zombie Conga project. Make sure that **Copy items if needed** and the **ZombieConga** target are checked, then click **Finish**.

At this point, you should double check that the font has been added into the correct build phase for your project. To check this, select **ZombieConga** in the project navigator, select the **ZombieConga** target, select **Build Phases**, expand the **Copy Bundle Resources** area and check that **GLIMSTIC.TTF** is listed there. If not, click the + button and select it manually.

Next, open **Info.plist** and click on the last entry in the list, and you'll see plus (+) and minus (-) buttons appear next to that title.

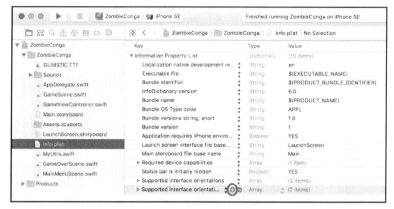

Click the plus button and a new entry will appear in the table, along with a drop-down list of options:

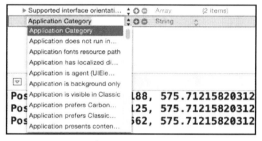

In the drop-down box, type **Fonts**, making sure to use a capital **F**. The first option that comes up will be **Fonts provided by application**. Press **Return** to select that option.

Click the triangle to the left of the new entry to expand it, and double-click inside the value field.

Inside the textbox that appears, type **GLIMSTIC.TTF**. This is the name of the font file you downloaded and the one you're going to use in the game. Be sure to spell it correctly or your app won't be able to load it.

Now, to try out this font! Open **GameScene.swift** and replace your line that declares the livesLabel property with the following:

```
let livesLabel = SKLabelNode(fontNamed: "Glimstick")
```

> **Note:** Note that the font filename (i.e. "GLIMSTIC.TTF") does not necessarily have to match the actual name of the font (i.e. "Glimstick"). You can find the actual name of the font by double-clicking the .TTF file.

Build and run, and you'll see your new font appear:

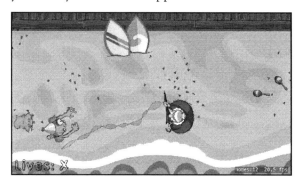

Updating the label text

One last thing: The label is still showing the placeholder text. To update the text, simply add this line to update(_:) after moveCamera():

```
livesLabel.text = "Lives: \(lives)"
```

Build and run, and now your lives will properly update!

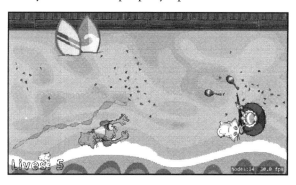

Challenges

This is your final challenge for Zombie Conga. Your game is 99% complete, so don't leave it hanging!

As always, if you get stuck, you can find the solutions in the resources for this chapter — but give it your best shot first!

Challenge 1: A cat count

Your challenge is to add a second label to the game to keep track of the count of cats in your conga train. This label should be in the bottom-right of the playable area.

Here are a few hints:

- Create a property named `catsLabel` like you did for the `livesLabel`.

- In `didMove(to:)`, configure the `catsLabel` similarly to the `livesLabel`. However, you'll have to change the `text`, `horizontalAlignmentMode` and `position`

- For the `position`, refer to the diagram earlier in the chapter if you get stuck.

- Finally, in `moveTrain()`, update the `catsLabel.text` based on `trainCount`.

If you've made it this far, a huge congratulations — you've completed your first SpriteKit minigame, from scratch! Think of everything you learned. You now know how to:

- Add sprites to a game.

- Move them around manually.

- Move them around with actions.

- Create multiple scenes in a game.

- Make it a scrolling game with a camera.

- Add labels to the game.

Believe it or not, this knowledge is sufficient to make 90% of SpriteKit games. The rest is just icing on the cake! :]

Section II: Physics and Nodes

In this section, you'll learn how to use the built-in 2D physics engine included with SpriteKit to create movement as realistic as that in Angry Birds or Cut the Rope. You'll also learn how to use special types of nodes which allow you to play videos and create shapes in your game.

In the process, you'll create a physics puzzle game named Cat Nap, where you take the role of a cat who's had a long day and just wants to go to bed.

Chapter 7: Scene Editor

Chapter 8: Beginning Physics

Chapter 9: Intermediate Physics

Chapter 10: Advanced Physics

Chapter 11: Crop, Video and Shape Nodes

Chapter 7: Scene Editor

By Marin Todorov

In this chapter, you'll begin to build the second minigame in this book: a puzzle game named Cat Nap. Here's what it will look like when you're finished:

In Cat Nap, you take the role of a cat who's had a long day and just wants to go to bed.

However, a thoughtless human has cluttered the cat's bed with scrap materials from his recent home renovation. This silly human's bad choices are preventing the cat from falling asleep! Of course, since cats don't care much about — well, anything — he sits on top of the scrap anyway.

Your job is to destroy the blocks by tapping them so the cat can comfortably fall into place. Be careful, though: If you cause the cat to fall on the floor or tip onto his side, he'll wake up and get really cranky.

The puzzle is to destroy the blocks in the correct order, so the cat falls straight down. One wrong choice and — queue evil music — you face the Wrath of Kitteh!

You'll build this game across the next six chapters, in stages:

1. **Chapter 7, Scene Editor**: You are here! You'll begin by creating the first level of the game, pictured above. By the end, you'll have a better understanding of Xcode's scene editor.

2. **Chapter 8, Beginning Physics**: In this chapter, you're going to make a little detour in order to learn the basics of creating physics simulations for your games. As a bonus, you'll learn how to prototype games inside an Xcode playground.

3. **Chapter 9, Intermediate Physics**: You'll learn about physics-based collision detection and create custom classes for your SpriteKit nodes.

4. **Chapter 10, Advanced Physics**: You'll add two more levels to the game as you learn about interactive bodies, joints between bodies, composed bodies and more.

5. **Chapter 11, Crop, Video and Shape Nodes**: You'll add special new blocks to Cat Nap while learning about additional types of nodes that allow you to do amazing things — like play videos, crop images and create dynamic shapes.

It's time to get started — there's nothing worse (or perhaps funnier) than an impatient cat!

Getting started

Start Xcode and select **File > New > Project...** from the main menu. Select the **iOS/Application/Game** template and click **Next**.

Enter **CatNap** for the Product Name, **Swift** for the Language, **SpriteKit** for the Game Technology and **Universal** for the Devices. Click **Next**, then choose a place on your hard drive to save your project and click **Create**.

You want this app to run in landscape rather than portrait mode. Just like you did in Chapter 1, "Sprites", select the **CatNap** project in the project navigator and then select the **CatNap** target. Go to the **General** tab and verify that under Device Orientation only **Landscape Left** and **Landscape Right** are checked.

You also need to modify this in one more spot. Open **Info.plist** and find the **Supported interface orientations (iPad)** entry. Delete the entries for **Portrait (bottom home button)** and **Portrait (top home button)** so that only the landscape options remain.

To get this game started on the right foot, or should we say paw, you need to set up an app icon. To do this, select **Assets.xassets** in the project navigator on the left and then select the **AppIcon** entry. Then, in the resources for this chapter, drag all of the files from the **starter/Resources/Icons/iOS** folder into the area on the right.

> **Note:** If Xcode adds icons for CarPlay, remove those and make sure the box is unchecked for CarPlay in the Attributes Inspector. You might need to drag a few individual files until Xcode properly matches all required icons.

You'll see the following when you're done:

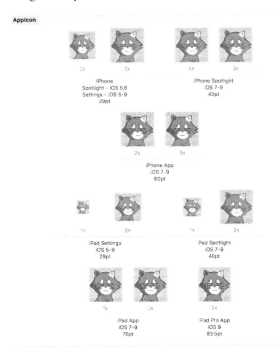

There's one final step. Open **GameViewController.swift** and modify the line that sets `skView.ignoresSiblingOrder` from `true` to `false`:

```
view.ignoresSiblingOrder = false
```

This makes it so nodes with the same `zPosition` are drawn in the order in which they are added to the scene, which will make developing Cat Nap a bit simpler. Keep in mind, though, that there's a performance cost incurred by changing this setting to `false`. Luckily, for a simple game like this, it's not a problem.

Build and run the project in iOS Simulator. You'll see the "Hello, World!" message nicely positioned in the center of the screen, in landscape mode.

Introducing texture atlases

Before you can add sprites to the scene, you need images for them, right? In the resources for this chapter, locate the **Resources** folder; this includes all the images, sounds and other files you'll need for Cat Nap; it's the folder where the project icons were located.

In Xcode, open **Assets.xcassets** and drag in all of the images from the **Resources/Images** folder. Also delete **Spaceship** from the asset catalog; this cat prefers both paws on the ground! At this point, your asset catalog should look like this:

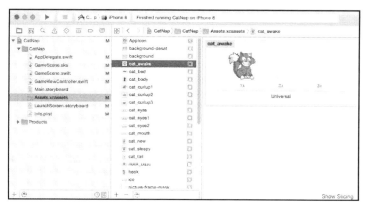

Next, drag the **Resources/Sounds** folder into your project and make sure that **Copy items if needed**, **Create groups** and the **CatNap** target are all checked. At this point, your project navigator should look like this:

Woo-hoo! You've finished setting up your project. Now it's time to fire up the scene editor.

Getting started with the scene editor

As mentioned previously, Cat Nap is a puzzle game in which players need to solve one level after another. This is a perfect reason to learn how to use the scene editor, a built-in Xcode tool that you can use to build levels without having to write everything in code.

The default SpriteKit project template contains a scene file already. Look in the project navigator and you'll see a file named **GameScene.sks**. Select that file and you'll see a new editor panel that shows a very dark gray background and the "Hello, World!" label you saw previously in the simulator:

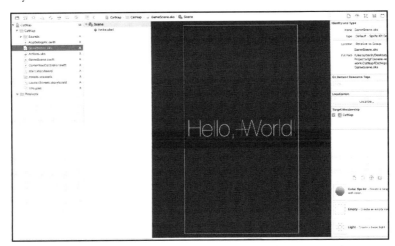

Click the minus (–) button in the mid-right corner several times until you see a white rectangle appear — you might need to click it five or six times if you're on a laptop. This is the boundary of your scene. The default size for a new scene is 750x1334 points.

Select the "Hello, World!" label and delete it (you can do that by simply pressing the Delete key on your keyboard while the label is selected).

Remember from Chapter 1, "Sprites", that the strategy we're taking for games in this book is to use a single set of images sized for a 2048x1536 scene and let SpriteKit downscale the images for all devices with smaller screen resolutions.

So let's resize the scene to our preferred 2048x1536 size. To do this, make sure the utilities editor on the right-hand side is open; if it's not, click **View > Utilities > Show Utilities.**

Within the Attributes Inspector for the scene, enter the new dimensions and set the scene anchor point to (0, 0) like so:

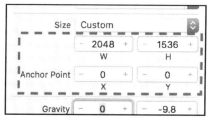

Now the scene has established a suitable size for supporting all devices.

The Object Library

At the bottom of the utilities editor, if it's not already selected, select the **Object Library**:

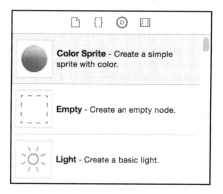

> **Note:** If the utilities editor on the right-hand side isn't open, click **View > Utilities > Show Object Library.**

The Object Library displays a list of objects that you can drop onto your scene and configure. When you load the scene file, those objects will appear in their correct positions based on the properties you set for them in the scene editor. That's much better than writing code to position and adjust every game object one by one, isn't it?

Here are some of the objects you can use:

- **Color Sprite:** This is the object you use to put sprites onscreen and the one you'll use most often throughout this chapter and the next.

- **Shape Node:** These are special types of nodes in SpriteKit that allow you to easily draw squares, circles and other shapes. You'll learn more about these in Chapter 11, "Crop, Video and Shape Nodes".

- **Label**: You already know how to create labels programmatically, but with the scene editor, you can create them simply by dragging and dropping them onto the scene.

- **Emitter**: These are special types of nodes in SpriteKit that allow you to create particle systems, which you can use for special effects like explosions, fire, or rain. You'll learn more about these in Chapter 16, "Particle Systems".

- **Light**: You can place a light node in your scene for a spotlight effect and have your scene objects cast shadows.

The best thing about the scene editor is that it's not just an editor — it also serves as a simulator, allowing you to easily preview scenes without running the app. You'll see this later.

Adding and positioning sprites

Make sure the yellow frame of your scene is visible and that it fits into the editor window. Drag and drop a **Color Sprite** object into the editor area.

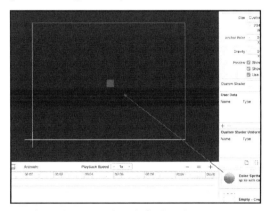

With the sprite selected, which happens by default when you create it, you'll see the available properties listed in the Attributes Inspector.

You may recognize a lot of these properties from before — you used many of them programmatically in your Zombie Conga project (such as `position` and `name`).

In the Attributes Inspector, you can set the sprite's name, parent node and the image file you want to use as the texture. You can also set the sprite's position, size and anchor point, either by hand or by dragging with the mouse.

Further down in the same panel, you'll see the controls to adjust the sprite's scale, z-position and z-axis rotation:

But wait! There's more! Even further down, listed in a section named **Physics Definition**, you'll find more properties you can set:

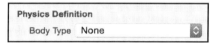

Notice that your sprite doesn't have a physics body, which means it is not taking part in a physics simulation. You'll be returning to this setting in future chapters, where you'll learn more about SpriteKit physics. In the meantime, let's begin by designing Cat Nap's first level.

Laying out your first scene

Select the sprite you just added to your scene and on the right-hand side, in the Attributes Inspector, set its properties to the following values:

- **Texture: background**
- **Position X: 1024**
- **Position Y: 768**

This should start you off nicely with the level's background image:

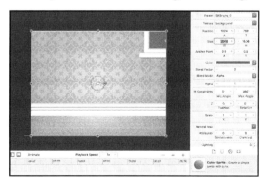

That was easy!

Next, you're going to add the cat bed to the scene. Drag another **Color Sprite** onto the scene and set its properties as follows:

- **Name: bed**
- **Texture: cat_bed**
- **Position: (1024, 272)** (enter X and Y into the respective boxes)

This will position the cat bed a bit off the bottom of the scene.

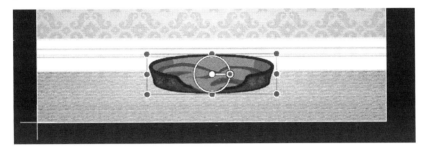

Now let's move on to those wooden blocks that get in the cat's way. There will be four blocks in total, but you'll add them two by two.

Drop two **Color Sprite** objects onto the scene. Edit their properties like so:

- **First block:** Texture **wood_vert1**, Position X **1024**, Position Y **330**
- **Second block:** Texture **wood_vert1**, Position X **1264**, Position Y **330**

Now you'll see this:

Take a moment to appreciate how much easier it is to put objects onscreen via the scene editor instead of through code. Of course, that doesn't mean you shouldn't understand what goes on behind the scenes. In fact, knowing how to do both is a huge plus.

OK! It's time to add the horizontal blocks. Drop two more **Color Sprite** objects onto the scene and adjust their properties as follows:

- **First block**: Texture **wood_horiz1**, Position X **1050**, Position Y **580**

- **Second block**: Texture **wood_horiz1**, Position X **1050**, Position Y **740**

Your scene continues to develop, and all of the obstacles are present now. At this point, you're only missing your main character:

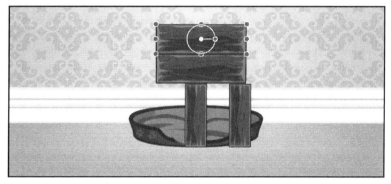

Drop one last **Color Sprite** object onto the scene. This will be the cat. Edit as follows:

- **Cat**: Texture **cat_sleepy**, Position X **1024**, Position Y **1036**

Finally, you've completed the basic setup of the first Cat Nap level:

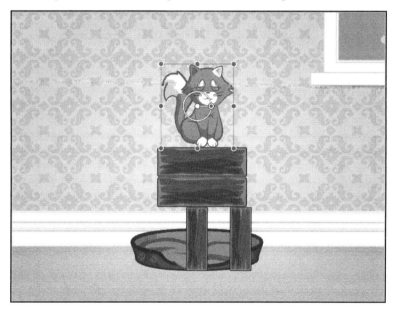

Build and run. Notice that your scene appears on the screen:

These are the basic skills you need to design levels using the scene editor. Luckily, it's capable of much more than laying down sprites on a scene. In the next section, you'll build more complex stuff!

File references

A cool feature (introduced in iOS 9) is that the scene editor allows you to reference content from other scene (.sks) files.

This means you can put together a bunch of sprites, add some effects like animations and then save those in a reusable .sks file. Then, you can reference the same content from multiple scenes, and they'll all dynamically load the same content from the reusable .sks file.

Now comes the best part: If you need to change the referenced content in *all* scenes, you only need to edit the original content and you're good to go.

As you may have guessed, this is perfect for level-based games where you often have characters or other parts of the scene recurring throughout the game. In Cat Nap, such a recurring character is everybody's favorite kitten:

In this section, you're going to extract the sleepy cat into its own .sks file and add more nodes and animations. Then you'll reference all of these as a bundle from within **GameScene.sks**.

First and foremost, since you're going to have more than one .sks file, it's time to organize them neatly. Control-click the yellow **CatNap** group and select **New Group**. Rename the group **Scenes**, and move **GameScene.sks** inside the newly created folder.

Once you're done, it should look like this:

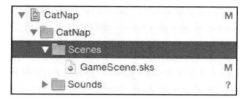

Next, control-click **Scenes** and from the pop-up menu, click **New File....** Choose the **iOS/Resource/SpriteKit Scene** file template and then click **Next**. Call the new file **Cat.sks** and save it in the project folder by clicking **Create**.

Xcode automatically opens the newly created **Cat.sks** file and presents you with an empty, dark gray editor window. In exactly the same way as before, your task is to resize the scene to your needs and add some sprites.

Set the scene size to **380x440** points (the size of the cat) and while you have that particular pane open, make sure the Anchor Point is set to (**0.5, 0.5**). Doing so lets you position the nodes inside the scene relative to the scene center; this is slightly easier than placing them relative to the lower left, as most nodes will be centered either horizontally or vertically:

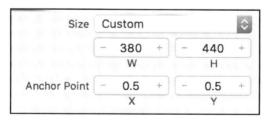

Now that the scene is ready for prime time, you need to add all of the cat's elements. First you'll add the torso. Drag in two **Color Sprite** nodes from the Object Library and set their properties like so:

- **Cat Body**: Name **cat_body**, Texture **cat_body**, Position X **22**, Position Y **-112**

- **Cat Head**: Name **cat_head**, Parent **cat_body**, Texture **cat_head**, Position X **18**, Position Y **192**

Note that you set the cat body as the parent of the cat head. Each SpriteKit node can have as many sub-nodes as needed, and sometimes it's handy to have one of your nodes act as the root node — that is, as a parent to other nodes. This way, if you need to copy or move all nodes, you only need to work with the root node, and the rest will move along with it.

Now your cat's body and head are nicely positioned within the scene while leaving space on the left for the big, fluffy tail that you're adding next.

Speaking of big, fluffy tails, drag in a **Color Sprite** from the Object Library and set its properties like so:

- **Tail**: Name **tail**, Texture **cat_tail**, Parent **cat_body**, Anchor Point (**0, 0**), Position (**-206, -70**), Z Position **-1**

Later in this chapter, you'll animate the tail so it rotates gently around its (**0, 0**) anchor point. This will make it appear as if the cat is swinging its tail slowly in the air, giving him that cat swagger.

So far the cat scene looks like this:

Now it's time to add the rest of the cat parts. Add two **Color Sprite** objects to the scene and adjust their properties like so:

- **Cat Mouth**: Name **mouth**, Parent **cat_head**, Texture **cat_mouth**, Position X **6**, Position Y **-67**

- **Cat Eyes**: Name **eyes**, Parent **cat_head**, Texture **cat_eyes**, Position X **6**, Position Y **2**

This completes the cat, and your scene will look like this:

Now you will remove the static cat image from **GameScene.sks** and use your newly designed cat scene.

To do this, open **GameScene.sks** and delete the static cat sprite. In its place, drop a **Reference** object from the Object Library:

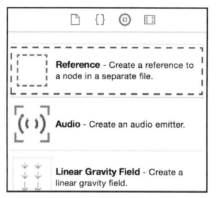

The empty reference node appears like a hollow, dashed rectangle:

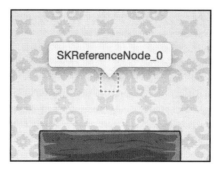

Set the following property values for the selected reference node:

- **Name: cat_shared**

- **Reference**: select **Cat.sks** from the drop-down menu

- **Position: (1030, 1045)**

- **Z Position: 10**

Here, you're loading the content of the file **Cat.sks** and positioning it where the static cat image used to be. Additionally, you're setting a higher z-position to make sure the contents of **Cat.sks** appear above the level's background image.

With this done, you've successfully created a reusable piece of content that you can use throughout your game. Nice job!

There's one problem with your cat — it doesn't do anything interesting. It's just a bunch of nodes stuck together!

It's time to correct that by creating what's called an "idle animation". This will help to make the scene come alive.

Animations and action references

So far, you've been creating node actions using code. As you saw in the previous chapters, with only a few lines of code, you can create an `SKAction` to move a sprite along the screen, rotate it and scale it. But sometimes it's nice to do that visually, especially when prototyping animations or level design.

In this section, you're going to learn how to add actions to the nodes in your scene. Later, you'll learn how to extract those actions into their own .sks files and reuse them to animate different sprites.

Adding actions to nodes

Open **Cat.sks** and find this button towards the bottom of Xcode's window:

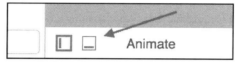

If the button is not selected, like in the screenshot above, click it to open the **action editor**:

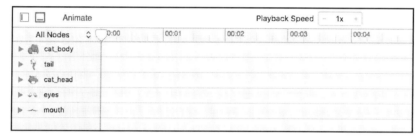

The action editor displays all the nodes in the scene and a timeline with rows corresponding to each node. If you've ever worked with animation or video software, you might be familiar with this type of user interface.

You're going to use the action editor to animate the cat's tail.

Grab a **RotateToAngle Action** object from the Object Library and drop it onto the timeline track for the **tail** node. While dragging the action over the tail track, a new strip will open and show you a live preview where the new action will appear when dropped.

Drop the action and position it at the beginning of the timeline — that is, at the 0:00 time mark:

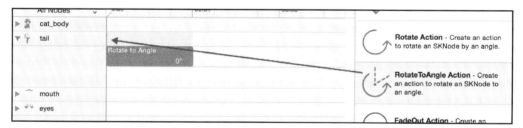

Cool! You've just added a rotate action to the tail sprite. You only need to polish the action a bit before giving it a try.

In the Attributes Inspector, set the following two values:

• **Duration:** 2

• **Degrees:** 5

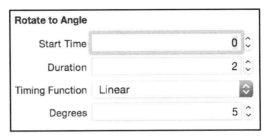

While you're at it, add one more action just after the first one.

Drag another **RotateToAngle Action** object to the **tail** node and snap it to the end of the first one; set its properties as follows:

• **Start Time:** 2

• **Duration:** 1.5

• **Degrees:** 0

This action will swing the cat's tail back to its initial position. The timeline will now look like so:

The best thing about the scene editor is that you don't need to run your game in the simulator or on a device in order to test your scenes.

Find the **Animate** button at the top of the action editor and click it; the scene editor will play the actions you just added. This allows you to quickly find any issues you may have with your animations.

If you want more control over the playback, you can simply grab the timeline scrubber and move it back and forth.

Notice how the **Animate** button turns into a **Layout** button. This indicates that you're currently animating the scene. If you'd like to work again on the layout, click on **Layout** to switch back to that mode.

When you click **Layout**, the timeline position resets, and you can again move sprites around and edit their properties.

More about the timeline

The **timeline** is very powerful when it comes to designing complex scenes and animations. Before moving on you will go on a quick tour.

To the right of the Animate button you will see a **Playback Speed** control. While you are playing back your actions you can choose the speed of replay. This makes sense since when you are loading those animations from code you can tell SpriteKit the speed you want to use for the animations.

Change the playback speed to **2x**.

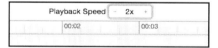

Click **Animate** and notice how the tail moves two times faster than before. This feature is very useful when you are prototyping animations in scene editor — if you are not really sure about the duration of some of your actions you can easily experiment by just changing the playback speed until you are satisfied.

Reset the playback speed to **1x** before moving on.

The timeline lists all views in your scene in the order you added them to the scene. You started with the cat body and added the eyes last so that is how they are ordered:

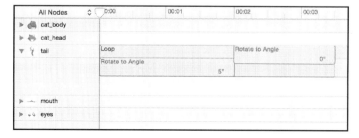

As you can imagine the more complex a scene is the more fields you will have in this list. Once you have so many nodes that you have to scroll continuously up and down to find the one you're looking for you will feel the need to navigate the list in a more convenient way.

You have two ways to filter the timeline node list. First, in the top left corner you will see a drop list menu:

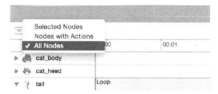

The item selected by default is All Nodes but you can choose from two more:

- **Nodes with Actions**: Filters the node list to show you only the nodes that already have actions attached. Using this option is useful when you want to modify an existing action and you want to see only the nodes that possibly run the action.

- **Selected Nodes**: This option will dynamically show you only the nodes you have currently selected in scene editor. This is a powerful mode as it shows you only the timeline for the selected scene items.

The second control allowing you to filter the node list is the search field at the bottom left corner:

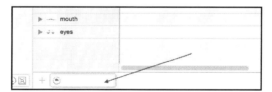

This field allows you to quickly filter the node list to only those nodes whose names contain the given search term. This comes in very handy when you want to work with a given node and you know its name off the top of your head.

Last but not least, in the bottom right corner there is a slider that allows you to scale up or down the timeline so you can see more or less actions without having to scroll through:

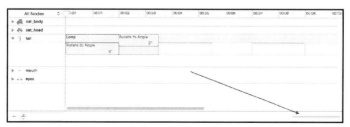

Repeating actions

You're almost done, but there's one more thing you need to do — make the cat's tail wave continuously. This cat refuses to sit still!

Making an action repeat a set number of times, or indefinitely, is easy to do using the action editor. For your tail animation, you'll first need to group the two actions you just created, and then repeat that action group so the tail can continuously swing back and forth.

First, select both actions in the action editor's timeline while pressing the **Command** key; if you do this properly, you'll see both actions appear highlighted:

While both actions are selected, Control-click on one of them and select **Create Loop** from the pop-up menu.

In the popover menu, click the infinity symbol ∞ to indicate that you want this action to repeat continuously (the button will remain highlighted to show you your current looping preference):

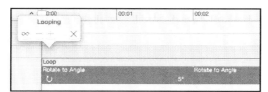

The timeline shows you the currently selected loop in blue and all of the repeats in an orange tint so you can easily distinguish between the "original" and its repetitions.

Besides an indefinitely repeating loop, you can choose from three more options.

When you first clicked **Create Loop** Xcode created a loop that plays once and repeats one more time. So if you wanted an action that plays a total of two times, you would not have had to do anything more.

The popup menu gives you a few more options to control the repeat count of the loop:

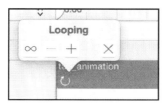

- ∞ loops the action forever;

- + adds one more repeat;

- - removes one repeat;

- X removes all repeats from the action.

If you ever need to edit it, you can see the menu by Control-clicking the loop and then selecting Edit Loop. For your tail-rotation action, you chose ∞ to make the cat gently swing its tail throughout the whole game.

> **Note:** It's natural to think that the X button closes the popup. In this case however it removes the looping from your animation instead. To close the popup window simply click somewhere outside of it and it will automatically go away.

That's pretty cool! And even cooler is that you've got a little content hierarchy going on in your game to maximize resource reuse:

1. **Cat.sks** contains sprites and actions, and configures the looping and duration of the actions.

2. **GameScene.sks** contains a complete level setup, and it also references the cat character from **Cat.sks**.

This setup allows you to load the cat with all its body parts and actions from any level in your game. In fact, you're going to load the cat in **each** level of your game!

Further, you're going to create more .sks files containing different cat animations, which you're going to load and use in different stages of the game.

Now build and run your project to see how far you've come:

Look at that cat swinging its tail like a boss.

This is a pretty long chapter, and you're probably a bit tired. If so, take a five minute break to fool around. Better yet, why not drag more reference nodes from the Object Library and load up the scene with more cats?

Good fun! Just make sure you remove all of the extra cats before going further. :]

In this chapter you have learned how to:

• find your way around the scene editor

• plan and design game scenes

• add and edit nodes and have them run basic actions

The interface of scene editor is fairly simple, yet it allows you to achieve quite a lot.

The next couple chapters will focus more on creating sprites and actions from code. It's important for you to know how to design and fine-tune your game's levels both from within scene editor and from your code so you can always use the best approach for your current project.

With that being said, make sure you really have a good command of the scene editor interface before moving on. The two challenges that follow are a perfect opportunity to exercise your newly acquired scene editor skills.

Challenges

There are two challenges for this chapter to give you some more practice creating actions and reusable .sks files.

As always, if you get stuck, you can find the solutions in the resources for this chapter — but give it your best shot first!

Challenge 1: Creating further cat actions

You've constructed the cat using a few nodes, including its body, head, tail, eyes and, of course, its gorgeous smile. So far, you've animated the tail by using a repeating sequence of two rotate actions.

In this challenge, you'll use additional types of actions to complete the cat's idle animation.

Follow the general steps below to create a new action inside **Cat.sks**. Add the actions listed below to the cat's **mouth** node, setting their properties like so:

- **Move Action**: Start Time **5**, Duration **0.74**, Timing **Ease Out**, Offset (**0, 5**)

- **Move Action**: Start Time **5.75**, Duration **0.75**, Timing **Ease In**, Offset (**0, -5**)

- **PlaySoundFileNamed Action**: Start Time **5.25**, Duration **1**

For the Filename of the sound action, select **mrreow** from the drop-down menu.

> **Note** Don't worry if the Duration changes. It may change to match the length of the sound file.

If you're wondering how you can make the actions overlap on the timeline, here's a hint for you; the final result will look like this:

Since you would like the actions to repeat including the 5 seconds of waiting time you need to do a little trick.

Add one more action at the beginning of the timeline for the **mouth** node:

- **Move Action**: Start Time **0**, Duration **1**, Offset (**0, 0**)

Then select all four actions and create a loop of them like you did earlier in this chapter. You should see the four actions grouped in a loop like so:

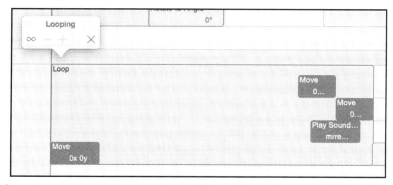

While you're at it, create one more action and drop it on the **eyes** node in the scene timeline. Drag in an **AnimateWithTextures Action** and set the Start Time to **6.5** and the Duration to **0.75**.

Then, in the fourth tab in the bottom right (the Media Library), drag **cat_eyes**, **cat_eyes1**, and **cat_eyes2** onto the Textures list of your newly created action.

Also, tick the **Restore** checkbox; this way when the animation completes, it will go back to its initial frame.

The final setup should look like this:

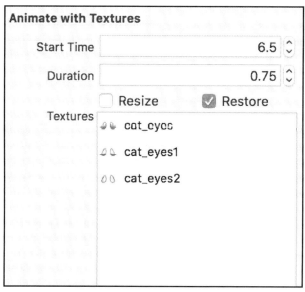

Once more, in order to trick SpriteKit to include the initial 6.5 seconds of waiting time in your loop, add another action:

• **Move Action**: Start Time **0**, Duration **1**, Offset (**0, 0**)

Select both actions you added to the cat eyes and create a loop that repeats forever.

Well done so far! Your complete timeline should now look similar to this:

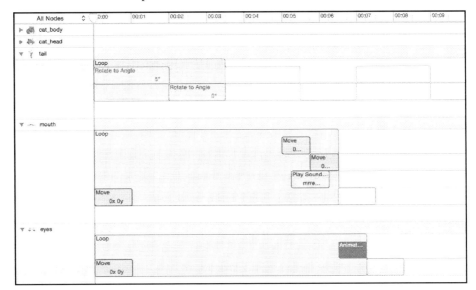

Build and run to enjoy the fruits of your labor. Watch as the cat sits quietly waving its tail, and every now and again, sleepily blinks and purrs. Neat, huh?

Challenge 2: Creating further cat scenes

In this challenge, you'll create two more .sks files, which you'll use later to load the cat's "win" and "lose" animations.

Create a new **CatCurl.sks** file and set the scene size to (**380, 440**), then set the Anchor Point to (**0, 0**). Add one **Color Sprite** object with the following properties:

• **Cat Curl**: Name **cat_curl**, Texture **cat_curlup1**, Position (**190, 220**), Size (**380, 440**)

In the actions editor, add one action to the **cat_curl** sprite node as follows:

• **AnimateWithTextures Action**: Start Time **0**, Duration **1**

Make sure Restore is **not** checked. For Textures, drag in the following files from the Media Library:

• **cat_curlup1**

• **cat_curlup2**

• **cat_curlup3**

You can scrub the timeline view to preview this animation; later you will load and run this when the player successfully solves a level in Cat Nap:

There's one more scene left to create: the animation to play when your player fails to solve a level. The process is similar to creating the winning sequence.

Create a new **CatWakeUp.sks** file and set the scene size to (**380, 440**) and Anchor Point to (**0, 0**). Add one **Color Sprite** object with the following properties:

- **Cat Awake**: Name **cat_awake**, Texture **cat_awake**, Position (**190, 220**), Size (**380, 440**)

In the actions editor, add one action to the **cat_awake** sprite node with the following properties:

- **AnimateWithTextures Action**: Start Time **0**, Duration **0.5**

Make sure Restore is **not** checked. For Textures, drag in the following files from the Media library:

- **cat_awake.png**

- **cat_sleepy.png**

Make the action repeat indefinitely.

You can scrub the timeline view to preview this animation; later you'll load and run this scene when the cat falls off a wooden block and onto the ground, causing the player to fail the level:

Whoever said cats always land on their feet?

Phew! That was a long chapter with lots of instructions. If you need to take another break, no one will blame you. However, the next chapter introduces you to the world of actions, collisions and crazy physics experiments, so don't wait too long to turn the page.

Chapter 8: Beginning Physics

By Marin Todorov

So far you've learned to move sprites by manually positioning them and by running actions. But what if you want to simulate more complex behavior, like a ball bouncing against a wobbly pillar, a chain of dominos falling down or a house of cards collapsing?

You could accomplish the above with plenty of math, but there's an easier way. SpriteKit contains a powerful and user-friendly physics engine that will help you move your objects realistically — in ways both simple and complex — without breaking a sweat.

With a physics engine, you can accomplish effects like those you see in many popular iOS games:

- **Angry Birds** uses a physics engine to simulate what happens when the bird collides with the tower of bricks.

- **Tiny Wings** uses a physics engine to simulate the bird riding the hills and flying into the air.

- **Cut the Rope** uses a physics engine to simulate the movement of the ropes and the effect of gravity on the candy.

Combing a physics engines with touch controls can give your games a wonderfully realistic dynamism — and as you can see in Angry Birds, sometimes in the name of destruction!

If you like this kind of lifelike behavior and want to know how to build your own physics-based game, you're in the right chapter.

Since you'll be playing around with physics — while learning, of course — a playground is the best place to get started. And I don't mean an actual playground; I mean an Xcode playground, which is perfect for experimenting with code.

In this chapter, you'll take a break from Cat Nap to learn the basics of SpriteKit physics in a playground. But don't worry — in the next two chapters you'll return to your old friend Cat Nap and integrate the physics engine there.

Physics in SpriteKit

Under the hood, SpriteKit uses a library named Box2D to perform all the physics calculations. Box2D is open-source, full-featured, fast and powerful. A lot of popular games already use Box2D — on the iPhone, Android, BlackBerry, Nintendo DS, Wii, OS X and Windows — so it's nice to see the library as a part of SpriteKit.

However, Box2D has two main drawbacks for iOS developers: it's written in C++, and it could stand to be more user-friendly, especially for beginners.

Apple doesn't expose Box2D directly; instead it abstracts it behind its own API in SpriteKit. In fact, Box2D is walled so well that Apple could choose to change the physics engine in a later version of iOS, and you wouldn't even know it.

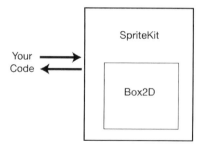

To make a long story short, in SpriteKit, you get access to all the power of a super-popular engine, but through a friendly, polished, Apple-style API.

Physics bodies

For the physics engine to control the movement of one of your sprites, you have to create a **physics body** for the sprite. You can think of a physics body as a rough boundary for your sprite that the engine will use for collision detection.

The illustration below depicts a typical physics body for a sprite. Note that the shape of the physics body doesn't need to match the boundaries of the sprite exactly. Usually, you'll choose a simpler shape to help the collision detection algorithms run faster.

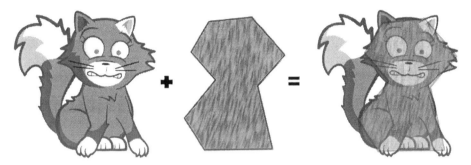

If you need a more precise shape, you can tell SpriteKit's physics engine to detect the shape of your sprite by ignoring all transparent parts of the image. This is a good strategy if you want a more lifelike collision between the objects in your game. For the cat, the automatically-detected, transparency-based physics body would look something like this:

You may be thinking, "Excellent! I'll just use that all the time."

Think twice. Before you rush into anything, understand that it takes *much* more processing power to calculate the physics for a complex shape like this one, as compared to a simpler polygonal shape.

Once you set a physics body for your sprite, it will move similarly to how it would in real life: it will fall with gravity, be affected by impulses and forces and move in response to collisions with other objects.

You can adjust the properties of your physics bodies, such as how heavy or bouncy they are. You can also alter the laws of the entire simulated world — for example, you can decrease gravity so that a ball, upon falling to the ground, will bounce higher and travel farther.

Imagine you throw two balls and each bounces for a while — the red one under normal Earth gravity and the blue one under low gravity, such as on the Moon. It would look something like this:

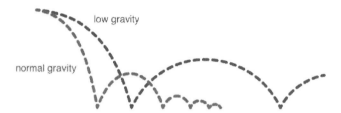

There are few things you should know about physics bodies:

- **Physics bodies are rigid**. In other words, physics bodies can't be squished or deformed under pressure and won't change shape as a consequence of the physics simulation. For example, you can't use a physics body to simulate a squishy ball that deforms as it rolls along the floor.

- **Complex physics bodies have a performance cost**. While it may be convenient to use the alpha mask of your images as the physics body, you should only use this feature when absolutely necessary. If you have many shapes onscreen colliding with each other, try using an alpha mask only for your main character or for two to three main characters, and set the rest to rectangles or circles.

- **Physics bodies are moved by forces or impulses**. Impulses, such as those that make two physics bodies bounce off each other, adjust the object's momentum immediately. Forces, such as gravity, affect the object gradually over time. You can apply your own forces or impulses to physics bodies as well — for example, you may use an impulse to simulate firing a bullet from a gun, but use a force to simulate launching a rocket. You'll learn more about forces and impulses later in this chapter.

SpriteKit makes all of these features, and many more, incredibly easy to manage. In Apple's typical manner, most of the configuration is fully pre-defined, meaning a blank SpriteKit project will already include lifelike physics with absolutely no set up required.

Getting started

Time to learn about physics in SpriteKit in the best way possible: by experimenting in real time inside an Xcode playground.

Launch Xcode and from its initial dialog, select **Get started with a playground**.

> **Note:** If you previously disabled the startup dialog, select **File > New > Playground...** from the main menu.

In the next dialog, enter **SpriteKitPhysicsTest** for the **Name** and select **iOS** for the **Platform**.

Click **Next** and select a location to save the playground.

Xcode will create a new, empty playground, importing only the UIKit framework, so you can use all of the data types, classes and structures you're used to working with in your iOS projects.

The empty playground window will look like this:

This view may seem a little strange if you haven't used playgrounds before. Don't worry — this next section covers the interface and how to experiment (play!) in a playground.

> **Note:** If you're already comfortable working in playgrounds, you can skip the next section and move on to "Creating a SpriteKit playgound".

Your first playground

In previous chapters, you've worked with Xcode projects, which usually include many source files, resources, storyboards, game scenes and so forth. A playground, on the other hand, is just a single bundle with a **.playground** extension.

Playgrounds allow you to experiment with code in real time. But before you do that, it's a good idea to get familiar with the interface.

Take a look at your empty playground window:

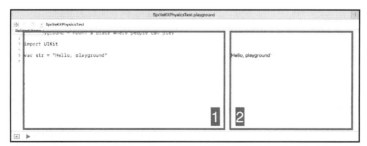

On the left-hand side is the source editor *(1)* and on the right-hand side is the results sidebar *(2)*. As you type code, Xcode evaluates and executes every line and produces the results in the results sidebar, as you'd expect.

For example, if you change "Hello, playground" to "Sprite Kit rules!", you'll immediately see the results sidebar update to reflect this change. You can experiment with anything you like, but right now give the code below a try:

```
let number = 0.4
let string = "Sprite Kit is #\(5-4)"
let numbers = Array(1...5)

var j = 0
for i in 1..<10 {
  j += i*2
}
```

As soon as you paste or type in the code, you'll see the results sidebar update and neatly align the output of every line against the corresponding code in the editor.

The first line of code produces the result you'd expect:

```
let number = 0.4
0.4
```

Note: For clarity, we'll display the code line followed by the corresponding result.

This is a static value, so to see the output of an expression, as well as prove the code really gets executed in real time, look at the result of the second line:

```
let string = "Sprite Kit is #\(5-4)"
"Sprite Kit is #1"
```

Xcode wraps the result in quotes to show you that the data type of that result is a String. The next example shows you the result of an even more elaborate piece of code:

```
let numbers = Array(1...5)
[1, 2, 3, 4, 5]
```

The code creates a new array containing Int elements with values from 1 to 5.

When you enter an expression like that, on a line by itself, Xcode will evaluate it and send the result to the results sidebar. This is incredibly useful for debugging purposes — rather than use a separate log function as you would in a project, simply write a variable name or an expression, and you'll immediately see its value to the right.

The final example produces a somewhat surprising result:

```
var j = 0
for i in 1..<10 {
    j += i*2
}

(9 times)
```

If you consider everything you've learned so far, you might expect this. The result is aligned to the code, so even though the line `j += i*2` is executed nine times in the loop, it can still produce only a single line of text.

The line tells you how many times the loop ran, but that's far from what would actually be useful to you: to see the values of the variables while the loop runs.

No fear — a playground is smarter than that! Hover with your mouse cursor over the text (**9 times**). You'll see an extra button appear along with a little tip:

Click the + button to show the history of the value over the nine loop iterations. This history is displayed directly under the line of code that calculates the value of j. Click on the points representing the loop iterations to see the value of your tracked expression in a little pop-up.

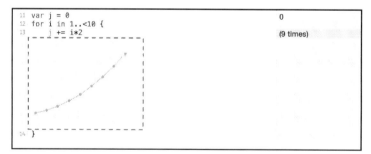

Good work. This is the basic knowledge you need to use an Xcode playground. Now comes the interesting part: conducting physics experiments in a playground.

Creating a SpriteKit playground

Delete any code you have in your playground and add these imports at the top:

```
import UIKit
import SpriteKit
import PlaygroundSupport
```

These import the basic **UIKit** classes, the SpriteKit framework and the handy **PlaygroundSupport** module, which will help you visualize your SpriteKit scene right inside the playground window.

Since you already know how to create a new game scene, you'll do that first.

Make sure Xcode's assistant editor is open; it usually stays in the right-hand side of the window. To show the Assistant editor, select **View > Assistant Editor > Show Assistant Editor** from Xcode's main menu.

Now, add the following to your playground's source code:

```
let sceneView = SKView(frame: CGRect(x: 0, y: 0, width: 480,
  height: 320))

let scene = SKScene(size: CGSize(width: 480, height: 320))
sceneView.showsFPS = true
sceneView.presentScene(scene)

PlaygroundPage.current.needsIndefiniteExecution = true
PlaygroundPage.current.liveView = sceneView
```

Most of this code is surely familiar, though you've never seen it in this context. Take a look at what you achieve above.

First, you create a new **SKView** instance and give it a frame size of 480 by 320 pixels. Then, you create an empty default **SKScene** instance and give it the same size. This is what the code in your view controllers has been doing for you in the previous chapters.

Next, you tell the SKView to present the scene.

Finally, you adjust the configuration of the current Playground page. As you can see, PlaygroundPage is quite handy and helps with a few things:

1. First and foremost, it tells Xcode *not* to abort executing your playground as soon as it runs through the source code. In a game prototype, you'd like things to keep running, right?

2. It renders the current state of the live view in the assistant editor.

3. Finally, it records the view over time so you can rewind, fast forward and skim through the recorded session. You'll see this momentarily.

In the assistant editor, you'll see your game scene:

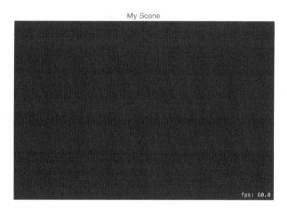

Do you see the frame rate label sometimes flickering as it renders different rates? This tells you that the scene is rendering live. (Well you might not see it flicker — there's not so much going on right now in the scene).

Playing with an empty game scene is not so much fun. Fortunately, that's easy to change! You have a nice, blank slate; your next step is to add sprites to the scene.

Add this code to the playground to create a new sprite with the image **square.png**:

```
let square = SKSpriteNode(imageNamed: "square")
```

If you open the Xcode console you will see the following error message:

```
SKTexture: Error loading image resource: "square"
```

That's because you didn't add any assets to your playground, and SpriteKit is letting you know that it couldn't find an image named **square.png**.

From Xcode's main menu, select **View > Navigators > Show Project Navigator**. Have a look at the file structure of your playground:

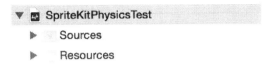

The playground contains two empty folders. The first, **Sources**, contains code you want to pre-compile and make available to your playground, while the second, **Resources**, contains assets you want to use, like images, sounds and so forth.

In the **Resources** folder for this chapter, you'll find a **Shapes** folder that includes all of the artwork you need for your playground. Grab all the files inside **Shapes** and drop them into the **Resources** folder in your playground.

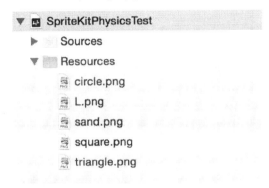

Excellent! Add this code to the end of the file:

```
square.name = "shape"
square.position = CGPoint(x: scene.size.width * 0.25,
  y: scene.size.height * 0.50)

let circle = SKSpriteNode(imageNamed: "circle")
circle.name = "shape"
circle.position = CGPoint(x: scene.size.width * 0.50,
  y: scene.size.height * 0.50)

let triangle = SKSpriteNode(imageNamed: "triangle")
triangle.name = "shape"
triangle.position = CGPoint(x: scene.size.width * 0.75,
  y: scene.size.height * 0.50)
```

This code creates three constants: `square`, `circle` and `triangle`. All of them are sprite nodes, and you initialize them with the images **square.png**, **circle.png** and **triangle.png**, respectively.

At this point, you can see in the results sidebar that the three sprites have been created successfully, but you still can't see them onscreen. You need to add them to your scene, so do that with the following code:

```
scene.addChild(square)
scene.addChild(circle)
scene.addChild(triangle)
```

This creates three sprites in the center of the screen: a square, a circle and a triangle. Check them out:

For the most part, this has been a review of creating sprites and positioning them manually onscreen, although this time, you've done it using a playground. But now it's time to introduce something new — controlling these objects with physics!

Circular bodies

Remember two things from earlier in this chapter:

1. For the physics engine to control the movement of a sprite, you must create a **physics body** for the sprite.

2. You can think of a physics body as a rough boundary for your sprite that the physics engine uses for collision detection.

Time to attach a physics body to the circle. Add this at the bottom of the file:

```
circle.physicsBody = SKPhysicsBody(circleOfRadius:
    circle.size.width/2)
```

SKPhysicsBody has a convenience initializer method,
SKPhysicsBody(circleRadius:), that creates a circular body. Because you need to
supply the radius of the circle, you'll be dividing the width of the circle sprite by 2.

> **Note:** The radius of a circle is the distance from the center of the circle to its edge.

Believe it or not, thanks to SpriteKit's pre-configured physics simulation, you're all done!

Once the playground re-executes your code you'll see the circle drop with gravity:

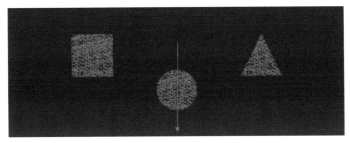

But wait a minute — the circle keeps falling offscreen and disappears! Not to mention
that by the time the scene is rendered, the circle is almost out of sight — you don't see
much of the fall happen.

The easiest way to fix this is to turn off gravity at the start of your scene and then turn it
back on a few seconds later. Yes — you heard me right — turn off gravity!

Skim through your Swift code and find the line where you call presentScene(_:) on
your SKView. Just before this line, add the code to turn off gravity:

```
scene.physicsWorld.gravity = CGVector(dx: 0, dy: 0)
```

Your scene has a property named physicsWorld that represents the basic physics setup
of your game. When you alter the gravity vector of your physics world, you change the
constant acceleration that is applied to every physics body in your scene each frame.

As soon as you enter the code to reset gravity to a zero vector, you'll see that now the
circle stays at its initial position without falling down. So far, so good.

Now you're going to create a little helper function named delay. Since you'll write it
once, and not need to re-compile it each time the playground executes, you may put it
aside in the **Sources** folder.

The easiest way to add a source file is to right-click on **Sources** and choose **New File**
from the pop-up menu.

Name the newly added file **SupportCode.swift** and then open it in the source editor. Once it's opened, add the following code to it:

```
import UIKit

public func delay(seconds: TimeInterval, completion: @escaping
() -> Void) {
    DispatchQueue.main.asyncAfter(deadline: .now() + seconds,
execute: completion)
}
```

Don't worry too much about this code. All you need to know is that you're using it to delay code execution, something you'll be doing throughout this chapter.

With that done, open the playground again by clicking on **SpriteKitPhysicsTest** in the project navigator, at the top.

Now scroll back down to the end of the code and add the following to re-establish gravity two seconds after the scene is created:

```
delay(seconds: 2.0) {
    scene.physicsWorld.gravity = CGVector(dx: 0, dy: -9.8)
}
```

> **Note:** Keep this piece of code at the bottom of the file — all the code you add from here on out, you'll add *just above* it.

Now that you've paused gravity, you'll be able to see the circle shape appear in the Assistant editor and then two seconds later, fall under the pull of gravity.

> **Note:** While you were editing **SupportCode.swift**, Xcode might have switched the contents of the assistant editor so you won't see the rendered scene. In that case, click on the quick jump bar at the top of the assistant editor and choose **Timeline/SpriteKitPhysicsTest.playground**.

But that's still not exactly what you want! For this demo, you want the circle to stop when it hits the bottom of the screen and stay there.

Luckily, SpriteKit makes this easy to do using something called an **edge loop body**.

Edge loop bodies

To put bounds around the scene, which is something you'll need to do in many physics-based games, add this line of code just before you present the scene:

```
scene.physicsBody = SKPhysicsBody(edgeLoopFrom: scene.frame)
```

First, you set the physics body for the scene itself. Any SpriteKit node can have a physics body, and remember, a scene is a node too!

Next, you create a different type of body — an edge loop rather than a circle. There is a major difference between these two types of bodies:

- The circle body is a **dynamic** physics body — that is, it moves. It's solid, has mass and can collide with any other type of physics body. The physics simulation can apply various forces to move volume-based bodies.

- The edge loop body is a **static** volume-less physics body — that is, it does not move. As the name implies, an edge loop only defines the edges of a shape. It doesn't have mass, cannot collide with other edge loop bodies and is never moved by the physics simulation. Other objects can be inside or outside its edges.

The most common use for an edge loop body is to define collision areas to describe your game's boundaries, ground, walls, trigger areas or any other type of unmoving collision space.

Since you want to restrict bodies to movement within the screen's edges, you create the scene's physics body to be an edge loop based on the scene's `frame`:

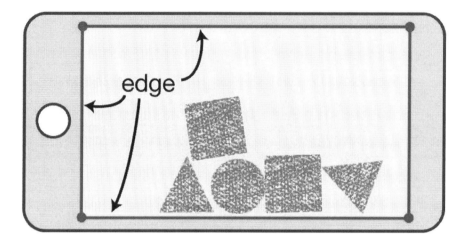

As you saw when Xcode ran your playground, the circle now stops when it hits the bottom of the screen and even bounces a little:

Rectangular bodies

Next, you'll add the physics body for the square sprite. Add the following line to your code:

```
square.physicsBody = SKPhysicsBody(rectangleOf:
    square.frame.size)
```

You can see that creating a rectangular physics body is very similar to creating a circular body. The only difference is that instead of passing in the radius of the circle, you pass in a `CGSize` representing the width and height of the rectangle.

Now that it has a physics body attached to it, the square will fall down to the bottom of the scene too… well, in two seconds, thanks to you having paused gravity — like a boss!

Custom-shaped bodies

Right now, you have two very simple shapes — a circle and a square. What if you needed a more complicated shape? For example, there's no built-in triangle shape.

You can create arbitrarily-shaped bodies by giving SpriteKit a **Core Graphics path** that defines the boundary of the body. The easiest way to understand how this works is by looking at an example — so try it out with the triangle shape.

Add the following code:

```
let trianglePath = CGMutablePath()
trianglePath.move(to: CGPoint(x: -triangle.size.width/2,
  y: -triangle.size.height/2))
trianglePath.addLine(to: CGPoint(x: triangle.size.width/2,
  y: -triangle.size.height/2))
trianglePath.addLine(to: CGPoint(x: 0, y: triangle.size.height/
2))
trianglePath.addLine(to: CGPoint(x: -triangle.size.width/2,
  y: -triangle.size.height/2))
triangle.physicsBody = SKPhysicsBody(polygonFrom: trianglePath)
```

Let's go through this step by step:

1. First, you create a new `CGMutablePath`, which you'll use to plot out the triangle's points.

2. Next, you move your virtual "pen" to the triangle's first point, which in this case is the bottom left, by using `move(to:)`. Note that the coordinates are relative to the sprite's anchor point, which by default is its center.

3. You then draw three lines, one to each of the three corners of the triangle, by calling `addLine(to:)`. Note the terms "draw" and "line" do not refer to things you'll see

onscreen — rather, they represent the notion of virtually defining the points and line segments that make up a triangle shape.

4. Finally, you create the body by passing the `trianglePath` to `SKPhysicsBody(polygonFrom:)`.

As expected, all three objects fall down once gravity is restored:

Visualizing the bodies

Each of the three objects now has a physics body that matches its shape, but at the moment, you can't prove that the physics bodies are indeed different for each sprite.

Before beginning the code for this section, add one more utility function to make your code shorter and easier to read. You'll need a random function that returns a `CGFloat` value in a given range, so open **Sources/SupportCode.swift** and add the following:

```
public func random(min: CGFloat, max: CGFloat) -> CGFloat {
  return CGFloat(Float(arc4random()) / Float(0xFFFFFFFF))
    * (max - min) + min
}
```

With that done, it's time to pour particles over the objects to observe their true physical shapes.

Return to your playground and add this function *before* your call to `delay(seconds:completion:)`:

```
func spawnSand() {
  let sand = SKSpriteNode(imageNamed: "sand")

  sand.position = CGPoint(
    x: random(min: 0.0, max: scene.size.width),
    y: scene.size.height - sand.size.height)

  sand.physicsBody = SKPhysicsBody(circleOfRadius:
    sand.size.width/2)
```

```
      sand.name = "sand"
      scene.addChild(sand)
   }
```

In this function, you make a small circular body, just like you did before, out of the texture named **sand.png** and position the sprite in a random location at the top of the scene. You also set the sprite's name to **sand** for easy access to it later.

Time to add 100 of these sand particles to see what happens. Modify your call to delay(seconds:completion:) by replacing what's there now with this:

```
  delay(seconds: 2.0) {
    scene.physicsWorld.gravity = CGVector(dx: 0, dy: -9.8)
    scene.run(
      SKAction.repeat(
        SKAction.sequence([
          SKAction.run(spawnSand),
          SKAction.wait(forDuration: 0.1)
          ]),
        count: 100)
    )
  }
```

Finally, some (SK-)action! :]

The new closure passed to delay(seconds:completion:) repeats a sequence of actions 100 times. The repeated sequence simply calls spawnSand and then waits for 0.1 seconds.

When the scene starts rendering in the Assistant editor, you'll see a "sand storm" as the 100 sand particles rain down and fill the spaces between the three bodies on the ground:

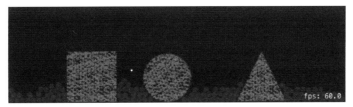

Observe how the sand bounces off of the shapes, proving that your shapes indeed have unique bodies.

After 30 seconds of execution, move the recording slider left and right to see the comical action of the sand going up and down and bouncing off the shapes.

Have some fun with that — you've earned it!

Bodies with complex shapes

The code to create `CGPath` instances is not easy to read, especially if it's been awhile since you wrote it. In addition, if you have a complex body shape to create, it's going to be a long and cumbersome process to create the path for it by code.

While it's useful to know how to create bodies out of custom paths, there's a much easier way to handle complex shapes.

Before you begin, there's one more shape you need to add to your scene, and it looks a bit like a rotated capital letter L:

Considering the code you wrote to define a triangular path, you probably already realize that the shape above will be painful to put together in code.

Go ahead and use the alpha mask of the image to create the physics body for the sprite. Add this to your code:

```
let l = SKSpriteNode(imageNamed: "L")
l.name = "shape"
l.position = CGPoint(x: scene.size.width * 0.5,
  y: scene.size.height * 0.75)
l.physicsBody = SKPhysicsBody(texture: l.texture!, size: l.size)
scene.addChild(l)
```

The initializer `SKPhysicsBody(texture:size:)` is the one that lifts the burden from your shoulders and automatically detects the shape of your sprite. It takes two parameters: `SKTexture` and `CGSize`.

In the example above, you use the texture of the sprite to generate the physics body for that sprite — but you aren't restricted to using the sprite's texture. If your sprite's texture has a very complex shape, you can also use a different image with a rough outline of your sprite to improve the performance of your game.

You can also control the size of the created body by adjusting the `size` parameter of `SKPhysicsBody(texture:size:)`.

Look at the scene now, and you'll see that the L shape automatically has a physics body that follows its outline. It conveniently falls onto the circle shape for a strong visual effect.

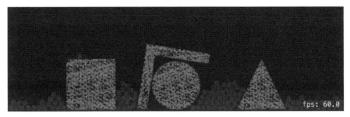

I'm sure you're already wondering how would you debug a real game scene with many complex shapes — you can't always have particles raining over your game objects!

Apple to the rescue!

The SpriteKit physics engine provides a very convenient feature: an API that enables physics debug output to your live scene. You can see the outlines of your objects, the joints between them, the physics constraints you create and more.

Find the line in your code that enables the "fps" label, `sceneView.showsFPS = true`, and add this line below it:

```
sceneView.showsPhysics = true
```

As soon as the scene starts rendering anew, you'll see the shapes of all your bodies drawn in bright green (it may be hard to see in this screenshot but it's there):

Thanks to this feature, you can do some serious debugging of your physics setup.

Properties of physics bodies

There's more to physics bodies than collision detection. A physics body also has several properties you can set, such as, colloquially speaking, slipperiness, bounciness and heaviness.

To see how a body's properties affect the game physics, you'll adjust the properties for the sand. Right now, the sand falls as though it's very heavy, much like granular rock. What if the pieces were made of soft, elastic rubber?

Add the following line to the end of spawnSand():

```
sand.physicsBody!.restitution = 1.0
```

The restitution property is used to determine how much energy the body loses when it bounces off of another body — a fancy way of saying "bounciness".

Values can range from 0.0, where the body does not bounce at all, to 1.0, where the body bounces with the same energy with which it started the collision. The default value is 0.2.

Oh my! The "sand" goes crazy:

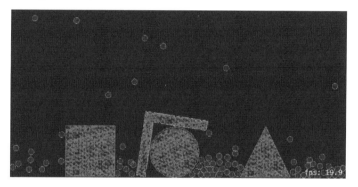

> **Note:** SpriteKit sets all properties of physics bodies to *reasonable* values by default. An object's default weight is based on how big it looks onscreen; restitution and friction ("slipperiness") default to values matching the material of most everyday objects, and so forth.

One more thing: While valid restitution values must be from 0 to 1, the compiler won't complain if you supply values outside of that range. However, think about what it would mean for a body to have a restitution value greater than 1, for example. The body would end a collision with *more* energy than it had initially. That's not realistic behavior and it would quickly break your physics simulation, as the values would grow too large for the physics engine to calculate accurately. It's not something I'd recommend in a real app, but give it a try if you want to have some fun.

Next, make the particles much more dense, so that they're effectively heavier than the other shapes. Given how bouncy they are now, it should be an interesting sight!

Add this line to the end of spawnSand():

```
sand.physicsBody!.density = 20.0
```

Density is defined as mass per unit volume — in other words, the higher the density of an object, the heavier it will be for its size. Density defaults to 1.0, so here you set the sand to be 20x as dense as usual.

This results in the sand being heavier than any of the other shapes — in comparison, the other shapes behave as if they're made of styrofoam. After the simulation settles down, you'll end up with something like this onscreen:

The red particles literally throw their considerable weight around and push the bigger, but lighter, blue shapes aside. When you control the physics, size doesn't necessarily matter!

Here's a quick tour of the rest of the properties on a physics body:

- **friction**: This sets an object's "slipperiness". Values can range from `0.0`, where the body slides smoothly along surfaces like an ice cube, to `1.0`, where the body quickly slows and stops when sliding along surfaces. The default value is `0.2`.

- **isDynamic**: Sometimes you want to use physics bodies for collision detection, but move the node yourself with manual movement or actions. If this is what you want, simply set `isDynamic` to `false`, and the physics engine will ignore all forces and impulses on the physics body and let you move the node yourself.

- **usesPreciseCollisionDetection**: By default, SpriteKit doesn't perform precise collision detection because it's often best to sacrifice some precision to achieve faster performance. However, this has a side effect: if an object is moving very quickly, like a bullet, it might pass through another object. If this ever happens, try turning this flag on to enable more accurate collision detection.

- **allowsRotation**: You might have a sprite you want the physics engine to simulate, but never rotate. If this is the case, simply set this flag to `false`.

- **linearDamping** and **angularDamping**: These values affect how much the linear velocity (translation) or angular velocity (rotation) decrease over time. Values can range from `0.0`, where the speed never decreases, to `1.0`, where the speed decreases immediately. The default value is `0.1`.

- **affectedByGravity**: All objects are affected by gravity by default, but you can turn this off for a body simply by setting this to `false`.

- **resting**: The physics engine has an optimization where objects that haven't moved in a while are flagged as "resting" so the physics engine doesn't have to perform calculations on them any more. If you ever need to "wake up" a resting object manually, simply set this flag to `false`.

- **mass** and **area**: These are automatically calculated for you based on the shape and density of the physics body. However, if you ever need to manually override the `mass`, you can. The `area` is read-only.

- **node**: The physics body has a handy pointer back to the `SKNode` to which it belongs. This is a read-only property.

- **categoryBitMask**, **collisionBitMask**, **contactBitMask** and **joints**: You'll learn all about these in Chapter 9, "Intermediate Physics" and Chapter 10, "Advanced Physics".

Applying an impulse

To wrap up this introduction to physics in SpriteKit, you're going to add a special effect to your test scene. Every now and then, you'll apply an impulse to the particles, making them jump.

The effect will look like a seismic shock that throws everything into the air. Remember, impulses adjust an object's momentum immediately, like a bullet firing from a gun.

To try it out, add this new method to your playground *before* your call to `delay(seconds:completion:)`:

```
func shake() {
  scene.enumerateChildNodes(withName: "sand") { node, _ in
    node.physicsBody!.applyImpulse(
      CGVector(dx: 0, dy: random(min: 20, max: 40))
    )
  }
}
```

This function loops over all of the nodes in your scene with the name **sand** and applies an impulse to each of them. You apply an upward impulse by having the x-component equal to zero and having a random positive y-component between 20 and 40.

You create the impulse as a `CGVector`, which is just like a `CGPoint` but named so that it's clear it's used as a vector. You then apply the impulse to the anchor point of each particle. Since the strengths of the impulses are random, the shake effect will look real.

Of course, you need to call the function before you'll see the particles jump. Locate the call to delay(seconds:completion:) and replace it with this one:

```
delay(seconds: 2.0) {
  scene.physicsWorld.gravity = CGVector(dx: 0, dy: -9.8)
  scene.run(
    SKAction.repeat(
      SKAction.sequence([
        SKAction.run(spawnSand),
        SKAction.wait(forDuration: 0.1)
        ]),
      count: 100)
  )
  delay(seconds: 12, completion: shake)
}
```

You call shake() 12 seconds after gravity is turned on, giving the scene time to settle down so you can observe the seismic shock.

It's a bit odd that the shapes don't jump by themselves but are rather "lifted" by the sand particles. Add this code to your shake() function to make the shapes jump, too:

```
scene.enumerateChildNodes(withName: "shape") { node, _ in
  node.physicsBody!.applyImpulse(
    CGVector(dx: random(min:20, max:60),
             dy: random(min:20, max:60))
  )
}

delay(seconds: 3, completion: shake)
```

First, you loop through all the shapes and apply a random vector impulse to each of them. Then, you call delay(seconds:completion:) and tell it to call shake() again in three seconds.

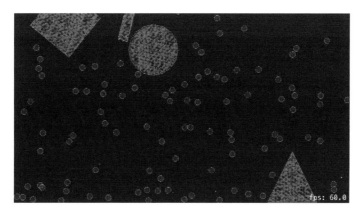

Well done. You've covered the basics of SpriteKit's physics engine, and you're almost ready to put these concepts to use in a real game. But first, it's time to push yourself to prove all that you've learned so far.

Challenges

This chapter has two challenges that will get you ready to create your first physics game. You'll learn about forces and create a dynamic sprite with collision detection.

As always, if you get stuck, you can find the solutions in the resources for this chapter — but do give it your best shot before peeking!

Challenge 1: Forces

So far, you've learned how to make the sand move immediately by applying an impulse. But what if you wanted to make objects move more gradually, over time?

Your first challenge is to simulate a very windy day that will blow your objects back and forth across the screen. Below are some guidelines for how to accomplish this.

First, add these variables:

```
var blowingRight = true
var windForce = CGVector(dx: 50, dy: 0)
```

Then, add this stub implementation of update():

```
extension SKScene {
  //1
  func applyWindForce() {
    enumerateChildNodes(withName: "sand") { node, _ in
      node.physicsBody!.applyForce(windForce)
    }
    enumerateChildNodes(withName: "shape") { node, _ in
      node.physicsBody!.applyForce(windForce)
    }
  }

  //2
  func switchWindDirection() {
    blowingRight = !blowingRight
    windForce = CGVector(dx: blowingRight ? 50 : -50, dy: 0)
  }
}

//3
Timer.scheduledTimer(timeInterval: 0.05, target: scene,
```

```
      selector: #selector(SKScene.applyWindForce),
      userInfo: nil, repeats: true)

  Timer.scheduledTimer(timeInterval: 3.0, target: scene,
      selector: #selector(SKScene.switchWindDirection),
      userInfo: nil, repeats: true)
```

Let's go over this section by section:

1. Inside `windWithTimer(_:)`, you enumerate over all sand particles and shape bodies and apply the current `windForce` to each. Look up the method named `applyForce(_:)`, which works in a similar way to `applyImpulse(_:)`, which you already know.

2. Inside `switchWindDirections(_:)`, you simply toggle `blowingRight` and update `windForce`.

3. You declare two timers. The first fires 20 times per second and calls `windWithTimer(_:)` on your scene — this is where you'll apply force to all the bodies. The second timer fires once every three seconds and calls `switchWindDirection(_:)`, where you'll toggle `blowingRight` and adjust the `windForce` vector accordingly.

Remember the difference between forces and impulses: You apply a force every frame while the force is active, but you fire an impulse once and only once.

If you get this working, you'll see the objects slide back and forth across the screen as the wind changes direction:

Challenge 2: Kinematic bodies

In your games, you might have some sprites you want to move with manual movement or custom actions, and others you want the physics engine to move. But you'll still want collision detection to work on all of these sprites, including the ones you move yourself.

As you learned earlier in this chapter, you can accomplish this by setting the isDynamic flag on a physics body to false. Bodies that you move yourself, but that still have collision detection, are sometimes called **kinematic bodies**.

Your second challenge in this chapter is to try this out for yourself by making the circle sprite move not by the physics engine, but by an SKAction. Here are a few hints:

- Set the isDynamic property of the circle's physics body to false after creating it.

- Create an SKAction to move the circle horizontally back and forth across the screen, and make that action repeat forever.

If you get this working, you'll see that everything is affected by the gravity, wind and impulses, except for the circle. However, the objects still collide with the circle as usual:

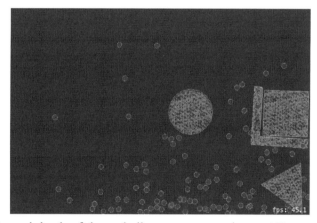

If you made it through both of these challenges, congratulations! You now have a firm grasp of the most important concepts of SpriteKit's physics engine, and you're 100% ready to put these concepts to use in Cat Nap. Meow!

Chapter 9: Intermediate Physics

By Marin Todorov

In Chapter 7, "Scene Editor", you got acquainted with SpriteKit's scene editor by building the first level of a game named Cat Nap.

Then in Chapter 8, "Beginning Physics", you took up physics in SpriteKit by experimenting in real time inside a playground. You learned how to add bodies to sprites, create shapes, customize physics properties and even apply forces and impulses.

In this chapter, you're going to use your newly acquired scene editor and physics skills to add physics into Cat Nap, creating your first fully playable level. By the end of this chapter, you'll finally be able to help the sleepy cat settle into his bed:

Purr-fect!

> **Note:** This chapter begins where Chapter 7's Challenge 2 left off. If you were unable to complete the challenges or skipped ahead from an earlier chapter, don't worry — simply open the starter project from this chapter to pick up where Chapter 7's Challenge 2 left off.

Getting started

Open your CatNap project, and make sure **GameScene.swift** is open.

First, you're going to do some more scene initialization by overriding the scene's `didMove(to:)`. Just as you did for Zombie Conga, you need to set the scene's playable area so that when you're finished developing Cat Nap, it will fully support both iPhone and iPad screen resolutions.

Get rid of all the default code added by Xcode by replacing the contents of **GameScene.swift** with the following:

```swift
import SpriteKit

class GameScene: SKScene {

  override func didMove(to view: SKView) {
    // Calculate playable margin

    let maxAspectRatio: CGFloat = 16.0/9.0
    let maxAspectRatioHeight = size.width / maxAspectRatio
    let playableMargin: CGFloat = (size.height
      - maxAspectRatioHeight)/2

    let playableRect = CGRect(x: 0, y: playableMargin,
      width: size.width, height: size.height-playableMargin*2)

    physicsBody = SKPhysicsBody(edgeLoopFrom: playableRect)
  }
}
```

Just as you did for Zombie Conga, you begin with a 16:9 aspect ratio and then define the frame of the playable area based on the current scene size.

Since Cat Nap is a physics-based game, you set the detected playable frame as the edge loop for the scene. That's all there is to it — SpriteKit will now automatically confine your game objects within the area you designated for the gameplay.

Now you're ready to take those sprites you placed in the scene editor and put them to work!

Custom node classes

When you place objects in the scene editor, you choose from the list provided in the Object Library.

As you already know, you can drag-and-drop a generic node, a sprite node showing an image or a label. At runtime, SpriteKit creates the nodes from the respective built-in type and sets them up the way you want.

This, however, leaves you with limited room for customization — you can't add new methods or simply override one of the built-in functionalities with your own implementation.

In this section, you'll learn how to create and employ your own custom node classes, which will give you exactly the behavior you need for your game from every node in your level.

You'll start by adding a simple class for the cat bed node. From Xcode's main menu, select **File > New > File...** and for the file template, choose **iOS/Source/Swift File**. Name the new file **BedNode.swift** and save it.

Replace the default contents with an empty `SKSpriteNode` subclass:

```
import SpriteKit

class BedNode: SKSpriteNode {
}
```

You've created an empty class that derives from `SKSpriteNode`; now you need to link this class to the bed sprite in the scene editor. To do this, open **GameScene.sks** in the scene editor and select the cat **bed.** In the Utilities Area, switch to the **Custom Class Inspector.**

For **Custom Class**, enter **BedNode**.

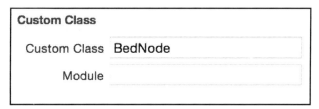

This way, when you launch your game, instead of creating a plain `SKSpriteNode` for the cat bed, SpriteKit will make a new instance of `BedNode`. Now you can customize your `BedNode` class to behave in the way you'd like.

Next, to understand how much you can do with custom node classes, you're going to add an event method that will get called when the node is added to the scene. If you're familiar with building `UIKit` apps for iOS, it will be similar to `UIView.didMoveToWindow()`.

First, you need a new protocol for all the nodes that will listen for this event. Open **GameScene.swift** and add the following after the `import` statement:

```
protocol EventListenerNode {
  func didMoveToScene()
}
```

Now, switch back to **BedNode.swift** to make the class conform to the new protocol and add a `didMoveToScene()` method stub that prints out a message. The class will now look like this:

```
import SpriteKit

class BedNode: SKSpriteNode, EventListenerNode {
  func didMoveToScene() {
    print("bed added to scene")
  }
}
```

For the final step, you need to call the new method. A good place to do that is at the bottom of the `didMove(to:)` of your scene class.

Back in **GameScene.swift**, add the following code at the end of `didMove(to:)`:

```
enumerateChildNodes(withName: "//*", using: { node, _ in
  if let eventListenerNode = node as? EventListenerNode {
    eventListenerNode.didMoveToScene()
  }
})
```

Here you use `enumerateChildNodes(withName:using:)`, an SKNode method that loops over all the nodes that exist in the scene. While `childNode(withName:)` finds the first node matching the given name or search pattern, `enumerateChildNodes(withName:using:)` returns an array containing all the nodes that match the name or pattern you're looking for.

As the first parameter, you can specify either a node name or a search pattern. If you've worked extensively with XML, you'll notice the similarities:

• **/name**: Search for nodes named "name" in the root of the hierarchy.

• **//name**: Search for nodes named "name" starting at the root and moving recursively down the hierarchy.

• *****: Matches zero or more characters; e.g. **name*** will match name1, name2, nameABC and name.

> **Note:** For additional examples, review the section "Advanced Searches" in Apple's SKNode docs: http://apple.co/1I9QfBz

Now you can decipher the search pattern from the last code block: //*. When your search pattern starts with //, the search is performed recursively from the top of the node hierarchy. Combine that with *, which means *any name*, and you loop over all existing nodes, regardless of their names or their locations in the node hierarchy.

As a second parameter, enumerateChildNodes(withName:using:) gets a closure; the code inside is executed once per each matching node. The first closure parameter is the matching node, and the second gives you an opportunity to stop the search at that node.

Build and run the game. You'll see your test message show up — your code looped over all nodes, matched the ones implementing EventListenerNode and called didMoveToScene() on each one:

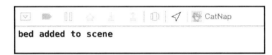

This proves that your game is using your custom BedNode SKSpriteNode subclass for the cat bed. w00t!

Now you can put all your node setup code in didMoveToScene() for each respective node class. That way, you won't clog your scene class with code that's relevant only to specific nodes. In your scene class, you'll add the code that has to do with the entire scene or interaction between nodes.

To give custom classes another try, add a custom class for the cat. From Xcode's main menu, select **File > New > File...** and for the file template, choose **iOS/Source/Swift File**. Name the new file **CatNode.swift** and save it.

Replace the default contents with the following SKSpriteNode subclass:

```
import SpriteKit

class CatNode: SKSpriteNode, EventListenerNode {
  func didMoveToScene() {
    print("cat added to scene")
  }
}
```

Just like before, you make sure that when the method gets called, it prints a statement.

One last thing before moving on: you don't want to change the class in **GameScene.sks**; you want to change the class in **Cat.sks**. Remember, **GameScene.sks** only holds a reference to **Cat.sks**, so you need to go to **Cat.sks** to set the appropriate class for your cat node.

Open **Cat.sks** and select the **cat_body** sprite node. In the Custom Class Inspector, set the **Custom Class** to **CatNode**.

Build and run the game again. The output in the console is now:

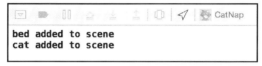

The cat is one step closer to taking a nap!

Next, you need to connect the nodes you created in the scene editor to variables so you can access the sprites in code.

Connecting sprites to variables

For those familiar with UIKit development, connecting nodes to variables is somewhat like connecting views in your storyboard to outlets.

Open **GameScene.swift** and add two properties to the GameScene class:

```
var bedNode: BedNode!
var catNode: CatNode!
```

catNode and bedNode are — or will be in a moment — the cat and cat bed sprite nodes, respectively. Notice that you use their custom classes, because the scene editor takes care to use the correct type when creating the scene nodes.

Open **GameScene.sks** and select the cat bed. In the Attributes Inspector, notice that the sprite has the name **bed**. This is how you'll find that sprite in the scene from code — by its name. The name of the sprite is much like a view's tag property in UIKit development.

Switch back to **GameScene.swift** and add the following code to didMove(to:):

```
bedNode = childNode(withName: "bed") as! BedNode
```

childNode(withName:) loops through a node's children and returns the *first* node with the required name. In this case, you loop through the scene's children, looking for the bed sprite, which is based on the name you set in the scene editor.

For the cat sprite, you need a different approach. You don't want to work with the cat reference; instead, you want to work with the cat body. After all, only the cat's body will have its own physics body — you don't need to apply physics simulation to the eyes or the whiskers!

Since the cat_body sprite is not a direct child of the scene, you can't simply provide the name cat_body to `childNode(withName:)` and expect to get it back. Instead, you need to recursively search through all the children of the children of the scene.

Consulting the search pattern table reference from earlier, you end up with the simple pattern **//cat_body**. That being the case, add this line to `didMove(to:)`:

```
catNode = childNode(withName: "//cat_body") as! CatNode
```

Now you have a reference to each sprite, so you can modify them in code. To test this, add the following two lines to the end of `didMove(to:)`:

```
bedNode.setScale(1.5)
catNode.setScale(1.5)
```

Build and run, and you'll see Giganto-Cat!

Now that you've proved you can modify the sprites in code, comment out those two lines to revert the cat and bed back to normal:

```
// bedNode.setScale(1.5)
// catNode.setScale(1.5)
```

Sorry about that, Giganto-Cat, but cats already have a big enough ego! :]

Congratulations — now you know how to connect objects in the scene editor to code. Now it's time to move onto physics!

Adding physics

Recall from the previous chapter that for the physics engine to kick in, you need to create physics bodies for your sprites. In this section, you're going to learn three different ways to do that:

1. Creating simple bodies in the scene editor

2. Creating simple bodies from code

3. Creating custom bodies

It's time try each of these methods, one at a time.

Creating simple bodies in the scene editor

Looking at your scene as it is now, you can't help but notice that those wooden blocks would be a perfect candidate for rectangular physics bodies.

From your experiments in the previous chapter, you already know how to create rectangular bodies in code; it's time to see how it's done in the scene editor.

Open **GameScene.sks** and select the four block sprites in your scene. Press and hold the **Command** key on your keyboard and click on each block until you've selected all of them:

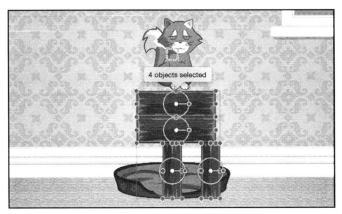

In the **Physics Definition** section of the Attributes Inspector, change the selection for **Body Type** to **Bounding rectangle**. This will open a section with additional properties, allowing you to control most aspects of a physics body. You read about each of these properties in the previous chapter.

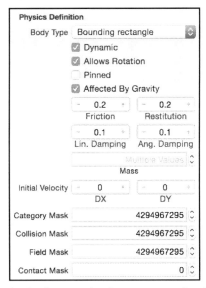

The default property values look about right for your wooden blocks: the bodies will be **dynamic**, can **rotate** when falling and are **affected by gravity**. The **Mass** field reads **Multiple Values**, because SpriteKit assigned a different mass to each wooden block based on its size.

That's all you need to do to set up the blocks' physics bodies. Notice now that when you deselect the blocks, they're faintly outlined in blue-green, indicating they have physics bodies:

There's one last thing to do: select all four wooden blocks again, scroll to the top of the Attributes Inspector and enter **block** in the **Name** field. Now you can easily enumerate all of the blocks in the scene and also easily see which ones are blocks when you debug the scene.

> **Note:** This kind of node configuration is something you could implement in a custom node class. Don't worry — you'll learn how to set up your bodies both from the scene editor and from code. But you can only do one at a time. :]
>
> In fact, you'll add a custom class for the block nodes later, when you add user interaction to them.

Simulating the scene

Let's quickly explore another feature of the scene editor.

You know that clicking the **Animate** button will run any sprite actions you add to sprites. But what about physics? Will the same button also fire up the good old physics engine? Click **Animate** and watch what happens:

You'll see the blocks fall down off the screen, but they won't stop at the edges. That's because the Animate button does not run the code that creates the edge loop that you added to GameScene. However, this is still a handy way to do some basic testing.

Creating simple bodies from code

What if you want a physics body to be smaller than a node's bounding rectangle or circle? For example, you might want to be "forgiving" in the collision detection between two objects to make the gameplay easier or more fun, similar to how you reduced the collision box for the crazy cat lady in Zombie Conga.

Making the physics body a different shape than the sprite itself is easy to do, and also gives you an opportunity to apply your skills from the previous chapter to Cat Nap.

The cat bed itself won't participate in the physics simulation; instead, it will remain static on the ground and exempt from collisions with other bodies in the scene. It will still have a physics body, though, because you need to detect when the cat falls onto the bed. So you're going to give the bed a small, non-interactive body for the purpose of detecting contacts.

Since you've already connected your bedNode instance variable to the bed sprite, you can create the body in code.

Switch to **BedNode.swift** and add the following to didMoveToScene():

```
let bedBodySize = CGSize(width: 40.0, height: 30.0)
physicsBody = SKPhysicsBody(rectangleOf: bedBodySize)
physicsBody!.isDynamic = false
```

As you learned in the previous chapter, a sprite's physics body doesn't necessarily have to match the sprite's size or shape. For the cat bed, you want the physics body to be much smaller than the sprite, because you only want the cat to fall happily asleep when he hits the exact center of the bed. Cats are known to be picky, after all!

Since you never want the cat bed to move, you set its dynamic property to false. This makes the body static, which makes calculations simpler for the physics simulation, because it can ignore any forces applied to this object.

> **Note:** You need to force unwrap the physicsBody property since it's an *optional* property. Generally you should use ! if you're sure there's a body attached to the sprite, or ? if you're not.

Open **GameViewController.swift** and add the following line inside `viewDidLoad()`, just after the code that declares `view`:

```
view.showsPhysics = true
```

Build and run the project, and you'll see your scene come alive:

Look at the little rectangle toward the bottom of the screen — that's the physics body of the cat bed. It's green to remind you it's not a dynamic physics body.

But your carefully built obstacle tower appears a little off-center. That happened because the bed body pushed aside your central wooden block. To fix this, you'll need to set the block bodies and the bed body so they don't collide with each other, something you'll learn how to do a bit later.

Creating custom bodies

Looking at the cat sprite, you can instantly guess that a rectangular or a circular body won't do — you'll have to use a different approach and create a custom-shaped physics body.

To do this, you'll load a separate image that describes the shape of the cat's physics body and use it to create the body object itself. Open **CatNode.swift** and add this code to `didMoveToScene()`:

```
let catBodyTexture = SKTexture(imageNamed: "cat_body_outline")
parent!.physicsBody = SKPhysicsBody(texture: catBodyTexture,
  size: catBodyTexture.size())
```

You create a new texture object out of an image named **cat_body_outline.png**. From the project navigator, open **cat_body_outline** from your **Assets.xcassets** catalog and you'll see it contains a vaguely cat-shaped blob.

This shape doesn't include the cat's head or tail, and it doesn't follow the outline of the paws. Instead, it uses a flat bottom edge, so the cat will remain stable on those wooden blocks.

Next, you create a body for the cat sprite using an SKPhysicsBody instance and the appropriate texture, scaling it to the texture's size. You're already familiar with how to do this from the previous chapter. Note how you add the physics body to the parent node (i.e. the compound node that holds all of the cat parts).

Build and run the project again, and check out the debug drawing of the cat's body. Excellent work!

Now that you've set up the first level, why don't you take a break from all this physics and get the player in the mood for puzzles by turning on some soothing and delightful music?

Introducing SKTUtils

In the first few chapters of this book, while you were working on Zombie Conga, you created some handy extensions to allow you to do things like add and subtract two CGPoints by using the + or − operators.

Rather than make you continuously re-add these extensions in each mini-game, we've combined them and created a library named SKTUtils.

Besides handy geometry and math functions, this library also includes a useful class that helps you easily play an audio file as your game's background music.

Now you're going to add SKTUtils to your project so you can make use of these methods throughout the rest of the chapter. Happy birthday!

Locate the **SKTUtils** folder in the root folder for this book and drag the entire folder into the project navigator in Xcode.

Make sure **Copy items if needed**, **Create Groups** and the **CatNap** target are all checked, and click **Finish**.

Take a minute to review the contents of the library. It should look quite familiar, with a few additions and tweaks:

Now every class in your project has access to these time-saving functions.

Background music

Now that you've added SKTUtils, it will be a cinch to add background music. Open **GameScene.swift** and add this code to didMove(to:) to start the music:

```
SKTAudio.sharedInstance()
  .playBackgroundMusic("backgroundMusic.mp3")
```

Build and run the project, and enjoy the merry tune!

Note: You still have many more build and runs ahead of you in this chapter. If at any time you feel like muting the background music, just comment out this last line.

Controlling your bodies

So far, you know how to create physics bodies for sprites and let the physics engine do its thing.

But in Cat Nap, you want a bit more control than that. For example:

- **Categorizing bodies:** You want to keep the cat bed from colliding with the blocks, and vice versa. To do this, you need a way to categorize bodies and set up collision flags.

- **Finding bodies:** You want to enable the player to destroy a block by tapping it. To do this, you need a way to find what bodies are at a given location in the scene.

- **Detecting contacts between bodies:** You want to detect when the cat hits the cat bed, so he can get his beauty sleep. To do this, you need a way to detect contacts.

You'll investigate these areas over the next three sections. By the time you're done, you'll have implemented the most important parts of this mini-game.

Categorizing bodies

SpriteKit's default behavior is for all physics bodies to collide with all other physics bodies. If two objects are occupying the same point, like the brick and the cat bed, the physics engine will automatically move one of them aside.

The good news is you can override this default behavior and specify whether or not two physics bodies should collide. There are three steps to do this:

1. **Define the categories:** The first step is to define categories for your physics bodies, such as block bodies, cat bodies and cat bed bodies.

2. **Set the category bit mask:** Once you have a set of categories, you need to specify the categories to which each physics body belongs, since a physics body can belong to more than one category. You do this simply by setting its category bit mask.

3. **Set the collision bit mask:** You also need to specify the collision bit mask for each physics body. This controls which categories of bodies the body will collide with.

As with most things, the best place to start is at the beginning — in this case, by defining the categories for Cat Nap. In **GameScene.swift**, add the category constants **outside** the GameScene class, preferably at the top:

```
struct PhysicsCategory {
  static let None:  UInt32 = 0
  static let Cat:   UInt32 = 0b1 // 1
  static let Block: UInt32 = 0b10 // 2
  static let Bed:   UInt32 = 0b100 // 4
}
```

Now you can comfortably access body categories like PhysicsCategory.Cat and PhysicsCategory.Bed.

You've probably already spotted that each of the categories turns on another bit. The following shows each value expressed in decimal and binary notations:

• **PhysicsCategory.None**: Decimal **0**, Binary **00000000**

• **PhysicsCategory.Cat**: Decimal **1**, Binary **00000001**

• **PhysicsCategory.Block**: Decimal **2**, Binary **00000010**

• **PhysicsCategory.Bed**: Decimal **4**, Binary **00000100**

This is very handy and allows you to easily combine categories. For example, when you want to specify that the cat should collide with all block bodies and the bed, you can say the collision bit mask for the cat is PhysicsCategory.Block | PhysicsCategory.Bed (read this as "block OR bed"), which produces the logical OR of the two values:

• **PhysicsCategory.Block | PhysicsCategory.Bed**: Decimal **6**, Binary **00000110**

> **Note:** If you aren't quite at ease with binary arithmetic, you can read more about bitwise operations here: https://en.wikipedia.org/wiki/Bitwise_operation

Now you can move on to steps two and three: setting the category and collision bit masks for each object, starting with the blocks.

Go back to **GameScene.sks** and select the **four wooden blocks**, as you did earlier. Look at the current **Category Mask** and **Collision Mask**:

Category Mask	4294967295
Collision Mask	4294967295
Field Mask	4294967295
Contact Mask	0

Both are set to the biggest integer value possible, thus making all bodies collide with all other bodies. If you convert the default value of 4294967295 to binary, you'll see that it has all bits turned *on*, and therefore, it collides with all other objects:

```
4294967295 = 11111111111111111111111111111111
```

Each bit corresponds to one category of physics bodies.

It's time to implement custom collisions. Edit the blocks' properties like so:

For **Category Mask**, enter the raw value of `PhysicsCategory.Block`, which is **2**.

For **Collision Mask**, enter the bitwise `OR` value of `PhysicsCategory.Cat | PhysicsCategory.Block`, which is **3**.

> **Note:** Just put the decimal values in the boxes — that is, for the Collision Mask, enter **3**.

| Category Mask | 2 |
| Collision Mask | 3 |

This means you've set each block's body to be of the `PhysicsCategory.Block` category, and you've set all of the blocks to collide with both the cat and other blocks.

Next, set up the bed. You created this body from code, so go back to **BedNode.swift** and add the following to the end of `didMoveToScene()`:

```
physicsBody!.categoryBitMask = PhysicsCategory.Bed
physicsBody!.collisionBitMask = PhysicsCategory.None
```

With the code above, you set the category of the bed body and then set its collision mask to `PhysicsCategory.None`, since you don't want the bed to collide with any other game objects.

> **Note:** As promised earlier, you're learning how to do things both from the scene editor and from code — when you're on your own, just pick whichever suits you. I personally like the code approach a little better, because you can use the defined enumeration members; in the scene editor, you have to use hard-coded integer values.

At this point, you've set up both the wooden blocks and the cat bed with the proper categories and collision masks.

Build and run the project one more time:

As expected, you see a block right in front of the bed's body without either body pushing the other away. Nice!

Finally, set the bit masks for the cat. Since you created the physics body for your cat sprite in code, you also have to set the category and collision masks in code, specifically in **CatNode.swift**. Open that file and add the following to the end of didMoveToScene():

```
parent!.physicsBody!.categoryBitMask = PhysicsCategory.Cat
parent!.physicsBody!.collisionBitMask = PhysicsCategory.Block
```

You placed the cat into its own category, PhysicsCategory.Cat, and set it to collide only with blocks.

> **Note:** A physics body's collisionBitMask value specifies which categories of objects will affect the movement of *that* body when those two bodies collide. But remember, you set the bed's isDynamic property to false, which already ensures that no forces will ever affect the bed — so there's no need to set the bed's collisionBitMask.
>
> Generally, there's never a reason to set the collisionBitMask for an object with its isDynamic property set to false. Likewise, there's never a reason to set the collisionBitMask for edge loop bodies. which are always treated as if their isDynamic property is false, even if it isn't.

Now you know how to make a group of bodies pass through some bodies and collide with others. You'll find this technique useful for many types of games. For example, in some games you want players on the same team to pass through each other, but collide with enemies from the other team. Often, you don't want game physics to imitate real life.

Handling touches

In this section, you'll implement the first part of the gameplay. When the player taps a block, you'll destroy it with a *pop*.

To distinguish nodes you can tap on from nodes that are just static decoration you will add a new protocol. Open **GameScene.swift** and add under the existing protocol declaration for `EventListenerNode`:

```
protocol InteractiveNode {
  func interact()
}
```

Since `SKNode` inherits from `UIResponder`, you can handle touches on each node from the node's own custom class by overriding `touchesBegan(_:with:)`, `touchesEnded(_:with:)` or other `UIResponder` methods.

Since right now you're interested in simple taps on the block nodes, a custom `BlockNode` class with just `touchesEnded(_:with:)` will suffice.

You're already quite familiar with creating custom node classes, so this should be a breeze. From Xcode's main menu, select **File > New > File...** and for the file template, choose **iOS/Source/Swift File**. Name the new file **BlockNode.swift** and save it.

Replace the default contents with the following:

```swift
import SpriteKit

class BlockNode: SKSpriteNode, EventListenerNode,
    InteractiveNode {
  func didMoveToScene() {
    isUserInteractionEnabled = true
  }

  func interact() {
    isUserInteractionEnabled = false
  }

  override func touchesEnded(_ touches: Set<UITouch>,
      with event: UIEvent?) {
    super.touchesEnded(touches, with: event)
    print("destroy block")
    interact()
  }
}
```

For this type of node, you did all the physics body setup using the scene editor, so inside `didMoveToScene()` all you need is to enable user interactions.

By default, `isUserInteractionEnabled` is off to keep the responder chain as light as possible — but for your blocks, you definitely want to handle touches, so you set it to `true`.

Further, you override `touchesEnded(_:with:)`, so you can handle simple taps on the block node — in the code above, you simply call `interact()` and leave it do all the work.

Since you will allow the players to destroy a block by simply tapping it once, as soon as `interact()` is being called you turn off `isUserInteractionEnabled` to ignore further touches on the same block.

The final step before you test that code is to set all block nodes to use this custom class in the scene editor. Open **GameScene.sks** and select the four wooden blocks just as you did before. In the Custom Class Inspector, enter **BlockNode** for the **Custom Class**:

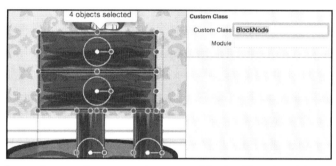

Build and run the project, and start tapping some blocks. You should see one line in the console for each of your taps on a block:

Now for the fun part! You want to destroy those blocks and remove them from the scene. Add this to `interact()` in **BlockNode.swift**:

```
run(SKAction.sequence([
  SKAction.playSoundFileNamed("pop.mp3",
    waitForCompletion: false),
  SKAction.scale(to: 0.8, duration: 0.1),
  SKAction.removeFromParent()
]))
```

Here you're running a sequence of three actions: the first action plays an amusing *pop* sound, the next scales down the sprite and the last removes it from the scene. This should be enough to make the level's basic physics work.

Build and run the project again. This time, when you tap the blocks, you've got your game on:

Detecting contacts between bodies

Very often in games, you'd like to know if certain bodies are in contact. Two or more bodies can "touch" or "pass through" each other, depending on whether or not they're set to collide. In both cases, they're in contact:

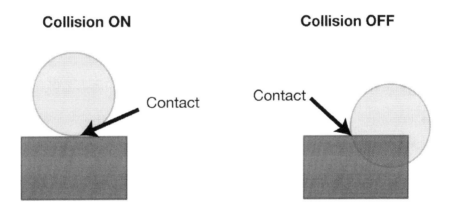

In Cat Nap, you want to know whether certain pairs of bodies touch:

1. If **the cat touches the floor**, it means he's on the ground, but out of his bed, so the player fails the level.

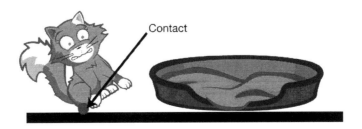

2. If **the cat touches the bed**, it means he landed successfully on the bed, so the player wins the level.

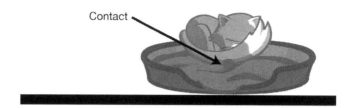

SpriteKit makes it easy for you to receive a callback when two physics bodies make contact. The first step is to conform to `SKPhysicsContactDelegate`.

In Cat Nap, you'll implement these methods in `GameScene`. Open **GameScene.swift** and add the `SKPhysicsContactDelegate` protocol to the class declaration line, so it looks like this:

```
class GameScene: SKScene, SKPhysicsContactDelegate {
```

The `SKPhysicsContactDelegate` protocol defines two methods you'll implement in `GameScene`:

*   `didBegin(_:)` tells you when two bodies first make contact.

*   `didEnd(_:)` tells you when two bodies end their contact.

The diagram below shows how SpriteKit would call these methods in the case of two bodies passing through each other:

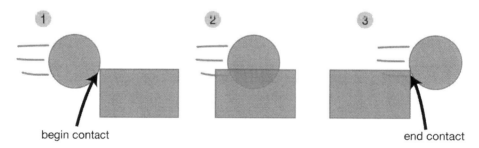

You'll most often be interested in `didBegin(_:)`, since much of your game logic will occur when two objects touch.

However, there are times you'll want to know when objects stop touching. For example, you may want to use the physics engine to test when a player is within a trigger area. Perhaps entering the area sounds an alarm, while leaving the area silences it. In a case such as this, you'll need to implement `didEnd(_:)`, as well.

To handle when the cat touches the floor, you first need to add a new category constant for the edges of the screen. Scroll to the top of **GameScene.swift** and add this new `PhysicsCategory` value:

```
static let Edge:  UInt32 = 0b1000 // 8
```

Then, find this line inside `didMove(to:)`:

```
physicsBody = SKPhysicsBody(edgeLoop: playableRect)
```

And just below it, add the following:

```
physicsWorld.contactDelegate = self
physicsBody!.categoryBitMask = PhysicsCategory.Edge
```

First, you set `GameScene` as the contact delegate of the scene's physics world. Then, you assign `PhysicsCategory.Edge` as the edge loop body's category.

Build and run the project to see the results of your actions so far.

Hmm... that's not right. All the blocks fall through the edge — but just seconds ago, the project worked fine!

The issue here is that the world edge now has a category, `PhysicsCategory.Edge`, but the blocks aren't set to collide with it. Therefore, they fall through the floor. Meanwhile, the cat bed's `isDynamic` property is set to `false`, so it still doesn't move at all.

With no blocks on the screen, you have no game! Open **GameScene.sks** in the scene editor and select the four wooden blocks, just as you did before. Then, change the **Collision Mask** for their bodies from 3 to **11**.

• **PhysicsCategory.Block | PhysicsCategory.Cat | PhysicsCategory.Edge:** Decimal **11**, Binary **00001011**

Build and run the project now, and you'll see the familiar scene setup. But try popping all the blocks out of the cat's way, and you'll see the cat fall through the bottom of the screen and disappear. Goodbye, Kitty!

By now, you probably know what's wrong: The cat doesn't collide with the scene's edge loop, of course.

Go to **CatNode.swift** and change the line where you set the cat's collision mask so that the cat also collides with the scene's boundaries:

```
parent!.physicsBody!.collisionBitMask = PhysicsCategory.Block
   | PhysicsCategory.Edge
```

This should keep that pesky feline from falling off the screen.

Build and run the project again, and everything will appear (and behave!) as it should.

Detecting contact between bodies

You've learned to use the `categoryBitMask` to set a physics body's categories, and the `collisionBitMask` to set the colliding categories for a physics body. Well, there's another bit mask: `contactTestBitMask`.

You use `contactTestBitMask` to define which categories of bodies should result in the physics contact delegate methods being called when a physics body comes into contact with another body.

It's easy to confuse `collisionBitMask` with `contactTestBitMask`. Just remember that *collision* refers to what's automatically handled by the physics simulation (i.e. when bodies bounce off each other), and *contact* simply refers to when two bodies make contact with each other.

In Cat Nap, you want to receive callbacks when the cat makes contact with either the edge loop body or the bed body, so switch to **CatNode.swift** and add this line to the end of `didMoveToScene()`:

```
parent!.physicsBody!.contactTestBitMask = PhysicsCategory.Bed
   | PhysicsCategory.Edge
```

That's all the configuration you need to do. Every time the cat body makes contact with either the bed body or the edge loop body, you'll get a callback.

Now to handle those contact callbacks. Back in **GameScene.swift**, add the following contact delegate protocol method to your class:

```
func didBegin(_ contact: SKPhysicsContact) {
  let collision = contact.bodyA.categoryBitMask
    | contact.bodyB.categoryBitMask

  if collision == PhysicsCategory.Cat | PhysicsCategory.Bed {
    print("SUCCESS")
  } else if collision == PhysicsCategory.Cat
      | PhysicsCategory.Edge {
    print("FAIL")
  }
}
```

Look at the parameter this method receives. It's of class SKPhysicsContact and tells you a lot about the contacting bodies:

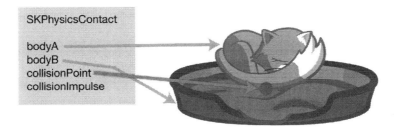

There's no way to guarantee a particular body will be set as bodyA or bodyB. But there are various ways you can find out, such as by checking the body's category or looking for some property of the body's node.

This simple game contains only four categories so far, which correspond to the integer values 1, 2, 4 and 8. And each body only belongs to one category. That makes it simple to check for contact combinations: simply use bitwise OR as you did to define the collision and contact bit masks.

Categories	2-Category Combinations
Cat: 1	Cat (1) | Block (2) = 3
Block: 2	Block (2) | Block (2) = 2
Bed: 4	Cat (1) | Bed (4) = 5
Edge: 8	... other combinations

> **Note:** If you feel the ground loosening under your feet when you think about comparing bitmasks, consider reading this short but informative article: https://en.wikipedia.org/wiki/Mask_(computing).

Inside your implementation of didBegin(_:), you first OR the categories of the two bodies that collided and store the result in collision. The two if statements check collision for the combinations of bodies in which you're interested:

- If the two contacting bodies are the **cat** and the **bed**, you print out "SUCCESS".

- If the two contacting bodies are the **cat** and the **edge**, you print out "FAIL".

Build and run the project to verify you've got this working thus far. You'll see a message in the console when the cat makes contact with either the bed or the floor.

> **Note:** When the cat falls on the ground, you'll see several FAIL messages. That's because the cat bounces off the ground just a little by default, so it ends up making contact with the ground more than once. You'll fix this soon.

Finishing touches

You're almost there — you already know when the player should win or lose, so you just need to do something about it.

There are three steps remaining in this chapter:

- Add an in-game message

- Handle losing

- Handle winning

Adding an in-game message

First, add the following new category value to the `PhysicsCategory` structure in
GameScene.swift:

```
static let Label: UInt32 = 0b10000 // 16
```

Next, you need a new custom class; it will inherit from `SKLabelNode`, the built-in
SpriteKit label class, but it will implement some custom behavior.

From Xcode's main menu, select **File > New > File...** and for the file template, choose
iOS/Source/Swift File. Name the new file **MessageNode.swift** and save it.

Replace the default code with the following:

```swift
import SpriteKit

class MessageNode: SKLabelNode {
  convenience init(message: String) {
    self.init(fontNamed: "AvenirNext-Regular")

    text = message
    fontSize = 256.0
    fontColor = SKColor.gray
    zPosition = 100

    let front = SKLabelNode(fontNamed: "AvenirNext-Regular")
    front.text = message
    front.fontSize = 256.0
    front.fontColor = SKColor.white
    front.position = CGPoint(x: -2, y: -2)
    addChild(front)

  }
}
```

First, you added a new `convenience init` that expects a parameter for the text to show
onscreen. To initialize the label node, you call another built-in `convenience init` that
sets the label with the AvenirNext font.

Next, you set the label's text, font size, color and z-position; you want the text to display
over all other scene nodes and 100 is an acceptable value.

To make things a bit more interesting, you add another label as a child to the current
one, the second one having a different color and offset by a few points. Essentially, you're
creating a poor man's drop-shadow for the text by combining dark and light copies of the
message.

Now, to make the message more amusing, add some physics to it by appending the following to the `convenience init`:

```
physicsBody = SKPhysicsBody(circleOfRadius: 10)
physicsBody!.collisionBitMask = PhysicsCategory.Edge
physicsBody!.categoryBitMask = PhysicsCategory.Label
physicsBody!.restitution = 0.7
```

You create a circular physics body for the label and set it to bounce off of the scene's edge. You also assign it to its own physics category, `PhysicsCategory.Label`.

When you add the label to the scene, it will bounce around until it rests on the ground, like so:

To make showing an in-game message even easier, add a short utility method to **GameScene.swift**:

```
func inGameMessage(text: String) {
  let message = MessageNode(message: text)
  message.position = CGPoint(x: frame.midX, y: frame.midY)
  addChild(message)
}
```

In this method, you create a new message node and add it at the center of the scene. Once that's done, the physics engine will take care of the rest.

Now you'll add the methods that run the winning and losing sequences, and you'll use `inGameMessage(text:)` from there.

Losing scenario

First of all, you're going to add a method to restart the current level. To do that, you'll simply call `presentScene(_:)` again on the `SKView` of your game, and it will reload the whole scene.

Still in **GameScene.swift**, add this new method:

```
func newGame() {
  let scene = GameScene(fileNamed:"GameScene")
  scene!.scaleMode = scaleMode
  view!.presentScene(scene)
}
```

In just a few lines of code, you:

- Create a new instance of `GameScene` by using the `init(fileNamed:)` initializer.

- Set the scale mode of the scene to match the scene's current scale mode.

- Pass the new `GameScene` instance to `presentScene(_:)`, which removes the current scene and replaces it with the shiny new scene.

With all preparations complete, it's time to add the initial version of the `lose` method to **GameScene.swift**:

```
func lose() {
  //1
  SKTAudio.sharedInstance().pauseBackgroundMusic()
  SKTAudio.sharedInstance().playSoundEffect("lose.mp3")

  //2
  inGameMessage(text: "Try again...")

  //3
  perform(#selector(newGame), with: nil, afterDelay: 5)
}
```

With this snippet of code, you do a few things:

1. You play a fun sound effect when the player loses. To make the effect more prominent, you pause the in-game music by calling `pauseBackgroundMusic()` on `SKTAudio`. Then, you use `playSoundEffect` in `SKTAudio` to play the effect.

2. You also spawn a new in-game message that reads "Try again…" to keep your players motivated. :]

3. Finally, you wait for five seconds and then restart the level by calling `newGame()`.

Locate `didBegin(_:)` and add the following line after `print("FAIL")`:

```
lose()
```

You now have a working fail sequence. Build and run the project, and give it a try.

Oops! Something isn't quite right, and it's a problem you've noticed before.

As the cat bounces off the floor, it produces numerous contact callbacks and you get many calls to your shiny, new lose() method.

To prevent this from happening, you need a mechanism to stop in-game interactions once the player has failed or completed the level. This calls for a state machine.

A basic state machine

Your Cat Nap state machine will handle two distinct states: when the level is playable, and when the level is inactive. In the latter state, contacts produced by bodies won't have any effect.

Add a new property to your GameScene class to hold the state of your level:

```
var playable = true
```

The level is playable as soon as it loads and appears onscreen. However, you want the level to become inactive as soon as you call lose(), because the player should never be able to lose multiple times without trying again. :]

Insert the following line at the top of lose():

```
playable = false
```

Finally, to prevent more successful contacts, insert the following at the top of didBegin(_:):

```
if !playable {
  return
}
```

This should suffice for now. Your level is playable at launch; then, as soon as the player fails, it becomes inactive. When the level restarts, it's playable again.

Build and run the program, and test it once more. You've solved the multi-message problem and the game restarts after a few seconds:

Good work — it was an easy fix that introduced you to the importance of handling your game state.

Playing an animation

There's something that feels incomplete about this losing sequence: the cat seems emotionless about his grand failure to comfortably sneak in a nap.

It's finally time to put the wake-up animation you designed in Chapter 7, "Scene Editor", to work.

Remember that you created the wake-up animation in **CatWakeUp.sks**? To wrap up this section, you're going to show the wake animation when the player fails to solve the level.

Open **CatNode.swift** and add a new method:

```
func wakeUp() {
  // 1
  for child in children {
    child.removeFromParent()
  }
  texture = nil
  color = SKColor.clear

  // 2
  let catAwake = SKSpriteNode(fileNamed:
"CatWakeUp")!.childNode(withName: "cat_awake")!

  // 3
  catAwake.move(toParent: self)
  catAwake.position = CGPoint(x: -30, y: 100)
}
```

You call this method on the cat node to "wake up" the cat. The method consists of two sections:

1. In the first section, you loop over all of the cat's child nodes — the cat "parts" — and remove them from the cat body. Then you set the current texture to `nil`. Finally, you set the cat's background to a transparent color, which effectively resets the cat to an empty node.

2. In the second section, you load **CatWakeUp.sks** and fetch the scene child named **cat_awake**. Review the contents of that .sks file, and you'll see that **cat_awake** is the name of the only sprite found there. This is also the sprite on which the **cat_wake** action runs.

3. Finally, you change the sprite's parent from the **CatWakeUp.sks** scene to the `CatNode`. You set the node's position to make sure that it will appear exactly over the existing texture.

> **Note:** I hope you noticed the use of `move(ToParent:)`. If a sprite already has a parent, you can't use `addChild(_:)` directly to add it elsewhere; `move(ToParent:)` removes it from its current hierarchy and adds it at the new location you specify.

That's it! Switch back to **GameScene.swift** and add the following at the bottom of `lose()`:

```
catNode.wakeUp()
```

Build and run the project and enjoy your complete sequence:

Winning scenario

Now that you have a losing sequence, it's only fair to give the player a winning sequence. Add this new method to your GameScene class:

```
func win() {
  playable = false

  SKTAudio.sharedInstance().pauseBackgroundMusic()
  SKTAudio.sharedInstance().playSoundEffect("win.mp3")

  inGameMessage(text: "Nice job!")

  perform(#selector(GameScene.newGame), with: nil,
    afterDelay: 3)
}
```

This code looks almost identical to what you did in lose(), with a few differences, of course. When you pause the music, you play an uplifting win song and show the rewarding "Nice job!" message.

Just like before, you'll add an extra method in your cat node class to load the winning animation. Open **CatNode.swift** and add the following:

```
func curlAt(scenePoint: CGPoint) {
  parent!.physicsBody = nil
  for child in children {
    child.removeFromParent()
  }
  texture = nil
  color = SKColor.clear

  let catCurl = SKSpriteNode(fileNamed:
"CatCurl")!.childNode(withName: "cat_curl")!
  catCurl.move(toParent: self)
  catCurl.position = CGPoint(x: -30, y: 100)
}
```

This is similar to wakeUp(), with a couple of differences:

1. You remove the cat's physics body as you'll animate the cat manually into the bed.

2. You load the happy curl animation from **CatCurl.sks**.

curlAt(scenePoint:) expects a single CGPoint argument, which is the bed location in the scene's coordinate system. To find the curl point in the cat coordinate system, you need to first convert the location. That's easy thanks to convert(_:from:), which converts a position from one node's coordinate system to another node's coordinate system.

Append to the bottom of curlAt(scenePoint:):

```
var localPoint = parent!.convert(scenePoint, from: scene!)
localPoint.y += frame.size.height/3
```

In the first line, you call convert(_:from:) on the cat body's parent. Since the cat body is what you will be moving and it lives in the parent's coordinate system, you want the target location to be converted to that system.

In the second line, you add one third of the cat's height to the curl point, which makes the curl happen toward the bottom of the bed, not in its center.

Finally, have the cat body run the animation at the bottom of curlAt(scenePoint:) in **CatNode.swift**:

```
run(SKAction.group([
  SKAction.move(to: localPoint, duration: 0.66),
  SKAction.rotate(toAngle: -parent!.zRotation, duration: 0.5)
  ]))
```

This action group animates the cat to the center of the bed, and it also straightens up the cat in case he was falling over. (Any rotations due to the physics simulation were applied to the cat parent!. This rotate action run by the cat body will counteract that.)

You've reached the final steps to put everything together. Open **GameScene.swift** and in win(), append this line at the bottom:

```
catNode.curlAt(scenePoint: bedNode.position)
```

Then, inside didBegin(_:), find the print("SUCCESS") line and add this line after it:

```
win()
```

Build and run the project. You now have a winning sequence in place (pun intended):

Believe it or not, you've completed another mini-game! And this time, your game also has a complete physics simulation. Give yourself a pat on the back.

Don't be sad that your game has only one level. You'll continue to work on Cat Nap in the next two chapters, adding two more levels as well as some crazy features before you're done.

Challenges

Make sure you aren't rushing through these chapters. You're learning a lot of new concepts and APIs, so iterating over what you've learned is the key to retaining it.

That's one reason why the challenges at the end of each chapter are so important. If you feel confident about everything you've covered so far in Cat Nap, move on to the challenge.

This chapter introduced a lot of new APIs, so in case you get stuck, the solutions are in the resources folder for this chapter. But have faith in yourself — you can do it!

Challenge 1: Count the bounces

Think about the in-game message you show when the player wins or loses the level. Your challenge is to fine-tune when it disappears from the scene.

More specifically, your challenge is to count the number of times the label bounces off the bottom margin of the screen and remove the message on exactly the fourth bounce. Working through this will teach you more about custom node behaviors, and it will be a nice review of what you've already learned.

Try implementing the solution on your own, but if you need a little help, follow the directions below.

1. Add a variable in `MessageNode` to keep track of the number of bounces. Also, add a `didBounce()` method that increases the counter and removes the node from its parent on the fourth bounce.

2. Enable contact notifications between the label's physics body and the edge of the screen. To do that you will need to set the `contactTestBitMask` of `MessageNode`.

3. In `didBegin(_:)` of your `GameScene` class, add a check for contact between two physics bodies with the categories `PhysicsCategory.Label` and `PhysicsCategory.Edge`. Keep in mind, you need to add this check *before* the line `if !playable {`; otherwise, your bounce contact messages will fire in vain. Locate the `MessageNode` by accessing the right body's `node` property.

For example:

```
let labelNode = contact.bodyA.categoryBitMask ==
    PhysicsCategory.Label ? contact.bodyA.node :
    contact.bodyB.node
```

4. Once you grab the node, you can cast it to a MessageNode and call your custom method that increases its bounce counter.

This exercise will get you on the right path to implementing more complicated contact handlers. Imagine the possibilities — all the custom actions you could make happen in a game depending on how many times two bodies touch, or how many bodies of one category touch the edge, and so forth.

Chapter 10: Advanced Physics

By Marin Todorov

In the last chapter, you saw how easy it is to create responsive game worlds with SpriteKit, especially when using the scene editor. By now, you're a champion of creating sprites and physics bodies and configuring them to interact under simulated physics.

But perhaps you're already thinking bigger. So far, you can move shapes by letting gravity, forces and impulses affect them. But what if you want to constrain the movement of shapes with respect to other shapes — for example, maybe you want to pin a hat to the top of the cat's head, and have it rotate back and forth based on physics? Dr. Seuss would be proud!

In this chapter, you'll learn how to do things like this by adding two new levels to Cat Nap — three, if you successfully complete the chapter's challenge! By the time you're done, you'll have brought your knowledge of SpriteKit physics to an advanced level and will be able to apply this newfound skill to your own apps.

> **Note:** This chapter begins where the previous chapter's Challenge 1 left off. If you were unable to complete the challenge or skipped ahead from an earlier chapter, don't worry — simply open the starter project from this chapter to pick up in the right place.

Getting started

To get you back on track with Cat Nap, you're going to add one last touch to Level 1: a smarter failure detection system.

Specifically, you want to detect whether the cat is leaning to either side by more than 25 degrees. If he is, you want to wake up the cat, at which point the player should fail the level.

To achieve this, you'll check the position of the cat every frame, but only after the physics engine does its job. That means you have to understand a bit more about the SpriteKit game loop.

Back in the third chapter of this book, you learned that the SpriteKit game loop looks something like this:

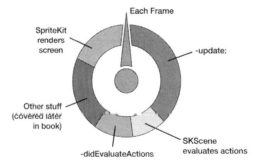

Now it's time to introduce the next piece of the game loop: simulating physics. Here's your new version of the loop:

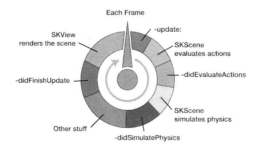

After evaluating the sprite actions, but just before rendering the sprites onscreen, SpriteKit performs the physics simulation and moves the sprites and bodies accordingly, which is represented by the yellow chunk in your new diagram.

At that point, you have a chance to perform any code you might like by implementing `didSimulatePhysics()`, represented by the red chunk.

This is the perfect spot to check if the cat is tilting too much!

> **Note:** The new loop also includes `didFinishUpdate()`. This is a method you can override if you want do something after all the other processing has been completed.

To write your code to check for the cat's tilt, you'll use a function from `SKTUtils`, the library of helper methods you added to the project in the previous chapter. In particular, you'll use a handy method that converts degrees into radians.

Make sure you have the CatNap project open in Xcode. Then inside **GameScene.swift**, implement `didSimulatePhysics()` as follows:

```
override func didSimulatePhysics() {
  if playable {
    if fabs(catNode.parent!.zRotation) >
        CGFloat(25).degreesToRadians() {
      lose()
    }
  }
}
```

Here you perform two tests:

• **Is the game currently playable?** You check if `playable` is `true` to see if the player is still solving the level.

• **Is the cat tilted too much?** Specifically, is the absolute value of the cat's `zRotation` property more than the radian equivalent of 25 degrees?

When both of these conditions are `true`, you call `lose()` right away, because the cat is falling over and should wake up immediately!

One more thing to note is that the `zRotation` of `catNode` never changes, since the cat's physics body is attached to `catNode`'s parent and not `catNode`. That's why you need to keep an eye on the rotation of the cat as a whole by referencing `catNode.parent!`.

Build and run, and then fail the level on purpose. The cat wakes up while he's still in the air, before he even touches the ground.

This is more realistic behavior, as it's hard to sleep when falling to the ground!

Introducing Level 2

So far, you've been working on a game with a single game scene. Cat Nap, however, is a level-based puzzle game.

In this section of the chapter, you're going to give the game the ability to present different levels onscreen, and you'll add a second level right away. Level 2 will feature new interactive physics objects, like springs, ropes and hooks.

Except in this game, you'll call the springs *catapults*. See what I did there? :]

Fortunately for the cat, this level will have just one catapult. Here's how the level will look when you're finished:

I know, I know. That catapult underneath the cat and the hook on the ceiling look rather nefarious, but I promise no animals will be harmed in the making of this game.

To win the level, the player first needs to tap the catapult. This will launch the cat upward, where the hook will catch and hold him suspended. With the cat safely out of the way, the player can destroy the blocks. Once the blocks are destroyed, the player can tap the hook to release the cat, who will then descend safely to his bed below.

On the other hand, if the player destroys the blocks first and then taps the catapult, the cat won't rise high enough to reach the hook, causing the player to lose the level.

Loading levels

Lucky for you, you're already loading levels in your game.

You have a single level so far, and the level file is named **GameScene.sks**. You load it, show it onscreen, and then you implement the game logic in your GameScene class.

You need to create another **.sks** file for each of Cat Nap's levels. Then, you need to load and display these new levels, one after the next, as the player solves them.

First of all, to avoid confusion, rename **GameScene.sks** to **Level1.sks**. You can simply edit the name in the project navigator.

Next, you need to add a factory method in your GameScene class that takes a level number and creates a scene by loading the corresponding **.sks** file from the game bundle.

To do this, add the following property and class function to GameScene:

```
//1
var currentLevel: Int = 0

//2
class func level(levelNum: Int) -> GameScene? {
  let scene = GameScene(fileNamed: "Level\(levelNum)")!
  scene.currentLevel = levelNum
  scene.scaleMode = .aspectFill
  return scene
}
```

You'll use the currentLevel property to hold the current level's number. The class method level(levelNum:) takes in a number and calls GameScene(fileNamed:). If the level file loads successfully, you set the current level number on the scene and scale correctly.

Now you need to make a few changes to your view controller. Open **GameViewController.swift** and find the following line in viewDidLoad():

```
if let scene = GameScene(fileNamed: "GameScene") {
```

Replace it with this:

```
if let scene = GameScene.level(levelNum: 1) {
```

That's much easier on the eyes, isn't it?

Next, open **GameScene.swift** and locate newGame(). To improve it with the new factory method, replace the complete method body with this:

```
view!.presentScene(GameScene.level(levelNum: currentLevel))
```

Build and run to verify the game works as usual.

Good work. Now you can focus on building Level 2.

Scene editor, round 2

After doing so much in code, it'll be nice to use the scene editor again.

From Xcode's menu, select **File > New > File….** Then choose **iOS/Resource/SpriteKit Scene** and click **Next.**

Name the new file **Level2.sks** and click **Create.**

As soon as you save the file, Xcode opens it in the scene editor. Zoom out until you see the scene border:

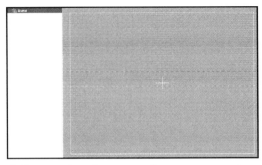

With the scene editor skills you already possess from previous chapters, setting up this scene will be easy, as well as a great way to review what you've learned.

First, resize the scene to **2048x1536**, and set the Anchor Point to **(0, 0)**:

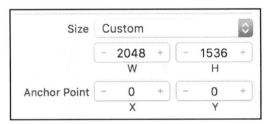

Next, add five **Color Sprite** objects to the scene and set their properties as follows:

- **Background**: Texture **background**, Position (**1024, 768**)

- **Bed**: Texture **cat_bed**, Name **bed**, Position (**1024, 272**), Custom Class **BedNode**

- **Block1**: Texture **wood_horiz1**, Name **block**, Position (**1024, 260**), Body Type **Bounding rectangle**, Category Mask **2**, Collision Mask **43**, Custom Class **BlockNode**

- **Block2**: Texture **wood_horiz1**, Name **block**, Position (**1024, 424**), Body Type **Bounding rectangle**, Category Mask **2**, Collision Mask **43**, Custom Class **BlockNode**

- **Spring**: Texture **spring**, Name **spring**, Position (**1024, 588**), Body Type **Bounding rectangle**, Category Mask **32**, Collision Mask **11**, Custom Class **SpringNode**

Whoa, that's a lot of objects! Much of what you're doing is recreating the elements from Level 1: a background image, a cat bed and some blocks.

For this level, you also added a sprite for the spring. It uses a new physics category, 32, and a new custom class, `SpringNode`. You don't have those yet, but you can quickly add them right now.

Open **GameScene.swift** and find the `PhysicsCategory` struct at the top of the file. Add a new constant to use for your springs:

```
static let Spring:UInt32 = 0b100000 // 32
```

> **Note:** For practice, see if you can figure out why you set the category mask to 43 for the two blocks in the level. If you get stuck, open Calculator on your Mac, switch to Programmer mode and enter in 43 to see the number in binary.

Next, create a new file by choosing **File > New > File...** and select **iOS/Source/Cocoa Touch Class** for the template. Name the new class **SpringNode**, make it a subclass of **SKSpriteNode** and click **Next**, then **Create**.

Xcode will automatically open the file. When it does, replace the contents of the file with the following:

```
import SpriteKit

class SpringNode: SKSpriteNode, EventListenerNode,
InteractiveNode {

  func didMoveToScene() {

  }

  func interact() {

  }
}
```

Look familiar? Your custom node class implements the `EventListenerNode` protocol and has an empty `didMoveToScene()` method, where you'll add some code momentarily. In addition, this class conforms to `InteractiveNode` because you want to let the player tap on the spring node and interact with it.

There's only one key component missing from your new level — the cat! Open **Level2.sks** and drag in a **Reference** object from the Object Library:

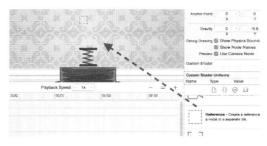

Give the Reference object the following properties, matching the cat's configuration in Level 1:

- Name **cat_shared**, Reference **Cat**, Position (**983**, **894**), Z Position **10**.

It's time to test the level.

Head over to **GameViewController.swift** and replace `if let scene = GameScene.level(levelNum: 1) {` with the following:

```
if let scene = GameScene.level(levelNum: 2) {
```

Now the game begins with Level 2, rather than Level 1. That's right: Not only does this make it quicker to test Level 2 — now you can cheat in your own game! ;]

Build and run the project, and you'll see the initial setup for your new level:

You'll see the cat pass straight through the spring. That happens because your existing code doesn't know about your new spring objects. You're about to change that.

Catapults (springs)

Since catapults are a new category of objects for your game, you need to tell your scene how other objects should interact with them. The code for this will be quite familiar to you, so I won't spell out all of the details; feel free to move through this part quickly.

> **Note:** In this chapter, I use the words **catapults** and **springs** interchangeably.

To make the cat sit on top of the catapult, you need to enable collisions between the cat and the catapult.

Open **CatNode.swift**, and in didMoveToScene(), change the line responsible for setting the cat's collisionBitMask to include PhysicsCategory.Spring:

```
parent!.physicsBody!.collisionBitMask = PhysicsCategory.Block
    | PhysicsCategory.Edge | PhysicsCategory.Spring
```

Now your catapult and cat should behave as expected.

Build and run the game; check to see how the cat and catapult get along:

One small change in code, one big step for sleepy cats!

Next, it's time to make the catapult hurl that kitty when the player taps on the spring sprite. It's actually quite easy; if the player taps on the catapult, you need to apply an impulse to the spring, which will then bounce the cat — if, of course, the cat is on top of the spring.

The first step is to enable user interaction on the spring node so it will react to taps.

Switch to **SpringNode.swift** and add the following line to didMoveToScene():

```
isUserInteractionEnabled = true
```

And just like you did for the block nodes, add the respective UIResponder method to detect taps:

```
override func touchesEnded(_ touches: Set<UITouch>,
    with event: UIEvent?) {
  super.touchesEnded(touches, with: event)
  interact()
}
```

Now, add the code for the interaction inside `interact()`:

```
isUserInteractionEnabled = false

physicsBody!.applyImpulse(CGVector(dx: 0, dy: 250),
                          at: CGPoint(x: size.width/2, y:
size.height))

run(SKAction.sequence([
  SKAction.wait(forDuration: 1),
  SKAction.removeFromParent()
  ]))
```

When the player taps a spring node, you apply an impulse to its body using `applyImpulse(_:at:)`.

This is similar to what you did with the sand particles in Chapter 8, "Beginning Physics". Because a spring can "jump" only once, you disable the user input on that node as soon as it receives a tap. Finally, you remove the catapult after a delay of one second.

Build and run the game again, and this time, tap on the catapult:

Houston, we have lift off... and a slight problem.

Right now, when catapulted, the kitty flips through the air and lands on its head. That's why you need to add the ceiling hook to grab him!

The idea is that the catapult will bounce the kitty right onto the hook, which will hold him while the player clears the blocks. Once the blocks are gone, you'll release the kitty so he falls straight into his bed. Mrrow!

An overview of Joints

To implement the ceiling hook, you need **joints**. In SpriteKit, there are five types of joints available, each of which lets you constrain the positions of two bodies relative to each other. This section describes them in turn.

> **Note:** Because joints are a heavily-used concept in physics-based games, it's a good idea to familiarize yourself with them.

Fixed joint

A fixed joint gives you the ability to attach two physics bodies together.

Imagine you have two objects and you nail them together with a few rusty nails. If you take one of the objects and throw it, the other one will fly right along with it.

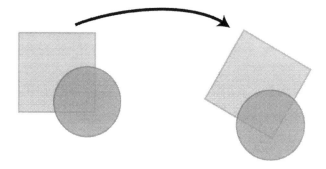

Sometimes, you want to make an object immoveable. The quickest way to do that is to fix it to the scene's edge loop, and you're ready to go.

Other times, you want a complex object a player can destroy — and perhaps break into many pieces. If that's the case, simply fix the pieces together, and when the player hits the object, remove the joints so the pieces fall apart.

Limit joint

You can use a limit joint to set the maximum distance between two physics bodies. Although the two bodies can move closer to each other, they can never be farther apart than the distance you specify.

Think of a limit joint as a soft but strong rope that connects two objects. In the diagram below, the ball is connected to the square via a limit joint; it can bounce around, but it can never move farther away than the length of the limit joint.

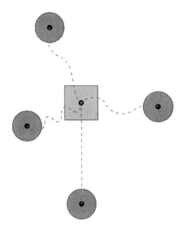

These types of joints are useful when you want to connect two objects, but let one move independently of the other within a certain radius — like a dog on a leash!

Spring joint

A spring joint is much like a limit joint, but the connection behaves more like a rubber band: elastic and springy.

A spring joint is useful for simulating rope connections, especially elastic ropes. If you have a bungee-jumping hero in your game, the spring joint will be of great help!

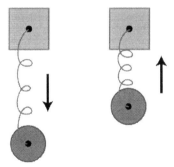

Pin joint

A pin joint fixes two physics bodies around a certain point, the anchor of the joint. Both bodies can rotate freely around the anchor point — if they don't collide, of course.

Think of the pin joint as a big screw that keeps two objects tightly together, but still allows them to rotate:

If you were to build a clock, you'd use a pin joint to fix the hands to the dial; if you were to build a physics body for an airplane, you'd use a pin joint to attach the propeller to the plane's nose.

Sliding joint

A sliding joint fixes two physics bodies on an axis along which they can freely slide; you can further define the minimum and maximum distances the two bodies can be from each other while sliding along the axis.

The two connected bodies behave as though they're moving on a rail with limits on the distance between them:

A sliding joint might come in handy if you're building a roller coaster game and you need the two car objects to stay on the track, but to stay some distance away from each other.

> **Note:** It's possible to apply more than one joint to a physics body. For example, you could use one pin joint to attach an hour hand to a clock face, and add a second pin joint to connect the minute hand to the clock face.

Joints in use

The easiest way to learn how to use joints is to try them out for yourself. And what better way to do that than by creating the hook object and attaching it to the ceiling?

Consider this blueprint for the hook object:

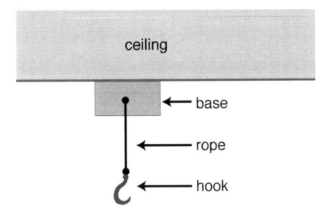

There's one body fixed to the ceiling (the base), another body for the hook and a third body that connects them together (the rope).

To make this structure work, you'll be using two types of joints:

- A **fixed joint** to fix the base to the ceiling.

- A **spring joint** to connect the hook to the base. The spring joint will be your rope.

Using a fixed joint

First, you need to add the relevant sprites in the scene editor. Open **Level2.sks** and add two **Color Sprites**, configured as follows:

- **Hook mount**: Texture **wood_horiz1**, Position (**1024, 1466**)

- **Hook base**: Texture **hook_base**, Name **hookBase**, Position (**1024, 1350**), Body Type **Bounding rectangle**, Custom Class **HookBaseNode**

hookBase is the node to which the hook and its rope will be attached. The base itself is going to be fixed on the ceiling by a joint to the scene edge body.

You might wonder what purpose the wood block serves. It doesn't even have a physics body!

Take a look at the playable area on an iPhone compared to that of an iPad:

On the smaller iPhone 5s, the scene cuts out somewhere just before the top edge of the hook base — it looks like the hook base is built into the ceiling. But remember that an iPad's screen aspect ratio is different, which is why you can see more of the scene on the iPad. If it weren't for the wood piece on top, it would look like the hook base were just floating in midair.

So the wood block's only role is to make things look nice. On an iPhone, it's outside of the screen bounds, so the player won't even see it.

Perhaps you've noticed that the hook has a custom node class; you're going to add that to the project now.

Create a new file by choosing **File > New > File...**, and select the file template **iOS/ Source/Cocoa Touch Class**. Name the new class **HookBaseNode**, make it a subclass of **SKSpriteNode** and click **Next** and then **Create**. Xcode will automatically open the file once it's created.

To clear the error you see in Xcode by default, replace `import UIKit` with:

```
import SpriteKit
```

`HookBaseNode` is a little different than the other custom nodes you've created so far. Since the hook structure is a compound object made of a base, a swinging rope and the hook itself, you'll use only one custom class for the whole structure.

You're also going to create the rope and the hook in code rather than in the scene editor.

First, you need a way to access the parts of the hook, so add the following properties in **HookBaseNode.swift**:

```
private var hookNode = SKSpriteNode(imageNamed: "hook")
private var ropeNode = SKSpriteNode(imageNamed: "rope")
private var hookJoint: SKPhysicsJointFixed!
```

```
var isHooked: Bool {
  return hookJoint != nil
}
```

The first two properties are the nodes you need in order to finish building the hook structure, and `hookJoint` is something you'll use later when the kitty bounces and is "hooked" by the rope. Finally, there's a dynamic property named `isHooked`; this checks if there's already a stored physics joint in `hookJoint`.

Next, make your new class conform to the `EventListenerNode` protocol by adding on to the class declaration:

```
class HookBaseNode: SKSpriteNode, EventListenerNode {
```

Also, add the initial stub for `didMoveToScene()`:

```
func didMoveToScene() {
  guard let scene = scene else {
    return
  }
}
```

You make sure that the node has already been added to the scene; if not, you bail out.

Now in `didMoveToScene()`, you're going to configure and add `hookNode` and `ropeNode`. Then, you're going to finish constructing the hook. You'll do this in a few steps.

First, add the following, after the `guard` statement, but not within it:

```
let ceilingFix = SKPhysicsJointFixed.joint(withBodyA:
  scene.physicsBody!, bodyB: physicsBody!, anchor: CGPoint.zero)
scene.physicsWorld.add(ceilingFix)
```

Here, you use a factory method of `SKPhysicsJointFixed` to create a joint instance between the current node's body and the scene's own body, which is the edge loop. You're also giving the joint an anchor point, which tells the scene at what location to create the connection between the two bodies.

You always specify the anchor point in scene coordinates. When you attach a body to the scene's body, you can safely pass any value as the anchor point, so you use `(0, 0)`.

Finally, you add the joint to the scene's physics world. Now these two bodies are connected until the end of time — or until you remove the joint.

> **Note:** When you create a fixed joint, the two bodies don't need to be touching — each body simply maintains its relative position from the anchor point.
>
> You *could* get this same behavior without using a joint at all. Instead, you could make the physics body static, either by unchecking the **Dynamic** field in the scene editor or by setting the isDynamic property of the physicsBody to false. This would be more efficient for the physics engine, but you're using a fixed joint here for learning purposes.

Build and run the game, and you'll see the hook base fixed securely to the top of the screen:

> **Note:** If you don't see the hook base, try running the game on an iPad or iPad Simulator.

Look at that line going from the bottom-left corner to the top of the scene — this is the debug physics drawing representing the joint you just created. It indicates there's a joint connecting the scene itself — with a position of (0, 0) — to the hook.

Since you're on a roll, add the sprite for the rope, too.

Back in **HookBaseNode.swift**, add the following to the end of didMoveToScene(),:

```
ropeNode.anchorPoint = CGPoint(x: 0, y: 0.5)
ropeNode.zRotation = CGFloat(270).degreesToRadians()
ropeNode.position = position
scene.addChild(ropeNode)
```

This sets the rope's anchor point to be one of its ends, positions the end on top of the hook base and rotates the rope so it points down.

Now it's time to add the hook itself, which will use a different type of joint.

Using a spring joint

First, you need one more body category for the hook, so switch back to
GameScene.swift and add the following new value to the `PhysicsCategory`:

```
static let Hook:  UInt32 = 0b1000000 // 64
```

Now, go back to **HookBaseNode.swift** and add the following to the end of
`didMoveToScene()`:

```
hookNode.position = CGPoint(
    x: position.x,
    y: position.y - ropeNode.size.width)

hookNode.physicsBody =
    SKPhysicsBody(circleOfRadius: hookNode.size.width/2)
hookNode.physicsBody!.categoryBitMask = PhysicsCategory.Hook
hookNode.physicsBody!.contactTestBitMask = PhysicsCategory.Cat
hookNode.physicsBody!.collisionBitMask = PhysicsCategory.None

scene.addChild(hookNode)
```

This sets the position of the hook and creates a physics body for it. It also sets the
category bit mask to `PhysicsCategory.Hook`, and sets the `contactTestBitMask` such
that contact notifications will occur for contacts between the hook and the cat.

The hook doesn't need to collide with any other objects. Later, you'll implement some
custom behavior for it that default SpriteKit physics doesn't provide.

> **Note:** You position the hook sprite just under the ceiling base because the distance
> between the base and the hook is precisely the length of the rope that will hold
> them together.

Now, create a spring joint to connect the hook and its ceiling holder by adding the
following to `didMoveToScene()`:

```
let hookPosition = CGPoint(x: hookNode.position.x,
    y: hookNode.position.y+hookNode.size.height/2)

let ropeJoint = SKPhysicsJointSpring.joint(
    withBodyA: physicsBody!, bodyB: hookNode.physicsBody!,
    anchorA: position,
    anchorB: hookPosition)
scene.physicsWorld.add(ropeJoint)
```

First, you calculate the position where the joint should attach itself to the hook and store that position in `hookPosition`.

Then, using a factory method similar to the one you used for the ceiling joint, you connect the hook base's body and the `hookNode` body with a spring joint. You also specify the precise points in the scene's coordinate system where the rope connects to the two bodies.

Build and run the game now. If all's well, you'll see your hook hanging in the air just under the ceiling:

The rope joint works fine, but that rope doesn't move.

The SpriteKit game loop, Round 4

At long last, it's time to introduce the final missing piece of the SpriteKit game loop.

As you can see below, after SpriteKit finishes simulating physics, it performs one last step: applying something named **constraints** to the scene and notifying your scene that this has happened.

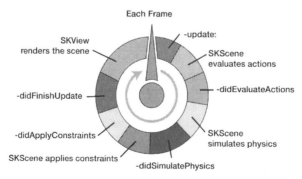

Let's take a look at how this works.

An overview of Constraints

Constraints are a handy SpriteKit feature that let you ensure certain constraints on the position and rotation of sprites within your game are met.

The best way to understand constraints is to see them in action.

Open **GameScene.swift** and add the following code to the end of `didMove(to:)`:

```
let rotationConstraint = SKConstraint.zRotation(
  SKRange(lowerLimit: −π/4, upperLimit: π/4))
catNode.parent!.constraints = [rotationConstraint]
```

There are two steps to using a constraint:

- **Create the constraint**. This example creates a constraint that limits `zRotation` from -45° to 45°, and applies it to the cat node.

- **Add the constraint to a node**. To add the constraint to a node, simply add it to the constraints array on the node.

> **Note:** To type π in your source code, press and hold the **Alt** key on your keyboard and press **P**. π is a constant defined in **SKTUtils**; Command-click on it in Xcode to jump to its definition. If you prefer, you can use `CGFloat(M_PI)` instead.

After SpriteKit finishes simulating the physics, it runs through each node's constraints and updates the position and rotation of the node so that the constraint is met.

Build and run to see this in action:

As you can see, even though the physics simulation sometimes determines that the cat should fall over beyond 45°, during the constraint phase of the game loop, SpriteKit updates the cat's rotation to 45° so the constraint remains `true`.

This was just a test, so comment out the previous code:

```
//let rotationConstraint = SKConstraint.zRotation(
// SKRange(lowerLimit: -π/4, upperLimit: π/4))
//catNode.parent!.constraints = [rotationConstraint]
```

You could also add constraints to do such things as:

• Limit a sprite so it stays within a certain rectangle.

• Make a turret in your game point in the direction in which it's shooting.

• Constrain a sprite's movement along the x-axis.

After this crash course in constraints, you're ready to use a real constraint in your Cat Nap game. Specifically, you'll finish the hook object by adding the final piece: the rope constraint.

Implementing a rope with a constraint

Now you're going to use a constraint to make sure the rope is always oriented toward the hook sprite, making it appear as if the rope is connected to the hook.

In **HookBaseNode.swift**, add the following code at the end of `didMoveToScene()`:

```
let range = SKRange(lowerLimit: 0.0, upperLimit: 0.0)
let orientConstraint = SKConstraint.orient(to: hookNode,
   offset: range)
ropeNode.constraints = [orientConstraint]
```

`SKConstraint.orient(to:offset:)` produces a constraint object that automatically changes the zRotation of the node to which it's being applied, so that the node always points toward another "target" node.

You can also provide an offset range to the constraint if you don't want to orient the node with perfect precision. Since you want the end of the rope and the hook to be tightly connected, you provide a zero range for the constraint.

Finally, you set the `orientConstraint` as the sole constraint for the `ropeNode`.

One last step. There's nothing that moves the hook — which makes it look kind of odd. Add this line to the end of `didMoveToScene()`:

```
hookNode.physicsBody!.applyImpulse(CGVector(dx: 50, dy: 0))
```

This applies an impulse to the hook node so that it will start swinging.

Build and run the game again. Check out your moving, customized level object:

Remember, there are two things going on here that make this behavior work:

- You set up a **joint** connecting the hook to the base. This makes the hook maintain a certain distance from the base, so it appears to "swing".

- You set up a **constraint** that makes the rope always orient itself toward the hook, so that it appears to follow the hook.

Together, this makes for a pretty sweet effect!

> **Note:** In the first edition of this book, this chapter instructed readers to manually orient the rope inside the scene's `update(_:)` method. On every invocation of `update(_:)`, the code calculated the angle between the base and hook sprites and set that angle as the `zRotation` of the rope.
>
> This is still a perfectly valid strategy, but since SpriteKit now has built-in constraints that can handle this for you, this edition uses the new approach. In your games, choose whichever is most suitable.

There's one thing I should mention to keep my conscience clear: Right now, the rope is represented by just one sprite. That means your rope is more like a rod.

If you'd like to create an object that better resembles a rope, you could create several shorter sprite segments and connect them to each other, like so:

In this case, you might want to create physics bodies for each rope segment and connect them to each other with pin joints.

More constraints

So far, you've seen examples of the zRotation(_:) and orient(to:offset:) constraints.

There are a number of other types of constraints you can create in SpriteKit beyond the ones you've already seen:

- positionX(_:), positionY(_:) and positionX(_:y:). These let you restrict the position of a sprite to within a certain range on the x-axis, y-axis or both. For example, you could use these to restrict the movement of a sprite to be within a certain rectangle on the screen.

- orient(to point:offset:) and orient(to:in:offset:). Just like you can make a sprite orient itself toward another sprite, as you made the rope orient itself toward the hook, you can make a sprite always orient itself toward a certain point. For example, you could use these to make a turret point toward where the user taps.

- distance(range:to node:), distance(range:to point:) and distance(range:to:in). These let you ensure that two nodes, or a node and a point, are always within a certain distance of each other. The function is similar to a limit joint, except these work on any node, whether or not it has a physics body.

Creating and removing joints dynamically

You need to add a few final touches to get the whole cat-hooking process to work. Firstly, you need to check for hook-to-cat contact. Secondly, you need to create and remove a joint to fix the cat to the rope dynamically.

Open **GameScene.swift** and scroll to didBegin(_). This is the place where you detect when object bodies in your game touch. You need to check if the two contacting bodies are the hook and the cat. You also need to do an additional check to see if they're already hooked together.

To perform these checks, you need a property for the hook node. Add a new property to **GameScene.swift**:

```
var hookBaseNode: HookBaseNode?
```

Next, you need to look through the scene hierarchy to find out if there's a hook node. Don't forget, the other levels don't have a hook, and that's why you need an optional value for that property.

Next, add the following to the bottom of `didMove(to:)`:

```
hookBaseNode = childNode(withName: "hookBase") as? HookBaseNode
```

That line should be familiar; you simply locate the node by name and assign it to the property you created earlier.

Now scroll back to `didBegin(_:)` and add the check for hook-to-cat contact right after the win/lose conditions (you can tack it on using `else if` if you like):

```
if collision == PhysicsCategory.Cat | PhysicsCategory.Hook
    && hookBaseNode?.isHooked == false {
  hookBaseNode!.hookCat(catPhysicsBody:
    catNode.parent!.physicsBody!)
}
```

You check if the collision bit mask matches the cat and hook categories, and that the two aren't hooked together already. If both are true, you call `hookCat(catPhysicsBody:)` on the hook node. Of course, this method doesn't exist yet, so you'll get an error. But that's an easy problem to fix.

Go back to **HookBaseNode.swift** and add a new method to hook the cat:

```
func hookCat(catPhysicsBody: SKPhysicsBody) {
  catPhysicsBody.velocity = CGVector(dx: 0, dy: 0)
  catPhysicsBody.angularVelocity = 0
}
```

First, you manually alter the physics simulation by forcing a velocity and angular velocity of zero on the cat's body. You do this to calm things down when the cat's about to get hooked; you don't want to make players wait too long before their next moves while they wait for the hook to stop swinging.

The important point here is that you can manually alter the physics simulation. How great is that? Don't be afraid to do this — making the game fun is your top priority.

Now, add the following to that same method:

```
let pinPoint = CGPoint(
  x: hookNode.position.x,
  y: hookNode.position.y + hookNode.size.height/2)

hookJoint = SKPhysicsJointFixed.joint(
  withBodyA: hookNode.physicsBody!, bodyB: catPhysicsBody,
```

```
    anchor: pinPoint)
  scene!.physicsWorld.add(hookJoint)

  hookNode.physicsBody!.contactTestBitMask = PhysicsCategory.None
```

With that block of code, you calculate the position where the two bodies will be anchored together. Using this position, you create a new `SKPhysicsJointFixed` to connect the hook and cat, and then you add it to the world.

You also need to make `didSimulatePhysics()` respect the fact that the kitty is "hooked", so that the game is OK with rotating to angles more than the margin of 45 degrees.

Open **GameScene.swift**, and inside `didSimulatePhysics()`, change the `if` condition from `if playable {` to this:

```
  if playable && hookBaseNode?.isHooked != true {
```

Now when the cat swings on the hook, he won't wake up.

Build and run the game, and play around with it to experience all your great physics effects:

When the cat hangs from the ceiling, you can safely destroy the blocks over the cat bed. But you're still missing one thing — the cat needs to fall off the hook and into the bed. To make that happen, you need to remove the joint you just added.

This time, add the method to destroy the joint before you call it. Open **HookBaseNode.swift** and add the following:

```
func releaseCat() {
  hookNode.physicsBody!.categoryBitMask = PhysicsCategory.None
  hookNode.physicsBody!.contactTestBitMask =
```

```
    PhysicsCategory.None
  hookJoint.bodyA.node!.zRotation = 0
  hookJoint.bodyB.node!.zRotation = 0
  scene!.physicsWorld.remove(hookJoint)
  hookJoint = nil
}
```

In this method, you simply undo what you did in `hookCat(catNode:)`. You remove the joint connecting the hook and the cat. Then, you straighten up the cat and the hook.

Next, you'll add the code to let the cat fall off the hook. In the game, the player will need to tap the cat while it swings in midair.

Here you encounter a new problem: The player needs to tap on the cat node, but the hook node needs to react to this action. You want to keep nodes decoupled if possible, since different levels feature different node combinations.

To keep the nodes independent from each other, you'll use notifications.

Each time the player taps on the cat, it will send a notification, and nodes that are interested in this event will have the chance to catch the broadcast and react in whatever way is necessary.

First, you're going to handle taps on the cat node. Open **CatNode.swift** and add the following to `didMoveToScene()`:

```
isUserInteractionEnabled = true
```

Just like before, you need to make this class adhere to `InteractiveNode`.

Add the protocol to the class declaration:

```
class CatNode: SKSpriteNode, EventListenerNode,
  InteractiveNode {
```

As soon as you do that, Xcode will complain about missing the required protocol method, so add a stub for now:

```
func interact() {
}
```

Then, just under the class declaration, define a new notification name as a type property:

```
static let kCatTappedNotification = "kCatTappedNotification"
```

Now, add the method to handle touches:

```
override func touchesEnded(_ touches: Set<UITouch>,
    with event: UIEvent?) {
  super.touchesEnded(touches, with: event)
  interact()
}
```

Each time the player taps on the cat, a notification needs to be sent via
NSNotificationCenter. To make that happen, add the following line of code inside
interact():

```
NotificationCenter.default.post(Notification(name:
  NSNotification.Name(CatNode.kCatTappedNotification),
  object: nil))
```

You'll do more in interact(), but for now, you simply broadcast a
kCatTappedNotification.

> **Note:** This time around, you don't disable user interactions inside interact().
> Since other nodes might implement custom logic based on taps on the cat, you
> can't speculate on whether further touches on that node would be of interest. To
> be safe, you keep accepting touches and broadcasting the same notification over
> and over again.

Next, you're going to observe for the kCatTappedNotification. If one is received,
you're going to release the cat from the hook, but — needless to say — only if the cat is
already hooked.

Open **HookBaseNode.swift** and add the following to didMoveToScene():

```
NotificationCenter.default.addObserver(
  self, selector: #selector(catTapped), name: Notification
  .Name(CatNode.kCatTappedNotification), object: nil)
```

This code "listens" for a notification named kCatTappedNotification. If it "hears" a
notification, it will invoke the catTapped() method. Add that method now:

```
func catTapped() {
  if isHooked {
    releaseCat()
  }
}
```

In `catTapped()`, you simply check if the cat is currently hanging from the hook, and in that case, you call `releaseCat` to let it go. That's all!

Build and run the game again, and try to land the cat on the bed. You probably don't need this advice, but: tap on the catapult, tap on all the blocks, and then tap the cat to solve the level.

Creating joints dynamically is a fun and powerful technique. I hope to see you use it a lot in your own games!

Compound shapes

It's time to move on to the third level of Cat Nap.

In this level, you'll tackle another game physics concept, one related to body complexity. With this in mind, have a look at the completed Level 3 and try to guess what's new compared to the previous levels:

You guessed right if you said that in Level 3, one of the blocks has a more complicated shape than your average wooden block.

Perhaps you also noticed that the shape is broken into two sub-shapes. Maybe you even wondered why it was done that way instead of being constructed as a polygon shape, like was done in Chapter 8, "Beginning Physics".

Sometimes in games, for reasons related to game logic, you need an object that's more complex than a single image with a physics body. To better understand the problem, let's go back in time, I mean — back in chapters.

Do you remember your old friend the zombie from the Zombie Conga minigame?

In a physics-based game, a zombie would have quite a complex shape, and you might be temped to use a single texture for it. But if you made the zombie body-parts separate nodes, with separate physics bodies, you could make him do such things as wave his hands or move his legs.

Also — everyone knows that when zombies don't keep a strict diet of fresh brains, they start losing limbs. You've surely seen your green friends drop an arm or a jaw while they chase the hero in the latest Hollywood horror movie.

If you use separate nodes for the zombie arms, you could simply "detach" them during any point in your game for an added comical effect.

Having said that, in this section you'll build a simple compound body for the next level of Cat Nap.

Designing Level 3

Just as before, replace the starting level in **GameViewController.swift**:

```
if let scene = GameScene.level(levelNum: 3) {
```

Creating the third level of Cat Nap in the scene editor will follow much the same process as for Level 2.

From Xcode's menu, select **File > New > File...** and then **iOS/Resource/SpriteKit Scene**. Click **Next**, save the file as **Level3.sks**, and click **Create**.

You'll be rewarded, as usual, with the sight of an empty game scene. Sorry, no flashing lights, screaming fans or bells and whistles. But hey, maybe they'll add that in a future release. :]

OK, first, resize the scene to **2048x1536** points and set the Anchor Point to **(0, 0)**. Then, add the following **Color Sprite** objects to the empty scene:

- **Background**: Texture **background**, Position (**1024, 768**)

- **Bed**: Texture **cat_bed**, Name **bed**, Position (**1024, 272**), Custom Class **BedNode**

- **Block1**: Texture **wood_square**, Name **block**, Position (**946, 276**), Body Type **Bounding rectangle**, Category Mask **2**, Collision Mask **11**, Custom Class **BlockNode**, Z Position **2**

- **Block2**: Texture **wood_square**, Name **block**, Position (**946, 464**), Body Type **Bounding rectangle**, Category Mask **2**, Collision Mask **11**, Custom Class **BlockNode**, Z Position **2**

- **Block3**: Texture **wood_vert2**, Name **block**, Position (**754, 310**), Body Type **Bounding rectangle**, Category Mask **2**, Collision Mask **11**, Custom Class **BlockNode**, Z Position **2**

- **Block4**: Texture **wood_vert2**, Name **block**, Position (**754, 552**), Body Type **Bounding rectangle**, Category Mask **2**, Collision Mask **11**, Custom Class **BlockNode**, Z Position **2**

- **Stone1**: Texture **rock_L_vert**, Name **stone**, Position (**1282, 434**), Custom Class **StoneNode**

- **Stone2**: Texture **rock_L_horizontal**, Name **stone**, Position (**1042, 714**), Custom Class **StoneNode**

Finally, drag in a **Reference** object from the Object Library. Give the reference object the following properties:

- Name **cat_shared**, Reference **Cat**, Position (**998, 976**).

This is the complete setup for Level 3. Build and run the game to see what you have so far:

The level in its current state doesn't look very good. The cat falls through the stone L-shaped block as if the block weren't in the scene at all. And no wonder — you didn't create any bodies for the two blocks used to build the L-shape. In the next section, you'll learn how to create a complex body that matches the shape of the new stone block.

Making compound objects

For your stone nodes, you'll have an even more elaborate initialization than for the hook.

You'll develop a custom class called StoneNode. When you add it to the scene, it will search for all stone pieces, remove them from the scene and create a new compound node to hold them all together. As you can see, when it comes to creating custom node behavior, the sky's the limit!

First, create a new file by choosing **File > New > File...** and selecting **iOS/Source/Cocoa Touch Class** for the template. Name the new class **StoneNode**, make it a subclass of **SKSpriteNode** and click **Next** and **Create**. Xcode will automatically open the new file.

To clear the error you see in Xcode, replace the default contents with the following:

```
import SpriteKit

class StoneNode: SKSpriteNode, EventListenerNode,
  InteractiveNode {

  func didMoveToScene() {

  }

  func interact() {

  }
}
```

This code looks familiar by now. You create a custom SKSpriteNode subclass and conform to your EventListenerNode protocol.

Next, add the method that will look through the scene nodes and bind together all the stone pieces. Make it a static method:

```
static func makeCompoundNode(in scene: SKScene) -> SKNode {
  let compound = StoneNode()

}
```

You first initialize an empty StoneNode object to hold your stone pieces.

> **Note:** Don't worry about the error. That will disappear after you finishing adding the rest of the code.

Next inside that method, find all the stone pieces and remove them from the scene. Then, add each one to `compound` instead:

```
for stone in scene.children.filter(
    { node in node is StoneNode}) {
  stone.removeFromParent()
  compound.addChild(stone)
}
```

You filter the scene child nodes, taking only the ones of type `StoneNode`. Then, you simply move them from their current places into the hierarchy of the `compound` node.

Next, you need to create physics bodies for each of these pieces. You'll just loop over all the stone nodes now contained in the `compound` node and create a physics body for each one:

```
let bodies = compound.children.map({ node in
  SKPhysicsBody(rectangleOf: node.frame.size,
    center: node.position)
})
```

With this code, you store all the bodies in the `bodies` array, because in the next bit of code, you'll be supplying them to the initializer of `SKPhysicsBody(bodies:)` and creating a compound physics body out of all the pieces.

Do that now by adding the following:

```
compound.physicsBody = SKPhysicsBody(bodies: bodies)
compound.physicsBody!.collisionBitMask = PhysicsCategory.Edge
  | PhysicsCategory.Cat | PhysicsCategory.Block
compound.physicsBody!.categoryBitMask = PhysicsCategory.Block
compound.isUserInteractionEnabled = true
compound.zPosition = 1

return compound
```

`SKPhysicsBody(bodies:)` takes all of the bodies you provide and binds them together; you set the result as the body of the `compound` node. Finally, you set the collision bit mask of the stone node so that it collides with the cat, the other blocks and the edge of the screen.

Before returning the ready-for-use `compound` node, you enable user interactions on it. The `compound` node will accept taps — not the individual pieces.

> **Note:** Now that you're returning a valid object, the error should be resolved.

All that's left to do is call the new method from `didMoveToScene()`, so do that now:

```
guard let scene = scene else {
  return
}

if parent == scene {
  scene.addChild(StoneNode.makeCompoundNode(in: scene))
}
```

For each node, you check if its parent is `scene`. If it is, that means the stone nodes haven't been moved to the `compound` node yet, in which case you call `makeCompoundNode(in:)`.

Build and run the game, and behold the coveted L-shaped stone in all its compound glory!

Destroy one of the **wooden** blocks on the left to see the two stone pieces now behave as one solid body:

Victory! You have a compound body in your scene.

If you try to solve the level, it won't work; that's because you haven't added interactivity to the stone blocks yet.

Switch back to **StoneNode.swift** and override the `UIResponder` method to react to touches:

```
override func touchesEnded(_ touches: Set<UITouch>,
    with event: UIEvent?) {
```

```
    super.touchesEnded(touches, with: event)
    interact()
}
```

Then add the relevant code to `interact()`:

```
isUserInteractionEnabled = false

run( SKAction.sequence([
  SKAction.playSoundFileNamed("pop.mp3",
    waitForCompletion: false),
  SKAction.removeFromParent()
  ]))
```

Note that `interact()` will be called on your compound node, so calling `removeFromParent()` will remove the compound node and both of the pieces it contains. Two for the price of one!

No matter which of the pieces the player taps, you remove *all* of the pieces by removing the node that holds them.

Build and run the game again. This time, you'll be able to solve the level.

Level progression

Until this point, you've worked on one level at a time, so you've manually specified which level to load. However, that won't work for players — they expect to proceed to the next level after winning!

This is quite easy to implement. Begin by setting the game to load Level 1. Change the line that loads the scene in **GameViewController.swift** so it looks like this:

```
if let scene = GameScene.level(levelNum: 1) {
```

Then, in **GameScene.swift**, add the following code **to the beginning** of win(). Make sure you add it before all of the other code:

```
if currentLevel < 3 {
  currentLevel += 1
}
```

Now, every time the player completes a level, the game will move on to the next one. Finally, to raise the stakes, add this **to the beginning** of lose():

```
if currentLevel > 1 {
  currentLevel -= 1
}
```

That'll certainly make the player think twice before tapping a block!

Congratulations — you now have three unique levels for Cat Nap. You've learned how to use the scene editor and how to create custom classes for your nodes. You've even learned how to implement custom physics behavior. From here on out, you're ready to start working on your own level-based physics game. The principles you learned in the last four chapters remain the same in any physics game.

There's one more chapter with Cat Nap to go, where you'll be learning about some more advanced types of nodes you can use in your game. But before you move on — try your hand at the challenge below!

Challenges

By now, you've come a long way toward mastering physics in SpriteKit.

And because I'm so confident in your skills, I've prepared a challenge for you that will require a solid understanding of everything you've done in the last three chapters — and will ask even more of you.

Challenge 1: Add one more level to Cat Nap

Your challenge is to develop an entirely new level by yourself. If you do everything just right, the finished level will look like this:

As you can see, this time, besides blocks, there's a seesaw between the poor cat and its bed. This cat sure has a hard life.

And yes, it's a real seesaw; it rotates about its center and is fully interactive. And you developed it all by yourself! Er, sorry — you *will* develop it all by yourself. See, I have confidence in you. :]

I'll lay down the main points and you can take it from there.

Your scene in **Level4.sks** should be **2048x1536** in size with Anchor Point at **(0, 0)**.

Here are the objects to add:

- **Background:** Texture **background**, Position **(1024, 768)**

- **Bed:** Texture **cat_bed**, Name **bed**, Position **(1024, 272)**, Custom Class **BedNode**

- **Block1:** Texture **wood_square**, Name **block**, Position **(1024, 626)**, Body Type **Bounding rectangle**, Category Mask **2**, Collision Mask **11**, Custom Class **BlockNode**

- **Block2:** Texture **wood_square**, Name **block**, Position **(1024, 266)**, Body Type **Bounding rectangle**, Category Mask **2**, Collision Mask **11**, Custom Class **BlockNode**

- **Seesaw base:** Texture **wood_square**, Name **seesawBase**, Position **(514, 448)**, Body Type **Bounding rectangle**, Uncheck **Dynamic** checkbox under Body Type, Category Mask **0**

- **Seesaw:** Texture **ice**, Name **seesaw**, Position **(518, 440)**, Body Type **Bounding rectangle**, Category Mask **2**, Collision Mask **11**

And, of course, the cat reference:

• Name **cat_shared**, Reference **Cat**, Position (**996, 943**), Z position **10**

Once you've placed these objects, the scene should look something like this:

There's not much left to do from here — I'll assume you've done everything perfectly so far!

You'll need to fix the seesaw board to its base on the wall. Do that by creating a pin joint that will anchor the center of the board to the center of the base and let the board rotate around that anchor, like so:

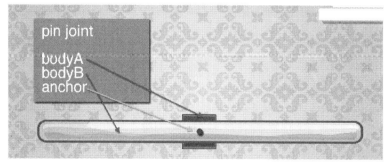

You can create a pin joint in two ways. First, create it in code using `SKPhysicsJointPin.joint(withBodyA:bodyB:anchor:)` to ensure you understand how it works. You'll need to find the node by name and use it to create the joint.

After that, you can remove that code and do the much simpler thing: Check the **Pinned** checkbox in the scene editor, in the seesaw's **Physics Definition** section. This will create a pin joint that connects the node to the scene at the node's anchor point.

That's it. Try solving the level yourself. I'm not going to give you any other tips besides the fact that the order in which you destroy the blocks matters — you got this!

Chapter 11: Crop, Video, and Shape Nodes

By Marin Todorov

In the very first chapter of this book, you learned that all of the visual elements in your game scene are nodes. You used a number of different nodes by creating instances of classes that inherit from SKNode.

Whether you create a node from code, or add them using the scene editor, they all inherit from the SKNode base class.

Here's a quick review of the nodes you've used so far:

- **SKNode**: An empty node that doesn't draw anything on the screen; use it to group other nodes by adding them as children to this node.

- **SKScene**: This node represents a single *screen* or a level in your game; add all your level nodes directly or indirectly to this node.

- **SKLabelNode**: From the game score to the player's remaining lives to any in-game messages — it's all done with this node.

- **SKSpriteNode**: You've been using this node quite often; it displays an image or a sequence of images onscreen via an action. This is generally the node you use the most when designing a scene.

In this chapter, you'll continue working on Cat Nap, and in the process, you'll learn about three advanced types of nodes:

- **SKCropNode**: This node lets you mask the contents of a node, including its child nodes. This comes in handy when you want to *crop out* part of a texture.

- **SKVideoNode**: This node lets you include videos in your games. As you've probably experienced, developers often use videos to create richer gameplay.

- **SKShapeNode:** This node lets you draw shapes onscreen. You can draw shapes of different complexities, from rectangles and circles to any arbitrary shape.

If these three nodes have anything in common, it's that they all let you add unique effects to your games. These nodes might not seem like much at first, but by the end of this chapter, you'll be able to create amazing and advanced things using them.

Make no mistake — advanced does not necessarily mean difficult. You'll probably find this chapter easier than you expect, and when you're done, you just might have the urge to celebrate with some disco moves.

Without further ado, it's time to add two more levels to Cat Nap.

> **Note:** This chapter begins where the previous chapter's Challenge 1 left off. If you were unable to complete the challenge or skipped ahead from an earlier chapter, don't worry — you can simply open the starter project from this chapter to pick up in the right place.

Getting started

Open the project in Xcode. Then, open the **Assets.xcassets** catalog.

To work through this chapter, you'll need some extra resources. Look in the **starter/ resources** folder for this chapter and drag the **textures** folder into the asset catalog. Included in this folder are additional textures you'll need to build this chapter's levels.

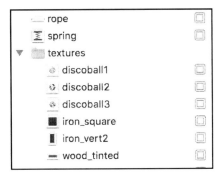

Then, drag the **media** folder into your project — *not* into the asset catalog, but into the **project navigator**. This folder contains a video that you'll use in this chapter to spice up one of the new levels and the audio track to go along with it.

Since you're already a pro with the scene editor, I won't ask you to create the last two levels of Cat Nap from scratch. Instead, open the **levels** folder inside **Resources** and drag **Level5.sks** and **Level6.sks** into your project.

To let the player progress to these new levels, open **GameScene.swift** and inside `win()`, change `if currentLevel < 4 {` to this:

```
if currentLevel < 6 {
```

Also, to save yourself some time while developing, open **GameViewController.swift** and inside `viewDidLoad()`, change `if let scene = GameScene.level(levelNum: 1) { ` to this:

```
if let scene = GameScene.level(levelNum: 5) {
```

With that, you've completed the project setup and you can lay your hands on `SKCropNode` to do some cutouts. Snip snip!

Crop nodes

In previous chapters, you used `SKSpriteNode` to show textures onscreen. For example, if you wanted to display a picture of the main character from this book's first mini-game, Zombie Conga, you could easily do that by creating a new `SKSpriteNode` and adding it to your scene like so (don't add this code; this is just an example):

```
let picture = SKSpriteNode(imageNamed: "picture")
picture.position = CGPoint(x: 200.0, y: 150.0)
addChild(picture)
```

You would see the picture show up at full size:

But what if you wanted to create a node that's not rectangular in shape? So far, you've used only rectangular textures; when you needed a different shape, you simply used images with transparent backgrounds.

Using transparency works most of the time, but if you're creating a more advanced game, you'll may need to take a normal rectangular texture and cut out an arbitrary piece of it to use in your scene.

To crop the contents of a texture, you can apply a mask and cut out only the content you want to keep:

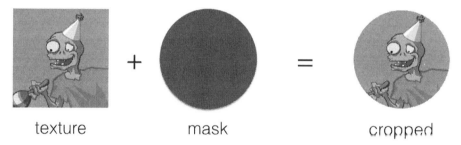

Imagine using a cookie cutter: You press the cutter onto the dough, and it cuts out a piece of the dough in the shape of the cutter. There's your cookie!

To use `SKCropNode` to achieve a similar effect, you follow four easy steps:

1. **Create a new SKCropNode**. This node doesn't display anything by default; it's only a container node.

2. **Add one or more child nodes** of any type you like to the crop node: labels, sprite nodes and so forth.

3. **Set the crop mask**. The mask is also a node and can be any type, such as a sprite node or a label. The mask node's contents should have transparent and opaque areas; opaque areas will result in content showing, while transparent areas will result in hidden, or cut out, content.

4. **Add the crop node to the scene.** Like any other node, you need to add the crop node to the scene to see its contents.

The process looks much like this:

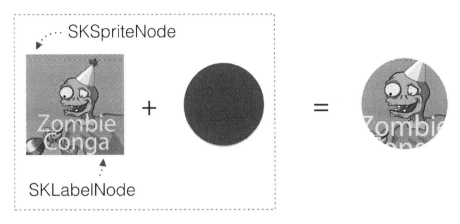

SKCropNode

In this example, a crop node has two child nodes: a sprite node and a label. When you apply a circular mask to the crop, you cut out all of the child nodes' content located in the transparent area of the mask.

With that in mind, you're good to start working on a very special part of Level 5: a dusty old picture of a zombie who likes the conga!

With a little help from my frames

Run Cat Nap and take a look at Level 5:

You can play around a bit, but here's the bad news: You can't solve the level as-is. You need to add some extra cool crop nodes to help the kitty get to his bed.

> **Note:** The black blocks are just like normal blocks, except they're indestructible; no matter how many times you tap them, they'll remain unharmed.

The new element in this level is obviously the picture frame on the wall. Open **Level5.sks** and select the picture frame node. Switch to the Custom Class inspector, and you'll see the node is already configured to be an instance of `PictureNode`.

Create a new file by choosing **File > New > File...** and selecting **iOS/Source/Cocoa Touch Class** for the file template. Name the new class **PictureNode**, make it a subclass of **SKSpriteNode** and click **Next** and **Create**. Xcode will automatically open the new file.

Replace the contents of **PictureNode.swift** with the following:

```
import SpriteKit

class PictureNode: SKSpriteNode, EventListenerNode,
  InteractiveNode {

  func didMoveToScene() {
    isUserInteractionEnabled = true

  }

  func interact() {

  }
}
```

This code enables touches on the picture node and gets you ready to add more custom content. At the moment, `PictureNode` only displays a hollow picture frame. Next, you're going to load the zombie picture and crop it to a circle so it will fit in the frame.

As a first step, add the following code to `didMoveToScene()`:

```
let pictureNode = SKSpriteNode(imageNamed: "picture")
let maskNode = SKSpriteNode(imageNamed: "picture-frame-mask")
```

These lines load images into two sprite nodes:

* In `pictureNode`, you load the zombie picture.

* In `maskNode`, you load an image of a circle with a transparent background. Tshis will be your mask.

Next, you need to add the crop node. Add the following lines:

```
let cropNode = SKCropNode()
cropNode.addChild(pictureNode)
cropNode.maskNode = maskNode
addChild(cropNode)
```

You create an empty `SKCropNode` and add `pictureNode` as a child. Then, you set your prepared `maskNode` to be the mask of the crop node. Finally, you add the configured crop node as child to the picture frame node — the one that came from the `.sks` file.

Build and run the game. You'll see the zombie picture cropped neatly inside the picture frame:

To see exactly what the crop node does, comment out the line `cropNode.maskNode = maskNode`.

This removes the mask so you can see the whole, uncropped content:

Now **uncomment** the line where you set the mask, and you'll have the zombie picture cropped once again and neatly tucked inside the picture frame.

Look more carefully at the picture: It features a green outline denoting a physics body.

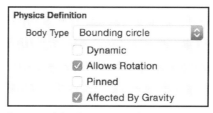

Switch back to the scene editor and look up the Physics Definition of the picture, and you'll notice two things:

- The picture has a **circular body** that matches the shape of the picture frame. Specifically, the body is a Bounding circle.

- The body isn't **dynamic**, because the Dynamic option is unchecked. This means the body isn't affected by the physics world — gravity doesn't pull it down, and when other bodies hit it, it doesn't move.

To finish up the level, you'll add just a bit of interactivity to this node. When the player taps on the picture frame, you'll set its physics body to be dynamic. Since the picture isn't pinned to the wall, it will fall down under the pull of gravity and help the player solve the level.

Open **PictureNode.swift** and add a new method to the `PictureNode` class:

```
override func touchesEnded(_ touches: Set<UITouch>,
    with event: UIEvent?) {
  super.touchesEnded(touches, with: event)
  interact()
}
```

Then, add the interaction code to `interact()`:

```
isUserInteractionEnabled = false
physicsBody!.isDynamic = true
```

Once the player taps the picture, you simply set the `isDynamic` property on its body to `true`.

Build and run the game. See if you can get kitty to his bed. Note that the seesaw block for this level is not a seesaw and is instead used as a `BlockNode`, so you can make it "pop" by tapping it.

Note: If you have difficulty solving the level, here's a hint: destroy all of the wooden blocks, then tap the picture; when the picture pushes kitty over the center of his bed, tap the seesaw block.

Crop nodes are straightforward: They let you cut out any shape you want from any texture or node. But you don't have to limit yourself to using images for the mask node. For example, you can use an SKLabelNode as a mask to produce some neat looking text. Here's what happens when you crop the level's background image, specifically the room's wallpaper, using a label node for a mask:

But enough about cutting and cropping — it's time to move on to the next stop on your advanced nodes tour: SKVideoNode.

Video nodes

Videos are everywhere in games — from a lively scene background to cutscenes. A video can give your game a number of advantages. For example:

- You can include **3D content** in your 2D game. Produce a scene in 3D modeling software, animate it in some way and finally, export it as video file. Alternatively, buy a cheap 3D royalty-free video online. Play the video in your 2D game and boom! — you have 3D content. :]

- You can **save GPU power**. Imagine you have a game taking place at the bottom of the ocean; in the background, you have 200 different fishes swimming happily about. You can create 200 sprite nodes and run 200 repeating actions on them to create the scene, but that would take a toll on the device's GPU and your game's frame rate. If you pre-record the scene and play the video as a background in your game, you can increase your game's performance.

- Finally, you can include content that is simply **a movie**. Is your player in command of hundreds of tiny 2D space ships? Then put on a hat and a fake mustache, become Space Admiral Zblorg and use your iPhone to record a video of the player's pep talk for the next level.

I'm sure you don't need any more convincing to get started with SKVideoNode or the next level of Cat Nap.

Creating a video node

Open **GameViewController.swift** and change the starting level to **6** to save yourself the trouble of having to solve Level 5 each time you want to test something:

```
if let scene = GameScene.level(levelNum: 6) {
```

Build and run the game to see this level's starting point:

Since you're familiar with Cat Nap's game mechanics, you'll quickly notice that you don't have a way to solve this level in its current state.

There are a bunch of wooden pieces lying around, but the kitty is way off the center of the screen; no matter how you destroy the wooden blocks, Kitty is just too far from his bed to make it in.

I bet you've also noticed a new element on the screen: a big, shiny disco ball! In this level, you're going to turn the quiet bedroom into a disco each time the player taps the ball. While the music and lights are on, if the player taps the kitty, he'll start to "dance". Each time the kitty dances, he'll end up a bit to the right of his original position.

If the player repeats this routine of tapping the disco ball and the kitty, the kitty will eventually find himself in the center of the screen. From there, getting into his bed will be as easy as tapping a couple of blocks.

If you look around the level file in the scene editor, you'll see that the custom class for the ball sprite is already set to `DiscoBallNode`.

So, what are you waiting for? You know the drill — create that class. :]

Create a new file by choosing **File > New > File...** and selecting **iOS/Source/Cocoa Touch Class** for the file template. Name the new class **DiscoBallNode**, make it a subclass of **SKSpriteNode** and click **Next** and **Create**.

Xcode will automatically open the file. Once it does, replace the contents of the file with the following:

```
import SpriteKit
import AVFoundation

class DiscoBallNode: SKSpriteNode, EventListenerNode,
  InteractiveNode {

  private var player: AVPlayer!
  private var video: SKVideoNode!

  func didMoveToScene() {
    isUserInteractionEnabled = true

  }

  func interact() {

  }
}
```

You lay down the class basics by inheriting from `SKSpriteNode` and implementing the `EventListenerNode` and `InteractiveNode` protocols, just as before. This time, though, you have two class variables as well:

- **player**: This is the `AVPlayer` class from the `AVFoundation` framework. It helps you load local or remote video files for playback. `AVPlayer` doesn't render the video itself; it only loads and manages the video file.

- **video**: This is the node responsible for displaying onscreen the video file you load via `AVPlayer`.

Incidentally, `AVPlayer` creates an instance of `AVPlayerItem`, which represents a single video file in the `AVPlayer` playlist:

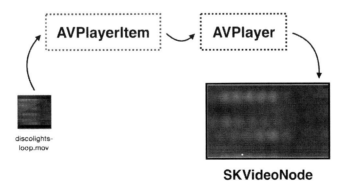

SKVideoNode can automatically load the video file without the help of a separate AVPlayer object, but in that case, you can only start and stop the video. You also lose fine-grained control of playback, such as seeking through and looping the video.

To instantaneously display the video, you'll load the file and have the video node ready when the game loads the level. Initially, you'll have the video node hidden, but when the player taps on the ball, you'll unhide the node and have the video play instantly.

It's time to get this show on the road. Add the following to didMoveToScene():

```
let fileUrl = Bundle.main.url(forResource: "discolights-loop",
  withExtension: "mov")!
player = AVPlayer(url: fileUrl)
video = SKVideoNode(avPlayer: player)
```

The first line gets the URL to the **discolights-loop.mov** video file included in your project. You use that URL to create a new AVPlayer instance. Then, SKVideoNode(avPLayer:) creates a video node that uses the aforementioned AVPlayer object.

And that's it! Your node is ready for prime time.

> **Note:** Did you notice that you didn't have to specify the video format codec the player needs in order to reproduce your file? AVPlayer is almost magical in the way it deals with videos. It looks up the video file meta information and decides on its own how to load and decode the video content. Besides being magical, AVPlayer loads and plays any MPEG4 (.mp4), Apple MPEG4 (.m4v) or QuickTime (.mov) file.

Video playback

Since you've loaded the video and initialized your video node, all that's left to do is position and size the node, and, of course, add it to the scene.

Still in didMoveToScene(), add the following lines:

```
video.size = scene!.size
video.position = CGPoint(
  x: scene!.frame.midX,
  y: scene!.frame.midY)
video.zPosition = -1
scene!.addChild(video)

video.play()
```

With this code, you make the video as big as the scene and then center it so it fills the whole screen. Further, you set its zPosition so that the video appears behind the cat, the bed and the blocks, but *in front* of the original background.

Finally, you add the video node to the scene and start playing it.

Build and run now to see the result:

Wow! I told you this would be amazing!

However, there's a slight problem with the video right now — it plays for few seconds, then stops as it reaches the end of the file.

You need to make the video loop, which happens to be a rather simple task.

When AVPlayer reaches the end of the video file, it posts a certain notification. You'll listen for that notification and simply rewind the video tape to its start position, and continue the playback from there. And by video tape, I mean the video file. :]

Add the following to didMoveToScene():

```
NotificationCenter.default.addObserver(self,
   selector: #selector(didReachEndOfVideo),
   name: NSNotification.Name.AVPlayerItemDidPlayToEndTime,
   object: nil)
```

You observe for a notification named AVPlayerItemDidPlayToEndTime. As the name suggests, this is the notification that's posted whenever AVPlayer reaches the end of the current video file.

Now, you need to add a didReachEndOfVideo() method to react to the playback having reached the end of the video.

Therefore, add a new method to **DiscoBallNode.swift**:

```
func didReachEndOfVideo() {
  print("rewind!")
  player.currentItem!.seek(to: kCMTimeZero)
  player.play()
}
```

The `currentItem` property on your player object is an instance of `AVPlayerItem`. This class gives you access to a lot of the aspects of the video player, like seeking through the video, audio mixing, video composition, loaded video buffers and much more.

Using `seek(to:)`, it's possible to move the current position in the video to a given time offset. The handy `kCMTimeZero` constant tells the player item to seek to the beginning of the file.

Additionally, just to make the looping more obvious for this demo, you print a message in the console whenever you jump from the end of the video to the beginning of the video.

Build and run the game on your device. Enjoy the glorious disco lights video on loop:

> **Note:** Isn't that video cool? I made it especially for this chapter's project. I built a small app using Core Animation and my favorite layer, `CAReplicatorLayer`, and then captured the video of the animation from my screen.
>
> If you want to learn how to create cool animations with Core Animation, check out my book about animations, *iOS Animation by Tutorials*:
>
> https://www.raywenderlich.com/store/ios-animations-by-tutorials

The previous screenshot doesn't do much justice to the video, but the output in the console clearly shows that the video loops and plays continuously:

```
☑  ▶  ‖  △  ↓  ↥  ⬚  ◁  ◎  🐱 CatNap
bed added to scene
cat added to scene
rewind!
rewind!
rewind!
rewind!
rewind!
rewind!
rewind!
rewind!
rewind!
```

Now, to make the video blend a little better, set its opacity to 75% by adding the following line to `didMoveToScene()`:

```
video.alpha = 0.75
```

The change in opacity makes for a more subtle effect that fits the scene perfectly.

As per your initial plan, you need to hide the video until the player taps the disco ball. Still in `didMoveToScene()`, replace `video.play()` with the following two lines:

```
video.isHidden = true
video.pause()
```

This will hide the video node as well as ensure it is paused, since there's no reason to keep `AVPlayer` busy while the video isn't visible.

Next, you need to add the code to react to touches on the disco ball.

Since the disco ball will work for just a few seconds at a time, you'll need to implement a timeout to turn it off again. The easiest way is to add a new instance property — call it `isDiscoTime` — and show or hide the video whenever the value of that property changes.

Add the following to `DiscoBallNode`:

```
private var isDiscoTime: Bool = false {
  didSet {
    video.isHidden = !isDiscoTime

  }
}
```

Any time you change the value of `isDiscoTime`, the `didSet` handler will show or hide the video node accordingly.

Now you can override `touchesEnded(_:withEvent:)` in your disco ball class, and simply toggle the value of `isDiscoTime`. Add this to `DiscoBallNode`:

```
override func touchesEnded(_ touches: Set<UITouch>,
    with event: UIEvent?) {
  super.touchesEnded(touches, with: event)
  interact()
}
```

And, as usual, add the code to handle user taps in `interact()`:

```
if !isDiscoTime {
  isDiscoTime = true
}
```

Build and run the game, and tap the disco ball to make sure everything works as planned:

When you tap the disco ball, the video appears and it's ready to play. Now, you just need to play the video and add a little extra "something" to the disco ball.

First, add a new property to keep a frame animation for your disco ball:

```
private let spinAction = SKAction.repeatForever(
  SKAction.animate(with: [
    SKTexture(imageNamed: "discoball1"),
    SKTexture(imageNamed: "discoball2"),
    SKTexture(imageNamed: "discoball3")
    ], timePerFrame: 0.2))
```

`spinAction` is a frame animation action that continuously loops over the `discoball1`, `discoball2`, and `discoball3` images. That should get you a nice and shiny rotating disco ball animation.

Back in didSet for isDiscoTime, add the following:

```
if isDiscoTime {
  video.play()
  run(spinAction)
} else {
  video.pause()
  removeAllActions()
}
```

This bit of code plays or pauses the video depending upon whether the player turns the disco music on or off. Notice the use of the play() and pause() methods from SKVideoNode; these handy methods control the underlaying AVPlayer and are, in fact, the only playback methods the node offers.

Now you have the scene and mood all set — you show the disco lights video and the disco ball starts spinning — but the player keeps listening to the mellow Cat Nap tune.

In the beginning of this chapter you added two new files to your project — the video of the disco lights and an audio file called *disco-sound.m4a*. Why not just have the audio track contained in the video you might ask? Well, the video is just a couple of seconds long, and it loops a number of times when you play it in the game. The audio track is longer, so to keep both files smaller in size, you will play it manually alongside the video.

You will simply replace the background music with the disco tune whenever you start the video and then bring back the default music whenever disco time is over.

Add just after the last chunk of code you inserted, still in didSet for isDiscoTime:

```
SKTAudio.sharedInstance().playBackgroundMusic(
  isDiscoTime ? "disco-sound.m4a" : "backgroundMusic.mp3")
```

This simple one-liner switches between the Cat Nap tune and disco depending on the current level state.

The final code to add to didSet will automatically turn off the disco mode after a few seconds. At the end of that method, append the following:

```
if isDiscoTime {
  video.run(SKAction.wait(forDuration: 5.0), completion: {
    self.isDiscoTime = false
  })
}
```

First, you check if the player is turning on the disco mode; if so, you run a wait action on the video node for 5 seconds. When this action completes, you simply set isDiscoTime to false, which triggers the didSet handler again and pauses and hides the video.

Build and run to see how it's coming together. With that, your video node crash course is complete!

> **Note:** If you'd like to know more about fine-grained playback control, streaming video from the Internet or playing video on iOS, consult the `AVPlayer` class documentation: http://apple.co/1JZPhds.
>
> If you want to learn more about recording and playing video, you can follow this fun tutorial online that will take you on an `AVFoundation` tour: http://bit.ly/1Lnyhh8

Disco kitty

To wrap up this section, you'll add a bit of custom behavior to your cat node. It's time for some sick dance moves!

You need to handle taps on the cat node, and you need to check if it's currently disco time. If it is, you'll make the cat "dance" for a while. To expose the `isDiscoTime` property of `DiscoBallNode` to other classes, you'll add a static property.

In **DiscoBallNode.swift**, and the following properyy:

```
static private(set) var isDiscoTime = false
```

Further, inside `didSet` for the instance property `isDiscoTime`, and below all of the other code in the `didSet` handler, add the following line:

```
DiscoBallNode.isDiscoTime = isDiscoTime
```

This code will keep the static property `isDiscoTime` in sync with the instance property of the same name.

Now, each time the player taps on the cat node, you can check the static property on `DiscoBallNode` and see if there's a disco happening.

Open **CatNode.swift** and add a property to keep track of whether or not the cat is currently dancing:

```
private var isDoingTheDance = false
```

Now, append the following lines to `interact()`:

```
if DiscoBallNode.isDiscoTime && !isDoingTheDance {
  isDoingTheDance = true
  //add dance action
}
```

In `interact()`, you check if `DiscoBallNode.isDiscoTime` is on, and whether the cat is currently *not* dancing. When both conditions are fulfilled, it's dance time!

Wrapping up this method is as simple as adding a few actions to the cat node. First, replace `//add dance action` with this:

```
let move = SKAction.sequence([
  SKAction.moveBy(x: 80, y: 0, duration: 0.5),
  SKAction.wait(forDuration: 0.5),
  SKAction.moveBy(x: -30, y: 0, duration: 0.5)
  ])
let dance = SKAction.repeat(move, count: 3)
```

The first action, `move`, represents a single dance move: It moves the cat 80 points to the right, then waits half a second and moves the cat back 30 points.

The complete dance action, `dance`, repeats `move` three times. When the action has finished running, the cat will effectively have moved to the right by 150 points.

This is exactly what you want, since the ultimate goal is to move the cat to the center of the screen and just over the bed.

Finally, you want to run the `dance` action, and when it completes, toggle the Boolean flag back to `false`. To get that working, add this bit of code just after the `let dance` line:

```
parent!.run(dance, completion: {
  self.isDoingTheDance = false
})
```

This runs the move action on the compound cat node. And that's it. You're ready to check out kitty's dance moves!

Build and run the game. Tap the disco ball a few times, and while the lights are on, tap on the cat to get him moving:

Can you figure out how to solve the level on your own? Give it a try!

Once you're over the center of the bed, you can make your way in:

When you're done with disco moves and fooling around, *dance* on over to the next and final section of this chapter!

Shape nodes

A shape node lets you draw any kind of shape onscreen, from a simple circle or rectangle, to any arbitrary shape you can define with a `CGPath`.

Speech bubbles are a great example of shape nodes used in games, because they need to have different widths or heights depending on the current phrase the character is speaking. Based on the amount of text that needs to fit in the bubble, you can easily create a smaller or a larger rectangle, like so:

In fact, you've already used an SKShapeNode to draw a shape onscreen. In Chapter 2, "Manual Movement", you drew a rectangle onscreen to visualize the playable area:

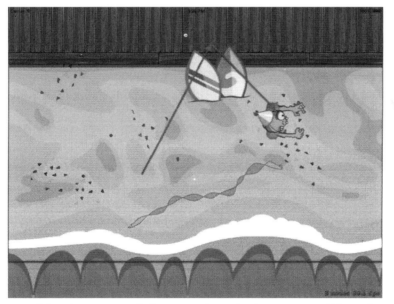

In this section of the chapter, you'll dive into that a little more. You'll learn how to set the stroke, color and width of the shape; how to make it hollow or filled; and finally, how to use a texture to make the shape look at home in the scene.

The final goal for this chapter is to add a dynamic hint arrow to show the player where to begin solving the level. Most games have hints or tutorials of some sort, and you'd like Cat Nap to be on par with them.

When you finish working through this section, you'll have a nice bouncing arrow floating next to the disco ball:

Adding a shape node

It's possible to add shape nodes in the scene editor, but the options for you to customize them are rather limited. Since you're a pro at developing custom nodes, you'll develop your own awesome node class for the hint arrow.

> **Note:** The shape node available in the scene editor's Object Library seems to be a bit buggy. For example, even if its textures render fine in the editor, when you run the project, the texture might be missing. For the time being, until Apple fixes the issue, use your own shape classes.

You'll still use the scene editor, but just to position a placeholder for your new node. Open **Level6.sks** and drag a new **Color Sprite** into the scene. It appears by default as a small red square, and that's good enough for a placeholder. You're going to hide the placeholder anyway, so the player will never see it.

Before leaving the scene editor, adjust the node like so:

• Name **hint**, Position (**1300, 1200**), Custom Class **HintNode**

Custom node class

time!

Now, create a new file by choosing **File > New > File...** and selecting **iOS/Source/Cocoa Touch Class** for the file template. Name the new class **HintNode**, make it a subclass of **SKSpriteNode** and click **Next** and **Create**.

When Xcode automatically opens the file, replace the contents with the following:

```
import SpriteKit

class HintNode: SKSpriteNode, EventListenerNode {

  func didMoveToScene() {
    color = SKColor.clear

  }
}
```

As soon as the node is added to the scene, you set its color to `clear()` and effectively make it fully transparent:

With the placeholder out of the way, you can create your own shape.

Shape node basics

First, you're going to try something simple. `SKShapeNode` has a number of convenience initializers that let you easily create the most commonly used shapes. You'll start with a simple rectangle with rounded corners.

In `didMoveToScene()`, and the following:

```
let shape = SKShapeNode(rectOf: size, cornerRadius: 20)
shape.strokeColor = SKColor.red
shape.lineWidth = 4
addChild(shape)
```

Hey, that's easy! Here you create a shape node, which is a rectangle that fits into the current node's size and has rounded corners with a radius of **20** points. You configure the shape node to outline the shape with a 4-points thick red line, and add it onscreen.

A quick build and run shows you the result:

Looking good. Try adjusting some more properties on your shape node by adding a few things to `didMoveToScene()`:

```
shape.glowWidth = 5
shape.fillColor = SKColor.white
```

To make the outline a bit "fuzzier", you add a glow effect by increasing `glowWidth`, which defaults to `0`.

Finally, an easy win is to set `fillColor` and have SpriteKit fill in the shape with a color automatically, like so:

Before moving on to the real task at hand, watch how easy it is to change the shape of the node.

Find `SKShapeNode(rectOf: size, cornerRadius: 20)` and replace it with a call to another convenience initializer:

```
let shape = SKShapeNode(circleOfRadius: 120)
```

This will make your node a different shape, but the rest of the properties you use to "beautify" it can remain the same.

Build and run to see how it looks now.

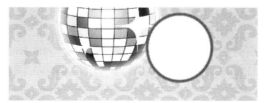

That's better. The path is now a circle.

I bet you're already asking, "Can't I just set my own custom path instead of using rectangles and circles?" Why, yes, you can. Now that you've covered the basics, you're going to move on to working with custom shapes.

Adding the hint arrow

SKShapeNode includes a property named path that you can set to an arbitrary CGPath. Then you can make the node draw anything you want.

You already worked with CGPath back in Chapter 8, "Beginning Physics", where you created a triangular shape for your triangle sprite's physics body.

Back then, you created this triangle in code: You started at the bottom-left corner, drew a line to the bottom-right corner, continued drawing to the top, and then back to where you started, closing the shape.

Coming up with the precise coordinates to draw a triangle is a pleasant brain tease, but how about more complex shapes, like a star, a truck or a space station? Unless you're a geometry genius and calculate π for breakfast, finding the coordinates by hand might be a bit too much.

Luckily, there's a neat app named PaintCode that lets you draw with your mouse, and then translates your drawings into Swift code using CGPath. I used that app to prepare the code for the arrow shape, so you don't have to draw it yourself:

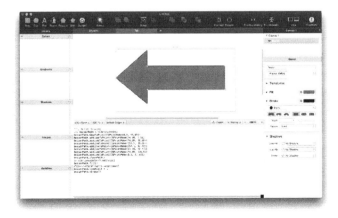

In PaintCode, the Swift code appears in the lower panel as you draw on the canvas. How cool is that!

For your Cat Nap arrow shape, you'll add a dynamic property on the `HintNode` class that will give you the arrow `CGPath`. With that said, add the following to `HintNode`:

```
var arrowPath: CGPath = {
  let bezierPath = UIBezierPath()

  bezierPath.move(to: CGPoint(x: 0.5, y: 65.69))
  bezierPath.addLine(to: CGPoint(x: 74.99, y: 1.5))
  bezierPath.addLine(to: CGPoint(x: 74.99, y: 38.66))
  bezierPath.addLine(to: CGPoint(x: 257.5, y: 38.66))
  bezierPath.addLine(to: CGPoint(x: 257.5, y: 92.72))
  bezierPath.addLine(to: CGPoint(x: 74.99, y: 92.72))
  bezierPath.addLine(to: CGPoint(x: 74.99, y: 126.5))
  bezierPath.addLine(to: CGPoint(x: 0.5, y: 65.69))
  bezierPath.close()

  return bezierPath.cgPath
}()
```

Here, you create an empty `UIBezierPath` and execute a series of line-drawing instructions, which ultimately, when combined one after the other, draw an arrow.

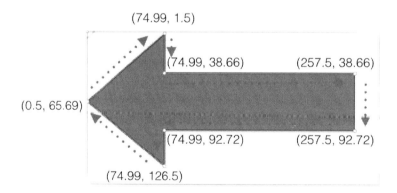

At the bottom of the method, you return the `CGPath` property on your Bézier path object.

Now you have to get rid of all the test code you wrote. To do that, simply replace the complete `didMoveToScene()` method with this one:

```
func didMoveToScene() {
  color = SKColor.clear

  let shape = SKShapeNode(path: arrowPath)
  shape.strokeColor = SKColor.gray
```

```
    shape.lineWidth = 4
    shape.fillColor = SKColor.white
    addChild(shape)
}
```

This code will get you started with a fresh, new arrow shape. This time around, you use a convenience initializer that takes a `CGPath` parameter, and you supply it with the path stored in your `arrowPath` property:

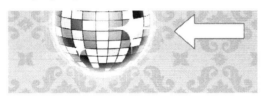

In this way, you can create any `CGPath` value and make `SKShapeNode` draw it onscreen. You can adjust the points of the path dynamically from your code, or even generate it on the fly based on the user's input.

There are a few final touches you need to make, and then you'll be ready.

In `didMoveToScene()`, add this:

```
  shape.fillTexture = SKTexture(imageNamed: "wood_tinted")
  shape.alpha = 0.8
```

This simply makes the hint arrow a better fit for your scene; you fill it with a wooden texture and give it a bit of transparency:

To quickly wrap up the level, add a few actions to the arrow to make it a bit more pleasant to the eye. Do so by adding these lines to `didMoveToScene()`:

```
  let move = SKAction.moveBy(x: -40, y: 0, duration: 1.0)
  let bounce = SKAction.sequence([
    move, move.reversed()
    ])
  let bounceAction = SKAction.repeat(bounce, count: 3)

  shape.run(bounceAction, completion: {
    self.removeFromParent()
  })
```

This creates a bouncing animation action and runs it three times on the arrow node. When the action completes, you remove the node from the scene.

Build and run one last time, and enjoy your new hint arrow. Notice how it appears as the level begins, and then disappears after three bounces.

And that's a wrap!

You gained some extensive experience with the scene editor, you learned about physics in SpriteKit and how to create your own game worlds, you created some complex physics-based mechanisms and finally, you used fantastic picture frames, videos and custom shapes! I think both you *and* the cat deserve a nap! :]

And of course, you can always add more levels to Cat Nap on your own. Why not come back and revisit Cat Nap once you learn about all the exciting APIs from the chapters in the rest of the book?

But before moving on, there are two quick challenges waiting for you.

Challenges

Challenge 1: Hints all around!

Now that your HintNode is fully functional, you can add it to the other levels in Cat Nap. Consider how you added the node in the last level, and then add it to Level 1, as well:

And then to Level 2:

That should definitely make the game easier to understand! Can you think of other game levels where you could add this hint?

Challenge 2: fillColor meets fillTexture

One aspect of SKShapeNode not covered in this chapter is the relationship between fillColor and fillTexture. As you made your way through the chapter, it might have seemed like only one of the two could be seen at any one time — as soon as you set the texture, you didn't see the white fill any more.

Indeed, the documentation for SKShapeNode says that once the texture is set, the value of fillColor is ignored. But that's not entirely true — you can use fillColor to tint the texture and produce a different color for the texture.

In this challenge, you'll try that on your own.

Enable user interaction for the hint arrow, and each time the player taps on it, change the fillColor of the shape node. Keep an array of SKColor objects: red, yellow and orange colors. Upon each tap, pick a random color from the list and set it as the fill color.

I hope this challenge will make you feel like you're back in art class at school. What color would a blue texture mixed with a yellow fill color produce?

Section III: Tile Maps

In this section, you'll learn about the new features in Xcode 8 that make creating tile map games even easier than before!

In the process, you'll create a game named Pest Control, where you take control of a vigorous, impossibly ripped he-man named Arnie. Your job is to lead Arnie to bug-fighting victory by squishing all those pesky bugs.

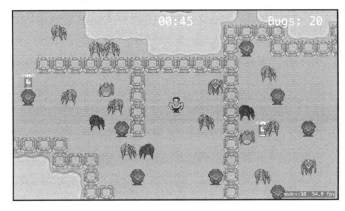

Chapter 12: Beginning Tile Maps

Chapter 13: Intermediate Tile Maps

Chapter 14: Saving and Loading Games

Chapter 12: Beginning Tile Maps

By Caroline Begbie

Tile maps were introduced nearly forty years ago when computers were unable to process fullscreen images in real time. Breaking up large images — such as the background map of a game — into small, tiled images used less memory and let programmers create complex games on the hardware of the time. Tile maps are the secret behind some of the amazing effects in games such as *Civilization* and *FarmVille*, which still use the classic, retro tiled game maps.

Tiles are not only useful for saving memory; there are lots of reasons to use them:

- **Flexibility**: Individual tiles can be addressed in code. You can swap out tiles and add special power-ups.

- **Layers**: Imagine an app that has a background layer, a buildings layer and an obstacles layer. Then, you could create a different background layer for each season of the year, and simply swap out the background layer to reflect the current season.

- **Procedural levels**: You can create unique, randomly-generated levels. No more painting each level individually by hand!

- **Performance**: As well as being memory-efficient, a tile map is a single SKNode. In previous versions of Xcode you'd have to add an SKNode for each tile.

- **Control**: You can paint tiles to indicate the initial positions of players and then easily replace the tiles in code.

- **Fun**: Bring out your inner artist and let a tile map be the canvas on which you paint your imaginary worlds! :]

Up to now, you've only been able to create tile maps in external apps, but Xcode 8 lets you paint tile maps *directly* in the SpriteKit scene editor.

Over the next three chapters, you'll develop a game named **Pest Control** using tile maps and simple pixel art. Here's what it will look like when you've finished all three chapters:

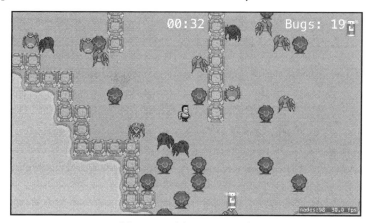

Your avatar is a vigorous, impossibly ripped he-man — let's call him Arnie. Arnie's more brawn than brain, but, like you, is awesome at squashing bugs. Here's what to expect over the next few chapters:

- Chapter 12, "Beginning Tile Maps": You'll learn how to create a tile set and paint a background tile map.

- Chapter 13, "Intermediate Tile Maps": You'll access tile maps in code, learn how to change tile images and create a tile map with randomly placed tiles.

- Chapter 14, "Saving and Loading Games": You'll put finishing touches on the game, such as a winning end state and a heads-up display. You'll also automatically save the game when you leave it and then reload it from where you left off.

By the end of these chapters, you'll know how to use tile map nodes in any game, and how to load and save your games. Along with Arnie, you'll rid your world of bugs!

Getting started

This chapter has a starter project which includes all the resources necessary for the chapters ahead. In Xcode, open **PestControl.xcodeproj** located in the **projects/starter/ PestControl** folder for this chapter.

Here's your starting point for the project: All the boilerplate code has been removed from Pest Control, it's been set to be landscape-only and all icons and images are in **Assets.xcassets**. The project also includes **SKTUtils**, as you'll need some of the math utilities later on.

Select **Assets.xcassets** in the project navigator. You'll see three sprite atlas folders: **Background**, **Characters** and **Scenery**.

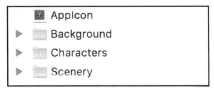

You'll use images from **Background** and **Scenery** to create your tile maps. **Characters** holds the images and animations for the players in your game.

All the images here are 32x32 pixels. One great thing about pixel art, as you will discover later, is that it scales well to Retina screens — so you don't have to worry about 2x and 3x images.

> **Note:** The background tiles are from http://kenney.nl, where you'll find a wonderland of different tiles and tilesets.

Build and run the app and you'll get a gray screen. Roll up your sleeves — you've got some work to do!

Creating a tile set

A tile map is a grid that you fill with tiles. Pest Control's grid will be squares, but grids can be isometric or even hexagonal, depending on the look you want to achieve. Sid Meier's *Civilization* is my favorite game series — *Civilization II* used isometric tiles and evolved into using a hexagonal grid in *Civilization V*.

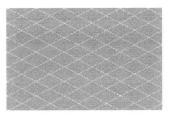
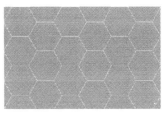

```
    Isometric          Hexagonal Flat      Hexagonal Pointy
```

The new **tile set** file is where you define your tiles. A tile set contains all the building blocks required for your map.

To start with, you'll create a simple tile set with two tiles. You'll then paint a tile map using these tiles.

Choose **File > New > File...**, select **iOS** and scroll down to **SpriteKit Tile Set**.

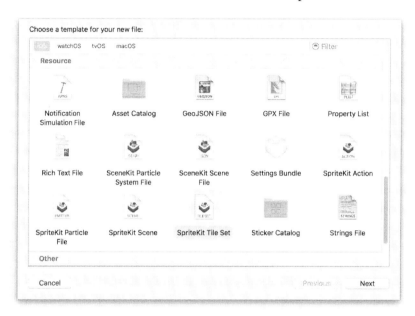

Click **Next**, name the file **TileSets**, ensure the Target for **PestControl** is checked and click **Create**.

Your new tile set contains one tile set called **Tile Set**, which in turn contains a tile group named **new tile group**.

In the Attributes Inspector, rename **Tile Set** to **Background** and **new tile group** to **grass tile**.

> **Note:** Instead of using the inspector, you can also double-click the name in the tile set pane, or select the name and press Return and then rename it.

Down at the bottom-right of the screen, find the **Media Library**:

This is a list of all media in your app; it's a great way to find all the images that you'll need for your tiles. You can even filter the images so that only relevant ones show up in the list.

Select the **grass tile** group and locate the **grass1** image in the Media Library. Drag it onto the tile slot in the center of the scene.

If you were to paint tiles with only one grass texture, a repeating pattern would form on the tile map. To overcome this, you can create tile variants with different textures.

Select the tile slot image to see a list of the tile variant definitions.

Drag **grass2** to the + slot to add a new variant. Then drag **grass3** to the new + slot. You now have three grass variants. When you paint grass on the map, one of these three tile variants will be randomly chosen.

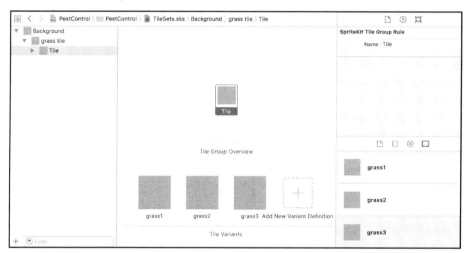

Now to create a water tile.

Select **Background** in the tile set pane, and click the + at the bottom of the pane. Choose **New Single Tile Group** from the popup menu. Rename **new tile group** to **water tile**.

Select the **water tile** group, locate the **water** image in the Media Library and drag it onto the tile slot.

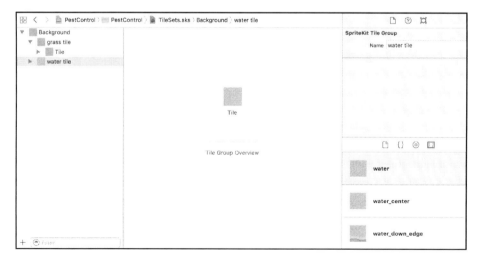

> **Note:** At the time of writing, there's a bug in Xcode 8 where you will need to create and then delete a third blank tile to be able to paint in the Tile Editor. Select **Background** in the tile set pane, and click the **+** at the bottom of the pane. Choose **New Single Tile Group** from the popup menu. You don't need to rename this or add an image to the tile. Select this new tile group and press **delete**. Until the bug is fixed, you'll need to take this step every time you add a new tile group or tile set.

You've created a tile set containing two tile groups — one for grass, and one for water — so you're now able to create a tile map in your scene.

Creating a tile map

Select **GameScene.sks** in the project navigator. Change the scene's **Size** to a width of 1024 and the height to 768.

As Pest Control is a top-down game, there will be no gravity required in the physics simulations. Change **Gravity** to **(0, 0)**.

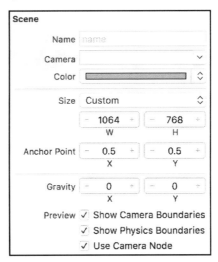

At the bottom right, show the **Object Library**, and locate the **Tile Map Node** object. This object is new in Xcode 8. Drag the tile map node on to the scene and select it in the scene navigator.

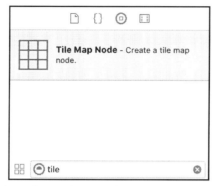

With the tile map node selected, use the Attributes Inspector to change the following properties:

- Name: **background**

- Position: **(0, 0)**

- Map Size - Columns: **40**, Rows: **30**

You only have one tile set in the app, so the Background tile set has automatically been chosen for you in the Tile Sets dropdown. The Tile Size has been taken from the Background tile set and automatically set to a width of 32 and a height of 32.

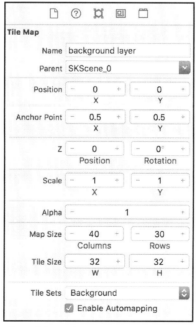

Using the - at the bottom right of the editor pane, zoom out until you can see the whole node. Notice that the tile map node is larger than the scene.

Now for the exciting part!

Double-click the **background** node in the main scene editor to enter the tile painter. You should see a grid, but if not, zoom in using the + at the bottom right until you do. Each square in this grid can contain a tile. Click and drag, and paint grass onto your background.

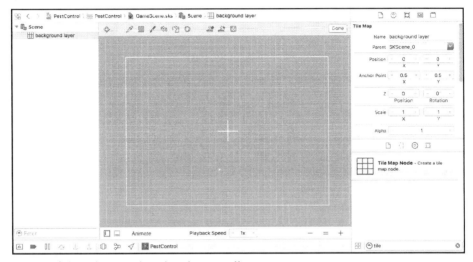

At the top of the editor is the tile editor toolbar:

You'll find these tools are very similar to other painting apps you may have used. From left to right, here's what the tools do:

Hand: Pans the scene around. If you're painting, you can click and drag outside the node to pan instead of choosing this tool, but the Hand tool is convenient when you're zoomed in on your node.

Eyedropper: Selects a painted tile as the current tile to paint with.

Select Tile: Shows a pop-up of all the tile groups in the tile set. Choose a tile from this pop-up to paint with.

Brush: Paints with the currently selected tile.

Flood Fill: Fills similarly painted connected squares with the selected tile. Use this to quickly fill in the entire background with one tile.

Erase: Removes painted tiles.

Select Brush Size: Changes the size of the Brush tool. Useful for painting large areas.

Create Stamp: Selects an area and saves it as a stamp. Click at the top left of the pattern and then click at the bottom right of the pattern to complete the stamp. If you have painted an intricate tile pattern, you can create a stamp of this pattern and then repeatedly paint it.

Select Stamp: Shows a pop-up of all the stamps you have created. Select one and then click on the map to paint the stamp. Right-click the stamp to delete it from the pop-up.

Randomize: Clears the grid and randomly paints the selected tile all over the grid.

Done: Finishes painting and exits the tile map editor.

To get a feel for how the tools work, practice painting a tile map with water and grass. Select the different tiles from the Select Tile pop-up. Paint the water areas with the Brush and then use Flood Fill with the grass tile to fill all tiles in the tile map node.

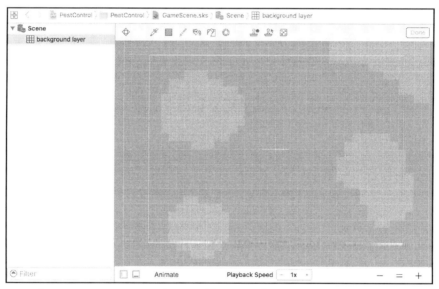

Zoom in and examine your grass tiles; you'll notice that they're not all the same. Each of the three variants you added to the grass tile is used randomly, which adds a subtle variation to the grass.

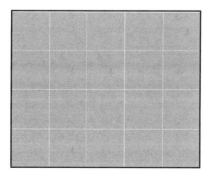

When you've finished, click **Done** at the top right of the editor to exit painting.

Build and run your app to see your tile map in action. Not all the tile map will appear onscreen at once, but later on in this chapter, when your hero is running about the scene, you'll follow him into the parts of the map that you can't yet see.

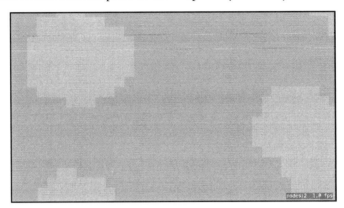

Adjacency groups

So far you've created tile groups with only a single tile. The water tiles in your tile map connect directly to the grass tiles, which makes the background look like a grid. Adjacency groups let you define a tile group with edge tiles. For example, when you paint the water, adjacency groups will paint the adjacent edge grass tiles automatically, instead of painting a single water tile. This joins the water to the grass in a more natural fashion.

Select **TileSets.sks** in the project navigator. Control-click the tile set **Background** and choose **New > 8-Way Adjacency Group** from the menu.

Change the name of the new tile group to **water**.

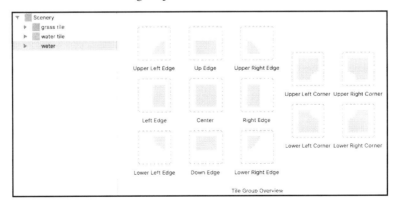

Instead of the single tile, you'll need to fill in all the thirteen slots for this tile group.

Included in Pest Control's assets are the edge and corner tiles:

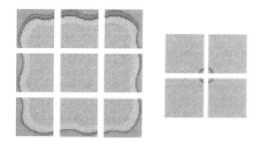

Your task is to match the images with the tile slots.

The shaded area of the slot thumbnail indicates where the main part of the tile should be. For example, in the water group the shaded areas indicate where water should show. The non-shaded areas indicate where grass should show.

In the **Media Library**, filter all the water tiles by entering **water** in the filter field:

The water images have particular names to make this task a little easier. Drag the **water_center** image from the Media Library onto the **Center** tile slot. Drag **water_down_edge** to the **Down Edge** slot. Drag **water_left_edge** to the **Left Edge** slot.

Continue dragging the water tiles to their corresponding slots. If you make a mistake, just drag the correct tile to the slot and choose **Replace tile variant texture** from the pop-up menu. The corner tiles should show just a tiny amount of grass in the corner.

When you've finished, your tile layout should look like this:

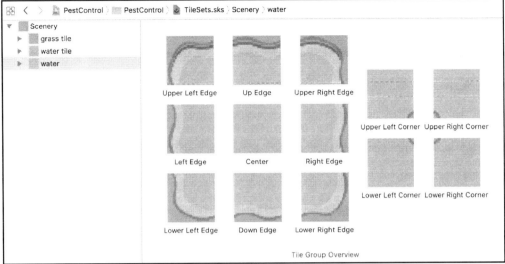

Choose **GameScene.sks** in the project navigator to return to the scene to paint your new tiles.

Double-click the **background** tile map node to edit it. You'll find your new tile group on the Select Tile pop-up.

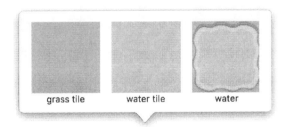

Select this group and start painting. As you paint, the edge and corner tiles automatically paint around your painted tiles.

When you've finished experimenting with painting archipelagos, select the grass tile and flood fill the background so that all of the tile map is painted.

Build and run your app to admire it in the simulator.

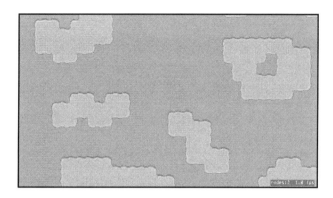

Adding the player

So far, Pest Control is missing two vital ingredients — the player and the bug enemies! In this section you'll add a `Player` class and add the player to the game.

To keep the project organized, first create a new group. In the project navigator, control-click **GameScene.swift** and select **New Group**. Rename the group to **Characters**. This group is where you'll create your `Player` and `Bug` classes.

Control-click **Characters** and choose **New File...**. Select **iOS/Source/Swift File** and click **Next**. Name the file **Player** and click **Create**.

Add this to **Player.swift**:

```
import SpriteKit

class Player: SKSpriteNode {

  required init?(coder aDecoder: NSCoder) {
    fatalError("Use init()")
  }
}
```

This defines `Player` as a subclass of `SKSpriteNode`.

You're about to add a custom initializer, so here you implement the required `SKSpriteNode` initializer and have it fail with a fatal error.

Add the custom initializer to `Player`:

```
init() {
  let texture = SKTexture(imageNamed: "player_ft1")
  super.init(texture: texture, color: .white,
            size: texture.size())
  name = "Player"
```

```
    zPosition = 50
  }
```

You've now created the initializer for the player sprite node. The player has a `zPosition` of 50 which, as befits the star, should always keep him in front of other nodes.

In **GameScene.swift**, add a property to `GameScene` for the background tile map so that you can address it in code.

```
var background: SKTileMapNode!
```

Override the required initializer:

```
required init?(coder aDecoder: NSCoder) {
  super.init(coder: aDecoder)
  background =
    childNode(withName: "background") as! SKTileMapNode
}
```

Here, you set `background` as the background tile map node from the scene editor.

Add a property for the player to `GameScene`:

```
var player = Player()
```

Then, override `didMove(to:)`:

```
override func didMove(to view: SKView) {
  addChild(player)
}
```

Here, you tell the scene to add the player to the scene hierarchy when the scene is added to the presenting view.

Build and run, and your brave hero Arnie is now ready for action!

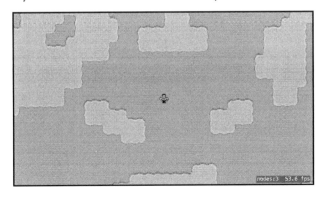

Scene scale modes

You'll notice that Arnie looks very tiny in the center of the screen.

That's because the scene is currently scaled to the size of the view. Pest Control's levels are intended to be larger than the viewport, so, unlike the other games in this book, the scene does not need to be scaled.

To show the different `scaleMode`s, I've created a scene with width 300 and height 1330, and added a red sprite of width 300 in the center. These are screenshots on an iPhone 6 which has a width of 320 points and a height of 568 points:

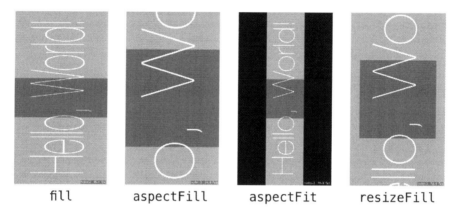

fill   aspectFill   aspectFit   resizeFill

Take a look at each one:

- `fill`: The default `scaleMode` that scales the scene to fit the view in both directions. As you can see, the result is deformed.

- `aspectFill`: Scales both directions uniformly, so that the size of the smaller dimension fits the view. In this case, the width fits the view, and the height is scaled to be larger than the view.

- `aspectFit`: Scales both directions uniformly, but ensures that the whole scene fits inside the view. In this case, black bands show because the width is too small for the view.

- `resizeFill`: Doesn't scale the scene at all, and crops the scene outside the view.

In **GameViewController.swift**, in `viewDidLoad()`, locate this code:

```
scene.scaleMode = .aspectFill
```

Replace that line with:

```
scene.scaleMode = .resizeFill
```

Now the scene won't scale at all; the 32x32 pixel images will take up exactly 32x32 points on the screen.

Build and run the app to see Arnie in his full glory:

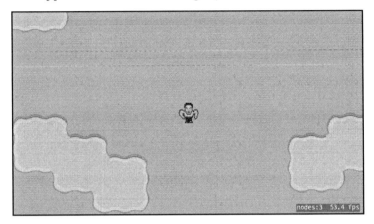

Moving the player

To make Arnie do your bidding, tap the screen and he'll run to that spot. You'll use the player's physics body velocity for this.

Add the following to **Player.swift** at the end of `init()`:

```
physicsBody = SKPhysicsBody(circleOfRadius: size.width/2)
physicsBody?.restitution = 1.0
physicsBody?.linearDamping = 0.5
physicsBody?.friction = 0
physicsBody?.allowsRotation = false
```

Here, you create a circular physics body for the player. A circle is the most efficient shape for physics simulation, and will do just fine for this game. You'll use circular bodies for all the characters.

The player should have the following physics characteristics:

- Bounce off everything without losing energy (`restitution`)

- Gradually lose velocity (`linearDamping`)

- Slide like butter with no friction (`friction`)

- Not rotate (`allowsRotation`)

Check out Chapter 8, "Beginning Physics" if you need a refresher on what these properties do.

At the top of **Player.swift** before the `Player` class declaration, add an enum which will hold all the player settings:

```
enum PlayerSettings {
  static let playerSpeed: CGFloat = 280.0
}
```

This will be the player's speed. You can change this value to tweak how fast your player moves.

Create a new method in `Player`:

```
func move(target: CGPoint) {
  guard let physicsBody = physicsBody else { return }

  let newVelocity = (target - position).normalized()
                            * PlayerSettings.playerSpeed
  physicsBody.velocity = CGVector(point: newVelocity)
}
```

This method makes the player move toward `target`. `newVelocity` describes the new velocity of the player; the speed is determined by the `playerSpeed` constant, and the direction is calculated from the desired new location less the player's current position.

Finally, in **GameScene.swift**, override the touch method to tell Arnie where he should run.

```
override func touchesBegan(_ touches: Set<UITouch>,
                      with event: UIEvent?) {
  guard let touch = touches.first else { return }

  player.move(target: touch.location(in: self))
}
```

This method takes the touch location and sends it to the Player's `move(target:)` method.

Build and run your app; Arnie now runs to wherever you tap on the screen. But he's a bit too earnest, because he keeps running and disappears off the edge of the screen!

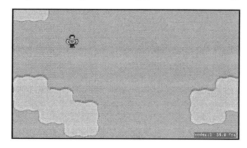

Just as you did in Zombie Conga, you'll create a camera which follows the player. An advantage of using a camera is that you'll be able to choose the zoom level. You'll be able to zoom out to see the whole level at one time, which is useful for testing. You could even change zoom levels to suit the size of the device.

Adding a camera

In **GameScene.sks**, drag a **Camera** from the **Object Library** onto the scene.

Name the camera **camera** and set Position to **(0, 0)**.

Select **Scene** in the scene editor navigator and select **camera** in the Camera drop-down.

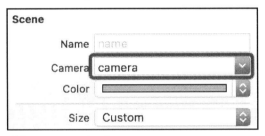

In **GameScene.swift**, add a new method to GameScene to constrain the camera to follow the player:

```
func setupCamera() {
  // 1
  guard let camera = camera else { return }

  // 2
  let zeroDistance = SKRange(constantValue: 0)
  let playerConstraint = SKConstraint.distance(zeroDistance,
                                               to: player)
  // 3
  camera.constraints = [playerConstraint]
}
```

With this method, you:

1. Check that the scene has a camera assigned to it.

2. Create a constraint to keep zero distance to the player.

3. Assign that constraint to the camera, so the camera will always follow the player and keep him centered onscreen.

Call this new method at the end of didMove(to:):

```
setupCamera()
```

Build and run the app. The camera now follows Arnie, but he escapes from the scene and disappears into the gray wilderness beyond. Perhaps he's searching for bugs to eliminate? :]

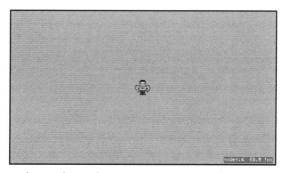

You'll need to set up a physics boundary so Arnie stays within the scene bounds.

Add this new method to GameScene:

```
func setupWorldPhysics() {
  background.physicsBody =
      SKPhysicsBody(edgeLoopFrom: background.frame)
}
```

By giving an edge loop physics body to the background tile map node, you make sure the player will never leave the map.

Call this new method at the end of didMove(to:):

```
setupWorldPhysics()
```

Build and run, and the player bounces around inside the background tile map searching for bugs.

However, because the camera stays centered on the player, you can see the grayness beyond the scene's bounds. Time to fix that.

Constraining the camera

The camera should follow the player only as far as it can until it reaches the edge. This will require a second set of constraints for the camera.

The camera's viewport size is the same as the view's bounds size. Here's the scene as an iPhone 6 would see it, with the camera moved to the top left of the scene:

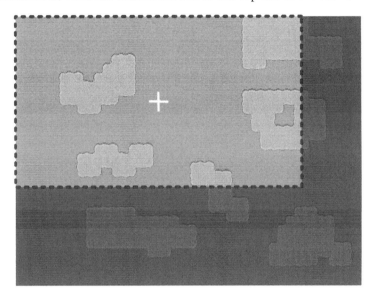

To exclude the gray area outside the boundary, the camera (positioned at the cross) should be distanced from the edge by half its width and half its height.

In `GameScene`, change `setupCamera()` to the following:

```
func setupCamera() {
  guard let camera = camera, let view = view else { return }

  let zeroDistance = SKRange(constantValue: 0)
  let playerConstraint = SKConstraint.distance(zeroDistance,
                                               to: player)
  // 1
  let xInset = min(view.bounds.width/2 * camera.xScale,
                   background.frame.width/2)
  let yInset = min(view.bounds.height/2 * camera.yScale,
                   background.frame.height/2)

  // 2
  let constraintRect = background.frame.insetBy(dx: xInset,
```

```
                                              dy: yInset)
  // 3
  let xRange = SKRange(lowerLimit: constraintRect.minX,
                       upperLimit: constraintRect.maxX)
  let yRange = SKRange(lowerLimit: constraintRect.minY,
                       upperLimit: constraintRect.maxY)

  let edgeConstraint = SKConstraint.positionX(xRange, y: yRange)
  edgeConstraint.referenceNode = background
  // 4
  camera.constraints = [playerConstraint, edgeConstraint]
}
```

Here's what you're doing in the previous code:

1. First, you determine the smallest distance from each edge that you can position the camera to avoid showing the gray area. However, in the event the camera viewport is larger than the map — when it's impossible to avoid showing the gray area — you take the minimum of that distance and half the background width/height. That way the map will stay centered.

2. Now that you know the smallest distance from each edge, you can use insetBy(dx:dy:) to get a rectangular boundary constraint.

3. Then, you set up a constraint for x and y with lower and upper limits.

4. Finally, you constrain the camera with the player constraint first and the edge constraint second. The edge constraint has higher priority, so it goes last.

To see the constraints in action, go to **GameScene.sks**. Select **camera** in the scene editor navigator and change Scale to (**2.5, 2.5**). Run the app in the iPhone SE simulator:

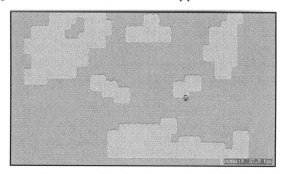

The camera is now zoomed way out. The background width is less than the width of the view, but the background height isn't. Tap the screen to make your tiny player run up and down, and you'll see the camera is constrained to follow the player in the y-direction until it reaches the edge. If you make the player run side to side, the camera will not follow the player in the x-direction, because the edge constraint has higher priority than the player constraint.

Once you've tested that, set the camera scale in **GameScene.sks** back to (**1, 1**).

> **Note:** Even at (1, 1) scale, the 12.9-inch iPad Pro will show the entire map along with some gray area. Feel free to use this for testing. Of course, before releasing a game like this, you would want to make sure no gray area shows. There are different ways you could do this, such as scaling the camera, making the map bigger, adding some border tiles or changing the scale mode.

Player animations

Now that your hero's running about, he really ought to be able to see where he's going. You'll give him an animation depending upon the direction he's traveling.

Arnie's mortal enemies are bugs, which will also be animated. You'll create a protocol that describes these animations, and both `Player` and `Bug` will conform to this protocol.

First create a new file to hold the game's global constants.

Control-click **AppDelegate.swift** and choose **New File…**. Select **iOS/Source/Swift File** and click **Next**. Name the file **Types** and click **Create**.

Add the following to **Types.swift**:

```
enum Direction: Int {
  case forward = 0, backward, left, right
}
```

This defines all directions in which a character is allowed to move.

Create another new **Swift File**, this time in the **Characters** group, called **Animatable.swift**.

Add this to the end of the file:

```
import SpriteKit

protocol Animatable {
}
```

All characters conforming to `Animatable` will have a different animation depending upon their direction. By creating a method in a protocol extension, you can provide a default method to calculate this direction.

Add the following code to the end of **Animatable.swift**:

```
extension Animatable {
  func animationDirection(for directionVector: CGVector)
    -> Direction {
    let direction: Direction
    if abs(directionVector.dy) > abs(directionVector.dx) {
      direction = directionVector.dy < 0 ? .forward : .backward
    } else {
      direction = directionVector.dx < 0 ? .left : .right
    }

    return direction
  }
}
```

This method takes in a vector and returns the direction of this vector — forward, backward, left or right. It does so by determining if the x-component or y-component of the vector is greater, and if that component is positive or negative. A bigger, negative x-component means that the direction is towards the left, and a bigger, negative y-component means down, which in this case, is forward.

Add the following to the end of **Player.swift**, outside the class definition:

```
extension Player : Animatable {}
```

Player now conforms to Animatable and can use Animatable's protocol extension methods.

Add the following to Player, at the end of move(target:):

```
print("* \(animationDirection(for: physicsBody.velocity))")
```

Build and run the app, and the direction of the player will print out in the debug console.

All you need to do now is load the corresponding animation for that direction.

In **Animatable.swift**, add the following property to Animatable (inside the protocol definition, not the extension):

```
var animations: [SKAction] {get set}
```

This property will hold the character's animations, and each class that conforms to this protocol will need to define this property.

`Player` needs to conform to `Animatable`, so in **Player.swift** add the property below to the top of the `Player` class:

```
var animations: [SKAction] = []
```

Now take a look at **Assets.xcassets**. In the **Characters** sprite atlas folder, you'll find the animation images for both the player and the bugs.

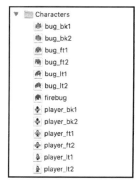

Notice the careful naming. The character is the first part of the filename, and the direction makes up the second part of the filename. This makes it easier to use the animation images in code.

Create a method to fill the animations array. In **Animatable.swift**, add this method to the `Animatable` protocol extension:

```
func createAnimations(character: String) {
  let actionForward: SKAction = SKAction.animate(with: [
          SKTexture(imageNamed: "\(character)_ft1"),
          SKTexture(imageNamed: "\(character)_ft2")
          ], timePerFrame: 0.2)
  animations.append(SKAction.repeatForever(actionForward))

  let actionBackward: SKAction = SKAction.animate(with: [
          SKTexture(imageNamed: "\(character)_bk1"),
          SKTexture(imageNamed: "\(character)_bk2")
          ], timePerFrame: 0.2)
  animations.append(SKAction.repeatForever(actionBackward))

  let actionLeft: SKAction = SKAction.animate(with: [
          SKTexture(imageNamed: "\(character)_lt1"),
          SKTexture(imageNamed: "\(character)_lt2")
          ], timePerFrame: 0.2)
  animations.append(SKAction.repeatForever(actionLeft))

  animations.append(SKAction.repeatForever(actionLeft))
}
```

> **Note:** Xcode will give you some compile errors — don't worry, you'll fix those soon!

Here, you create animate `SKActions` for each direction using the name of the character passed into the method. Notice the strict order they're added to the array. The order corresponds to the `Direction` enum. For example, `Direction.forward` is set to `0`, `Direction.backward` is `1` and so on.

The `Direction.right` animation will be a flipped version of the `Direction.left` animation. This will be done at the time that the direction is calculated.

Unfortunately, the protocol no longer compiles. Protocols assume that conforming types may have value semantics (i.e. structures and enumerations) which would make `animations` immutable. In this situation, the Characters (`Player` and `Bug`) are the only classes which will conform to `Animatable` and, being classes, they have reference semantics. So you can safely inform `Animatable` that only class types will conform.

Change the definition of `Animatable` to:

```
protocol Animatable: class {
```

`animations` is now mutable and the compile errors will go away.

In **Player.swift**, set up the player's animations by adding this to the end of `init()`:

```
createAnimations(character: "player")
```

This will call the default implementation of `createAnimations(character:)` in `Animatable` and set up the player's `animations` array with all the necessary `SKAction` animations.

Create the following new method in `Player`:

```
func checkDirection() {
  guard let physicsBody = physicsBody else { return }
  // 1
  let direction =
      animationDirection(for: physicsBody.velocity)
  // 2
  if direction == .left {
    xScale = abs(xScale)
  }
  if direction == .right {
    xScale = -abs(xScale)
  }
  // 3
```

```
    run(animations[direction.rawValue], withKey: "animation")
}
```

The above code is fairly straightforward:

1. You calculate the direction from the player's velocity using `Animatable`'s default implementation.

2. If the direction is returned as `right`, you set the player's `xScale` to negative so that the `left` animation is reversed.

3. You run the appropriate animation for the direction.

At the end of `move(target:)`, replace the `print` statement with a call to your new method:

```
checkDirection()
```

Build and run, and test the different animations for each direction:

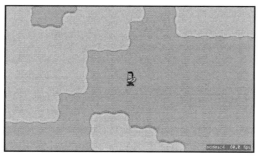

Bounce the player off the edge, and he backtracks instead of turning. Hmm. Apparently you'll need to react to physics collisions and correct the player's direction if necessary. You'll add this in the next chapter, after you've added physics categories to all the game elements.

Texture filtering mode

If you have good eyes, you'll notice that Arnie's textures look fuzzy.

He *should* look as sharp as the Arnie on the right in the above image. What's going on?

There are several **filtering modes** you can use when scaling up a SKTexture:

- **Linear**: The color of any added pixels is blended between the colors of the original pixels. This is the better option for photos.

- **Nearest**: The color of any added pixels is derived from the nearest existing pixel. This is the better option for pixel art.

The Arnie texture is using default linear filtering mode. As all your textures need the nearest filtering mode in Pest Control, you'll create an extension to SKTexture.

Control-click **Types.swift** and create a new **Swift File** named **Extensions.swift**.

Add this to the end of the file:

```
import SpriteKit

extension SKTexture {
  convenience init(pixelImageNamed: String) {
    self.init(imageNamed: pixelImageNamed)
    self.filteringMode = .nearest
  }
}
```

Here, you add a convenience initializer to SKTexture that will automatically set the texture's filtering mode to .nearest.

Now you'll change the places where you initialized textures to call this new initializer.

In **Player.swift**, in init() change:

```
let texture = SKTexture(imageNamed: "player_ft1")
```

to the following:

```
let texture = SKTexture(pixelImageNamed: "player_ft1")
```

In Animatable's createAnimations(character:), change all the instances of

```
SKTexture(imageNamed: "\(character)_ft1"),
```

to call the convenience initializer:

```
SKTexture(pixelImageNamed: "\(character)_ft1"),
```

Build and run, and Arnie should look as sharp as ever:

Challenges

In this chapter, you set up a tile map for the background. This background uses substantially fewer resources than one large image would. You've also set up the basic gameplay for your player.

These two challenges will consolidate your knowledge of painting a tile map and adding characters. Arnie will need obstacles to overcome and bugs to destroy!

As always, if you get stuck, you can find the solutions in the resources for this chapter — but give it your best shot first!

Challenge 1: Obstacles

In your first challenge, you'll set up a tile map of walls. In the next chapter, you'll add physics bodies to these walls and Arnie will have to go around them to get at the bugs.

You'll create a new tile set for Obstacles containing a wall tile. You'll then create a new tile map node in the game scene and paint walls on the tile map.

Follow these steps:

1. In **TileSets.sks**, add a new **Grid Tile Set** and name it **Obstacles**. Add a new **Single Tile Group** to that set for the wall. Name it **wall** and set the tile texture to the wall image.

2. In **GameScene.sks**, add a new **Tile Map Node** named **obstacles**. Make sure you set to the Position to (**0, 0**) and use your new tile set **Obstacles**. Change the map size dimensions of **Obstacles** to be the same as the background tile map node and paint some walls.

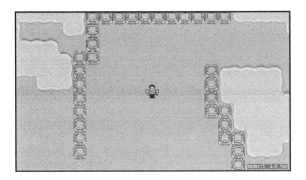

Challenge 2: Adding enemies

In the next chapter, you'll set up a tile map laying out positions of the enemy bugs. The bug tile map will be a placeholder for your hero's bug nemeses, and you'll replace those tiles with sprite nodes. Your challenge is to create a Bug class which is very similar to the Player class. Don't add the animations — you'll do this in the next chapter.

To test the Bug class, you can add a single bug node to the scene. You should be able to get your player to kick it around. After you've completed the next chapter, he'll be able to squash it! :]

Follow these steps:

1. Create a new subclass of SKSpriteNode named Bug. It should use the **bug_ft1** texture and have a circular physics body. Disallow rotation and give the physics body restitution a value of 0.5 to make the bug a little bouncy.

2. In didMove(to:) inside GameScene, create and add a bug node. Set the bug's position to (60, 0), which will place the bug just to the right of Arnie.

3. Run the app and let Arnie kick the bug around the scene.

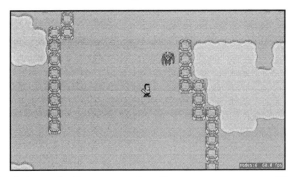

When you've finished these challenges, you're all set to move on to Chapter 13, "Intermediate Tile Maps", where you'll use and create tile maps in code — and help Arnie to fulfill his life's ambition of squashing all the bugs!

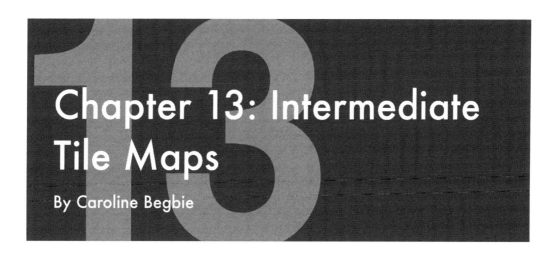

Chapter 13: Intermediate Tile Maps

By Caroline Begbie

In Chapter 12, "Beginning Tile Maps", you discovered how easy it is to create backgrounds out of tiles instead of using large images. You also painted obstacle tiles (that aren't quite obstacles yet) and created a bug you can kick around the scene.

In this chapter, you'll use tile maps to lay out the initial positions for the enemy bugs, and then create a tile map of power-ups completely in code. You'll also get those bugs swarming over the map, to the absolute *delight* of your protagonist Arnie!

> **Note:** This chapter begins where the previous chapter's Challenge 2 left off. If you were unable to complete the challenge or skipped ahead from an earlier chapter, don't worry — simply open the starter project from this chapter to pick up where the previous chapter left off.

Here's what the game will look like at the end of this chapter:

Tile map classes

A tile map gives you a visual way to lay out your enemy positions when the level starts.

You'll first create a tile set for the enemy bugs and then create a tile map node that maps out their starting positions for the level. In code, you'll use the position of the painted tiles to add your bug sprites to the scene and then discard the tile map.

Below is a diagram of the Background tile set you created earlier with the corresponding SpriteKit classes:

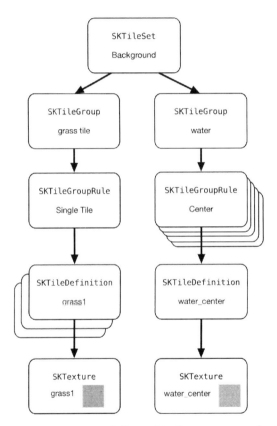

You'll go through the same process you followed before to create the Enemies tile set:

1. **SKTileSet**: Create a new tile set for enemies in **TileSets.sks**.

2. **SKTileGroup**: Create a new tile group for the bug.

3. **SKTileGroupRule**: Create the adjacency rule for the group: the bug tile will be a single tile with no adjacent tiles. Previously, you created a water group that had multiple adjacent tiles, such as Upper Left, Lower Right, Center, etc.

4. `SKTileDefinition`: Each rule can have a number of tile definitions that are variants for the tile. Earlier, you defined a grass tile with three different variants. Each variant can hold user data where you can define your own properties.

5. `SKTexture`: Each variant can hold a number of textures. Up to now, you've assigned one texture to one variant. But if you want your tile to be animated, the tile definition can hold a number of textures.

As you create the tile set and tile map, you'll learn how each step corresponds to a `SpriteKit` class.

Arnie is anxiously waiting for some bugs to squash, so you'd better get started!

Editors and classes

First, create the `SKTileSet`. In **TileSets.sks**, control-click **Background** and add a new **Grid Tile Set**. Name this tile set **Enemies**.

Next, create your `SKTileGroup`. Control-click **Enemies**, create a new **Single Tile Group**, and name this tile group **bug**.

Since you chose a Single Tile Group, the tile editor automatically created a single `SKTileGroupRule` with adjacency mask `adjacencyAll` and assigned it to the `rules` array property of the **bug** tile group.

Now to create two instances of `SKTileDefinition`. Locate the image **bug_ft1** in the Media Library and drag it to the tile slot. Click on the tile slot and then drag **bug_ft2** to the **Add New Variant Definition** slot:

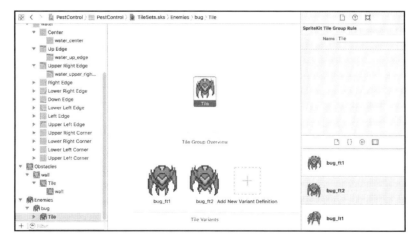

Click on the first variant and open the Attributes Inspector. Drag **bug_ft2** from the Media Library to the textures list in the Attributes Inspector. Change **Time Per Frame** to **0.2**. Your first bug will start animating.

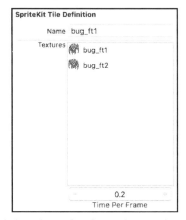

Select the second variant and drag **bug_ft1** from the Media Library to the textures list in the Attributes Inspector. Change **Time Per Frame** to **0.3**. Both bugs will be animating, but in slightly different fashions.

Create a third variant by dragging **firebug** from the Media Library to the **Add New Variant Definition** slot. This will be the super-bug that will try to bring your hero to his knees.

To distinguish this mighty bug from ordinary bugs, you'll give him some user data.

With the **firebug variant** selected, switch to the Attributes Inspector and scroll down to the **User Data** section. Click on the + to add a new attribute and name it `firebug`. The type of the attribute doesn't *really* matter, as you'll simply be checking for existence of the attribute. But to future-proof your app, change the type to **Boolean** with a value of **1** to represent `true`.

When you paint your bugs, you'll want more ordinary bugs than firebugs. Select the **bug_ft1 variant** and change **Placement Weight** to **10**. Repeat for the **bug_ft2 variant**.

Now the firebug will be 20 times less likely to be painted than ordinary bugs.

You're now ready to paint a new tile map with bugs.

In **GameScene.sks** drag a **Tile Map Node** from the Object Library to the scene.

With the new tile map node selected, change the following properties in the Attributes Inspector:

- Name: **bugs**

- Position: (**0, 0**)

- Map Size - Columns: **40**, Rows: **30**

- Tile Sets: **Enemies**

Double-click the bugs tile map node to enter the tile painter. Using the brush tool, paint some bugs on the map. If the bugs don't paint, restart Xcode and try again. Notice as you paint, that only about one in twenty bugs is a firebug.

Untick **Enable Automapping** in the Attributes Inspector and choose **Select Tile** in the tile painter tool bar.

With Automapping unchecked, you can select each one of the variants individually and paint them. Paint a few more firebugs on the bug tile map node. When you've finished, click **Done** in the tile editor toolbar.

> **Note:** You've been double-clicking the tile maps to edit them. However, this allows you to edit only the top tile map. If you want to edit a different tile map, select the node in the scene navigator and then go to **Editor > Edit Tile Map**.

Build and run and you'll see your ordinary bugs animating according to the variants you set up. The firebug, in all his majesty, doesn't yet animate.

There's one orange bug that's just sitting there, like a dead, er, bug. This is the bug you added to the scene to test the Bug class in the previous chapter's challenge. To exterminate him for good, remove the following code at the end of didMove(to:) in GameScene:

```
let bug = Bug()
bug.position = CGPoint(x: 60, y: 0)
addChild(bug)
```

Replacing tiles with SKNodes

Your tile map bugs can't move about because they're tied down to a tile. You'll now process the bugs tile map node and wherever you find a bug, you'll replace it with an SKNode.

Since you'll be using row and column references quite often in this process, create the following new typealias in **Types.swift**:

```
typealias TileCoordinates = (column: Int, row: Int)
```

In **GameScene.swift**, add the following new SKNode property to GameScene to serve as the parent for all bug sprites:

```
var bugsNode = SKNode()
```

Still in `GameScene`, create this new helper method:

```
func tile(in tileMap: SKTileMapNode,
          at coordinates: TileCoordinates)
          -> SKTileDefinition? {
  return tileMap.tileDefinition(atColumn: coordinates.column,
                                   row: coordinates.row)
}
```

This method returns a tile definition at a row–column coordinate.

Add the following new method to create the bug sprite nodes:

```
func createBugs() {
  guard let bugsMap = childNode(withName: "bugs")
    as? SKTileMapNode else { return }
  // 1
  for row in 0..<bugsMap.numberOfRows {
    for column in 0..<bugsMap.numberOfColumns {
      // 2
      guard let tile = tile(in: bugsMap,
                            at: (column, row))
        else { continue }
      // 3
      let bug = Bug()
      bug.position = bugsMap.centerOfTile(atColumn: column,
                                          row: row)

      bugsNode.addChild(bug)
    }
  }
  // 4
  bugsNode.name = "Bugs"
  addChild(bugsNode)
  // 5
  bugsMap.removeFromParent()
}
```

Here's what you're doing in the code above:

1. Cycle through the rows and columns of the tile map node.

2. Get the tile definition at the row–column coordinate. If it's not `nil`, then there must be a bug painted on that tile. You will use the `tile` variable shortly, but until then you'll get a compiler warning.

3. Create a bug sprite node and get the center point of the tile to position the bug, and add the bug to the scene.

4. Add `bugsNode` with all its child bugs to the scene.

5. Remove the tile map node from the scene as you no longer need it.

Call this method at the end of `didMove(to:)`:

```
createBugs()
```

Build and run; your bugs are now sprite nodes and they are all standing at attention, not moving at all. You'll also notice the firebugs have changed into ordinary non-super-bugs.

You'll fix all this in the next section.

Animating enemies

These bugs are made for walking, and that's just what they'll do. Just like `Player`, they will conform to `Animatable` and have a `move()` method.

First, conform `Bug` to `Animatable` just as you did with `Player`. Add an extension to the end of **Bug.swift**:

```
extension Bug : Animatable {}
```

Add this property to `Bug` to hold the bug animations:

```
var animations: [SKAction] = []
```

Still in `Bug`, at the end of `init()`, add the following:

```
createAnimations(character: "bug")
```

Now you've conformed `Bug` to `Animatable` and set up the animation actions in the `animations` array.

At the top of **Bug.swift**, before defining the Bug class, add an enum to hold the bug settings:

```
enum BugSettings {
  static let bugDistance: CGFloat = 16
}
```

In Pest Control, each bug will move randomly in one direction, before wandering off in another direction. bugDistance affects how big the movements can be. You can tweak this to change the bugs' speed.

In Bug, create a new move() method:

```
func move() {
  // 1
  let randomX = CGFloat(Int.random(min: -1, max: 1))
  let randomY = CGFloat(Int.random(min: -1, max: 1))

  let vector = CGVector(dx: randomX * BugSettings.bugDistance,
                        dy: randomY * BugSettings.bugDistance)
  // 2
  let moveBy = SKAction.move(by: vector, duration: 1)
  let moveAgain = SKAction.run(move)
}
```

The above code is fairly straightforward:

1. Here you create a vector with a random direction. Each component of the vector can be 0, bugDistance, or –bugDistance.

2. You create a moveBy action for the bug with this vector, and a second action to call move() again.

Add the following code to the end of move():

```
// 1
let direction = animationDirection(for: vector)
// 2
if direction == .left {
  xScale = abs(xScale)
} else if direction == .right {
  xScale = -abs(xScale)
}
// 3
run(animations[direction.rawValue], withKey: "animation")
run(SKAction.sequence([moveBy, moveAgain]))
```

Taking it comment-by-comment:

1. First, you determine the animation direction using the
    `animationDirection(for:)` from `Animatable`.

2. Then, if the direction is `right`, scale the bug so it appears to be going right.

3. Finally, run the appropriate animation action and kick off the sequence of move
    actions. The bug will perform the move, and then repeat `move()` indefinitely.

To start the bugs moving, go to **GameScene.swift**. In `createBugs()`, locate where you
add the bug to `bugsNode`:

```
bugsNode.addChild(bug)
```

After this line add the following:

```
bug.move()
```

Build and run, and your bugs should start wandering all over the place:

Physics categories

When the player collides with a bug, you need to remove the bug from the scene. As
you've learned in earlier chapters, you need to set up category bit masks to define which
contacts you want to listen for.

In **Types.swift**, add all the category bit masks you will need for the game:

```
struct PhysicsCategory {
  static let None:      UInt32 = 0
  static let All:       UInt32 = 0xFFFFFFFF
```

```
    static let Edge:      UInt32 = 0b1
    static let Player:    UInt32 = 0b10
    static let Bug:       UInt32 = 0b100
    static let Firebug:   UInt32 = 0b1000
    static let Breakable: UInt32 = 0b10000
}
```

You now have categories for the map edge, player, bug, firebug and a "breakable" category which you will use later.

In **Player.swift**, in init(), locate where you create the physics body. Just after that, add the following:

```
physicsBody?.categoryBitMask = PhysicsCategory.Player
physicsBody?.contactTestBitMask = PhysicsCategory.All
```

Your player now has the category of Player, and you'd like contact notifications for everything he hits.

Inside **Bug.swift**, find init() and locate where you create the physics body. Just after that, add the code below:

```
physicsBody?.categoryBitMask = PhysicsCategory.Bug
```

Your bugs now have a category of Bug.

> **Note:** There is no need to set the contactTestBitMask here. The only bug collisions you care about are ones with Arnie, and the contactTestBitMask of the player physics body already takes care of this.

Go to **GameScene.swift**. At the end of setupWorldPhysics(), add:

```
background.physicsBody?.categoryBitMask = PhysicsCategory.Edge

physicsWorld.contactDelegate = self
```

Here, you set the physics category of the map edge. You also set the game scene as the physics contact delegate to handle contact notifications.

At the end of **GameScene.swift**, after the class definition, add the extension:

```
extension GameScene : SKPhysicsContactDelegate {
}
```

Whenever there is contact between the player and a bug, you'll want to remove the bug from the scene.

In the `SKPhysicsContactDelegate` extension you just created, add this new method to `GameScene`:

```
func remove(bug: Bug) {
  bug.removeFromParent()
}
```

Add the physics contact delegate method:

```
func didBegin(_ contact: SKPhysicsContact) {
  let other = contact.bodyA.categoryBitMask
    == PhysicsCategory.Player ?
      contact.bodyB : contact.bodyA

  switch other.categoryBitMask {
  case PhysicsCategory.Bug:
    if let bug = other.node as? Bug {
      remove(bug: bug)
    }
  default:
    break
  }
}
```

Here, you check if `contact` is between the player and a bug. If so, remove the bug. You can refer back to Chapter 10, "Advanced Physics" to refresh your memory on the physics contact delegate methods.

Build and run the app and — at last — let Arnie loose on those bugs!

The bugs' demise is rather fast — it would be more dramatic with a lingering fade. In **Bug.swift**, add this method to Bug:

```
func die() {
  // 1
  removeAllActions()
  texture = SKTexture(pixelImageNamed: "bug_lt1")
  yScale = -1
  // 2
  physicsBody = nil
  // 3
  run(SKAction.sequence([SKAction.fadeOut(withDuration: 3),
                         SKAction.run(removeFromParent)]))
}
```

Here's how you're planning the demise of those bugs:

1. You remove all animations and make the bug lie on its back by reversing the sprite's yScale.

2. There's no need for a dead bug to participate in the physics simulation, so remove the physics body.

3. Run an action sequence to fade out and remove the bug from the scene.

To call this method, in **GameScene.swift**, locate this line in remove(bug:):

```
bug.removeFromParent()
```

Currently you simply remove the bug from its parent. To add the lingering fade, you could just replace this line by calling die().

However, later on you'll want to know the count of live bugs, and you can calculate this based on the number of children that bugsNode has. If you leave dead bugs parented by bugsNode, you won't be able to retrieve the correct number of live children.

So, instead of replacing the bug.removeFromParent() line, add these two lines right after:

```
background.addChild(bug)
bug.die()
```

You'll still remove the bug from its parent bugsNode, but then add it to background instead and call die(). The bug will be removed from background by the SKAction at the end of the die() sequence.

Build and run the app to see your bugs roll over and fade away when your hero squashes them.

Now that you're listening for contacts between the player and bugs, you can add a single line to make Arnie change direction when he bounces into something.

At the end of didBegin(_:) add:

```
if let physicsBody = player.physicsBody {
  if physicsBody.velocity.length() > 0 {
    player.checkDirection()
  }
}
```

When any contact notification occurs — and remember, you are only listening for contacts involving the player — you check the direction of the player to ensure Arnie is animating in the correct direction. If he's not moving at all, such as at the start of the game, do nothing.

Obstacles and physics

In the previous chapter's first challenge, you created an obstacles tile map node with walls on it.

You'll now access the obstacles node in code and create a physics body for the walls so Arnie can't just run over them in his haste to squish bugs.

In **GameScene.swift**, add a property to GameScene for the obstacles:

```
var obstaclesTileMap: SKTileMapNode?
```

obstaclesTileMap should be optional because some levels may not have obstacles.

Load up this property by adding this code at the end of init(coder:):

```
obstaclesTileMap = childNode(withName: "obstacles")
  as? SKTileMapNode
```

Add this new method to load up the physics bodies for the obstacles:

```
func setupObstaclePhysics() {
  guard let obstaclesTileMap = obstaclesTileMap else { return }
  // 1
  var physicsBodies = [SKPhysicsBody]()
  // 2
  for row in 0..<obstaclesTileMap.numberOfRows {
    for column in 0..<obstaclesTileMap.numberOfColumns {
      guard let tile = tile(in: obstaclesTileMap,
                        at: (column, row))
        else { continue }
      // 3
      let center = obstaclesTileMap
        .centerOfTile(atColumn: column, row: row)
      let body = SKPhysicsBody(rectangleOf: tile.size,
                              center: center)
      physicsBodies.append(body)
    }
  }
  // 4
  obstaclesTileMap.physicsBody =
    SKPhysicsBody(bodies: physicsBodies)
  obstaclesTileMap.physicsBody?.isDynamic = false
  obstaclesTileMap.physicsBody?.friction = 0
}
```

Reviewing each part:

1. Here you create an array to hold all the physics bodies.

2. You then cycle through all the rows and columns in the obstacles tile map node.

3. If a tile definition exists at the specified row–column, create a rectangular physics body of the same size as the tile. Add it to the physicsBodies array.

4. Create a physics body for the obstacles tile map node using physicsBodies. The separate physics bodies are compounded into a single physics body.

Call this new method at the end of didMove(to:):

```
setupObstaclePhysics()
```

In **GameViewController.swift** in `viewDidLoad()`, find the following lines:

```
view.showsFPS = true
view.showsNodeCount = true
```

After those lines, add:

```
view.showsPhysics = true
```

This will display thin green lines around physics bodies.

Build and run the app; pilot your hero around the map and he'll bounce off the walls, which also keep the marauding bugs at bay.

Tile user data

Remember the red firebug that isn't red any more? In this section, you'll restore the color to the bug and give it firebug super-powers.

If you remember when you created the bug tile group, you set some user data with key "firebug" to the firebug tile definition variant. You'll use this shortly.

First, create a new class for your firebug. This will be a simple `Bug` subclass.

Create a new **Swift File** in the **Characters** group and call it **Firebug.swift**.

Replace the code in **Firebug.swift** with the following:

```
import SpriteKit

class Firebug: Bug {

  required init?(coder aDecoder: NSCoder) {
    fatalError()
  }

  override init() {
```

```
    super.init()
    name = "Firebug"
    color = .red
    colorBlendFactor = 0.8
    physicsBody?.categoryBitMask = PhysicsCategory.Firebug
  }
}
```

Here you initialize a `Firebug` and give it a red tint. You'll have to kill this super-bug in a different way than just squashing it, so you also set its physics category to `Firebug`. You'll now be able to recognize a firebug during collisions.

Now, add a counter for the number of firebugs in the scene at the top of the `GameScene` class in **GameScene.swift**:

```
var firebugCount:Int = 0
```

You'll be killing the firebugs with specially formulated bug spray, so you need to know how many firebugs there are to give your hero enough super-bug spray.

Still in `GameScene`, locate `createBugs()`. In the `for` loop where you create the bug, *replace* this line:

```
let bug = Bug()
```

with the following:

```
let bug: Bug
if tile.userData?.object(forKey: "firebug") != nil {
  bug = Firebug()
  firebugCount += 1
} else {
  bug = Bug()
}
```

Here, you check the tile definition's user data. If there is a value for key `firebug`, create a firebug and increment the fire bug count. Otherwise create a normal bug.

Build and run the app. Firebugs are now red. And... they don't die! Arnie just bounces off them.

Looks like Arnie needs to pick up some of that super-bug spray — *stat*!

Creating tile maps in code

Games often have objects for the hero to pick up that give him extra abilities. For example, Mario turns into Fire Mario after picking up a Fire Flower. These are called power-ups; they might confer invincibility for a time or give the player extra speed or an extra life. In Pest Control, when Arnie picks up the bug spray, he'll be able to kill a firebug.

In this section you'll create a bug spray tile map node with randomly placed bug spray power-ups.

Up to now, you've been addressing existing tile maps in code and extracting data from them. In this section you'll create a tile map node entirely from scratch.

In **GameScene.swift** add a property for the bug spray tile map node to `GameScene`:

```
var bugsprayTileMap: SKTileMapNode?
```

When you created a tile set visually in the tile editor, you started by creating the tile set and working your way down to the tile definition. But when you create them in code, you work backwards: you create the tile definition first, and using that, build up to the tile set.

Add a new method to `GameScene`:

```
func createBugspray(quantity: Int) {
  // 1
  let tile = SKTileDefinition(texture:
    SKTexture(pixelImageNamed: "bugspray"))
  // 2
  let tilerule = SKTileGroupRule(adjacency:
    SKTileAdjacencyMask.adjacencyAll, tileDefinitions: [tile])
  // 3
  let tilegroup = SKTileGroup(rules: [tilerule])
  // 4
  let tileSet = SKTileSet(tileGroups: [tilegroup])
}
```

Straightforward code, so far:

1. Create the tile definition from the bug spray image.

2. Create the adjacency rule using the tile definition just created.

3. Create the tile group using the adjacency rule.

4. Create the tile set using the tile group.

Add this code to the end of createBugspray(quantity:):

```
// 5
let columns = background.numberOfColumns
let rows = background.numberOfRows
bugsprayTileMap = SKTileMapNode(tileSet: tileSet,
                                columns: columns,
                                rows: rows,
                                tileSize: tile.size)
// 6
for _ in 1...quantity {
  let column = Int.random(min: 0, max: columns-1)
  let row = Int.random(min: 0, max: rows-1)
  bugsprayTileMap?.setTileGroup(tilegroup,
    forColumn: column, row: row)
}
// 7
bugsprayTileMap?.name = "Bugspray"
addChild(bugsprayTileMap!)
```

Now, you populate the tile map as follows:

5. Create the bug spray tile map node using the new tile set. Make the bugsprayTileMap the same size as the background tile map node.

6. Place a tile randomly for each bug spray.

7. Name the bug spray node and add it to the scene.

Call this method from the end of didMove(to:):

```
if firebugCount > 0 {
  createBugspray(quantity: firebugCount + 10)
}
```

Here, you call the bug spray creation method, if there are any firebugs in the scene. If you create multiple levels at some point, you might save firebugs for more difficult levels.

Build and run the app and you'll see randomly placed bug spray all over the level:

You may see bug spray on top of walls where you can't pick them up due to the physics boundaries. You'll fix this later by getting Arnie to break down the wall to retrieve the bug spray.

Your next task is to get the player to pick up the bug spray when he runs over it.

Power-ups with tile maps

You won't be using physics contacts to detect when Arnie grabs the bug spray; instead, you'll determine if he runs over the tile containing the bug spray.

GameScene's update(_:) is performed each frame, so this is where you'll check the tile under the player's current position.

In **Player.swift**, add a property to determine whether the player is carrying bug spray:

```
var hasBugspray: Bool = false
```

Then, in **GameScene.swift**, add the following helper method:

```
func tileCoordinates(in tileMap: SKTileMapNode,
                     at position: CGPoint) -> TileCoordinates {
  let column = tileMap.tileColumnIndex(fromPosition: position)
  let row = tileMap.tileRowIndex(fromPosition: position)
  return (column, row)
}
```

This returns the row and column coordinates for a given position.

Still in GameScene, add the method below:

```
func updateBugspray() {
  guard let bugsprayTileMap = bugsprayTileMap else { return }
  let (column, row) = tileCoordinates(in: bugsprayTileMap,
                                      at: player.position)
  if tile(in: bugsprayTileMap, at: (column, row)) != nil {
    bugsprayTileMap.setTileGroup(nil, forColumn: column,
                                 row: row)
    player.hasBugspray = true
  }
}
```

Here you get the row and column for the player's position in the bug spray tile map. If the tile at this row and column is not `nil`, that means it has bug spray. Set the tile to `nil` and mark the player as having bug spray.

Next, override update(_:) with the following:

```
override func update(_ currentTime: TimeInterval) {
  if !player.hasBugspray {
    updateBugspray()
  }
}
```

In every frame, if the player is not already carrying bug spray, you call
updateBugspray() to check if the player is on a bug spray tile.

Build and run the app. When Arnie travels over the first bug spray, he'll pick it up and
ignore other bug sprays.

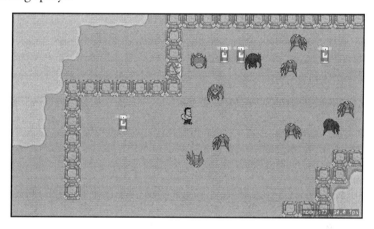

Visual cues

To let the user know if Arnie's already carrying bug spray, you're going to make him glow
green like the Hulk. You'll create an action to scale the player up and turn him flashing
green while he's carrying bug spray. Then those firebugs will have to run for their lives!

In **Player.swift**, add a new method to Player:

```
func blink(color: SKColor, on: Bool) {
  // 1
  let blinkOff = SKAction.colorize(withColorBlendFactor: 0.0,
                                   duration: 0.2)
  if on {
    // 2
    let blinkOn = SKAction.colorize(with: color,
                                    colorBlendFactor: 1.0,
                                    duration: 0.2)
    let blink = SKAction.repeatForever(SKAction.sequence(
      [blinkOn, blinkOff]))
    xScale = xScale < 0 ? -1.5 : 1.5
    yScale = 1.5
```

```
        run(blink, withKey: "blink")
    } else {
      // 3
      xScale = xScale < 0 ? -1.0 : 1.0
      yScale = 1.0
      removeAction(forKey: "blink")
      run(blinkOff)
    }
  }
}
```

This method takes in a color and a Boolean to turn the blinking on or off.

1. Create an action to reset the player to a clear color. You do this by setting the color blend factor to 0. The hero will still be colorized, but you can't see it. You'll always use this action regardless of whether you're turning the blink on or off.

2. If you're turning the blink on, create the color blend action with the appropriate color. The blink action will be a sequence of this color blend plus the clear color blend action you created in step 1. If the player is running right, xScale will be negative, so check xScale and scale accordingly. Run the action forever.

3. If you're turning the blink off, reset the player's scale, remove the blink action and then run the clear color action.

Still in **Player.swift**, change the property hasBugspray to:

```
var hasBugspray: Bool = false {
  didSet {
    blink(color: .green, on: hasBugspray)
  }
}
```

Whenever you set hasBugspray, the player will blink green if he has bug spray and return to normal if he doesn't.

Build and run the app to see Arnie grow and turn a menacing shade of green when he picks up a bug spray.

Those pesky firebugs still won't die though! You need some collision detection to make that happen.

In **GameScene.swift**, find GameScene's SKPhysicsContactDelegate extension and locate the switch statement in didBegin(_:).

Add a second case statement to check if the collision is with a firebug:

```
case PhysicsCategory.Firebug:
  if player.hasBugspray {
    if let firebug = other.node as? Firebug {
      remove(bug: firebug)
      player.hasBugspray = false
    }
  }
```

If the collision is with a firebug and the player is holding bug spray, you remove the firebug. By setting the player's hasBugspray property to false, you'll remove the green blinking action from the player.

Build and run the app; Arnie now leaves a buggy trail of destruction behind him!

Notice the bug spray only lasts for one firebug. Each time the player makes a kill, he'll have to resupply himself with bug spray to kill the next firebug.

Breakables

Arnie is a little frustrated that he can't get the bug spray on the walls. All he can do is bounce off the wall tile in vain:

But nothing, not even stone, should be able to resist Arnie's mighty force. You're going crack the wall when Arnie smashes into it, then disintegrate it into rubble.

You'll add new wall tiles and change the wall tile's user data to name the broken tile that will replace it. Most of the steps should already be familiar to you.

In **TileSets.sks** select the **Obstacles** tile set. Add two new **Single Tile Groups** named **wall-cracked** and **wall-broken**. Find the appropriate images in the Media Library and drag them to the tile slots.

Select the **wall** tile group and then the **wall** tile variant. In the Attributes Inspector, click the + under User Data and name the attribute "obstacle". Give it a Type of **Boolean** and a Value of **1** (true). When you come to create physics bodies later, you'll check this attribute.

In addition to this, each wall tile will hold a user data "breakable" attribute which will point to the next tile in the chain.

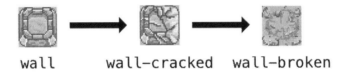

wall   wall-cracked   wall-broken

Add a second user data attribute named **breakable**. Make "breakable" a **String** with a Value of **wall-cracked**. This value is the name of the tile that will show when the wall is broken.

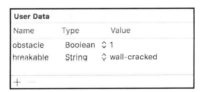

Select the **wall-cracked** tile variant under the tile group with the same name and add a user data attribute named **breakable**. Give it a Type of **String** and a Value of **wall-broken**. This tile will not need a physics body; you'll check the player's position instead of detecting contact.

Physics bodies for breakables

When Arnie crashes into a wall tile, you want to change the tile and remove the physics body from that tile. However, the obstacles tile map node's physics body is made up of a union of all the wall tiles' physics bodies, and it's impossible to remove just one wall physics body from this union.

So instead of creating one physics body, you'll modify GameScene's
setupObstaclePhysics() to create an SKNode with a physics body for each wall tile.
This sounds as if it would be inefficient, but in reality, you'll probably find even your
most complex levels will still run close to 60 frames per second.

Replace GameScene's setupObstaclePhysics() with the following:

```
func setupObstaclePhysics() {
  guard let obstaclesTileMap = obstaclesTileMap else { return }
  // 1
  for row in 0..<obstaclesTileMap.numberOfRows {
    for column in 0..<obstaclesTileMap.numberOfColumns {
      // 2
      guard let tile = tile(in: obstaclesTileMap,
                            at: (column, row))
        else { continue }
      guard tile.userData?.object(forKey: "obstacle") != nil
        else { continue }
      // 3
      let node = SKNode()
      node.physicsBody = SKPhysicsBody(rectangleOf: tile.size)
      node.physicsBody?.isDynamic = false
      node.physicsBody?.friction = 0
      node.physicsBody?.categoryBitMask =
        PhysicsCategory.Breakable

      node.position = obstaclesTileMap.centerOfTile(
        atColumn: column, row: row)
      obstaclesTileMap.addChild(node)
    }
  }
}
```

This code should be familiar to you by now:

1. Cycle through the tiles in the obstacles tile map node.

2. Test to see if a tile exists at the row–column. If it does, check if it is an "obstacle".

3. If the tile's user data has key obstacle, create an SKNode with a physics body at the
    tile's position. The node is simply used to hold the physics body, so a plain SKNode
    works fine. The physics body has the Breakable category and you only care about
    contact with the player.

Build and run and verify the green outlines are correct for the wall physics bodies. They
should not look any different than the obstacles tile map node's previous compound
physics body; however, because you have created an SKNode for each wall tile, the nodes
total at the bottom right of the screen has increased by the number of wall tiles you
painted. Mine increased from 47 to 98.

Breaking the breakables

When there is a contact between the player and a wall tile, you'll remove the wall SKNode, thereby removing the physics body. You'll also change the tile texture from `wall` to `wall-cracked`.

Add a new helper method to GameScene:

```
func tileGroupForName(tileSet: SKTileSet, name: String)
    -> SKTileGroup? {
  let tileGroup = tileSet.tileGroups
    .filter { $0.name == name }.first
  return tileGroup
}
```

This method returns a named tile group within a tile set. You'll use this method to replace the tile texture.

Add the following new method to GameScene:

```
func advanceBreakableTile(locatedAt nodePosition: CGPoint) {
  guard let obstaclesTileMap = obstaclesTileMap else { return }
  // 1
  let (column, row) = tileCoordinates(in: obstaclesTileMap,
                                      at: nodePosition)
  // 2
  let obstacle = tile(in: obstaclesTileMap,
                      at: (column, row))
  //3
  guard let nextTileGroupName =
      obstacle?.userData?.object(forKey: "breakable") as? String
    else { return }
  // 4
  if let nextTileGroup =
    tileGroupForName(tileSet: obstaclesTileMap.tileSet,
```

```
                    name: nextTileGroupName) {
    obstaclesTileMap.setTileGroup(nextTileGroup,
       forColumn: column, row: row)
  }
}
```

Stepping through the method:

1. Get the tile's row and column from the supplied position.

2. Retrieve the tile definition located at that row and column.

3. Get the value for key `breakable` from the obstacle's user data; the obstacle will change to this named tile group.

4. Use the helper method to get the tile group with that name. Set the tile group for the obstacle to this new tile group.

Locate the `switch` statement in `didBegin(_:)`.

Add a third `case` statement to check if the contact is with an obstacle:

```
case PhysicsCategory.Breakable:
    if let obstacleNode = other.node {
       // 1
       advanceBreakableTile(locatedAt: obstacleNode.position)
       // 2
       obstacleNode.removeFromParent()
    }
```

With this code, you do the following:

1. If the node is for a "breakable" obstacle, advance it to its next tile group. The **wall** tile will change to the **wall-cracked** tile here.

2. Remove the `SKNode` from its parent. This will also remove the physics body, so the player will no longer bounce off the obstacle and contact notifications will stop for this obstacle.

Replacing tile textures

Now that the wall physics body has been removed, you'll need to check the player's position in `update(_:)` to know when he crashes into the wall again.

Add this code to the end of `update(_:)`:

```
advanceBreakableTile(locatedAt: player.position)
```

If Arnie is running over a "breakable" obstacle, that means the obstacle does not have a physics body and the tile group should be replaced. For example, the **wall-cracked** tile will be replaced with the **wall-broken** tile.

Build and run the app, and the first time Arnie crashes into a wall tile, he rebounds. But if you look carefully, the physics body outline is no longer there, indicating the SKNode has been removed, and the tile texture is now cracked.

When Arnie hits the wall again, he bursts straight through and the tile changes from cracked to broken.

Challenge: Add a breakable tree

You've created a breakable wall, but the map would be more interesting with more objects. In this challenge you'll add breakable trees to the obstacles tile map node.

When Arnie collides with a tree, the tree should disintegrate and leave a stump. The process will be similar to what you did for the wall tiles:

1. Add two new tile groups to your **Obstacles** tile set in **TileSet.sks**: one with a tree tile and one with a tree-stump tile, using the appropriate images in the Media Library. Name them **tree** and **tree-stump**, respectively.

2. Add a "breakable" attribute to the User Data of the tree tile variant to mark it as a breakable. Make "breakable" a String and set "tree-stump" as the Value.

3. In **GameScene.sks** paint the tree tiles on the obstacles layer. Because the obstacles layer is not the top layer, you'll have to enter the tile painter via **Editor > Edit Tile Map**.

You've already written the code that handles the "breakable" attribute. All you need to do now is run the app, and Arnie will tear through trees, leaving nothing but a stump.

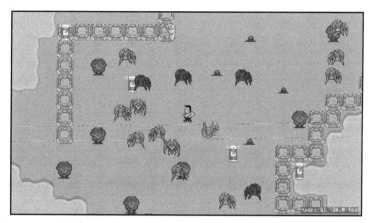

Congratulations — you almost have a complete game! Arnie squashes bugs with abandon, collects bug spray power-ups and crashes through obstacles.

But what if, amidst all the action, you get an inconvenient phone call? You'll lose all that bug-killing goodness!

In the next chapter you'll auto-save your game so you can resume it from where you were interrupted. You'll also add a timer, making the game more challenging.

Chapter 14: Saving and Loading Games
By Caroline Begbie

In the previous two chapters, you learned how to easily create game levels with the tile map editor for your epic bug-squashing game where tough guy Arnie chases down vicious marauding insects.

In this chapter, you'll improve Pest Control by adding new levels and a time challenge so that you can win or lose the game. You'll also learn how to save your progress when you leave the game — and restore it when you return.

This is what your app will look like at the end of this chapter:

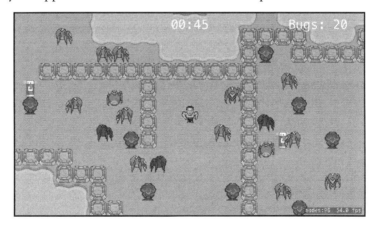

Note: The starter project for this chapter has an extra three levels already built for you. You can continue using your existing project, but if you do, you'll have to create your own three levels later.

Head-up display

You'll need a user interface component to tell the player how much time she has left in the level and whether she's won or lost.

This user interface is often called the head-up display, or HUD. This term came from military aviation, where the aircraft's instruments are projected up near the windscreen so the pilot doesn't have to lower their head to view the readings in-flight.

Control-click **GameScene.swift** and create a new **Swift File** called **HUD.swift**. Replace the contents of **HUD.swift** with this code:

```
import SpriteKit

class HUD: SKNode {

  override init() {
    super.init()
    name = "HUD"
  }

  required init?(coder aDecoder: NSCoder) {
    super.init(coder: aDecoder)
  }
}
```

Here, you declare HUD as a subclass of SKNode and set name in the default initializer.

At the top of **HUD.swift**, before the class definition, add the HUD constants:

```
enum HUDSettings {
  static let font = "Noteworthy-Bold"
  static let fontSize: CGFloat = 50
}
```

You can easily tweak the font and the font size here. Next, add the following new method to HUD:

```
func add(message: String, position: CGPoint,
         fontSize: CGFloat = HUDSettings.fontSize) {
  let label: SKLabelNode
  label = SKLabelNode(fontNamed: HUDSettings.font)
  label.text = message
  label.name = message
  label.zPosition = 100
  addChild(label)
  label.fontSize = fontSize
  label.position = position
}
```

This will display a generic message in the HUD. The high `zPosition` of the label ensures that these messages are on top of all the other nodes.

In **GameScene.swift**, add a property to `GameScene` for the HUD node:

```
var hud = HUD()
```

Then, add a new method to `GameScene` to set up the HUD:

```
func setupHUD() {
  camera?.addChild(hud)
  hud.add(message: "Howdy", position: .zero)
}
```

Because you want the HUD to stay in the same position on the screen, even as the camera moves to different areas of the map, you add it as a child of the camera instead of the scene. You also add a test message positioned at (0, 0) — the center of the camera.

Call this method at the end of `didMove(to:)`:

```
setupHUD()
```

Build and run your game, and it will welcome you:

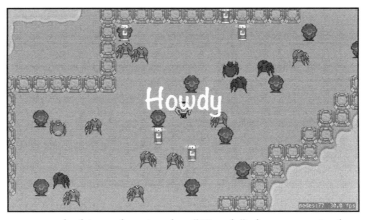

Make Arnie run around a bit, and notice that "Howdy" always stays in the center of the screen.

> **Note:** The label actually displays just above the center of the screen. This is because the default `verticalAlignmentMode` of a label is `baseline`. See Chapter 6, "Labels" for a review of label alignments.

Game timers

Arnie is becoming a little relaxed about the time he's taking to kill all these bugs. To make things interesting, you'll introduce a level timer to really get him moving. This timer will be displayed on the HUD.

First, get rid of the "Howdy" test message. Remove this line from the end of setupHUD():

```
hud.add(message: "Howdy", position: .zero)
```

Then, add a time limit property to GameScene:

```
var timeLimit: Int = 10
```

You're storing this as a variable rather than a constant because later you'll work with multiple levels, and each level will have a different time limit. In the first level, you're giving Arnie ten seconds to get rid of all those bugs!

Next, in **HUD.swift** add a new label property to HUD:

```
var timerLabel: SKLabelNode?
```

This is one message you'll want to keep a handle to, as you will be updating the time every frame.

Still in HUD, add a new method to update the timer label:

```
func updateTimer(time: Int) {
  let minutes = (time/60) % 60
  let seconds = time % 60
  let timeText = String(format: "%02d:%02d", minutes, seconds)
  timerLabel?.text = timeText
}
```

Here, you calculate the minutes and seconds from the given time and format the text for the label.

Add a new method to HUD to initialize the timer label:

```
func addTimer(time: Int) {
  guard let scene = scene else { return }
  // 1
  let position = CGPoint(x: 0,
                         y: scene.frame.size.height/2 - 10)
  add(message: "Timer", position: position, fontSize: 24)
  // 2
```

```
    timerLabel = childNode(withName: "Timer") as? SKLabelNode
    timerLabel?.verticalAlignmentMode = .top
    timerLabel?.fontName = "Menlo"
    updateTimer(time: time)
  }
```

Going over the code:

1. Here, you create the timer label just like any other message, positioning it at the top of the screen.

2. You then change properties to customize the look of the timer and update the time to the given start value.

Calculating the time

Back in **GameScene.swift**, add two properties to GameScene to store the passing time:

```
var elapsedTime: Int = 0
var startTime: Int?
```

Set up the HUD's timer at the end of setupHUD():

```
hud.addTimer(time: timeLimit)
```

Still in GameScene, add the following new method to update the HUD's timer:

```
func updateHUD(currentTime: TimeInterval) {
  // 1
  if let startTime = startTime {
    // 2
    elapsedTime = Int(currentTime) - startTime
  } else {
    // 3
    startTime = Int(currentTime) - elapsedTime
  }
  // 4
  hud.updateTimer(time: timeLimit - elapsedTime)
}
```

Taking each numbered comment in turn:

1. Here, you check to see if startTime has been instantiated; if startTime is nil, it means that the game has not started yet.

2. If the game has started, calculate the elapsed time from the game's current time less the start time.

3. If `startTime` is `nil`, instantiate it using the game's current time less elapsed time. At the start of the scene, `elapsedTime` is zero, but later on, when you reload saved scenes `elapsedTime` will be restored from that save.

4. Update the HUD with the time left for bug-killing.

Call this method from the end of `update(_:)`:

```
updateHUD(currentTime: currentTime)
```

`update(_:)` is called every frame, so this is where you want to recalculate the elapsed time and update the HUD timer.

Build and run to see the seconds ticking down. Great! But once the timer reaches zero, it keeps going....

Winning the game

All good games have a lose condition and, more importantly, a win condition. In this section, you'll add the ability to win or lose the game. Finally!

Add this new method to `GameScene`:

```
func checkEndGame() {
  if bugsNode.children.count == 0 {
    print("* YOU WON!!!")
  } else if timeLimit - elapsedTime <= 0 {
    print("* YOU LOST :(")
  }
}
```

The win condition is met when there are no more bugs left to kill. You added all the bugs to `bugsNode`, so you only need to check whether it has children or not.

The lose condition is met when Arnie has run out of time.

Call this method at the end of `update(_:)`:

```
checkEndGame()
```

Here, in every frame you check whether you've won or lost.

Build and run and wait ten seconds to lose the game for the very first time. You'll see the output in the debug console.

To win the game, squash all those bugs before the timer is up! If you didn't use the starter project for this chapter, you may want to paint fewer bugs in **GameScene.sks** to be able to win.

```
* YOU LOST :(
* YOU LOST :(
* YOU LOST :(
* YOU LOST :(
* YOU LOST :(
* YOU LOST :(
* YOU LOST :(
* YOU LOST :(
* YOU LOST :(
* YOU LOST :(
```

Game state management

Now that Pest Control is becoming a fully-fledged game, there are various game conditions that you'll have to handle:

- Initial run of the game
- Level start
- Currently playing the game
- Player has won
- Player has lost
- Game progress is paused
- Game can reload from a saved state

By knowing what "state" the game is in, you can handle user interactions accordingly. For example, you know at the start of the game that everything should be paused. A tap should start the game. Whereas if you're actually playing the game, a tap should move the player.

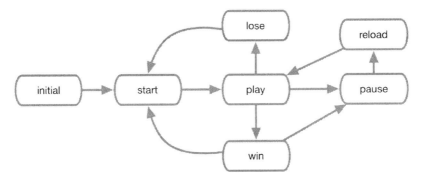

This diagram shows all the game states that are possible in Pest Control and how they lead to one another. You can't go straight from `start` to `win`, for example. The game has to go through the `play` state first.

State machines, as they are called, can get complex, and GameplayKit provides `GKStateMachine` to deal with them. However, in this game, the states are fairly simple, and you will keep track of them with a single property and an enum.

Add this to **Types.swift**:

```
enum GameState: Int {
  case initial=0, start, play, win, lose, reload, pause
}
```

Each of the game states will require a different message in the user interface. At the top of **HUD.swift**, before defining `HUD`, add message constants for all the necessary messages:

```
enum HUDMessages {
  static let tapToStart = "Tap to Start"
  static let win = "You Win!"
  static let lose = "Out of Time!"
  static let nextLevel = "Tap for Next Level"
  static let playAgain = "Tap to Play Again"
  static let reload = "Continue Previous Game?"
  static let yes = "Yes"
  static let no = "No"
}
```

Whenever the game state changes, you will need to update the HUD messages correspondingly. Add the following methods to `HUD`:

```
func updateGameState(from: GameState, to: GameState) {
  clearUI(gameState: from)
  updateUI(gameState: to)
```

```
  }

  private func updateUI(gameState: GameState) {
    // add messages for the new state
  }

  private func clearUI(gameState: GameState) {
    // clear previous state messages
  }

  private func remove(message: String) {
    childNode(withName: message)?.removeFromParent()
  }
```

These methods will keep the user interface in sync with the game state. Before updating the UI with the current state's messages, you'll clear out the previous state's messages. You'll flesh out these methods as you go through the chapter.

In **GameScene.swift**, add the game state property to GameScene:

```
var gameState: GameState = .initial {
  didSet {
    hud.updateGameState(from: oldValue, to: gameState)
  }
}
```

Placing an observer on gameState lets you update the user interface with the appropriate message whenever the state changes.

In HUD, add the following code to updateUI(gameState:):

```
switch gameState {
case .win:
  add(message: HUDMessages.win, position: .zero)
  add(message: HUDMessages.nextLevel,
      position: CGPoint(x: 0, y: -100))
case .lose:
  add(message: HUDMessages.lose, position: .zero)
  add(message: HUDMessages.playAgain,
      position: CGPoint(x: 0, y: -100))
default:
  break
}
```

And add this to clearUI(gameState:):

```
switch gameState {
case .win:
  remove(message: HUDMessages.win)
  remove(message: HUDMessages.nextLevel)
```

```
case .lose:
  remove(message: HUDMessages.lose)
  remove(message: HUDMessages.playAgain)
default:
  break
}
```

For the moment, you're simply handling win and lose states by displaying or removing messages as appropriate.

In GameScene in checkEndGame(), change the winning condition code:

```
print("* YOU WON!!!")
```

to:

```
player.physicsBody?.linearDamping = 1
gameState = .win
```

And change the losing condition code:

```
print("* YOU LOST :(")
```

to:

```
player.physicsBody?.linearDamping = 1
gameState = .lose
```

gameState has the property observer, which will handle displaying the appropriate messages. Setting linearDamping to 1 brings Arnie to a halt at the end of the level.

Build and run the game and test out both the winning and losing states. Currently you can still win after losing the game, but you'll fix that up shortly. No cheating for Arnie!

Starting the game

Currently the bugs start moving immediately when you start the game, without waiting for you to say you're ready.

You'll now set up the start game state where the whole game pauses until the user taps the screen.

First, update the user interface. In HUD, add this to the switch statement in updateUI(gameState:):

```
case .start:
  add(message: HUDMessages.tapToStart, position: .zero)
```

And add this to the switch statement in clearUI(gameState:):

```
case .start:
  remove(message: HUDMessages.tapToStart)
```

That handles displaying and removing the "Tap to Start" message.

In GameScene, at the end of didMove(to:), set the game state:

```
gameState = .start
```

Again, by setting gameState you will automatically update the HUD.

Add this code to the start of update(_:):

```
if gameState != .play  {
  isPaused = true
  return
}
```

Whenever the game state is not set to play, the scene's isPaused should be true. This will stop any actions running on nodes; additionally, the scene will not call update(_:) any more and Arnie won't be able to cheat by squash bugs after the timer has run out.

Next, replace touchesBegan(_:with:) with this code:

```
override func touchesBegan(_ touches: Set<UITouch>,
                           with event: UIEvent?) {
  guard let touch = touches.first else { return }
  switch gameState {
  // 1
  case .start:
    gameState = .play
    isPaused = false
    startTime = nil
```

```
    elapsedTime = 0
// 2
case .play:
    player.move(target: touch.location(in: self))
default:
    break
  }
}
```

This code is relatively straightforward:

1. If `gameState` is `start`, you move to the next game state `play` and unpause the scene. You also initialize `startTime` and `elapsedTime` to ensure the timer is in its initial state.

2. When `gameState` is `play`, you move the player by tapping just as before.

Build and run, and now you can get in the proper bug-bashing mentality before you start the game!

Changing levels

You now have a user interface to start the game, and tell you when you have won or lost. But playing one level can get tedious. it's time to move on to harder levels.

> **Note:** If you didn't use the starter project for this chapter, you'll need to create your own new levels called **Level1.sks**, **Level2.sks** and **Level3.sks**. To avoid reconfiguring the whole scene, duplicate **GameScene.sks** three times and repaint all the tile map nodes. Feel free to use your imagination! :]

I chose not to have firebugs in Level 1, but instead introduced them in Level 2. In Level 3 I built a lot of walls that Arnie has to break through to be able to kill the bugs.

  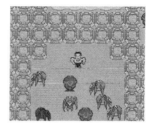

In **GameViewController.swift**, change:

```
if let scene = SKScene(fileNamed: "GameScene") {
```

to

```
if let scene = SKScene(fileNamed: "Level1") {
```

This will load **Level 1** instead of the **GameScene.sks** scene.

In **GameScene.swift**, add the following property to `GameScene`:

```
var currentLevel: Int = 1
```

This property will always contain the current level of the game.

Still in `GameScene`, create this new method:

```
func transitionToScene(level: Int) {
  // 1
  guard let newScene = SKScene(fileNamed: "Level\(level)")
      as? GameScene else {
    fatalError("Level: \(level) not found")
  }
  // 2
  newScene.currentLevel = level
  view!.presentScene(newScene,
    transition: SKTransition.flipVertical(withDuration: 0.5))
}
```

Here's what's going on in the code above:

1. You check that the scene for the new level exists. As you only have 3 levels, your game will currently crash when you try to go to Level 4.

2. You set the `currentLevel` property on the new scene and present the level with a flip vertical transition.

Next, in touchesBegan(_:with:), add two new cases to the switch statement:

```
case .win:
  transitionToScene(level: currentLevel + 1)
case .lose:
  transitionToScene(level: 1)
```

Here, you'll transition to the correct level. That will be the next level, if Arnie's good enough to win; otherwise, you'll restart the game from the beginning. For testing purposes, you can choose to transition to currentLevel instead of Level 1 when you lose.

Build and run and when you win Level 1 you'll be able to tap the screen to continue. Level 2 will load and wait for your tap to begin. Betcha can't win Level 2 in 10 seconds! :]

Scene user data

You've hard-coded ten seconds for each level, and you're probably frustrated at not being able to win Level 2. To overcome this, you can attach a unique time limit to each level.

Open **Level1.sks**.

With **Scene** selected in the scene navigator, open the Attributes Inspector and click the + under **User Data**. Name the property timeLimit and give it a Type of **Integer** with a Value of **12**. This value will be the number of seconds to complete the level.

Press **Command-S** to save the scene.

Repeat these steps for the other level scene files, changing the time limit as follows:

- **Level2.sks**: 45 seconds

- **Level3.sks**: 90 seconds

Then, in **GameScene.swift**, add this to the end of init(coder:):

```
if let timeLimit =
    userData?.object(forKey: "timeLimit") as? Int {
  self.timeLimit = timeLimit
}
```

Here, you load the time limit from the level scene instead of hard-coding it.

Build and run the app. Notice that the timer for Level 1 now starts at 12, and the time limits for the other two levels should be generous enough for you to beat all of them. (If not, feel free to adjust.)

Your game is finally complete! You have several levels, you have the skills to build plenty more and you can win and lose the game. But what happens when you get to Level 43, and you get a call from a co-worker because you're late for an important meeting? Are you going to lose all your progress? The rest of this chapter will show you how to overcome annoying interruptions by saving your game.

Opening and closing the app

You'll have to handle temporary interruptions like as a phone call, and more permanent ones such as the user leaving the game by pressing the Home button or closing the app. The app should recover the game when the user returns.

In summary, the different cases to handle are:

- **App launch**: If there is a saved game, load it.

- **Temporary interruption**: Pause the game and resume when the user returns.

- **Leaving the app**: Save the game.

Just as your game has states, so does your app. All the three situations above result in an app state change and you can handle these changes in two ways:

1. `AppDelegate` has delegate methods such as `application(_:didFinishLaunchingWithOptions:)`.

2. The system also broadcasts app state change notifications that you can observe. This is the method you'll use in Pest Control.

Observing notifications

You'll first deal with the temporary interruption. You actually don't need to save the game to disk in this case, because even though the app loses focus and becomes inactive, it still continues to run.

When a phone call comes through, the app broadcasts a `UIApplicationWillResignActive` notification. Here you can pause the game.

The observer for `UIApplicationDidBecomeActive` can then detect whether the game is paused or a new game and handle accordingly.

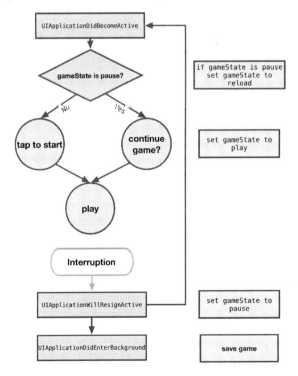

When the user presses the Home button, the app broadcasts
`UIApplicationWillResignActive` followed by
`UIApplicationDidEnterBackground`, where you'll want to save the game to disk when
the app enters the background.

For the moment though, you can test pause and resume for temporary interruptions by
pressing the Home button, as you can't simulate a phone call on the simulator.

Time for some code. Add a new extension to the end of **GameScene.swift** to separate
out the notification code:

```
// MARK: - Notifications
extension GameScene {
}
```

Add these methods to print out to the debug console:

```
func applicationDidBecomeActive() {
  print("* applicationDidBecomeActive")
}

func applicationWillResignActive() {
  print("* applicationWillResignActive")
}

func applicationDidEnterBackground() {
  print("* applicationDidEnterBackground")
}
```

Then add:

```
func addObservers() {
  NotificationCenter.default.addObserver(self,
    selector: #selector(applicationDidBecomeActive),
    name: .UIApplicationDidBecomeActive, object: nil)
  NotificationCenter.default.addObserver(self,
    selector: #selector(applicationWillResignActive),
    name: .UIApplicationWillResignActive, object: nil)
  NotificationCenter.default.addObserver(self,
    selector: #selector(applicationDidEnterBackground),
    name: .UIApplicationDidEnterBackground, object: nil)
}
```

This method will configure `GameScene` to observe the app state change notifications and
call the appropriate method. Call `addObservers()` at the end of `init(coder:)`:

```
addObservers()
```

Your app will now observe these three notifications. However, when you add observers, you must remember to remove them when the observer object is deallocated. Add the following deinitializer to GameScene:

```
deinit {
  NotificationCenter.default.removeObserver(self)
}
```

> **Note:** If your app targets iOS 9 or later, then you don't need to explicitly unregister observers when the observers are deallocated. But it doesn't hurt!

Build and run on the simulator. The system broadcasts UIApplicationDidBecomeActive when the app first starts. Tap to start the game and then select **Hardware > Home** or press **Command-Shift-H** to leave the app.

UIApplicationWillResignActive will fire first, quickly followed by UIApplicationDidEnterBackground. The appropriate messages appear in the debug console.

```
* applicationDidBecomeActive
* applicationWillResignActive
* applicationDidEnterBackground
```

However, the game continues, even though the app is in the background. Open the app again after 12 seconds have passed and you'll have lost your game even though you weren't playing it. Unfair!

You can fix this. Add the following to `applicationWillResignActive()`:

```
isPaused = true
if gameState != .lose {
  gameState = .pause
}
```

Here, you pause the game when it loses focus. By changing `gameState` to `pause`, you'll clear all messages from the HUD and be able to respond appropriately when the app becomes active again.

Next, add this to `applicationDidBecomeActive()`:

```
if gameState == .pause {
  gameState = .reload
}
```

If a game is in progress when the app becomes inactive, you'll ask the user whether she wants to continue playing the previous game instead of diving straight into killing bugs.

In **HUD.swift**, add this to the `switch` statement in `updateUI(gameState:)`:

```
case .reload:
  add(message: HUDMessages.reload, position: .zero,
      fontSize: 40)
  add(message: HUDMessages.yes,
      position: CGPoint(x: -140, y: -100))
  add(message: HUDMessages.no,
      position: CGPoint(x: 130, y: -100))
```

And add this code to the `switch` statement in `clearUI(gameState:)`:

```
case .reload:
  remove(message: HUDMessages.reload)
  remove(message: HUDMessages.yes)
  remove(message: HUDMessages.no)
```

Here, you use HUD messages to prompt the user if they want to continue the previous game.

In `GameScene`, add this to the `switch` statement in `touchesBegan(_:with:)`:

```
case .reload:
  // 1
  if let touchedNode =
      atPoint(touch.location(in: self)) as? SKLabelNode {
    // 2
    if touchedNode.name == HUDMessages.yes {
      isPaused = false
```

```
    startTime = nil
    gameState = .play
    // 3
  } else if touchedNode.name == HUDMessages.no {
    transitionToScene(level: 1)
  }
}
```

Going over this code:

1. Check if the touched node is a label.

2. If the user taps "Yes" to continue the game, change the game state to play. You reset startTime so you can continue the timer without including all the time that the game was paused.

3. If the user taps "No", start the game from Level 1.

Build and run again and start the game. At that point, the gameState is play. Select **Hardware > Home**. gameState is now pause.

Return to the application; the game state will go from pause to reload and you'll get the "Continue Previous Game?" message. You can choose "Yes" to continue the game or "No" to start a new one.

Saving games with NSCoding

You've taken care of a temporary interruption to the game. But if the app goes to the background — for example, by pressing the Home button — the system may terminate the app at any time. If this happens (or the user simply quits the app), you'll lose all the game states and the app will start from the beginning. You can verify that this happens by doing a build and run, stopping the app in Xcode and opening it again.

There are several ways you can save data permanently. For saving simple data such as high scores, you could save to disk using NSUserDefaults. You'll use NSUserDefaults in Chapter 23, "ReplayKit". At the other extreme, if you have a complex game structure with lots of data, you'll want to look into Core Data.

Pest Control only needs to persist the state of the game at a particular time. NSCoding is perfect for this.

NSCoding is a protocol for archiving object graphs such as your game scene. You define what you want encoded and then, using NSKeyedArchiver, a subclass of NSCoder, you can archive GameScene along with the whole hierarchy of SKNodes attached to it. You can choose to archive custom properties too.

Most Apple classes already conform to NSCoding, and you'll take advantage of this to easily store your game scene and current game state.

In **GameScene.swift**, add a new extension to GameScene to separate out all the saving and loading game methods that you will create:

```
// MARK: - Saving Games
extension GameScene {
}
```

Saving to disk

Whenever you store files to disk, you have to decide whether the user needs to have access to them. These are the available directories on the iPhone with their appropriate usage:

- **Documents**: Can be shared with the user via iTunes sharing.
- **Library**: Hidden from the user, but is backed up whenever the iPhone is backed up.
- **Caches**: For cached files that can easily be re-created. The system might delete this to free up space.
- **tmp**: Only for temporary data. Delete these files as soon as they are not needed any more. This directory is not backed up and can be emptied by the system at any time.

In Pest Control, the saved game shouldn't be deleted by the system, but the user doesn't need access to it outside of the app. So you'll save the game to the app's **Library** directory.

Add this new method to GameScene's **Saving Games** extension:

```
func saveGame() {
  // 1
  let fileManager = FileManager.default
```

```
  guard let directory =
    fileManager.urls(for: .libraryDirectory,
                    in: .userDomainMask).first
    else { return }
  // 2
  let saveURL = directory.appendingPathComponent("SavedGames")
  // 3
  do {
    try fileManager.createDirectory(atPath: saveURL.path,
      withIntermediateDirectories: true,
      attributes: nil)
  } catch let error as NSError {
    fatalError(
      "Failed to create directory: \(error.debugDescription)")
  }
  // 4
  let fileURL = saveURL.appendingPathComponent("saved-game")
  print("* Saving: \(fileURL.path)")
  // 5
  NSKeyedArchiver.archiveRootObject(self, toFile: fileURL.path)
}
```

Taking it comment-by-comment:

1. Here, you retrieve the app's Library directory by interacting with the file system using the singleton `FileManager`.

2. Next, you set up the directory URL for the new file.

3. Creating directories can fail for any number of reasons; for example, the file system may be full. Enclosing this in a `try...catch` allows you to catch and display any errors that occur. This won't fail if the directory already exists.

4. Then you set up the final path for the new file. Printing the name of the file is useful so that you can later locate it in the file system.

5. Finally, you archive the scene into the file. `NSKeyedArchiver` starts at the scene level and serializes every node in the scene object graph.

You only want to save the game if the game can be won. Add this to the end of `applicationDidEnterBackground()`:

```
if gameState != .lose {
  saveGame()
}
```

If the player has already lost, you'll start the game from the beginning when she re-enters the app.

Build and run the app on the simulator, tap to start, and press **Command-Shift-H** before losing the game.

You should see something like this in the debug console:

```
* applicationDidBecomeActive
* applicationWillResignActive
* applicationDidEnterBackground
* Saving: /Users/caroline/Library/Developer/CoreSimulator/Devices/
11B18709-4041-415C-86EB-0C6E77B8BC8D/data/Containers/Data/Application/
50ABD0B3-233D-47B3-87C5-B4051B91B10B/Library/SavedGames/saved-game
```

> **Note:** You may see an error message in the console that says `SKAction: Run block actions can not be properly encoded`. You'll fix this later.

You can use **Finder** to locate the directory listed in the debug console. Highlight from `/ Users` to `Application/[UUID]` — in this case, the UUID is `50ABD0B3-23...B10B` — and press **Command-C** to copy the directory path. In Finder, select **Go > Go To Folder...** and paste the directory path.

Here, you will see the app's **Documents**, **Library** and **tmp** directory.

Select the Library directory and your SavedGames directory. The file **saved-game** you just wrote should be in this directory. At this point, my file is 42KB.

Drag the UUID-named directory to your Finder sidebar for quick access. You'll be able to jump straight to the app's directory and delete the **SavedGames** directory when you want to do further testing.

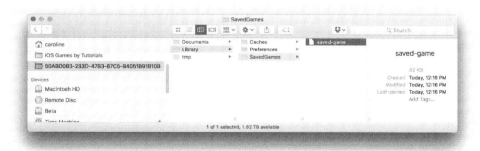

Override encode(with:)

As you've seen, it's very easy to serialize a SKScene with all its child nodes. However, currently none of GameScene's properties are being archived.

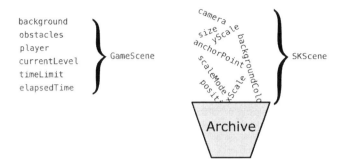

NSCoding has two methods:

- encode(with:): Serializes data

- init(coder:): Restores serialized data

SKScene conforms to NSCoding and implements encode(with:), but GameScene does not; therefore GameScene's properties aren't archived. You will need to override encode(with:) and archive the extra properties for all your custom classes: GameScene, Player and Bug.

Not all properties have to be archived though; you can recreate some properties when the scene starts up. For example, because SKScene archives the whole hierarchy of nodes, you don't have to explicitly archive the HUD's timer label — you just need to set the property to the appropriate node in init(coder:). You'll do this a bit later.

Override encode(with:) in GameScene's **Saving Games** extension:

```
override func encode(with aCoder: NSCoder) {
  aCoder.encode(firebugCount,
                forKey: "Scene.firebugCount")
  aCoder.encode(elapsedTime,
                forKey: "Scene.elapsedTime")
  aCoder.encode(gameState.rawValue,
                forKey: "Scene.gameState")
  aCoder.encode(currentLevel,
                forKey: "Scene.currentLevel")
  super.encode(with: aCoder)
}
```

This will archive these four specified properties from GameScene. You assign each property a unique key you can use to read it back in init(coder:). This key can be any string.

Similarly, you should override encode(with:) in your other custom classes. Add this to Player:

```
override func encode(with aCoder: NSCoder) {
  aCoder.encode(hasBugspray, forKey: "Player.hasBugspray")
  aCoder.encode(animations, forKey: "Player.animations")
  super.encode(with: aCoder)
}
```

And add this to Bug:

```
override func encode(with aCoder: NSCoder) {
  aCoder.encode(animations, forKey: "Bug.animations")
  super.encode(with: aCoder)
}
```

The custom classes Firebug and HUD have no extra properties, so they don't need to override encode(with:).

Build and run the app, tap to start the app and press **Command-Shift-H** to move the app to the background before you lose.

You shouldn't notice any difference in the output in the debug console, but if you look at your **saved-game** file, it should be bigger because it's saving more items. My file is now 54KB.

Loading the game

When the app first launches, GameViewController is responsible for presenting the first scene. If there's a saved game, then GameViewController should present the saved game instead of **Level1.sks**.

You'll create a factory method in GameScene to load a saved game if it exists. In the **Saving Games** extension in GameScene, add this new method:

```
class func loadGame() -> SKScene? {
  print("* loading game")
  var scene: SKScene?
  // 1
  let fileManager = FileManager.default
  guard let directory =
    fileManager.urls(for: .libraryDirectory,
                     in: .userDomainMask).first
    else { return nil }
  // 2
  let url = directory.appendingPathComponent(
```

```
     "SavedGames/saved-game")
   // 3
   if FileManager.default.fileExists(atPath: url.path) {
     scene = NSKeyedUnarchiver.unarchiveObject(
       withFile: url.path) as? GameScene
     _ = try? fileManager.removeItem(at: url)
   }
   return scene
 }
```

This is a type method that loads and returns a scene from the **saved-game** file. Step-by-step:

1. Get the **Library** directory.

2. Create the URL for the saved game.

3. If a saved game exists, unarchive the scene from the game file. After unarchiving, delete the saved file.

In **GameViewController.swift**, in viewDidLoad(), change this line:

```
   if let scene = SKScene(fileNamed: "Level1") {
```

to the following:

```
   if let scene = GameScene.loadGame()
             ?? SKScene(fileNamed: "Level1") as? GameScene {
```

Here, you try to load the scene from a saved game. If there isn't a saved game, load **Level1.sks**.

Build and run the app. The print message * loading game appears in the debug console, but the app crashes with a fatal error in init(coder:) in either Player or Bug.

```
         required init?(coder aDecoder: NSCoder) {
   ▶      fatalError("Use init()")
         }
```

Remember that init(coder:) is the other half of NSCoding. NSKeyedUnarchiver.unarchiveObject(withFile:) invokes init(coder:) to deserialize the properties that you archived with NSKeyedArchiver in encode(with:). For each of the classes that you archived, you'll now need to implement init(coder:) to unarchive them.

You already have an implementation of init(coder:) in GameScene. When there's no saved game, GameViewController loads the game scene with SKScene(fileNamed: "Level1").

This is a convenience initializer that calls GameScene's init(coder:) to unarchive **Level1.sks**.

When there is a saved game, NSKeyedUnarchiver calls that same init(coder:).

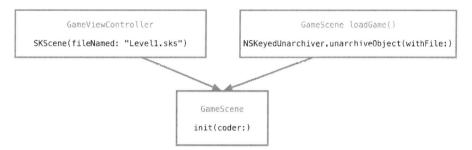

By checking whether aDecoder contains a gameState property set to pause, you can tell whether init(coder:) is loading **Level1.sks** or your saved game.

In GameScene, add this to init(coder:) just before calling addObservers():

```
// 1
let savedGameState = aDecoder.decodeInteger(
  forKey: "Scene.gameState")
if let gameState = GameState(rawValue: savedGameState),
    gameState == .pause {
  self.gameState = gameState
    firebugCount = aDecoder.decodeInteger(
      forKey: "Scene.firebugCount")
    elapsedTime = aDecoder.decodeInteger(
      forKey: "Scene.elapsedTime")
    currentLevel = aDecoder.decodeInteger(
      forKey: "Scene.currentLevel")
    // 2
    player = childNode(withName: "Player") as! Player
    hud = camera!.childNode(withName: "HUD") as! HUD
    bugsNode = childNode(withName: "Bugs")!
    bugsprayTileMap = childNode(withName: "Bugspray")
      as? SKTileMapNode
}
```

Here's the play-by-play:

1. If gameState is set to pause in aDecoder, that's a signal to load all the properties from the archive and restore the game state.

2. You didn't have to explicitly archive these properties because all nodes in an SKScene are automatically archived, but you do need to re-link GameScene's properties to these nodes.

Now you need to update init(coder:) in all your other custom classes. Replace init(coder:) in HUD with:

```
required init?(coder aDecoder: NSCoder) {
  super.init(coder: aDecoder)
  timerLabel = childNode(withName: "Timer") as? SKLabelNode
}
```

Replace init(coder:) in Player with:

```
required init?(coder aDecoder: NSCoder) {
  super.init(coder: aDecoder)
  animations = aDecoder.decodeObject(forKey:
"Player.animations") as! [SKAction]
  hasBugspray = aDecoder.decodeBool(
    forKey: "Player.hasBugspray")
}
```

Replace init(coder:) in Bug with:

```
required init?(coder aDecoder: NSCoder) {
  super.init(coder: aDecoder)
  animations = aDecoder.decodeObject(forKey: "Bug.animations")
    as! [SKAction]
}
```

Replace init(coder:) in Firebug with:

```
required init?(coder aDecoder: NSCoder) {
  super.init(coder: aDecoder)
}
```

Then, in GameScene, replace didMove(to:) with this code:

```
override func didMove(to view: SKView) {
  if gameState == .initial {
    addChild(player)
    setupWorldPhysics()
    createBugs()
    setupObstaclePhysics()
    if firebugCount > 0 {
      createBugspray(quantity: firebugCount + 10)
    }
    setupHUD()
    gameState = .start
  }
  setupCamera()
}
```

Whew! Good work, team. When `gameState` is set to `initial`, you execute the same code as before. However, when you load the scene from a saved game, much of the setup is already done. You only need to set up the camera constraints again. The existing camera constraints are stale and need to be updated to point to the newly unarchived `player` and `background` nodes, so you can simply rebuild the constraints.

Build and run; if you have a saved game, the message will ask you whether to continue that game. If you answer "Yes", the game should resume from that saved point.

You're almost finished!

Cleaning up

Believe it or not, your game has a couple of bugs — and not the insect kind! When you run your app from Xcode and you load a saved game, your bugs move for a second or two, and then stop moving. In the debug console you'll get an error:

```
2016-08-09 14:36:44.000 PestControl[14129:5492937] SKAction: Run block actions can not be
properly decoded, Objective-C blocks do not support NSCoding.
```

Take a look at `move()` in **Bug.swift**. You'll see this line:

```
let moveAgain = SKAction.run(move)
```

`moveAgain` is an `SKAction` that runs a block of code. `NSCoding` doesn't support archiving of blocks, so it produces the above error.

Instead of archiving a block, you can use `SKAction`'s `perform(_:onTarget)`. It's a subtle distinction. `SKAction.run(_:)` takes in a block to run, whereas `SKAction.perform(_:onTarget)` asks for the name of a method to call.

There is a second problem here. The method is currently called `move()`. Using `perform(_:onTarget)`, the compiler is not able to distinguish this `move()` from `SKNode`'s `move(toParent:)`, so you'll need to rename the method.

First, rename move() in Bug to moveBug(). You'll also need to change the method name where you call it in GameScene's createBugs().

Then, in moveBug(), change:

```
let moveAgain = SKAction.run(move)
```

to:

```
let moveAgain = SKAction.perform(#selector(moveBug),
                                 onTarget: self)
```

The app linker may still try to link to move(), so select **Product > Clean** to clean the project.

Similarly, in die(), in the SKAction run sequence, find:

```
SKAction.run(removeFromParent)
```

You could use perform(_:onTarget) here too, but there is also a built-in SKAction for removeFromParent. Replace the action with:

```
SKAction.removeFromParent()
```

This should remove the errors in the debug console, and your bugs should continue moving when the game is restored.

The second non-insect bug shows up in Level 2 when Arnie is blinking green and you save the game. Upon restoring the game, Arnie's blink is flashing really fast.

Actions start whenever their node is added to the scene. Unfortunately, because of this, any currently running action with a duration will have its timing messed up on restore. In this case, it's easy to fix by removing and re-adding the blink animation; but if you have more complex situations you'll need to take this limitation into account.

In Player, add the following to the end of init(coder:):

```
if hasBugspray {
  removeAction(forKey: "blink")
  blink(color: .green, on: hasBugspray)
}
```

If Arnie's in possession of bug spray, this removes the blink action and restores it.

Congratulations! You've completed Pest Control with all the gameplay and the ability to continue from saved progress. You're a winner!

Challenge

In larger scenes, it's difficult to know how many bugs are left for Arnie to hunt down. So your final challenge is to add a bug counter to the HUD that keeps track of all the remaining bugs in the scene.

This will be a process similar to adding the timer label.

1. In HUD, add a bug count label.

2. Create add and update methods for the bug count just as you did for the timer.

3. In GameScene, call the add method when you set up the HUD. Call the update method when you remove a bug.

4. In HUD's init(coder:) restore the node reference to the bug count label just as you did with the timer label.

If necessary, you'll find the solution in this chapter's challenge project.

Over the next chapters, you'll learn how to add some juice to your games. You might want to return to Pest Control and add some particle effects when you spray firebugs! In the **resources** folder for this chapter, you'll find some sound files to add some audible bounce and squash effects to your game.

Section IV: Juice

In this section, you'll learn how to take a good game and make it great by adding a ton of special effects and excitement — a.k.a. "juice."

In the process, you'll create a game named Drop Charge, where you're a space hero with a mission to blow up an alien space ship — and escape with your life before it explodes. To do this, you must jump from platform to platform, collecting special boosts along the way. Just be careful not to fall into the red hot lava!

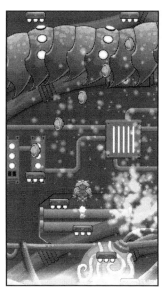

Chapter 15: Making Drop Charge

Chapter 16: Particle Systems

Chapter 17: Juice Up Your Game

Chapter 15: Making Drop Charge

By Michael Briscoe

In this section of the book, you'll take what you've learned so far and use that knowledge to create an endless, platform jumper game named Drop Charge. You'll also learn how to take a game from good to great by adding "juice" — those special details that collectively make your game shine brightly among the pack.

You'll do all of this and more in multiple stages across the next three chapters:

1. **Chapter 15, "Making Drop Charge"**: You'll put together the basic gameplay using the scene editor and code, flexing the SpriteKit muscles you've developed working through previous chapters.

2. **Chapter 16, "Particle Systems"**: You'll learn how to use particle systems to create amazing special effects.

3. **Chapter 17, "Juice Up Your Game"**: You'll trick out your game with music, sound, animation, more particles and other special effects, experiencing for yourself the benefits of mastering the details.

When you're finished, Drop Charge will look like this:

In Drop Charge, you're a space hero with a mission to blow up an alien space ship — and escape with your life before it explodes. To do this, you must jump from platform to platform, collecting special boosts along the way. Just be careful not to fall into the red hot lava!

Note: This chapter is optional; it is a review of what you have learned in the previous chapters. You should read this chapter if you'd like to get some additional practice while making a cool new game, but if you feel confident that you understand the material covered already, feel free to skip to the next chapter.

Getting started

As you've done in previous sections, start Xcode and create a new project with the **iOS/Application/Game** template. Enter **DropCharge** for the Product Name and verify that the Language is set to **Swift**, the Game Technology to **SpriteKit** and the Devices to **Universal**.

Drop Charge is designed to run in portrait mode. Therefore, click **DropCharge** in the project navigator, make sure the **General** tab is selected, click the **DropCharge** target and make **Portrait** the only selected option in the Device Orientation section.

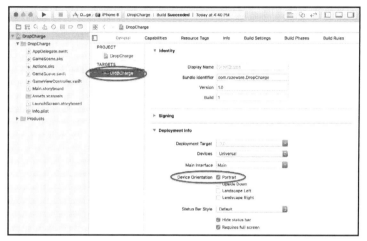

Also, open **Info.plist** and locate the **Supported interface orientations (iPad)** entry. Delete the entries for **Portrait (top home button)**, **Landscape (left home button)** and **Landscape (right home button)**.

Adding the art

In Xcode, open **Assets.xcassets** and delete the **Spaceship** entry. Then, select **AppIcon** and drag the appropriate icon from **starter/resources/icons** into each slot.

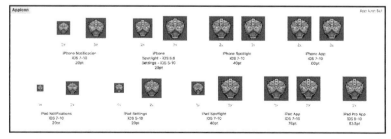

Finally, import the artwork you need for this game by dragging the files and folders from **starter/resources/images** into the left sidebar of **Assets.xcassets**.

> **Optional:** This would be a good point to set up your launch screen. You can find the launch art in **starter/resources/images**. Refer to Chapter 1 if you need help.

Building the game world in the scene editor

Now that you've got your project set up and your art at hand, you're ready to start working in the scene editor. This section is a review of the material from Chapter 7, "Scene Editor".

The first step is to configure your scene for the appropriate mode, which in this case is portrait mode.

Configuring the scene

Open **GameScene.sks** and select the **Attributes Inspector**. Set the **Size** to **W: 1536** and **H: 2048**. Be sure to set the **Anchor Point** to **(0, 0)**, and remove the **helloLabel** node.

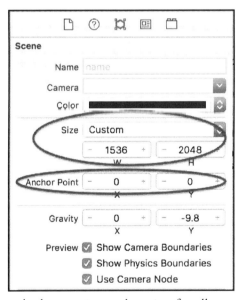

Remember, this is the standard scene size you're using for all games in this book, just in portrait mode instead of landscape mode.

From the **Object Library**, drag an **Empty** node into the scene. Name this node **World** and set its Position to **(768, 1024)**. All other nodes will be children of this node. This is a handy trick to use, because it will allow you to easily move all objects in the scene at once by moving the World node — which will be useful later on when you implement a screen shake effect.

Next, drag another **Empty** node into the scene. Name this node **Background**, and set its Parent to **World** and its Position to **(0, 0)**. You will add all backgrounds as descendants of this node, so that it will be easy to move all backgrounds at once by moving the Background node.

Add one last **Empty** node. This time, name it **Overlay**. Set its Parent to **Background** and its Position to **(0, 0)**. This node will hold all of your background textures. The reason you are adding them to the Overlay node rather than directly to the Background node is that you will eventually be creating multiple copies of the Overlay node, in order to implement continuous scrolling backgrounds.

Adding the background sprites

Now for some pretty pictures. Because Drop Charge will scroll up and down as the game progresses, you're going to make a background composed of several textures. Later, in code, you'll duplicate the Overlay node to repeat the background as needed.

In the **Utilities Area**, select the **Media Library**. Drag **bg_1** into the scene. Name it **bg1**, set its Parent to **Overlay**, its Position to **(0, -1024)** and its Anchor Point to **(0.5, 0.0)**.

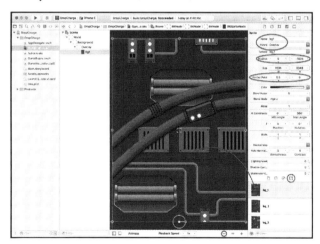

> **Note:** While you're laying out the scene, the artwork will appear quite large. Remember, to better visualize your scene, you can zoom out by clicking the **minus** (-) button at the bottom-right of the scene editor.

Add the remaining two **bg** nodes as children of the **Overlay** node with the following settings:

Media	Name:	Position		Anchor Point	
		X:	Y:	X:	Y:
bg_2	bg2	0	1024	0.5	0
bg_3	bg3	0	3072	0.5	0

Note: Setting the anchor point to the center-bottom of the bg nodes aids in positioning the stacked background, because you can simply add the texture's height to the y-position for each additional texture.

To make the background a little more interesting you'll add some decorations. Add the **midground** sprites as children of the **Overlay** node using the following settings:

Media	Name:	Position		Z Position:
		X:	Y:	
midground_1	m1	0	0	1
midground_2	m2	0	1690	1
midground_3	m3	0	3088	1
midground_4	m4	0	4726	1

Your complete background node will look like this:

How's that for a payoff? Build and run to see your progress.

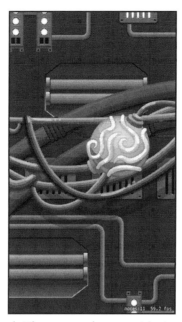

You've finished the background. That can only mean it's time to work on the foreground!

Adding the foreground sprites

Begin by adding another **Empty** node to your scene. Name it **Foreground**, set its Parent to **World**, its Position to **(0, 0)** and its Z Position to **2**. Here you're continuing your strategy of using an empty node to represent a "layer" of your game, this time for objects in the foreground like the title text, player and bomb.

From the Media Library, add four sprites as children of the **Foreground** node using these settings:

Media	Name:	Position		Scale		Z Position:
		X:	Y:	X:	Y:	
DropCharge_title	Title	0	410	1	1	1
Ready	Ready	0	0	0	0	1
player01_jump_1	Player	0	-460	1	1	3
bomb_1	Bomb	25	-417	1	1	1

Here's how you'll use these sprites:

- **Title** is the game's title, which you'll display until the player taps the screen to start.

- **Ready** is what you'll display once the game has loaded and is ready to play.

- **Player** is the space marine — the player's avatar.

- **Bomb** is what the space marine will drop to explode the alien spaceship and get the action started!

Next, you're going to add your last foreground node: the lava.

Lava is the enemy! It continuously rises as your marine strives for escape. The player must avoid falling in the lava, or risk a smoldering end.

From the Object Library, drag a **Color Sprite** into the scene. In Chapter 16, you'll attach an awesome particle system to this sprite, but you'll keep it simple for now. Name the sprite **Lava**, set its Parent to **Foreground**, its Position to (**0, -1024**), its Size to W: **1536** and H: **2048**, its Anchor Point to (**0.5, 1**) and its Z Position to **4**. Also, change the Color to **Orange** and set its Opacity to 75%.

Build and run to make sure you're still on track.

The lava is calmly resting just off-screen, waiting to be agitated by a bomb blast.

You're almost ready to start coding, but you don't want to leave your hero hanging in midair with a lit bomb behind him. You need some platforms — and as extra incentive to get him jumping, some shiny coins.

Creating platforms

To keep your players coming back, the game should be different every time they play. Later in this chapter, you'll add code that will randomly place platforms and coins in the level as the player moves up the screen. You could create your platform configurations entirely in code, but it's a lot easier — and more fun — to do it in the scene editor!

Control-click on your **DropCharge** folder, select **New Group**, and rename the group to **Scene Files**. You'll be creating lots of these, so it will be nice to keep them organized.

Control-click your new **Scene Files** group and select **New File....** Select the **iOS/ Resource/SpriteKit Scene** template and click **Next**. Save your scene as **Platform5Across.sks**.

Set the scene's Size to W: **900** and H: **200**, and its Anchor Point to (**0, 0**). Now drag a **Color Sprite** from the Object Library, name it **Overlay**, set its Position to (**450, 100**) and set its Size to W: **900** and H: **200**. This sprite is merely a container, so you don't need to see it; therefore, set its Opacity (via Color) to **0%**.

> **Note:** You're using a Color Sprite and not an Empty node here because you want to set the overlay node's exact dimensions, keeping the spacing between platforms consistent.

For this node, you want five platforms evenly spaced across the scene. Start by dragging **platform01** from the Media Library. Set its Name to **p1**, its Parent to **Overlay** and its Position to (**-360, 0**).

This time, you're also going to add a physics definition to the sprite, because you want the player to interact with the platform rather than just fall through it.

Scroll the Attributes Inspector down until you see the **Physics Definition** heading. Choose **Bounding rectangle** for the Body Type and make sure each of the following are unchecked: **Dynamic**, **Allows Rotation**, **Pinned** and **Affected By Gravity**. Set the Category Mask to **2** (the bit flag for a platform), the Collision Mask to **0**, the Field Mask to **0** and the Contact Mask to **1** (the bit flag for the player).

Note: Remember that you use the category mask to identify objects in didBegin(_:) of SKPhysicsContactDelegate.

Now that you have the first platform set up, click on **p1** and **duplicate** (**Command-D**) it four times with the following changes:

Name:	Position	
	X:	Y:
p2	-180	0
p3	0	0
p4	180	0
p5	360	0

When you're done, your platform scene will look like this:

Creating coins

Now you're going to create some coins that will give the marine a boost, and then you'll write some code.

As you did before, create a new file in your **Scene Files** group with the **iOS/Resource/ SpriteKit Scene** template. This time, name it **CoinArrow.sks** and set the scene Size to W: **900** and H: **600**, and its Anchor Point to **(0, 0)**.

Drag a **Color Sprite** from the Object Library and name it **Overlay**. Set its Position to **(450, 300)**, its Size to W: **900** and H: **600**, and its Opacity to **0%**.

This coin node will consist of five coins in an arrow pattern. From the Media Library, drag **powerup05_1** into the scene. Set its Name to **c1**, its Parent to **Overlay** and its Position to **(-360, -200)**.

Under Physics Definition, choose **Bounding circle** for the Body Type. Again, uncheck **Dynamic**, **Allows Rotation**, **Pinned** and **Affected By Gravity**. Set the Category Mask to **8** (the bit flag for a coin), the Collision Mask to **0**, the Field Mask to **0** and the Contact Mask to **1** (the bit flag for the player).

With that done, click on **c1** and **duplicate (Command-D)** it four times with the following changes:

Name:	Position	
	X:	Y:
c2	-180	0
c3	0	200
c4	180	0
c5	360	-200

Your finished coin arrow scene will look like this:

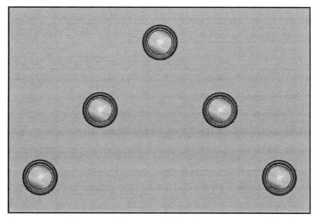

You're done with the scene editor — for now. It's time to get coding!

Writing the gameplay code

In this section, you'll implement Drop Charge's basic gameplay by:

1. Adding randomized platforms and coins.

2. Implementing touch events to drop the bomb.

3. Adding physics and collision detection so the marine can jump on platforms and collect coins.

4. Implementing code to read the device accelerometer data to steer the marine.

5. Creating methods to handle the camera node so that it follows the player sprite.

6. Implement code to get the lava flowing.

7. Adding code to continuously repeat the background, platforms and coins.

8. Track the game state and end the game when the hero has exhausted his lives.

Most of these things you've done before, so crack your knuckles and let's get started!

Adding platforms

Your hero is still floating in midair. Put some platforms under his feet to give the guy a rest — he'll need it when he finds out his ship's about to explode.

Begin by dragging **SKTUtils** into the project navigator. Verify **Copy items if needed**, **Create groups**, and the **DropCharge** target are all selected, and click **Finish**. You'll be using these utilities here to generate random numbers.

Open **GameScene.swift**. Delete everything and replace it with the following:

```
import SpriteKit

class GameScene: SKScene {

  // MARK: - Properties

  // 1
  var bgNode: SKNode!
  var fgNode: SKNode!
  var backgroundOverlayTemplate: SKNode!
```

```
    var backgroundOverlayHeight: CGFloat!
    var player: SKSpriteNode!

    // 2
    var platform5Across: SKSpriteNode!
    var coinArrow: SKSpriteNode!
    var lastOverlayPosition = CGPoint.zero
    var lastOverlayHeight: CGFloat = 0.0
    var levelPositionY: CGFloat = 0.0

    // 3
    override func didMove(to view: SKView) {
      setupNodes()
    }

    func setupNodes() {
      let worldNode = childNode(withName: "World")!
      bgNode = worldNode.childNode(withName: "Background")!
      backgroundOverlayTemplate = bgNode
        .childNode(withName: "Overlay")!.copy() as! SKNode
      backgroundOverlayHeight = backgroundOverlayTemplate
        .calculateAccumulatedFrame().height
      fgNode = worldNode.childNode(withName: "Foreground")!
      player = fgNode.childNode(withName: "Player") as!
        SKSpriteNode
      fgNode.childNode(withName: "Bomb")?.run(SKAction.hide())
    }

}
```

Let's go over this in sections:

1. Create properties for the background/foreground nodes and one for the background overlay that you set up in the scene editor. And another property to hold the background overlay height and one for the player node.

2. There are also properties here for the platform/coin overlays and to keep track of the last foreground overlay's position and height, making it possible for the game logic to properly position future overlays in a random manner once gameplay begins.

3. Inside `didMove(to:)`, you call `setupNodes()` which loads the children nodes from the **World** node into their respective properties, calculates the height of the background overlay and hides the **Bomb** node.

Note that when you retrieve the Overlay node (containing the background images) from the scene file, you use `copy()` to make a new copy of the node. This is because the background overlay will be used over and over again as needed.

Now implement the methods that load and create the platforms:

```
// MARK: - Overlay nodes

// 1
func loadForegroundOverlayTemplate(_ fileName: String) ->
  SKSpriteNode {
  let overlayScene = SKScene(fileNamed: fileName)!
  let overlayTemplate =
    overlayScene.childNode(withName: "Overlay")
  return overlayTemplate as! SKSpriteNode
}

// 2
func createForegroundOverlay(_ overlayTemplate:
  SKSpriteNode, flipX: Bool) {
  let foregroundOverlay = overlayTemplate.copy() as!
    SKSpriteNode
  lastOverlayPosition.y = lastOverlayPosition.y +
    (lastOverlayHeight + (foregroundOverlay.size.height / 2.0))
  lastOverlayHeight = foregroundOverlay.size.height / 2.0
  foregroundOverlay.position = lastOverlayPosition
  if flipX == true {
    foregroundOverlay.xScale = -1.0
  }
  fgNode.addChild(foregroundOverlay)
}

// 3
func createBackgroundOverlay() {
  let backgroundOverlay = backgroundOverlayTemplate.copy() as!
    SKNode
  backgroundOverlay.position = CGPoint(x: 0.0,
    y: levelPositionY)
  bgNode.addChild(backgroundOverlay)
  levelPositionY += backgroundOverlayHeight
}
```

Let's review this method by method:

1. loadForegroundOverlayTemplate(_:) takes the name of a scene file (such as
    Platform5Across) and looks for a node called "Overlay" inside, and then returns that
    node. Remember that you created an "Overlay" node in both of your scenes so far,
    and all the platforms/coins were children of this.

2. createForegroundOverlay(_:flipX:) positions a new overlay node from a given
    template node right above where any previous overlay node was placed. It also has a
    parameter to flip the node along its x-axis (which you will use later to add more
    variability into the level).

3. createBackgroundOverlay() makes a copy of the background overlay and places it right above the last added background overlay. You will use this to keep the background continuously cycling.

Add these lines to setupNodes() to load the overlays:

```
platform5Across =
  loadForegroundOverlayTemplate("Platform5Across")
coinArrow = loadForegroundOverlayTemplate("CoinArrow")
```

Next, add the following code immediately after setupNodes():

```
func setupLevel() {
  // Place initial platform
  let initialPlatform = platform5Across.copy() as! SKSpriteNode
  var overlayPosition = player.position
  overlayPosition.y = player.position.y -
    ((player.size.height * 0.5) +
    (initialPlatform.size.height * 0.20))
  initialPlatform.position = overlayPosition
  fgNode.addChild(initialPlatform)
  lastOverlayPosition = overlayPosition
  lastOverlayHeight = initialPlatform.size.height / 2.0
}
```

This method places the platform right below the player, and updates lastOverlayPosition and lastOverlayHeight appropriately.

Finally, add this line to didMove(to:):

```
setupLevel()
```

Now give your game a build and run.

Nice work! Your hero is standing his ground, looking like a boss — for now.

More platforms!

But you want more than one set of platforms in your level — and what about those coins? Add the following method after `createForegroundOverlay(_:flipX:)`:

```
func addRandomForegroundOverlay() {
  let overlaySprite: SKSpriteNode!
  let platformPercentage = 60
  if Int.random(min: 1, max: 100) <= platformPercentage {
    overlaySprite = platform5Across
  } else {
    overlaySprite = coinArrow
  }
  createForegroundOverlay(overlaySprite, flipX: false)
}
```

This bit of code generates a random number and adds a platform 60% of the time; otherwise, it adds the arrow of coins. Later, as a challenge, you'll build on this method to add other platform and coin configurations.

Now, add these lines to the bottom of `setupLevel()`:

```
// Create random level
levelPositionY = bgNode.childNode(withName: "Overlay")!
  .position.y + backgroundOverlayHeight
while lastOverlayPosition.y < levelPositionY {
  addRandomForegroundOverlay()
}
```

This continuously calls `addRandomForegroundOverlay()` to fill up content equal to the background overlay's height.

Build and run. You'll see something like this (your screen might look slightly different):

Dropping the bomb

Your hero looks a little bored — time to give him some motivation to get jumping!

Still working inside **GameScene.swift**, add the following enum definitions between the import statements and the class declaration:

```
// MARK: - Game States
enum GameStatus: Int {
  case waitingForTap = 0
  case waitingForBomb = 1
  case playing = 2
  case gameOver = 3
}

enum PlayerStatus: Int {
  case idle = 0
  case jump = 1
  case fall = 2
  case lava = 3
  case dead = 4
}
```

This code will help you keep track of the various states of the game, such as whether the game is idle, playing or over. Now, add the following properties with the others below the class declaration:

```
var gameState = GameStatus.waitingForTap
var playerState = PlayerStatus.idle
```

These two properties hold instances of your defined state enums, and you set them to their initial state. You'll use these throughout the game.

You'll want the player to know that the game has loaded and is ready to play, so add these lines to didMove(to:):

```
let scale = SKAction.scale(to: 1.0, duration: 0.5)
fgNode.childNode(withName: "Ready")!.run(scale)
```

This uses an action to display the "Ready" sprite. Next, add the following methods:

```
// MARK: - Events
override func touchesBegan(_ touches: Set<UITouch>, with event:
  UIEvent?) {
  if gameState == .waitingForTap {
    bombDrop()
  }
}
```

```
func bombDrop() {
  gameState = .waitingForBomb
  // Scale out title & ready label.
  let scale = SKAction.scale(to: 0, duration: 0.4)
  fgNode.childNode(withName: "Title")!.run(scale)
  fgNode.childNode(withName: "Ready")!.run(
    SKAction.sequence(
      [SKAction.wait(forDuration: 0.2), scale]))

  // Bounce bomb
  let scaleUp = SKAction.scale(to: 1.25, duration: 0.25)
  let scaleDown = SKAction.scale(to: 1.0, duration: 0.25)
  let sequence = SKAction.sequence([scaleUp, scaleDown])
  let repeatSeq = SKAction.repeatForever(sequence)
  fgNode.childNode(withName: "Bomb")!.run(SKAction.unhide())
  fgNode.childNode(withName: "Bomb")!.run(repeatSeq)
  run(SKAction.sequence([
    SKAction.wait(forDuration: 2.0),
    SKAction.run(startGame)]))
}

func startGame() {
  fgNode.childNode(withName: "Bomb")!.removeFromParent()
  gameState = .playing
}
```

You're already familiar with touch events from Chapter 2, "Manual Movement". Here you only need touchesBegan(_:with:) to monitor for a screen tap. Once you detect a touch, this method checks to make sure gameplay hasn't already started, and if it hasn't, calls bombDrop() to animate the bomb and start the game.

Build and run to try it out. You'll see the bomb pulse briefly then disappear, along with the ready message and title.

Physics for the player

If there was a bomb behind you, wouldn't you get moving real fast? Your hero needs to get moving. You'll fix that by configuring **GameScene.swift** to handle some basic physics.

In this section, you'll practice the skills you developed in Chapters 8, 9 and 10 — the three chapters on SpriteKit physics. If at any point you get confused about what you're doing, please review those chapters.

Insert this method just below `setupLevel()`:

```swift
func setupPlayer() {
  player.physicsBody = SKPhysicsBody(circleOfRadius:
    player.size.width * 0.3)
  player.physicsBody!.isDynamic = false
  player.physicsBody!.allowsRotation = false
  player.physicsBody!.categoryBitMask = 0
  player.physicsBody!.collisionBitMask = 0
}
```

This configures the physics properties for your `player` node, aka your hero. Now add this line to `didMove(to:)` to call that method:

```swift
setupPlayer()
```

Since `player` now has a `physicsBody`, you can turn it on when the game starts. Add the following line to `startGame()`:

```swift
player.physicsBody!.isDynamic = true
```

Build and run to see what happens.

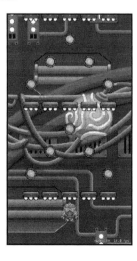

Oops! It looks like your marine is a bit clumsy, falling off the platform like that. Help him out by giving him a boost with the following methods:

```
func setPlayerVelocity(_ amount:CGFloat) {
  let gain: CGFloat = 1.5
  player.physicsBody!.velocity.dy =
    max(player.physicsBody!.velocity.dy, amount * gain)
}

func jumpPlayer() {
  setPlayerVelocity(650)
}

func boostPlayer() {
  setPlayerVelocity(1200)
}

func superBoostPlayer() {
  setPlayerVelocity(1700)
}
```

These methods set the vertical velocity of the `player` node's physics body, giving him thrust. When the marine lands on a platform or collides with a coin, `jumpPlayer()` will fire. You'll use `boostPlayer()` when the player collects a special coin.

Call `superBoostPlayer()` at the start of the game when the bomb explodes, by adding this line to `startGame()`:

```
superBoostPlayer()
```

Now give your game a build and run.

He goes up — and he comes down! Your marine needs to know about those coins and platforms before he becomes lava food.

Contact detection

First, add the following `struct` definition between the `import` statements and the `class` declaration:

```
struct PhysicsCategory {
  static let None: UInt32              = 0
  static let Player: UInt32            = 0b1       // 1
  static let PlatformNormal: UInt32    = 0b10      // 2
  static let PlatformBreakable: UInt32 = 0b100     // 4
  static let CoinNormal: UInt32        = 0b1000    // 8
  static let CoinSpecial: UInt32       = 0b10000   // 16
  static let Edges: UInt32             = 0b100000  // 32
}
```

Here you define the various physics categories for collision detection. This is why earlier in the scene editor you set the platform's category to 2, the coin's category to 8, and both of them to register a contact with 1 (the player).

Next, change the `class` declaration to read as follows:

```
class GameScene: SKScene, SKPhysicsContactDelegate {
```

Then add this line to `didMove(to:)`:

```
physicsWorld.contactDelegate = self
```

This declares your class as a `SKPhysicsContactDelegate`, and sets it as the delegate of `physicsWorld`.

Now implement this method in **GameScene.swift**:

```
func didBegin(_ contact: SKPhysicsContact) {
  let other = contact.bodyA.categoryBitMask ==
    PhysicsCategory.Player ? contact.bodyB : contact.bodyA
  switch other.categoryBitMask {
  case PhysicsCategory.CoinNormal:
    if let coin = other.node as? SKSpriteNode {
      coin.removeFromParent()
      jumpPlayer()
    }
  case PhysicsCategory.PlatformNormal:
    if let _ = other.node as? SKSpriteNode {
      if player.physicsBody!.velocity.dy < 0 {
        jumpPlayer()
      }
```

```
    }
  default:
    break
  }
}
```

This method handles collision detection and how it affects the player in various circumstances. Now when the marine makes contact with the platforms and coins, he'll get that boost he needs to get moving. There's just one more thing to do first.

In setupPlayer() change the line that reads:

```
player.physicsBody!.categoryBitMask = 0
```

To the following:

```
player.physicsBody!.categoryBitMask = PhysicsCategory.Player
```

This is to make sure didBegin(_:) can differentiate between the player node and other game objects.

Perform a build and run.

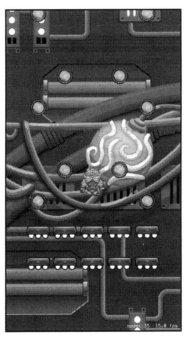

Yay! Now your hero is grabbing coins and bouncing happily off of the platforms.

> **Note:** Note there is a chance that your hero could get stuck offscreen based on the configuration of your random coins and platforms. If this happens, build and run again until you verify that the bouncing is working.

Using Core Motion to steer the player

You're going to use a framework called Core Motion to control your marine.

Core Motion is the framework responsible for receiving and processing motion data from device hardware, including both accelerometer and gyro-based data. In the games you created in earlier chapters of this book, you controlled your player sprites with touch events. In Drop Charge, you'll control the marine by tilting your device right or left.

Core Motion is beyond the scope of this book, but it's easy to set up and will be quite useful in controlling your marine's movement.

Begin by adding this `import` statement just below `import SpriteKit` in **GameScene.swift**:

```
import CoreMotion
```

Add these properties:

```
let motionManager = CMMotionManager()
var xAcceleration = CGFloat(0)
```

Here you're declaring an instance of the `CMMotionManager` that you'll poll for motion data, and adding a variable to track the acceleration.

Next, implement `setupCoreMotion()`, just after `setupPlayer()`:

```
func setupCoreMotion() {
  motionManager.accelerometerUpdateInterval = 0.2
  let queue = OperationQueue()
  motionManager.startAccelerometerUpdates(to: queue,
    withHandler:
    {
      accelerometerData, error in
      guard let accelerometerData = accelerometerData else {
        return
      }
      let acceleration = accelerometerData.acceleration
      self.xAcceleration = (CGFloat(acceleration.x) * 0.75) +
        (self.xAcceleration * 0.25)
  })
}
```

This method sets up the `motionManager` to periodically check the accelerometer and update the `xAcceleration` variable based on how much the user is tilting the device right or left. You'll use the `xAcceleration` property in an `updatePlayer()` method that you'll add shortly.

Add this line to `didMove(to:)`, just before `physicsWorld.contactDelegate...`:

```
setupCoreMotion()
```

Then add this helper method:

```
func sceneCropAmount() -> CGFloat {
  guard let view = self.view else {
    return 0
  }
  let scale = view.bounds.size.height / self.size.height
  let scaledWidth = self.size.width * scale
  let scaledOverlap = scaledWidth - view.bounds.size.width
  return scaledOverlap / scale
}
```

This determines how much of the scene width is cropped off the screen.

Finally, implement the `updatePlayer()` method:

```
func updatePlayer() {
  // Set velocity based on core motion
  player.physicsBody?.velocity.dx = xAcceleration * 1000.0

  // Wrap player around edges of screen
  var playerPosition = convert(player.position, from: fgNode)
  let leftLimit = sceneCropAmount()/2 - player.size.width/2
  let rightLimit = size.width - sceneCropAmount()/2
    + player.size.width/2
  if playerPosition.x < leftLimit {
    playerPosition = convert(CGPoint(x: rightLimit, y: 0.0),
      to: fgNode)
    player.position.x = playerPosition.x
  }
  else if playerPosition.x > rightLimit {
    playerPosition = convert(CGPoint(x:
      leftLimit, y: 0.0), to: fgNode)
    player.position.x = playerPosition.x
  }
  // Check player state
  if player.physicsBody!.velocity.dy < CGFloat(0.0) &&
      playerState != .fall {
    playerState = .fall
    print("Falling.")
  } else if player.physicsBody!.velocity.dy > CGFloat(0.0) &&
      playerState != .jump {
```

```
    playerState = .jump
    print("Jumping.")
  }
}
```

This updates the velocity of the player's physics body based on the `xAcceleration` property you set based on the accelerometer. Note it multiplies the value by 1000 — this felt right through trial and error. This also contains code to wrap the player around the edges of the screen.

Lastly, the player state is checked to see if the hero is falling or jumping. For now you're just printing the state to the console — you'll be adding code here in Chapter 17, "Juice Up Your Game".

You'll call `updatePlayer()` continuously to steer your marine; to do that you'll need to override the scene's `update(_:)` method:

```
override func update(_ currentTime: TimeInterval) {
  updatePlayer()
}
```

Build and run — but this time be sure to use an actual device, as Core Motion isn't supported in iOS Simulator.

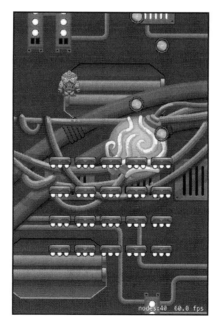

> **Note:** For more information about Core Motion, visit Apple's iOS Developer Library: http://apple.co/1F4DjCH. I highly recommend you acquaint yourself with this framework because it's often handy to add accelerometer-based input into your games.

Camera tracking

Now that you've got the marine jumping, you may have noticed that he frequently moves out of view. To fix that, you'll add an SKCameraNode and some methods to track the hero as he jumps his way to safety. This is a review of the material from Chapter 5, "Camera".

Begin by adding this to **GameScene.swift**, where the rest of the properties are:

```
let cameraNode = SKCameraNode()
```

Next, add the following lines to setupNodes():

```
addChild(cameraNode)
camera = cameraNode
```

These lines add the SKCameraNode to the scene, and sets its camera property.

Implement this method to track the camera:

```
func updateCamera() {
  // 1
  let cameraTarget = convert(player.position,
    from: fgNode)
  // 2
  let targetPositionY = cameraTarget.y - (size.height * 0.10)

  // 3
  let diff = targetPositionY - camera!.position.y
  // 4
  let cameraLagFactor = CGFloat(0.2)
  let lagDiff = diff * cameraLagFactor
  let newCameraPositionY = camera!.position.y + lagDiff

  // 5
  camera!.position.y = newCameraPositionY
}
```

Let's review this section by section:

1. The player's position is relative to its parent (fgNode), so you use this method to convert the position to scene coordinates.

2. Set the target camera position to the player's Y position less 10% of the scene's height.

3. Calculate the difference between the target camera position and its current position.

4. Rather than updating the camera straight to the target, move the camera toward the target. This will make the camera appear to take a while to catch up to the player when the player moves quickly, for a cool effect.

5. Update the camera's position.

Now add the following line to the bottom of `didMove(to:)`:

```
camera?.position = CGPoint(x: size.width/2, y: size.height/2)
```

This code will center the camera. To make sure that the camera is tracking your hero at all times, add this line to the top of `update(_:)`:

```
updateCamera()
```

Build and run to see how the camera tracks the hero, always keeping him onscreen.

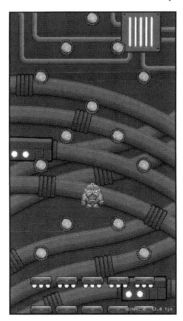

Note: You may notice that if you jump far enough, the background disappears! Don't worry, you'll fix that soon.

Let the lava flow

You've almost got all of the gameplay for Drop Charge in place. It's time to set the antagonist — lava — into motion.

Begin by adding this property to **GameScene.swift**:

```
var lava: SKSpriteNode!
```

Then, add this line to `setupNodes()`:

```
lava = fgNode.childNode(withName: "Lava") as! SKSpriteNode
```

You use this property to hold your "Lava" node that you set up in the scene editor. Now add the following method:

```
func updateLava(_ dt: TimeInterval) {
  // 1
  let bottomOfScreenY = camera!.position.y - (size.height / 2)
  // 2
  let bottomOfScreenYFg = convert(CGPoint(x: 0, y:
    bottomOfScreenY), to: fgNode).y
  // 3
  let lavaVelocityY = CGFloat(120)
  let lavaStep = lavaVelocityY * CGFloat(dt)
  var newLavaPositionY = lava.position.y + lavaStep
  // 4
  newLavaPositionY = max(newLavaPositionY, (bottomOfScreenYFg -
    125.0))
  // 5
  lava.position.y = newLavaPositionY
}
```

Here's what's going on with `updateLava(_:)`:

1. Calculate the Y position at the bottom of the viewable part of the screen.

2. The Lava's parent is `fgNode`, so convert the position to the coordinate system of `fgNode`.

3. Here you are defining a base velocity for the lava, and then determining the distance traveled for the current time step. You then add it to the lava's position.

4. The `max` method returns the highest Y position between `newLavaPositionY` and a position slightly below the visible area of the screen. This keeps the lava in sync with the camera position; otherwise it could fall behind as the hero climbs his way up.

5. Finally, you set the lava's Y position to the calculated `newLavaPositionY`.

Next, add this method:

```
func updateCollisionLava() {
  if player.position.y < lava.position.y + 90 {
    playerState = .lava
    print("Lava!")
    boostPlayer()
  }
}
```

This pseudo collision detector doesn't actually detect contact between the lava and player nodes, but rather compares their proximity to each other. If the marine falls too close to the lava, he'll jump up as if his feet are afire! In Chapter 16, "Particle Systems", you'll make use of playerState to add a smoke trail.

Now you need to modify the camera to accommodate the lava. Scroll back to updateCamera() and change targetPositionY to a var. Then add these lines right after:

```
let lavaPos = convert(lava.position, from: fgNode)
targetPositionY = max(targetPositionY, lavaPos.y)
```

These modifications get the current lava position and compare it to the camera target; choosing the larger of the two values. This keeps the lava from appearing higher than the middle of the screen.

Before you build and run, it's time to properly set up your update(_:) method. Start by adding the following properties:

```
var lastUpdateTimeInterval: TimeInterval = 0
var deltaTime: TimeInterval = 0
```

Then replace update(_:) with:

```
override func update(_ currentTime: TimeInterval) {
  // 1
  if lastUpdateTimeInterval > 0 {
    deltaTime = currentTime - lastUpdateTimeInterval
  } else {
    deltaTime = 0
  }
  lastUpdateTimeInterval = currentTime
  // 2
  if isPaused {
    return
  }
  // 3
  if gameState == .playing {
    updateCamera()
```

```
      updatePlayer()
      updateLava(deltaTime)
      updateCollisionLava()
    }
  }
```

Here's a quick overview:

1. Calculate `deltaTime` which is the time between the last `update(_:)` call and the current one. This value will be used in the `updateLava(_:)` method.

2. Next you check to see if the scene is paused, and if so, exit the method.

3. Then check to see if the game is playing, and if it is, call your update methods, including your new lava methods.

Now go ahead and build and run, and play your game for a bit. Everything is looking great. You've got some hot lava, the marine is collecting coins and jumping from platform to platform, then — hey! Houston, we've got a problem....

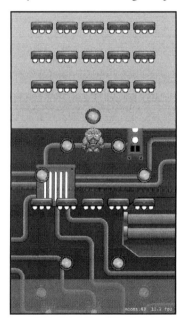

Repeating the background, coins and platforms

You've got one more method to add. To make this game a continuous platform jumper, there should be a never ending supply of coins and platforms.

Implement the following method in **GameScene.swift**:

```
func updateLevel() {
  let cameraPos = camera!.position
  if cameraPos.y > levelPositionY - (size.height * 0.55) {
    createBackgroundOverlay()
    while lastOverlayPosition.y < levelPositionY {
      addRandomForegroundOverlay()
    }
  }
}
```

This tracks the camera's position and adds a new background node, as well as a random platform or coin overlay node when needed. Now call it by adding this line to update(_:), just below the call to updateCamera():

```
updateLevel()
```

Game over, man!

So far, you've been playing an endless game, suffering no consequences when the hero falls into the lava. You'll fix that by adding code to track the hero's lives, and when to end the game.

First, add this line to the properties at the top of **GameScene.swift**:

```
var lives = 3
```

Now, add the gameOver() method as follows:

```
func gameOver() {
  // 1
  gameState = .gameOver
  playerState = .dead
  // 2
  physicsWorld.contactDelegate = nil
  player.physicsBody?.isDynamic = false
  // 3
  let moveUp = SKAction.moveBy(x: 0.0, y: size.height/2.0,
    duration: 0.5)
  moveUp.timingMode = .easeOut
  let moveDown = SKAction.moveBy(x: 0.0,
    y: -(size.height * 1.5),
    duration: 1.0)
  moveDown.timingMode = .easeIn
  player.run(SKAction.sequence([moveUp, moveDown]))
  // 4
```

```
    let gameOverSprite = SKSpriteNode(imageNamed: "GameOver")
    gameOverSprite.position = camera!.position
    gameOverSprite.zPosition = 10
    addChild(gameOverSprite)
}
```

Here's an overview of what's going on:

1. Setting the `gameState` to `.gameOver` stops the updates to the camera, level, player, and lava, effectively stopping gameplay.

2. Next, turn off collision detection, and make the hero's body no longer dynamic so he won't respond to physics forces, such as gravity.

3. Then, create an animation for the hero that removes him off the screen.

4. Lastly, display the "Game Over" sprite.

To decrement the hero's lives after a collision with the lava, add these lines to `updateCollisionLava()`, just below the call to `boostPlayer()`:

```
lives -= 1
if lives <= 0 {
    gameOver()
}
```

When your hero touches the lava, you decrement his lives by 1. If the number of lives is less than or equal to 0, then you call `gameOver()` to end the game.

Restarting Drop Charge

Once the game is over, you'll need a way to restart Drop Charge to play again. All that you need to do is update `touchesBegan(_:with:)` like so:

```
override func touchesBegan(_ touches: Set<UITouch>, with event:
UIEvent?) {
    if gameState == .waitingForTap {
        bombDrop()
    } else if gameState == .gameOver {
        let newScene = GameScene(fileNamed:"GameScene")
        newScene!.scaleMode = .aspectFill
        let reveal = SKTransition.flipHorizontal(withDuration: 0.5)
        self.view?.presentScene(newScene!, transition: reveal)
    }
}
```

Finishing touch

The marine needs a little more pop in his jump now that everything is properly set up. Scroll to setPlayerVelocity(_:) and change gain to:

```
let gain: CGFloat = 2.5
```

Now that you've completed the basic gameplay for Drop Charge, build and run to see everything you've accomplished.

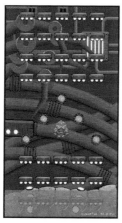

Congratulations — you now have the core gameplay for Drop Charge complete, and have reviewed everything you've learned about SpriteKit so far!

Now that you have a solid understanding of the basics of SpriteKit, it's time to move onto some new techniques, such as particle systems, and adding Juice. Across the next two chapters, you'll take this basic gameplay and make it shine!

Challenges

You only created two foreground overlays for Drop Charge: a standard five-across platform and an arrow pattern of coins. It would be a lot more interesting if your game had a variety of platform and coin patterns.

You're going to practice what you've learned on your own by creating additional object overlays. This mission is divided into four challenges. As you begin to work through them, keep in mind that each object has its own physics category to differentiate itself in didBegin(_:).

And remember, if you get stuck with any of these challenges, you can find the solutions in the resources for this chapter. But give them your best shot first!

Challenge 1: Create a five-across breakable platform

In Drop Charge, there will be platforms that break when the marine lands on them. Using the **block_break01** art from the Media Library, create a **Break5Across.sks** file. Don't worry about making the platform break — you'll do that in the next chapter.

Challenge 2: Create a "special" coin arrow

When your hero collects a "special" coin, you want him to get a bigger boost! Using the **powerup01_1** art from the Media Library, create a **CoinSArrow.sks** file, making only the top coin "special".

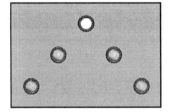

> **Important:** Be sure to name your special coins "special", as certain methods will look for this name in Chapter 17, "Juice Up Your Game".

Challenge 3: Create additional platform and coin patterns

> **Hint:** You can save yourself a bit of work by duplicating and renaming existing **.sks** files from the finder and using them as the basis for your new ones.

- **PlatformArrow.sks:** an arrow pattern of five standard platforms.

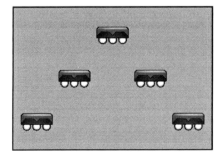

- **PlatformDiagonal.sks**: a diagonal pattern of five standard platforms.

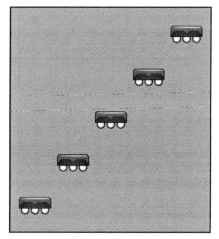

- **BreakArrow.sks**: an arrow pattern of five breakable platforms.

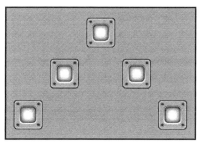

- **BreakDiagonal.sks**: a diagonal pattern of five breakable platforms.

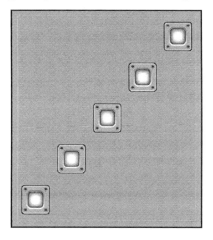

- **Coin5Across.sks**: a pattern of five coins across.

- **CoinDiagonal.sks**: a diagonal pattern of five coins.

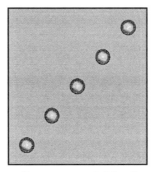

- **CoinCross.sks**: a cross pattern of nine coins. Make five coins horizontal and five vertical — no need to duplicate the center coin.

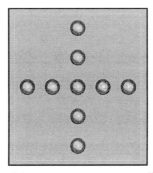

- **CoinS5Across.sks**: a pattern of five coins across, two of them special coins.

- **CoinSDiagonal.sks**: a diagonal pattern of five coins, two of them special.

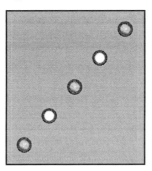

- **CoinSCross.sks**: a cross pattern of nine coins just like the standard coin cross, but include three special coins in the horizontal bar.

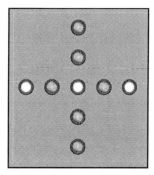

- **Optional**: Can you think of other interesting platform/coin patterns for your game? Using what you learned, come up with your own pattern!

Challenge 4: Add code for new foreground overlays

Now that you've created additional platform and coin overlays, update **GameScene.swift** to use the new objects.

Here are a few hints:

- Add properties to hold the templates for your `SKSpriteNode` overlays.

- Load the overlays in `setupNodes()`.

- Update `addRandomForegroundOverlay()` to accommodate the new overlays. Use logic statements to choose regular platforms 75% of the time and breakable platforms for the remaining 25%. Do the same for regular coins versus special coins.

- Update `didBegin(_:)` to add a new case for `.CoinSpecial` that boosts the player (rather than jumping the player).

- Update `didBegin(_:)` to add a new case for `.PlatformBreakable` that is just like `.PlatformNormal` except it also removes the platform from the game.

If you get this working, congratulations — you have truly mastered the material so far in this book!

In the next chapter, you'll learn about **particle systems** and how they can be used to create stunning visual effects like explosions and smoke — and lava!

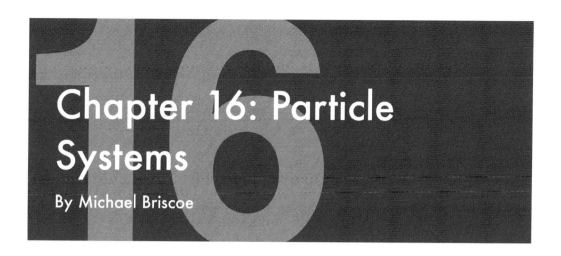

Chapter 16: Particle Systems

By Michael Briscoe

Nothing can "juice" up your game quite like a particle system:

Particle systems, such as this spectacular explosion, are an easy way to create a variety of special effects in your games. Here are just a few of the things you can simulate with a particle system:

Smoke	Water	Fog
Star Fields	Snow	Rain
Fire	Explosions	Fireworks
Sparks	Blood	Bubbles

And this is only the beginning. It's impossible to imagine all you could do with a particle system, and it pays to be creative. For instance, say you want to simulate subatomic particles emanating from a rip in the space–time continuum. That's easy!

Without particle systems, you'd probably resort to traditional frame-by-frame animation techniques to achieve a special effect like the explosion above. This would require many sprites, likely taking up significant memory — not to mention being tedious to create — and the results might not look very realistic.

In a particle system, the effects are created with a small image texture and a configuration file, making things much simpler. The particles are also handled efficiently for improved performance. This allows for real-time editing and rendering, resulting in greater realism.

In this chapter, you'll continue preparing Drop Charge for its juice-up by using particle systems to create three dazzling special effects. You'll learn how to implement particle systems programmatically, as well as by using the Xcode editor.

> **Note:** This chapter begins where the previous chapter's challenge left off. If you were unable to complete the challenge or skipped ahead from an earlier chapter, don't worry — simply open the starter project for this chapter to pick up where the previous chapter left off.

Getting started

Before you start coding, it's important to know how particle systems work, both in theory and within SpriteKit.

A single particle in SpriteKit is simply two triangles put together to create a square or quad. This quad is then textured, colored and rendered to the screen. For example, here's a raindrop depicted as a particle:

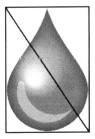

During each frame, the particle system looks at each individual particle it owns and advances it according to the system's configuration. For example, the configuration might say, "Move each particle between 2 to 10 pixels toward the bottom of the screen." You can see the effects of this configuration in the following diagram:

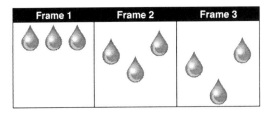

When it's initialized, a particle system will typically create a cache of particles known as the **particle pool**. When it's time for a new particle to be born, the particle system will obtain an available particle from its particle pool, set the initial values of the new particle and then add it to the rendering queue.

When the particle has reached the end of its life, the system will remove it from the render queue and return it to the particle pool, to be used at a later time.

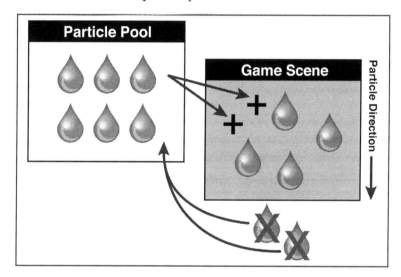

Particle systems in practice

SpriteKit makes it incredibly easy to create and use particle systems by giving you a special node named SKEmitterNode, the sole purpose of which is to make particle systems and render them as quickly as possible.

This section will give you a quick overview of how to use particle systems in SpriteKit. You'll begin by reading through this information without doing anything in Xcode. This will likely get you excited to try it out for yourself. Later in the chapter, you'll do just that.

To use an SKEmitterNode programmatically, you simply declare an instance of the node and configure its properties, like so:

```
let rainTexture = SKTexture(imageNamed: "Rain_Drop.png")
let emitterNode = SKEmitterNode()
emitterNode.particleTexture = rainTexture
emitterNode.particleBirthRate = 80.0
emitterNode.particleColor = SKColor.white
emitterNode.particleSpeed = -450
emitterNode.particleSpeedRange = 150
emitterNode.particleLifetime = 2.0
```

```
emitterNode.particleScale = 0.2
emitterNode.particleScaleRange = 0.5
emitterNode.particleAlpha = 0.75
emitterNode.particleAlphaRange = 0.5
emitterNode.position = CGPoint(x: frame.width / 2, y:
frame.height + 10)
emitterNode.particlePositionRange = CGVector(dx: frame.maxX, dy:
0)
addChild(emitterNode)
```

For now, don't worry about what these properties mean — you'll learn about them shortly. To see the effects of this code, open and run the **Rain** project included in the **starter/examples** folder.

You can also use Xcode's built-in editor to visually create and configure a particle system:

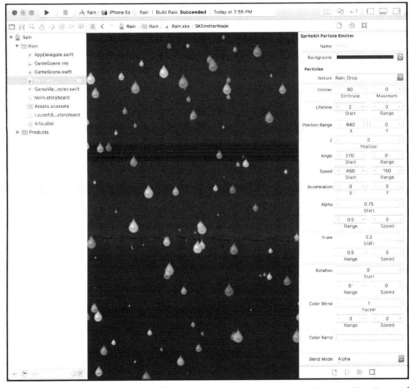

To do this, you simply create a new file with the **iOS/Resource/SpriteKit Particle File** template, resulting in an **.sks** file that you can edit with the built-in particle emitter editor.

Then, in code, you create an SKEmitterNode with the file, like this:

```
let rainEmitter = SKEmitterNode(fileNamed: "Rain.sks")!
rainEmitter.position = CGPoint(x: 320, y: 960)
addChild(rainEmitter)
```

This visual editor is super convenient because it lets you visualize the particle system in real time as you tweak its properties, making it quick and easy to get the exact effects you want.

There's much more to discover, but it's time to begin to learn by doing. You'll create your first particle system for Drop Charge by implementing an SKEmitterNode programmatically. Later, you'll create additional effects using the visual editor.

Programmatic particle systems

Wouldn't it be great if the bomb in Drop Charge actually exploded instead of just winking off the screen? In this section, you'll get your first taste of particle systems by creating an explosion at the start of the game. You'll create it programmatically to help you understand what's going on behind the scenes.

Open your **DropCharge** project in Xcode. If you skipped the previous chapter, open the project located in **starter**.

SpriteKit renders every particle displayed onscreen using a single texture attached to the particle system. This texture can be anything you wish, giving you great freedom to customize the look of your particles.

From the project navigator, open the **Assets.xcassets** catalog. Drag the **spark.png** file from **starter/resources** into the left sidebar. This is a white circular image that you will tint orange, and create a ton of copies of to look like an explosion.

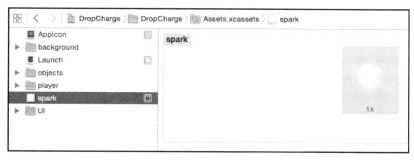

Now that you have an image for your texture, you can create the particle system.

Core properties of particle systems

Open **GameScene.swift** and implement the following method:

```
// MARK: - Particles
func explosion(intensity: CGFloat) -> SKEmitterNode {
  let emitter = SKEmitterNode()
  let particleTexture = SKTexture(imageNamed: "spark")

  emitter.zPosition = 2
  emitter.particleTexture = particleTexture
  emitter.particleBirthRate = 4000 * intensity
  emitter.numParticlesToEmit = Int(400 * intensity)
  emitter.particleLifetime = 2.0
  emitter.emissionAngle = CGFloat(90.0).degreesToRadians()
  emitter.emissionAngleRange = CGFloat(360.0).degreesToRadians()
  emitter.particleSpeed = 600 * intensity
  emitter.particleSpeedRange = 1000 * intensity
  emitter.particleAlpha = 1.0
  emitter.particleAlphaRange = 0.25
  emitter.particleScale = 1.2
  emitter.particleScaleRange = 2.0
  emitter.particleScaleSpeed = -1.5
  emitter.particleColor = SKColor.orange
  emitter.particleColorBlendFactor = 1
  emitter.particleBlendMode = SKBlendMode.add
  emitter.run(SKAction.removeFromParentAfterDelay(2.0))

  return emitter
}
```

This method creates, configures and returns an `SKEmitterNode` based on an "Intensity factor" representing how strong you would like the explosion to be, allowing you to reuse this method to add additional explosions later in the game.

You first create a new `SKEmitterNode` and an `SKTexture`. Then, after setting the emitter's `zPosition`, you set the following properties:

- **particleTexture**: The texture to use for each particle, and probably the most important property to set. The default value is `nil`, and if you don't set a texture, the emitter uses a colored rectangle to draw the particle.

- **particleBirthRate**: The rate at which the emitter generates the particles per second. It defaults to `0.0`. If you leave the birth rate at `0.0`, the emitter won't generate any particles. In your method above, you set the `particleBirthRate` to a high value of `4000` so that the emitter generates its particles very quickly, creating an explosive effect.

- **numParticlesToEmit**: The number of particles the emitter will generate before stopping. The default value is `0`, which means the emitter will generate an endless stream of particles. You want this emitter to stop after generating a few particles.

- **particleLifetime**: The duration of time, in seconds, that each particle is active. The default value is `0.0`; if you don't change this, the emitter won't generate any particles.

- **emissionAngle**: The angle from which the particles are emitted. The default value is `0.0`, which is directly right. In your method, you set the particles to initially emit straight up. Controlling the emission angle can be useful when you want to create effects like fountains or geysers, where the water should move up the screen before slowing and falling back down the screen, as if affected by gravity.

- **emissionAngleRange**: The range of randomness of the emission angle, which varies plus or minus half the range value. This is really useful when simulating explosions. The default value is `0.0`. By setting it to `360`, you give the explosion a more realistic round shape.

- **particleSpeed**: The initial speed for a new particle in points per second. The default value is `0.0`. In your method, you scale the speed to create explosions of varying intensity.

- **particleSpeedRange**: The range of randomness of the particle speed that varies plus or minus half the range value. The default value is `0.0.` This property is especially important for simulating turbulence, without which your explosion would look like an "O".

- **particleAlpha**: The average starting alpha value for each particle, which determines the transparency of your particles. The default value is `1.0`, which is fully opaque.

- **particleAlphaRange**: The range of randomness of the particle alpha, which varies plus or minus half the range value. The default value is `0.0`; you set it to `0.25` which makes some of the particles slightly transparent.

- **particleScale**: The scale at which the emitter renders each particle. The default value is `1.0`, which means the emitter renders the texture for each particle at the texture's full size. Values greater than `1.0` scale up the particles while values less than `1.0` scale them down.

- **particleScaleRange**: The range of randomness of the particle scale, which varies plus or minus half the range value. The default value is `0.0`; you set it to `2.0` which varies the size of your particles for a more convincing explosion.

- **particleScaleSpeed**: The rate at which a particle's scale factor changes per second. The default value is `0.0`. In your method, you use a negative number so that the particles quickly shrink and wink out of sight.

- **particleColor**: The color the emitter blends with the particle texture using the `particleColorBlendFactor` (see below). The default value is `SKColor.clear()`. In your method, you set this to orange so that the particles look more like fire and sparks.

- **particleColorBlendFactor**: The amount of color the emitter applies to the texture when rendering each particle. It defaults to `0.0`, which means the emitter uses the color of the texture and blends none of the color specified in `particleColor`. A value greater than `0.0` blends the texture color with the `particleColor` using the defined `particleBlendMode` (see below).

- **particleBlendMode**: The blending mode used to blend particles with the other colors onscreen. The default value is `SKBlendMode.alpha`, which means that the particles and other objects are blended by multiplying the particles' alpha values. In your method, you set the blend mode to `SKBlendMode.add`, which adds the particles' and objects' colors together — making it seem like the particles give off light.

After setting the emitter's properties, you attach an action to remove the emitter after a two-second delay. The method then returns the configured emitter node.

As you can see, there are a lot of properties you can set on an `SKEmitterNode` — and there are even more you'll learn about very soon.

Now that you have a method that can create and configure a particle system, add one to your scene to see what it looks like.

Update `startGame()` as follows:

```
func startGame() {
  let bomb = fgNode.childNode(withName: "Bomb")!
  let bombBlast = explosion(intensity: 2.0)
  bombBlast.position = bomb.position
  fgNode.addChild(bombBlast)
  bomb.removeFromParent()
  gameState = .playing
  player.physicsBody!.isDynamic = true
  superBoostPlayer()
}
```

This bit of code grabs a reference to the bomb sprite and creates an explosion particle system. Then it places the explosion at the bomb's position, adds the particle system to the scene and removes the bomb sprite.

Build and run to see this in action.

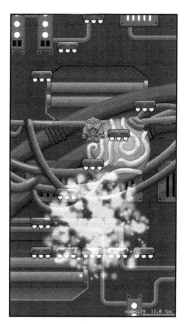

Now that's an explosive start! I'm sure you don't need any more convincing that particle systems can really juice up your game!

Advancing simulations in time

At times, your particle system simulations will need to start from some point in the future, as in the case of a star field or weather. In other words, you may want the simulation to begin with a screen full of stars, rain or snowflakes — not wait for them to slowly fall from the top of the screen.

To demonstrate this, open and run the **Starfield** project located in **starter/examples**. Notice that it takes a few seconds for the screen to fill with stars.

Not very convincing, is it?

Still in the **Starfield** project, open **GameScene.swift** and uncomment the following line in `didMove(to_:)`:

```
emitter.advanceSimulationTime(15)
```

This property advances the particle system by 15 seconds, effectively filling the sky with stars.

Build and run to see the difference.

Now you see a screen full of stars, as if you were traveling on a starship at warp speed! Any time you want to advance a particle system to a point beyond its initial state, you'll find this method handy.

More core properties of particle systems

There are a number of other core particle system properties. Here's a list of what's available:

> **Note:** Unless stated otherwise, all of these properties default to 0.

- **particleZPosition**: The starting z-position for each particle.

- **particleColor[Red/Green/Blue/Alpha]Speed**: The rate at which each color component changes per second, for each particle.

- **particleColorBlendFactorSpeed**: The rate at which the blend factor changes per second.

- **xAcceleration**: The amount of x-acceleration to apply to the velocity of each particle. This property is useful for simulating wind.

- **yAcceleration**: The amount of y-acceleration to apply to the velocity of each particle. This property is useful for simulating gravity.

- **particleRotation**: The starting rotation to apply to each particle.

- **particleRotationSpeed**: The rate at which the amount of rotation should change over one second.

- **particleSize**: The initial size of each particle. It defaults to `CGSizeZero`, causing the particle to use the assigned texture size as its initial size. If you haven't assigned a texture to your particle, you must set this property to a non-empty size or you won't see anything.

- **particleScaleSpeed**: The rate at which to modify the scale of each particle over one second.

- **particleAlphaSpeed**: The rate at which to modify the alpha value of each particle over one second.

- **targetNode**: This lets you render particles as if they belong to another node instead of the emitter node. It's an important property that you can use to create some unique effects. You'll learn more about this property later.

Range properties

There is another set of properties on `SKEmitterNode` that let you add random variance to a related property. You've seen examples of this already, when you used `emissionAngleRange`, `particleSpeedRange`, `particleAlphaRange` and `particleScaleRange` to add random values to the explosion emitter. Without these properties, your explosion would look more like an electric candle flame.

These range properties are very important when you're trying to simulate real world objects and phenomena. By adding a bit of randomness to the way your system generates particles, you're introducing *turbulence* and adding realism to your effects.

Here are other properties that can have random variance:

- **particleLifetimeRange**: This randomizes the lifetime of each particle, meaning some particles will live longer than other particles.

- **particlePositionRange**: This starts every particle in a random position. It defaults to `(0.0, 0.0)`, meaning all particles will originate from the same position.

- **particleRotationRange**: This randomizes the initial rotation of each particle.

- **particleColor[Red/Green/Blue/Alpha]Range**: This creates each particle with random red/green/blue/alpha component values, according to the range.

- **particleColorBlendFactorRange**: This randomizes the initial blend factor for each particle.

Keyframe properties

There are four properties on `SKEmitterNode` that provide a very cool technique referred to as **key framing**. Instead of varying the property between a single value and a random range, the idea with key frames is to change a property to several specific values over time.

For example, there is a keyframe property on SKEmitterNode of type SKKeyframeSequence named particleColorSequence:

```
var particleColorSequence: SKKeyframeSequence?
```

To use a keyframe property, you first initialize it and then add one or more keyframes. Each keyframe has two properties:

- **value**: This is the value the property takes when this keyframe occurs. particleColorSequence expects an SKColor instance for the value, such as SKColor.yellow(). Other properties may expect different types of values.

- **time**: This is the time the keyframe occurs within the lifetime of the particle, with a value ranging from 0 (the moment the particle is created) to 1 (the moment the particle is destroyed). For example, if the lifetime of a particle is 10 seconds and you specify 0.25 for time, the keyframe would occur at 2.5 seconds.

Give key framing a shot by using the particleColorSequence to make the explosion more lifelike.

Switch back to your **DropCharge** project and open **GameScene.swift**. Add the following code to explosion(intensity:), before the return statement:

```
let sequence = SKKeyframeSequence(capacity: 5)
sequence.addKeyframeValue(SKColor.white, time: 0)
sequence.addKeyframeValue(SKColor.yellow, time: 0.10)
sequence.addKeyframeValue(SKColor.orange, time: 0.15)
sequence.addKeyframeValue(SKColor.red, time: 0.75)
sequence.addKeyframeValue(SKColor.black, time: 0.95)
emitter.particleColorSequence = sequence
```

Also **remove** the emitter.particleColor = SKColor.orange line, as you no longer need it.

The code you just added does the following:

1. Creates an SKKeyframeSequence and initializes it with a capacity of 5, since you'll be adding five color keyframes.

2. Adds an SKColor.white when the particle is first generated.

3. Adds an SKColor.yellow when 10% of the particle's life has passed.

4. Adds an SKColor.orange when 15% of the particle's life has passed. This is the dominant color.

5. Adds an `SKColor.red` when 75% of the particle's life has passed.

6. Adds an `SKColor.black` just before the particle is destroyed.

Build and run to see your modified explosion.

The explosion starts out brighter than before and then fades away to glowing embers. It's a subtle effect, but remember, adding juice is all about the details — especially the subtle ones!

There are three other properties that support keyframe sequences:

- **particleColorBlendFactorSequence**: This lets you accurately control the blend factor applied to each particle during its lifetime.

- **particleScaleSequence**: This lets you scale each particle up and down multiple times during its lifetime.

- **particleAlphaSequence**: This gives you full control over each particle's alpha channel during its lifetime.

Sequence properties

There are two important properties to mention for `SKKeyframeSequence`: the `interpolationMode` and the `repeatMode`.

The `interpolationMode` property specifies how to calculate the values for times between each keyframe.

The available `interpolationMode` values are:

- **linear**: This mode calculates the interpolation values linearly. This is the default mode.

- **spline**: This mode calculates the interpolation values using a spline, which gives the effect of easing at the start and end of a keyframe sequence. If you were to scale a particle with this mode, then the scaling would begin slowly, pick up speed and then slow down until coming to the end of the sequence, providing a smooth transition.

- **step**: This mode does *not* interpolate the time values between keyframes. It simply calculates the value as that of the most recent keyframe.

The `repeatMode` property specifies how to calculate values if they're outside of the keyframes defined in the sequence. It's possible to define keyframes from `0.0` all the way to `1.0`, but you don't have to; you could have a keyframe that runs from `0.25` to `0.75`. In that case, the `repeatMode` property defines what values to use from `0.0` to `0.25` and from `0.75` to `1.0`. The available `SKRepeatMode` values are:

- **clamp**: This mode clamps the value to the range of time values found in the sequence. If, for example, the last keyframe in a sequence had a time value of `0.5`, any time from `0.5` to `1.0` would return the last keyframe value. This is the default mode.

- **loop**: This mode causes the sequence to loop. If, for example, the last keyframe in a sequence had a time value of `0.5`, any time from `0.5` to `1.0` would return the same value as from `0.0` to `0.5`.

Visually-created particle systems

Now that you've got a big explosion to start the game, you can heat up the lava! This time, you're going to create the lava particle system within Xcode's particle emitter editor.

Creating the .sks file

Adding particle systems programmatically is not your only option. SpriteKit also supports configuring particle emitters via a `.sks` file. This file lets you store all of the necessary settings for a particle system in a single file as part of your project, so you can take full advantage of the built-in Xcode editor, as well as of easy loading and saving via `NSCoding`.

OK! It's time to create a new group to hold all of your particle systems. With **GameScene.swift** highlighted, select **File > New > Group** from the main menu. Name this group **Particles** and press Enter to confirm.

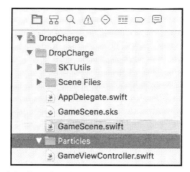

With the **Particles** group highlighted, select **File > New > File...** from the main menu. Select **iOS/Resource/SpriteKit Particle File**.

Click **Next**. On the next screen, you'll see a drop-down that contains a number of different particle templates.

These templates give you a handy starting point from which to create your own particles. The items in the list are common particle configurations that you can adapt to your own needs. The following images show what each template looks like:

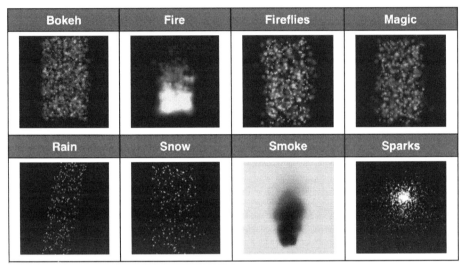

Generally you should choose whichever is closest to the effect you're trying to make and then tweak it from there. Although you could use any of these templates to get started on the lava, fire is the closest thing to lava, so select the **Fire** template from the list.

Click **Next** once more and enter **Lava** for the file name. Then click **Create** to create the file.

> **Note:** When you add your first particle file to a project, Xcode automatically adds a second file, **spark.png**, alongside it. This image file is the default texture for all particle templates built into Xcode, apart from one: the Bokeh template has its own default image called **bokeh.png**. You don't have to use this texture for your particle system. If you want to use your own texture, simply add it to your project and select it in the Xcode particle emitter editor (see below).

The Xcode particle emitter editor

Not all properties of an SKEmitterNode are configurable through Xcode's built-in particle editor, such as the sequence properties for scale, blend factor and alpha, However, you can configure the most important properties of a node. To access the editor, select **Lava.sks** and verify that the Attributes Inspector is visible on the right.

Feel free to take a moment to play around with the settings in the inspector to see how the particle system behaves in response.

Notice the **Texture** property? It's set to use the default texture file, **spark.png**. This is where you could set the texture to one of your own, if you desired.

Making lava

The best way to begin making lava is by changing the color of the template. The default color is close to what you want, but you'll get a softer lava effect if the color ramps up from black to a reddish-orange glow.

Locate the **Color Ramp** property in the editor and click on the color stop at the left of the color selection panel. This will display a standard macOS color picker. Change the color in the picker and watch the color of the particles change.

Select the **Color Sliders** tab in the color picker and make sure that the drop-down shows **RGB Sliders**. Now set the first color stop to **black** by setting the red, green and blue sliders all to **0**. The color ramp in the editor is actually editing the emitter's `particleColorSequence`. You're going to add two more stops (keyframes) to the sequence.

Click at about the **25%** mark of the color ramp to create a new color stop. Enter **99** for the red value, **50** for the green and **0** for the blue. Next, click at the end of the color ramp to create another color stop. Enter **219** for the red value, **66** for the green and **0** for the blue.

Your color ramp will look something like the following:

With the color sequence set, you can start to edit the shape, speed and position of the emitter. At the top of the particle editor pane, find **Emitter Birthrate** and change the value to **50** with a **Maximum** of **0**. Then set **Lifetime Start** to **1.5** with a **Range** of **0**.

This causes the emitter to generate 50 particles per second, with each particle living for 1.5 seconds. To optimize performance, you want to keep the number of particles as low as possible while still getting the effect you want. So 50 particles per second * 1.5 seconds of lifetime per particle means only about 75 particles will be onscreen at one time.

For now, set **Position Range X** to **128** and **Y** to **0**. You'll change this in code later.

Change **Angle** to **90** with a **Range** of **360**. This causes the particles to emit in every direction.

Next, set the **Speed Start** and **Range** to **0**. Lava is thick and slow, so you don't need any speed here.

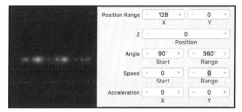

Now, set **Alpha Start** to **1** with a **Range** of **0.2** and a **Speed** of **-0.2**. The particles will start with an opacity from 80–100% and then fade out slowly.

Finally, give your lava some mass by setting **Scale Start** to **9** with a **Range** and **Speed** of **0**. Your particle system is beginning to look a lot more like hot lava!

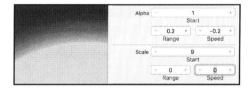

Loading the .sks file

The `SKEmitterNode` is fully compliant with `NSCoding`, which makes the loading process simple. When you edit and save a particle system using Xcode, your `.sks` file will be updated and included in the app bundle, ready to be deployed to a device. To load a particle system in code, simply initialize an `SKEmitterNode` with the name of the `.sks` file.

Now that you've configured your lava particle system, it's time to see it in action. Switch to **GameScene.swift** and implement the following method:

```
func setupLava() {
  lava = fgNode.childNode(withName: "Lava") as! SKSpriteNode
  let emitter = SKEmitterNode(fileNamed: "Lava.sks")!
  emitter.particlePositionRange = CGVector(dx: size.width
    * 1.125, dy: 0.0)
  emitter.advanceSimulationTime(3.0)
  lava.addChild(emitter)
}
```

First, you grab a reference to the lava `SKSpriteNode` that you created in the scene editor; you're going to attach the emitter to this. Then you create an `SKEmitterNode`, providing the filename of the `.sks` file you created.

The next line sets the `particlePositionRange` property so that particles are generated along the entire width of the scene, plus a little bit more. Next, you advance the simulation time so your lava is extra hot!

Finally, you add the emitter to the lava `SKSpriteNode`.

Now scroll to `setupNodes()` and find this line:

```
lava = fgNode.childNode(withName: "Lava") as! SKSpriteNode
```

Replace that line with a call to set up your lava particle system:

```
setupLava()
```

While you're at it, modify `updateCollisionLava()` to better accommodate your particle system.

```
func updateCollisionLava() {
  if player.position.y < lava.position.y + 180 {
    playerState = .lava
    print("Lava!")
    boostPlayer()
    lives -= 1
    if lives <= 0 {
      gameOver()
    }
  }
}
```

If you completed the challenge from the last chapter, or you are using the starter project, the only thing you are changing is the `lava.position.y` offset to `180`.

This places the marine a little higher above the lava when they collide. Without this modification, the marine sinks a little too far into the lava before his boost.

Build and run to see your new particle system defined from a `.sks` file!

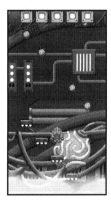

Wow! That's some hot lava!

> **Note:** Be sure to test on an actual device rather than the simulator, as particle systems do not perform well on the simulator.

Continuous and play-once systems

So far, you've created two particle systems for Drop Charge: a bomb explosion and a lava pit. The explosion you created in code is an example of a **play-once** system, which generates particles until it reaches a designated number, at which point, it stops. The lava system, on the other hand, emits particles **continuously**.

The difference is in the **Particles: Maximum** setting, or the `numParticlesToEmit` property in code. Remember, if this property is set to `0`, the particles will emit continuously, and any number greater than `0` will only render the specified number of particles. For the rest of this chapter, you'll be creating a few play-once particle systems.

Where there's fire, there's smoke

When the space hero collides with the lava, he jumps up vigorously — as we all would if we were game heroes! That works, but wouldn't it be cool to make the collision a bit more obvious by giving him a hot foot?

Highlight the **Particles** group in the project navigator and select **File > New > File...** from the main menu. Select **iOS/Resource/SpriteKit Particle File**, and then select **Spark** from the list of templates and click **Next**. Name the file **SmokeTrail.sks** and click **Create**.

You now have a new particle file you can edit. Notice the spark template emits particles continuously. For this effect, you only want the smoke to last for a second or two. To accomplish this, start by setting **Emitter Birthrate** to **200** and **Maximum** to **200**. Then set **Lifetime Start** to **1** and **Range** to **0.5**.

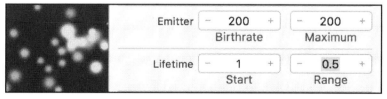

Set both the **Position Range** X and the **Position Range** Y to 24. Set **Angle** to 0 and **Angle Range** to 360. These settings give your smoke a little turbulence.

Now to slow things down a bit, set **Speed Start** to **50** and **Range** to **100**. Smoke tends to float, so remove the gravity effect by setting both **Acceleration** X and Y to 0.

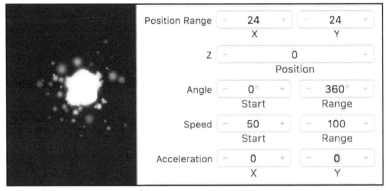

You want the smoke particles to start fairly large, then shrink and fade out. To do this, set **Alpha Start** to **1**, **Range** to **0** and **Speed** to **-0.25**. Then set **Scale Start** to **1.6**, **Range** to **1** and **Speed** to **-2**.

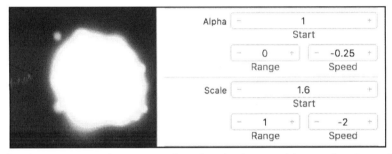

Next, you'll color your particles gray so that they look more like smoke. Begin by setting **Color Blend Factor** to **1** and **Range** to **1**. This will apply random factors of color to the existing texture color. Now click on the left-most color stop on the **Color Ramp** to bring up the color picker, and set **Red**, **Green** and **Blue** all to **100**.

Click at about the 75% mark to create a new color stop, and set **Red**, **Green** and **Blue** to **177**.

Finally, create a third color stop at the right-most edge of the color ramp and set **Red**, **Green** and **Blue** to **255**. Lastly, you don't want the smoke to glow, so set **Blend Mode** to **Alpha**.

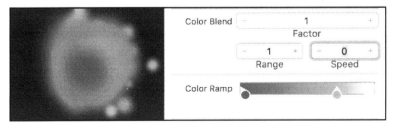

You now have your smoke particles, so it's time to set them loose. Switch back to
GameScene.swift. You'll be creating another trail effect for your hero later, so add these
helper methods:

```
func addTrail(name: String) -> SKEmitterNode {
  let trail = SKEmitterNode(fileNamed: name)!
  trail.zPosition = -1
  player.addChild(trail)
  return trail
}

func removeTrail(trail: SKEmitterNode) {
  trail.numParticlesToEmit = 1
  trail.run(SKAction.removeFromParentAfterDelay(1.0))
}
```

The first method helps by creating an SKEmitterNode with the specified .sks file and
attaching it to the player sprite. It then returns the SKEmitterNode so that you can clean
it up later by passing it to removeTrail(trail:).

Now update the updateCollisionLava() method as follows:

```
func updateCollisionLava() {
  if player.position.y < lava.position.y + 180 {
    if playerState != .lava {
      playerState = .lava
      let smokeTrail = addTrail(name: "SmokeTrail")
      run(SKAction.sequence([
        SKAction.wait(forDuration: 3.0),
        SKAction.run() {
          self.removeTrail(trail: smokeTrail)
        }
      ]))
    }
    boostPlayer()
    lives -= 1
    if lives <= 0 {
      gameOver()
    }
  }
}
```

You create a smoke trail particle system, add it to the player, and after three seconds,
remove it.

Build and run, and let the hero fall into the lava.

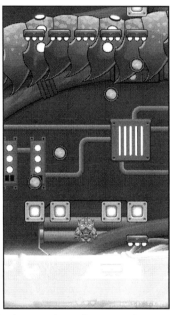

Hey, what's going on? Where's the smoke? The particle system is there, but it's behind the player sprite, and there are no forces influencing the trajectory of the particles.

Targeted particle systems

Imagine you're traveling in a car with the windows rolled up, holding a smoke grenade. The smoke would stay contained within the car, probably making it hard to see and breathe! Observers watching your car pass by wouldn't see any smoke streaming from behind. Once you rolled down the window, though, air would rush in and out of the car, pulling the smoke out with it.

Something similar is going on with your particle system. You need to tell the emitter that there's a world outside of the sprite to which it's attached.

SKEmitterNode has a property called targetNode that lets you set the node that renders the emitter's particles.

Add the following line to addTrail(name:), right before adding the emitter to player:

```
trail.targetNode = fgNode
```

The particles will still initially spawn wherever the emitter node is, which is the same spot as player. But after that, since fgNode is set as the targetNode, they will be treated as if they were children of fgNode. Since the position of fgNode is not changing at all, the particles will stop following the player and instead hover near where they initially spawned.

Now build and run. Each time your hero touches the lava, a trail of smoke will appear!

Congratulations! Besides adding hefty doses of fire and smoke to Drop Charge, you've developed your understanding of particle systems and their usefulness. You've learned how to create particle systems and configure their properties, both programmatically and within the Xcode editor, and how to load them and deploy them in your game.

But probably what's made the biggest impression is the dramatic effect these systems can have on your player's experience — and this is just the beginning. In the next chapter get ready to make this game even sweeter — through the power of juice! :]

Challenges

Now it's time to practice creating particle systems on your own. With each challenge, you'll create a particle system for your game using Xcode's particle emitter editor.

If you get lost or feel stuck, have a look at the particle system .sks files in the **challenge/ particles** folder. But most importantly, have fun and feel free to experiment!

Challenge 1: Collecting normal coins effect

Create a **CollectNormal.sks** particle file to use when the player sprite collides with the normal coins. It should be a play-once system similar to your explosion. There is a **Star.png** texture located in **challenge/resources** for your use.

Challenge 2: Collecting special coins effect

Create a **CollectSpecial.sks** particle file to use when the player sprite collides with the special coins. It should be similar to the **CollectNormal** system, but slightly bigger and with more energy.

Challenge 3: Breaking platform effect

Create a **BrokenPlatform.sks** particle file to use when the player sprite lands on a breakable platform. Use the **block/_break01/_piece01** texture that's already included in the DropCharge project. It should be a short, play-once particle system.

Challenge 4: Player trail effect

Create a **PlayerTrail.sks** particle file to use when the player sprite is jumping. This should be similar to the smoke trail system. Use the **Star.png** texture and give it a bluish color.

> **Note:** Don't worry about adding the code to spawn these particle effects yet; you'll handle that in the next chapter.

Chapter 17: Juice Up Your Game

By Michael Briscoe

Pop quiz! What's the difference between a good game and a great game? Why does one game delight its players, while another is greeted with indifference? Why do some games have raving fans and stellar reviews, while others languish at the bottom of the App Store? And what is the magical potion named "polish" that you're supposed to sprinkle on your games to make them awesome?

The answer is all in the details.

Great games are filled to the brim with droves of details that are often so subtle you might not even consciously notice them while you're playing. Polishing a game means paying attention to these details. Don't stop developing once your game reaches a playable state, and don't rush it to the App Store. Push your game further. Spice it up! Add polish!

"Juice" is a special type of polish that is easy and fun to add, and serves to bring joy and exuberance to your game. When a game is *juicy*, it feels alive — every interaction between the player and the game world results in a stimulating response.

For example, when two objects collide, you shouldn't just see it happen on the screen — that collision should look so convincing that you can almost *feel* it in your body. Playing a juicy game is a visceral experience.

No Juice

With Juice

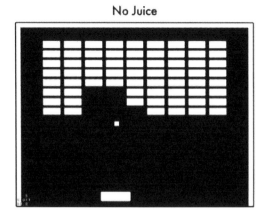
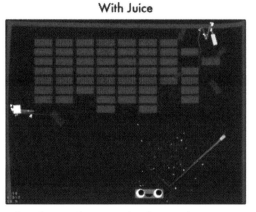

The great thing about juice is that you don't need to have a large art budget or hire expensive consultants with impressive resumes. Instead, you can use simple animation effects — such as scaling, rotation and movement — particle effects, music and sound effects. Most of these things are already in your toolkit; others, like music and sound effects, you can find online or create with free or inexpensive software. This is wonderful news for programmers like you and me!

On their own, none of these effects are terribly exciting, but when combined, every interaction within the game world results in a cascade of visual and audible feedback that keeps players coming back for more. That is what it means to make your game *juicy*.

In this chapter, you'll take Drop Charge and juice it up by adding a myriad of details to it. Although it's a good game now, adding juice will make it totally awesome!

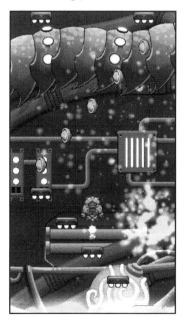

Getting started

This chapter begins where the previous chapter's challenge left off. If you were unable to complete the challenge or skipped ahead from an earlier chapter, don't worry — simply open the starter project for this chapter to pick up where the previous chapter left off.

Juicing up your game is like performing a magic trick. The results may look impressive to an unsuspecting audience, but it's really just sleight of hand. Fortunately, you don't need to go to a school of witchcraft and wizardry and study for years just to become a master of special effects.

Before you begin randomly adding effects, you need to know where to apply them. If you add them arbitrarily or without consideration, your game runs the risk of confusing and distracting players.

But there's good news! There's a simple three-step algorithm you can use to plan out your game's effects.

Three steps for adding juice

1. **List the actors**: First, make a list of all of the objects that play a role in your game, often called **actors**. For example, the space hero and a platform object are two of the actors in Drop Charge.

2. **List the interactions**: Second, make a list of the interactions that exist between the actors. For example, the hero collides with a coin to collect it. An object can also perform interactions with itself, like moving or changing state. For example, the hero could be moving upwards, or falling.

3. **Add effects to interactions**: Finally, add as many effects to these interactions as you can. This is what makes the player feel like they're making magic as they play. For example, in the previous chapter, when you created the smoke trail effect to mark the hero's collision with the lava, you were adding juice.

Simple enough, right? Good. You'll first carry out steps 1 and 2 with Drop Charge. Then later, you'll repeatedly apply step 3 until the game is as juicy as you can make it.

Step 1: List the actors

First, who or what are the actors in Drop Charge?

- **The hero**: Your space hero, frantically jumping to escape his exploding ship.

- **Normal platforms**: The hero's immediate destination and a place to rest.

- **Breakable platforms**: Fragile platforms that break when the hero lands on them, providing very little respite from his escape.

- **Normal coins**: These help the hero by providing a boost to his upward movement.

- **Special coins**: These provide a greater boost to the hero, propelling him closer to safety.

- **Lava**: The hero must avoid the rising lava at all costs or risk a serious hot foot!

- **Background**: This includes the scrolling images of the ship's machinery and vents. The images serve no real purpose in the game, other than to make it look more interesting.

- **The game world**: The game world is the container for all of the other actors.

- **Gameplay rules**: Certain gameplay rules might cause interesting things to happen. For example, in Drop Charge, if the marine falls in the lava three times, he dies, and the game is over.

- **The player**: Yes, the player is an actor in the game too. In fact, the player has the most important role! In this game, the hero is the player's avatar.

Step 2: List the interactions

Now that you've identified the gameplay actors, what interactions exist between them?

Here's a partial list:

- **The hero interacts with platforms** when he rests or jumps up the screen.

- **The hero interacts with coins** when he collects and destroys coins for a speed boost.

- **The hero interacts with the lava** when he gets a boost and a hot foot, or maybe even dies.

- **The hero interacts with the game world** when he performs an action like jumping, falling or changing direction.

- **The player interacts with the screen** when she moves the device or taps the screen.

- **A gameplay rule interacts with the game world** when the "game over" conditions are satisfied.

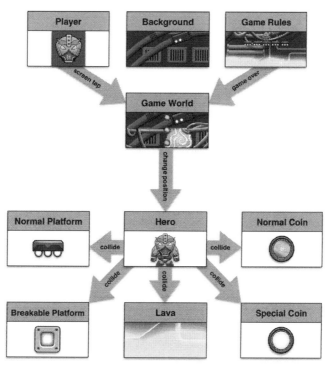

All of these interactions are opportunities for juice, like ripe fruit hanging from a tree, just waiting for you to pluck and squeeze. But what effects should you use?

Step 3: Add effects to interactions

Here are five basic effects you can use to add juice to your game:

1. **Music and sound effects**: Snappy music and sound effects can set the mood of your game and enhance your visual effects.

2. **Frame animation**: Animating the texture of your sprite to further convey an action or movement can have a dramatic impact.

3. **Particle systems**: You've already seen how adding particle effects, like explosions and smoke, can add high-octane juice.

4. **Screen effects**: Shaking and/or flashing the entire game world more deeply engages the player and conveys a sense of urgency.

5. **Sprite effects**: You can change a node's size, rotation, color and transparency to create interesting effects and enhance visual cues.

All of these effects can be temporary or permanent, immediate or animated, performed by themselves or — and this is where the magic happens — in combination with other effects. When you add a bunch of these effects together, you can make the entire screen jump and bounce. That's when things get juicy!

You can add most of these effects with a simple SKAction. That's the wonderful thing about these effects — they're incredibly simple to program, so adding them to your game is a quick win. Be warned, however: Once you start adding special effects, it's hard to stop!

Music and sound effects

Have you ever watched an action movie with the sound turned off? Besides the obvious fact that you can't hear the dialogue, the visuals seem a little flat and sometimes confusing. It's well established that music plays an important part in setting the tone and pace of a film. Sound effects can greatly enhance immersion as well. You can use this same concept to add juice to your game.

Once you have your project open, drag the **starter/resources/sounds** folder to the Xcode project navigator to import them. Make sure **Copy items if needed**, **Create groups**, and the **DropCharge** target are all checked. Once you're done, you should see them in your project navigator:

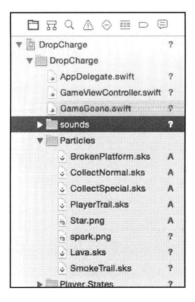

Queue the music

Drop Charge seems a little tepid without sound. To fix that, you'll start by adding music. iOS 9 introduced a new node to SpriteKit: SKAudioNode. This node makes it easy to play sound files from within your game. What used to take several lines of code can now be done in two!

> **Note:** In previous chapters, you used `SKTUtils` to play audio. This chapter shows how you can use `SKAudioNode` instead.

Open **GameScene.swift** and add the following helper method:

```
func playBackgroundMusic(name: String) {
  if let backgroundMusic = childNode(withName:
      "backgroundMusic") {
    backgroundMusic.removeFromParent()
  }
  let music = SKAudioNode(fileNamed: name)
  music.name = "backgroundMusic"
  music.autoplayLooped = true
  addChild(music)
}
```

The first part of this method checks to see if you've already added the `backgroundMusic` node to the scene, and if so, removes it. Next, you initialize an `SKAudioNode` with the file name passed into the method, setting its `autoplayLooped` property. Then, you add the node to your scene.

Because you set the `autoplayLooped` to `true`, your music file will automatically play once it's added to the scene; it will repeat until you remove it. Now you need to call this method with a sound file.

Scroll to `didMove(to:)` and add this line:

```
playBackgroundMusic(name: "SpaceGame.caf")
```

Build and run Drop Charge. If all went well, you'll hear a jazzy little tune welcoming you to the game.

Creating a change of pace

Your space hero seems a little laid back at the moment, chillin' to some tunes. But when that bomb drops, things get crazy real fast! This seems like a good time to switch to more frenetic music.

Add this line to the end of `startGame()`:

```
playBackgroundMusic(name: "bgMusic.mp3")
```

This code executes when the game enters the `playing` state, replacing the calmer music with a more frantic beat. Build and run to hear the results. Don't forget, you'll need to start the gameplay to hear the music change.

Not bad, but you can juice it up even more by adding some background noise.

Add the following to the end of `startGame()`:

```
let alarm = SKAudioNode(fileNamed: "alarm.wav")
alarm.name = "alarm"
alarm.autoplayLooped = true
addChild(alarm)
```

When the game enters the `playing` state you will also play an alarm noise in the background.

Now add this code to `gameOver()`:

```
playBackgroundMusic(name: "SpaceGame.caf")
if let alarm = childNode(withName: "alarm") {
  alarm.removeFromParent()
}
```

This changes the background music to the original music, and silences the alarm sound.

Build and run and notice the cool alarm sound effect as you play the game, and that the game reverts back to the peaceful music on game over.

Adding sound effects

Now you've got background music, and it's just as easy to add accompanying sound effects. Still within **GameScene.swift**, add the following constants to the class properties:

```
let soundBombDrop = SKAction.playSoundFileNamed("bombDrop.wav",
  waitForCompletion: true)
let soundSuperBoost = SKAction.playSoundFileNamed("nitro.wav",
  waitForCompletion: false)
let soundTickTock = SKAction.playSoundFileNamed("tickTock.wav",
  waitForCompletion: true)
let soundBoost = SKAction.playSoundFileNamed("boost.wav",
  waitForCompletion: false)
let soundJump = SKAction.playSoundFileNamed("jump.wav",
  waitForCompletion: false)
let soundCoin = SKAction.playSoundFileNamed("coin1.wav",
  waitForCompletion: false)
let soundBrick = SKAction.playSoundFileNamed("brick.caf",
  waitForCompletion: false)
let soundHitLava =
SKAction.playSoundFileNamed("DrownFireBug.mp3",
  waitForCompletion: false)
```

```
let soundGameOver =
SKAction.playSoundFileNamed("player_die.wav",
  waitForCompletion: false)

let soundExplosions = [
  SKAction.playSoundFileNamed("explosion1.wav",
    waitForCompletion: false),
  SKAction.playSoundFileNamed("explosion2.wav",
    waitForCompletion: false),
  SKAction.playSoundFileNamed("explosion3.wav",
    waitForCompletion: false),
  SKAction.playSoundFileNamed("explosion4.wav",
    waitForCompletion: false)
  ]
```

Here you define a series of `SKAction` constants, each of which will load and play a sound file. Because you define these actions before you need them, they are preloaded into memory, which prevents the game from stalling when you play the sounds for the first time. You also create an array of explosion sound effects that you'll use to play a random boom.

At the bottom of `bombDrop()`, modify the `run(SKAction.sequence...` statement as follows:

```
run(SKAction.sequence([
  soundBombDrop,
  soundTickTock,
  SKAction.run(startGame)
  ]))
```

When the game enters the `waitingForBomb` state, it will play **bombDrop.wav**, followed by **tickTock.wav**, before transitioning to the `playing` state.

But no bomb would be complete without an Earth-shattering *kaboom*, right? Add this line to `startGame()`, after the line that removes the bomb from the scene:

```
run(soundExplosions[3])
```

Build and run to hear the bomb tick, with a huge explosion!

Things are already getting juicy!

It's time to add the sound effects for when the player collides with the coins and platforms. Scroll to didBegin(_:). Replace the switch statement with the following:

```
switch other.categoryBitMask {
case PhysicsCategory.CoinNormal:
  if let coin = other.node as? SKSpriteNode {
    coin.removeFromParent()
    jumpPlayer()
    run(soundCoin)
  }
case PhysicsCategory.CoinSpecial:
  if let coin = other.node as? SKSpriteNode {
    coin.removeFromParent()
    boostPlayer()
    run(soundBoost)
  }
case PhysicsCategory.PlatformNormal:
  if let _ = other.node as? SKSpriteNode {
    if player.physicsBody!.velocity.dy < 0 {
      jumpPlayer()
      run(soundJump)
    }
  }
case PhysicsCategory.PlatformBreakable:
  if let platform = other.node as? SKSpriteNode {
    if player.physicsBody!.velocity.dy < 0 {
      platform.removeFromParent()
      jumpPlayer()
      run(soundBrick)
    }
  }
default:
  break
}
```

didBegin(_:) is pretty much the same, except you run some of the playSoundFileNamed actions you defined earlier. Now, when the hero makes contact with the platforms and coins, the game plays a nice and juicy sound effect.

Give it a go! Build and run, and listen to the sweet sound (effects) when you hit platforms and coins.

Final sound effects

Lastly, you'll add sound effects for when the marine collides with the lava and when the game reaches the "game over" state.

Scroll to `updateCollisionLava()` and modify the `run(SKAction.sequence...` by inserting the `soundHitLava` action:

```
run(SKAction.sequence([
  soundHitLava,
  SKAction.wait(forDuration: 3.0),
  SKAction.run() {
    self.removeTrail(trail: smokeTrail)
  }
  ]))
```

Next, add this to `gameOver()`, just after `player.run(SKAction.sequence...`:

```
run(soundGameOver)
```

Both of the lines you've added simply play their respective sound files after the marine collides with the lava or enters the `gameOver` state.

Build and run. Play your game for a bit, but then mute the sound and play the game again. The simple addition of sound greatly enhances your interactions with the game's actors. And you're just getting started with the juice!

Frame animation

Now you're going to get a bit more visual by adding texture animation.

At the moment, the game objects in Drop Charge seem a little static, and the coins blend in with the background. You can fix that by animating the textures of `SKSpriteNode`.

You can do this in code with `SKAction.animate(with:timePerFrame:)`, or you can set up animation actions visually in Xcode's scene editor. For Drop Charge, you'll take advantage of both methods.

Creating actions visually

To save yourself some work, you'll create two new scenes to act as animation references for all the coin overlays.

As you've done before, create a new file in your **Scene Files** group with the **iOS/ Resource/SpriteKit Scene** template. Name this scene **Coin.sks**.

Now from the Media Library, drag **powerup05_1** into the scene. Set its Name to **Coin**, and its Position to **(0, 0)**.

Under Physics Definition, choose **Bounding circle** for the Body Type. Also, make sure each of the following are unchecked: **Dynamic**, **Allows Rotation**, **Pinned** and **Affected By Gravity**.

Set the Category Mask to **8** (the bit flag for a coin), the Collision Mask to **0**, the Field Mask to **0** and the Contact Mask to **1** (the bit flag for the player).

From the Object Library, drag an **AnimateWithTextures Action** toward the scene; the action editor will expand if it's not already visible. Drop the action on **Coin** within the action editor.

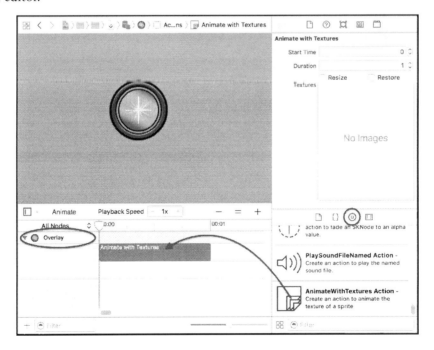

Within the Utilities Area, switch to the Media Library and drag and drop **powerup05_1** through **powerup05_6** into the **Textures** field of the Attributes Inspector. Set the Duration to **0.5**.

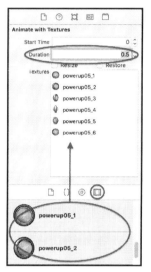

You can preview your animation action by clicking on the **Animate** button at the top of the action editor. The toolbar will turn blue, and the Animate button will change to **Layout**, as your animation begins to play.

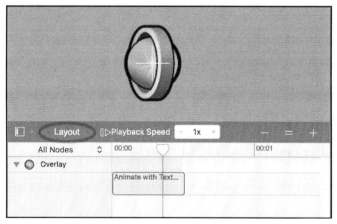

Next, click on the **circular arrow** icon on the bottom-left of the action to bring up the **Looping** pop-up. You want this action to loop over and over, so click on the **loop forever** icon on the left — like you did in Chapter 7. Notice how the action representation in the timeline has changed to reflect its looping status.

Click the **Animate** button to watch your coin spin continuously.

Now that you have your coin reference scene, you'll also need one for the *special* coin. As you did before, create a new scene and name it **CoinSpecial.sks**. This time drag the blue coin, **powerup01_1**, into the scene. Set its Name to **Coin**, and its Position to **(0, 0)**.

Under Physics Definition, choose **Bounding circle** for the Body Type. Also, make sure each of the following are unchecked: **Dynamic**, **Allows Rotation**, **Pinned** and **Affected By Gravity**. Set the Category Mask to **16** (the bit flag for a special coin), the Collision Mask to **0**, the Field Mask to **0** and the Contact Mask to **1**.

Repeat the process for adding an **AnimateWithTextures Action**. Be sure to use the **powerup01_1** through **powerup01_6** textures. Set the Duration to **0.5**, and make the action **loop forever**.

Using coin references

You've got a spinning coin now, but how do you get the rest of them going? Instead of replacing all the coins in each scene file with **reference nodes** like you did in Chapter 7, "Scene Editor", you'll swap out the old static coins for the new animated ones — in code.

Start by opening **GameScene.swift** and add the following variables to the class properties:

```
var coin: SKSpriteNode!
var coinSpecial: SKSpriteNode!
```

These will be set to the coin nodes from the two scenes you just created. Add a new method below `loadForegroundOverlayTemplate(_:)`:

```
func loadCoin(_ fileName: String) -> SKSpriteNode {
  let coinScene = SKScene(fileNamed: fileName)!
  let coinTemplate = coinScene.childNode(withName: "Coin")
  return coinTemplate as! SKSpriteNode
}
```

And add the following code to `setupNodes()` just after loading `breakDiagonal`:

```
coin = loadCoin("Coin")
coinSpecial = loadCoin("CoinSpecial")
```

This loads the coin nodes from the scene files. Next, implement this new method after `loadCoin(_:)`:

```
func loadCoinOverlayTemplate(_ fileName: String) ->
    SKSpriteNode {
  // 1
  let overlayTemplate = loadForegroundOverlayTemplate(fileName)
  // 2
  overlayTemplate.enumerateChildNodes(withName: "*",
      using: { (node, stop) in
    let coinPos = node.position
    let coin: SKSpriteNode
    // 3
    if node.name == "special" {
      coin = self.coinSpecial.copy() as! SKSpriteNode
    } else {
      coin = self.coin.copy() as! SKSpriteNode
    }
    // 4
    coin.position = coinPos
    overlayTemplate.addChild(coin)
    node.removeFromParent()
  })
  // 5
  return overlayTemplate
}
```

Here's what this function does:

1. First, it loads the coin overlay from its scene file.

2. Next, it enumerates through all of the children in the overlay node.

3. If the child node is named "special", then make a copy of the `coinSpecial` node, otherwise copy the `coin` node.

4. Position and add the new animated coin node, then remove the old static one.

5. Finally, return the overlay `SKSpriteNode`.

Now that you have the `loadCoinOverlayTemplate(_:)` method, it's time to use it.

Scroll to `setupNodes()` and replace the lines below:

```
coin5Across = loadForegroundOverlayTemplate("Coin5Across")
coinDiagonal = loadForegroundOverlayTemplate("CoinDiagonal")
coinCross = loadForegroundOverlayTemplate("CoinCross")
coinArrow = loadForegroundOverlayTemplate("CoinArrow")
coinS5Across = loadForegroundOverlayTemplate("CoinS5Across")
coinSDiagonal = loadForegroundOverlayTemplate("CoinSDiagonal")
coinSCross = loadForegroundOverlayTemplate("CoinSCross")
coinSArrow = loadForegroundOverlayTemplate("CoinSArrow")
```

...with the following:

```
coin5Across = loadCoinOverlayTemplate("Coin5Across")
coinDiagonal = loadCoinOverlayTemplate("CoinDiagonal")
coinCross = loadCoinOverlayTemplate("CoinCross")
coinArrow = loadCoinOverlayTemplate("CoinArrow")
coinS5Across = loadCoinOverlayTemplate("CoinS5Across")
coinSDiagonal = loadCoinOverlayTemplate("CoinSDiagonal")
coinSCross = loadCoinOverlayTemplate("CoinSCross")
coinSArrow = loadCoinOverlayTemplate("CoinSArrow")
```

Instead of using the `loadForegroundOverlayTemplate(_:)` as before, you are now using `loadCoinOverlayTemplate(_:)` to load the coin overlays. You've saved yourself a ton of work by stripping away all the old stationary coins and replacing them with brand new spinning ones — all at runtime!

Build and run to see your coin animation action at work in the game.

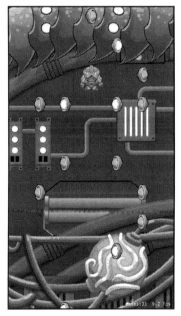

Whether or not you're a space marine, those coins now look a lot more enticing.

Animation actions in code

It's fun and easy to visually create animation actions in the scene editor. It's also great for looping animations, or for animations that occur at finite points along a timeline.

But what if you want the animation to occur when triggered by specific actions, such as when your brave space hero is jumping? That's when it makes more sense to create those animation actions in code.

In this section, you're going to add some animations to the space marine himself. To do this, open **GameScene.swift** and add the following variables to the class properties:

```
var playerAnimationJump: SKAction!
var playerAnimationFall: SKAction!
var playerAnimationSteerLeft: SKAction!
var playerAnimationSteerRight: SKAction!
var currentPlayerAnimation: SKAction?
```

These are empty SKAction variables that you'll initialize in just a moment. But before you do, add these two helper methods:

```
func setupAnimationWithPrefix(_ prefix: String, start: Int,
    end: Int, timePerFrame: TimeInterval) -> SKAction {
  var textures = [SKTexture]()
  for i in start...end {
    textures.append(SKTexture(imageNamed: "\(prefix)\(i)"))
  }
  return SKAction.animate(with: textures,
    timePerFrame: timePerFrame)
}

func runPlayerAnimation(_ animation: SKAction) {
  if currentPlayerAnimation == nil
      || currentPlayerAnimation! != animation {
    player.removeAction(forKey: "playerAnimation")
    player.run(animation, withKey: "playerAnimation")
    currentPlayerAnimation = animation
  }
}
```

The first method loads several textures into an array. Then, it creates an animate action using the textures and the timePerFrame as arguments.

The second method does the following:

- First, it checks to see if there's a current animation and if there is, makes sure it's not the same as the new animation.

- If the animation passes these tests, then the method removes any running animation actions.

- Then it runs the input animation action, animation.

- Finally, the method sets the currentPlayerAnimation to the input animation, so you can properly track it.

Scroll to `didMove(to:)` and add these lines to initialize your animation actions:

```
playerAnimationJump = setupAnimationWithPrefix(
  "player01_jump_", start: 1, end: 4, timePerFrame: 0.1)
playerAnimationFall = setupAnimationWithPrefix(
  "player01_fall_", start: 1, end: 3, timePerFrame: 0.1)
playerAnimationSteerLeft = setupAnimationWithPrefix(
  "player01_steerleft_", start: 1, end: 2, timePerFrame: 0.1)
playerAnimationSteerRight = setupAnimationWithPrefix(
  "player01_steerright_",  start: 1, end: 2, timePerFrame: 0.1)
```

Now that you've created your player animations, it's time to put them to use. Scroll to `updatePlayer()` and add the following lines to the end of the method:

```
// Animate player
if playerState == .jump {
  if abs(player.physicsBody!.velocity.dx) > 100.0 {
    if player.physicsBody!.velocity.dx > 0 {
      runPlayerAnimation(playerAnimationSteerRight)
    } else {
      runPlayerAnimation(playerAnimationSteerLeft)
    }
  } else {
    runPlayerAnimation(playerAnimationJump)
  }
} else if playerState == .fall {
  runPlayerAnimation(playerAnimationFall)
}
```

This checks the player body's horizontal velocity and plays the appropriate animation action for the `jump` state. If the player state is `fall`, it plays the single animation for falling. Build and run to see Drop Charge in all its animated glory!

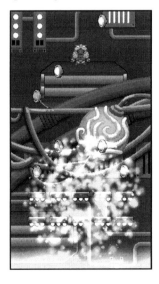

Things are really starting to get juicy, but you're going to take it up another notch by adding more particle systems.

Particle effects

It's time to put those particle systems you created in the last chapter's challenge to use, starting with a motion trails effect for the hero. This will enhance the illusion that he's moving quickly, eager to escape the ship.

For this effect, you want to temporarily turn off the trails when the hero has his hot foot. To do that, you need a reference to the player trail's `SKEmitterNode`.

Still within **GameScene.swift**, add this variable to the class properties:

```
var playerTrail: SKEmitterNode!
```

Next, add this line to `setupPlayer()`:

```
playerTrail = addTrail(name: "PlayerTrail")
```

Here, you use the `addTrail(name:)` method you created for adding the smoke trail, passing in the the PlayerTrail filename.

Build and run to see the hero's speedy motion trail.

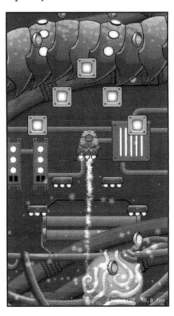

When the hero hits the lava, you currently can't see the smoke trail because the motion trail covers it.

To fix that, scroll to `updateCollisionLava()` and add the following line just after `playerState = .lava`:

```
playerTrail.particleBirthRate = 0
```

The `particleBirthRate` emitter property from the last chapter comes in handy here, stopping the flow of particles just before you add the smoke trail.

Next, within `updatePlayer()` replace `print("Falling.")` with these lines:

```
if playerTrail.particleBirthRate == 0 {
  playerTrail.particleBirthRate = 200
}
```

When the player state is `fall`, then you restore the `playerTrail` birthrate to `200`, provided it's not already `200`.

Build and run. Now you'll see the motion and smoke trails playing nicely together.

Random explosions

Time to up the chaos factor and add more juice by creating random explosions in the background; this will enhance the sense of the ship disintegrating.

Start by adding these property variables to the top of **GameScene.swift**:

```
var timeSinceLastExplosion: TimeInterval = 0
var timeForNextExplosion: TimeInterval = 1.0
```

You'll use these properties to track when to add your random explosions.

Next, add the following method just above `explosion(intensity:)`:

```
func createRandomExplosion() {
  // 1
  let cameraPos = camera!.position
  let sceneSize = self.size

  let explosionPos = CGPoint(x: CGFloat.random(min: 0.0,
    max: cameraPos.x * 2.0), y: CGFloat.random(min:
    cameraPos.y - sceneSize.height / 2,
    max: cameraPos.y + sceneSize.height * 0.35))
  // 2
  let randomNum = Int.random(soundExplosions.count)
  run(soundExplosions[randomNum])
  // 3
```

```
    let explode = explosion(intensity: 0.25
      * CGFloat(randomNum + 1))
  explode.position = convert(explosionPos, to: bgNode)
  explode.run(SKAction.removeFromParentAfterDelay(2.0))
  bgNode.addChild(explode)
}
```

Here's what you do in the above method:

1. First, you get the camera position and generate a random position within the viewable part of the game world, excluding a little breathing room toward the top of the scene.

2. Next, you get a random number to play a random explosion sound effect from the soundExplosions array.

3. Finally, you create an explosion with varying intensity. Then you set its position, removing it after two seconds, and add it to the background node of the game world.

Before you can see your explosions, you need to do a couple more things.

First, add this method just below updateCollisionLava():

```
func updateExplosions(_ dt: TimeInterval) {
  timeSinceLastExplosion += dt
  if timeSinceLastExplosion > timeForNextExplosion {
    timeForNextExplosion = TimeInterval(CGFloat.random(min:0.1,
      max: 0.5))
    timeSinceLastExplosion = 0

    createRandomExplosion()
  }
}
```

This method checks periodically to see when to set off an explosion by comparing the last explosion time with a randomly chosen time in the future.

When that time is reached, the method fires createRandomExplosion().

Lastly, go to update(_:) and add this just below updateCollisionLava():

```
  updateExplosions(deltaTime)
```

Build and run.

Woo-hoo! Explosions make *everything* better, don't they? :]

Power-up particles

There's another actor interaction that's begging for an effect: when the hero collides with the coins. Right now, the coins simply disappear from the screen and give him a boost. Wouldn't it be cool to add particles to the mix?

Start by adding this helper method:

```
func emitParticles(name: String, sprite: SKSpriteNode) {
  let pos = fgNode.convert(sprite.position,
    from: sprite.parent!)
  let particles = SKEmitterNode(fileNamed: name)!
  particles.position = pos
  particles.zPosition = 3
  fgNode.addChild(particles)
  particles.run(SKAction.removeFromParentAfterDelay(1.0))
  sprite.run(SKAction.sequence(
    [SKAction.scale(to: 0.0, duration: 0.5),
    SKAction.removeFromParent()]))
}
```

This method takes a filename and a sprite node, does all the work of creating and positioning your particle system and then removes the sprite.

Now, scroll to `didBegin(_:)` and make a few changes to the `switch` statement.

Within `case PhysicsCategory.CoinNormal:`, find this line:

```
coin.removeFromParent()
```

...and replace it with the following line:

```
emitParticles(name: "CollectNormal", sprite: coin)
```

Do the same within `case PhysicsCategory.CoinSpecial:` but replacing the original line with the following code:

```
emitParticles(name: "CollectSpecial", sprite: coin)
```

While you're there, add the particle system for contact with the breakable platforms. Within `case PhysicsCategory.PlatformBreakable:`, replace the following line:

```
platform.removeFromParent()
```

With this:

```
emitParticles(name: "BrokenPlatform", sprite: platform)
```

Game over, man

How about a big explosion when the game ends? Wait — what about a *huge* explosion?

Add the following code to the bottom of `gameOver()`:

```
let blast = explosion(intensity: 3.0)
blast.position = gameOverSprite.position
blast.zPosition = 11
addChild(blast)
run(soundExplosions[3])
```

This code creates a large explosion and positions it over the "Game Over" sprite, complete with sound effects.

Build and run to see your juicy power-ups, platforms, and particle mayhem. You'll see sparks and rubble flying everywhere!

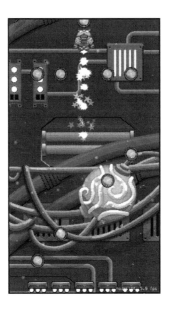

Screen effects

You've juiced things up with sound, animation and particles, so it's time to turn to screen effects, which can really bring things to life by affecting the entire game world. For Drop Charge, you'll implement a **screen shake** to simulate transient spatial movement similar to an earthquake — or in your case, a *shipquake*!

Open **GameScene.swift** and add this constant to the class properties:

```
let gameGain: CGFloat = 2.5
```

You'll learn more about this constant later. Next, add the following helper method:

```
func screenShakeByAmt(_ amt: CGFloat) {
  // 1
  let worldNode = childNode(withName: "World")!
  worldNode.position = CGPoint(x: size.width / 2.0, y:
    size.height / 2.0)
  worldNode.removeAction(forKey: "shake")
  // 2
  let amount = CGPoint(x: 0, y: -(amt * gameGain))
  // 3
  let action = SKAction.screenShakeWithNode(worldNode, amount:
    amount, oscillations: 10, duration: 2.0)
  // 4
  worldNode.run(action, withKey: "shake")
}
```

This method does the following:

1. It grabs a reference to the world node, resets its position and removes any previous "shake" actions. This code makes sure that only one screen shake action is running at a time — preventing pandemonium!

2. It creates a `CGPoint` based on the input `amount`. You only want the screen to shake vertically, so you set `x:` to `0`.

3. It creates a `screenShakeWithNode` action that oscillates the world by the input amount, 10 times in total, over the space of two seconds.

4. The method has the world node run the action using the "shake" key so that subsequent calls to the method can remove it.

> **Note:** `screenShakeWithNode` is a custom `SKAction` that's included with `SKTUtils`. You can learn more about this action and other useful screen effects by taking a look at the **SKAction+SpecialEffects.swift** file.

Now you need to put this helper method to use. Juicing up the bomb explosion is a good way to start!

Add this line to `startGame()`, just after `fgNode.addChild(bombBlast)`:

```
screenShakeByAmt(100)
```

Build and run. You'll see just how much shaking the screen can invigorate the game.

Shake, shake, shake

Let's sprinkle more juicy screen-shaking throughout the game. Add the following to `updateCollisionLava()` just after `boostPlayer()`:

```
screenShakeByAmt(50)
```

The next time the player hits the lava, she'll really know it!

Next, add this line to `boostPlayer()`:

```
screenShakeByAmt(40)
```

Now the screen will shake a little when the hero collects a special coin.

Lastly, juice up `createRandomExplosion()` by adding this code:

```
if randomNum == 3 {
  screenShakeByAmt(10)
}
```

Because it's possible to overuse the screen shake effect, you only shake the screen a small amount, and only with the largest explosion. You don't want to make the player queasy!

Build and run Drop Charge to admire your controlled chaos.

Sprite effects

There are a lot of sprite properties and actions you can use to achieve a variety of effects. For example, often games will change a sprite's scale to convey a sense of elasticity, like that of a bouncing ball, or change its color to indicate a transition to a new mode.

In the first section of this chapter, you added an alarm sound to create a sense of urgency. Now you'll juice that up by adding an oscillating red-light effect.

Still within **GameScene.swift**, add the following variable to the class properties:

```
var redAlertTime: TimeInterval = 0
```

Your red-light effect will use this to track its oscillation.

Next, add the following helper method:

```
func isNodeVisible(_ node: SKNode, positionY: CGFloat)
  -> Bool {
  if !camera!.contains(node) {
    if positionY < camera!.position.y - size.height * 2.0 {
      return false
    }
  }
  return true
}
```

You'll use this method to determine if a node is visible within the game world. This will help with performance and memory management, as you don't want unused objects taking up valuable resources.

Add the following method:

```
func updateRedAlert(_ lastUpdateTime: TimeInterval) {
  // 1
  redAlertTime += lastUpdateTime
  let amt: CGFloat = CGFloat(redAlertTime) * π * 2.0 / 1.93725
  let colorBlendFactor = (sin(amt) + 1.0) / 2.0
  // 2
  for bgChild in bgNode.children {
    for node in bgChild.children {
      if let sprite = node as? SKSpriteNode {
        let nodePos = bgChild.convert(sprite.position, to: self)
        // 3
        if !isNodeVisible(sprite, positionY: nodePos.y) {
          sprite.removeFromParent()
        } else {
          sprite.color = SKColorWithRGB(255, g: 0, b: 0)
          sprite.colorBlendFactor = colorBlendFactor
        }
      }
    }
    // 4
    if bgChild.name == "Overlay"
        && bgChild.children.count == 0 {
      bgChild.removeFromParent()
    }
  }
}
```

Here's what's going on in the above method:

1. This part of the code calculates the oscillation of color to apply to each background sprite.

2. Here, you loop to iterate through all of the background nodes in the game world.

3. If the node isn't visible, you remove it to free up resources; otherwise, you set its color to red and blend it according to the amount you calculated in step 1.

4. If a background overlay has had all of its children removed, then remove it from the scene.

Since this effect is generated over time, you need to add it to your game's update loop.

Add this line to update(_:) right after updateExplosions(deltaTime):

```
updateRedAlert(deltaTime)
```

Bouncing platforms

Finally, you're going to add a method to make the platforms bounce when the player lands on them — as if things weren't sketchy enough for our poor space marine!

Add the following code to **GameScene.swift**:

```
func platformAction(_ sprite: SKSpriteNode, breakable: Bool) {
  let amount = CGPoint(x: 0, y: -75.0)
  let action = SKAction.screenShakeWithNode(sprite,
    amount: amount, oscillations: 10, duration: 2.0)
  sprite.run(action)

  if breakable == true {
    emitParticles(name: "BrokenPlatform", sprite: sprite)
  }
}
```

This method takes a sprite node and uses the custom screenShakeWithNode(_:amount:oscillations:duration:) action to vertically shake the platform. It then checks to see if the platform is breakable, and if so, calls emitParticles(name:sprite:).

Next, scroll to didBegin(_:) and replace the case statements for PhysicsCategory.PlatformNormal and PhysicsCategory.PlatformBreakable to the following:

```
case PhysicsCategory.PlatformNormal:
  if let platform = other.node as? SKSpriteNode {
    if player.physicsBody!.velocity.dy < 0 {
      platformAction(platform, breakable: false)
      jumpPlayer()
      run(soundJump)
    }
  }
```

```
case PhysicsCategory.PlatformBreakable:
  if let platform = other.node as? SKSpriteNode {
    if player.physicsBody!.velocity.dy < 0 {
      platformAction(platform, breakable: true)
      jumpPlayer()
      run(soundBrick)
    }
  }
```

When the `player` sprite makes contact with either the normal or breakable platforms, `platformAction(_:breakable:)` is now called to bounce the platform.

Finishing touches

Before you build and run, you need to do some cleanup and a performance tweak.

First, scroll to `updateLevel()`. Once there, add the following lines of code:

```
// remove old foreground nodes...
for fgChild in fgNode.children {
  let nodePos = fgNode.convert(fgChild.position, to: self)
  if !isNodeVisible(fgChild, positionY: nodePos.y) {
    fgChild.removeFromParent()
  }
}
```

Like the code you used in the red-light effect, this code iterates through all of the platforms and coins in the scene and removes any obsolete objects. This avoids runaway memory usage — like a pile of offscreen cat ladies in Zombie Conga.

Now for one last tweak. Modify `setPlayerVelocity(_:)` as follows:

```
func setPlayerVelocity(_ amount:CGFloat) {
  player.physicsBody!.velocity.dy =
    max(player.physicsBody!.velocity.dy, amount * gameGain)
}
```

This moves the hard-coded `gain` property to the `gameGain` property you created earlier. In case you want to change the pace of the game and the amount of juice, you can simply change the value of this property.

Build and run your game, and behold the abundance of juice!

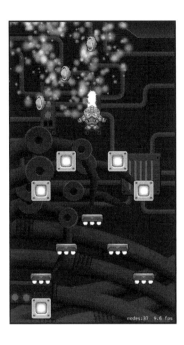

Challenge

Putting what you've learned into practice, here's a challenge for you.

As always, you can find the solution to this challenge in the **challenge** folder — but believe in yourself and try your very best first. Good luck!

Challenge: Create a "squash and stretch" effect

Create an effect that squashes and stretches the player sprite, enhancing his visual motion. This is a common technique used in traditional animation, where an object compresses as it hits the ground, then extends as it bounces up. Here are some hints to get you going:

- Create a `squashAndStretch` action property made up of a sequence of scale actions that squash and then stretch the player sprite.

- Use a scale factor of about 15%.

- The duration of each action should be relatively short.

- Use the `easeInEaseOut` timing mode.

- Run the action on the player sprite within the `updatePlayer()` method, when the `jump` and `fall` player states change.

Where to go from here?

In this chapter, you learned about the concept of "juice" and how it can turn a good game into a *great* game. You also have some great tools at your disposal: the three-step process to juice up your game and the five basic special effects.

For some ideas of more ways to add Juice to your game, check out Ray's AltConf talk on the matter here: http://bit.ly/1FViSbC

Also, check out what other developers are doing with their games. Make a list of the things you like about them. The best thing about adding juice is that you're only limited by your imagination!

Section V: Other Platforms

In this section, you'll learn how to create games that work on macOS, tvOS and watchOS.

In the process, you'll create a game named Zombie Piranhas. In this game, your goal is to catch as many fish as possible without hooking a zombie — because we all know what happens when zombies are around.

Chapter 18: macOS Games

Chapter 19: tvOS Games

Chapter 20: watchOS Games

Chapter 18: macOS Games

By Michael Briscoe

One of the biggest advantages of being an iOS developer is that you're not just an iOS developer — you're an *Apple* developer. In fact, your Apple Developer Program account lets you develop for all available Apple platforms!

This goes far beyond the scope of the developer program itself. The very same tools, languages and frameworks you use to build apps for the iPhone and iPad can be used to build apps for your Mac, Apple TV and Apple Watch, creating a cross-platform culture like no other.

Over the next three chapters, you'll learn how to leverage your iOS knowledge to build games for all Apple Platforms:

1. **Chapter 18, macOS Games**: You'll take a complete iOS game and add a **target** for macOS. Along the way, you'll learn some of the differences between the platforms, such as windows, mouse and keyboard events.

2. **Chapter 19, tvOS Games**: Building from Chapter 18, you'll add another target for tvOS. You'll learn concepts such as **Focus**, **parallax icons**, **Top Shelf** and how to work with the **Apple TV Remote**.

3. **Chapter 20, watchOS Games**: Finally, you'll add a target for watchOS. Here, you'll learn about **gestures**, the **Digital Crown**, **Haptic Feedback** and design considerations for small screens.

Cross-platform strategies

There are two approaches to cross-platform game development:

1. **Start with a cross-platform project**: Xcode 8 has a new **Cross-platform SpriteKit Game** template. If you plan for your game to be cross-platform from the start, this will save you time in the long run. You'll take a quick peek at how to do this in this chapter.

2. **Adding platform targets**: If you already have an existing game ready that works on a single OS, you can add support for other platforms by creating **targets**. This is the main approach you'll take over the next three chapters.

Cross-platform from scratch

To get an idea of how to make your next epic game cross-platform from the start, begin by opening the latest version of Xcode.

Choose **File > New > Project...** From the template panel, choose **Cross-platform/Application/Cross-platform SpriteKit Game**, then click **Next**.

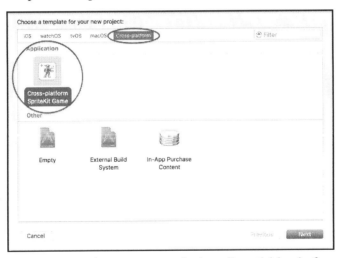

Enter **Hello World** for the Product Name, verify that all available platforms are checked, then click **Next**. Choose a location to save your project, then click **Create**.

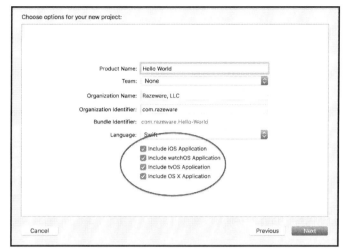

Take a moment to explore your new cross-platform game project.

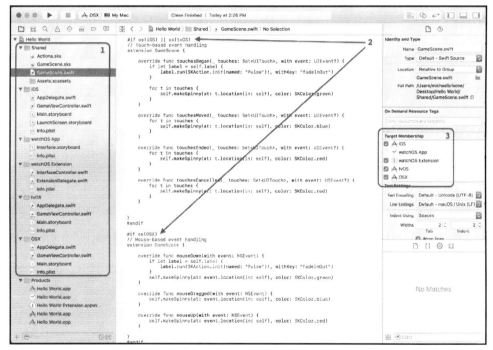

1. There are several new groups in the project navigator: a **Shared** group, and a group for each platform. The Shared folder is where all the source files and other resources shared between all platforms reside. This is where you'd put things like your main gameplay classes, graphic assets and sounds. The other groups contain platform-specific items.

2. Code that is specific to each platform is contained within **preprocessor directives** and class extensions. The directives tell the compiler which code to use depending on the selected active build scheme. You'll learn more about preprocessor directives in just a moment.

3. Target Membership is applied on a per-file basis to tell the compiler which files to compile for each platform target. In this case, **GameScene.swift** belongs to all platform targets.

Build and run each platform to see for yourself how easy it can be to create cross-platform games.

> **Tip:** A lot of developers will use one set of graphic assets for all platforms. Keep this in mind when creating your artwork. Usually it's best to design for the largest possible resolution, which minimizes the chance your art will be scaled upwards, which can result in distorted, blurry images.

Creating platform targets

For the rest of this chapter, you'll take a complete iOS game — Zombie Piranhas — and create a target for macOS that will run in a window on your Mac.

Getting started

Start by opening **projects/starter/Zombie Piranhas**. Take a moment to browse through the project to see how it's put together, especially the **GameScene.swift** and **GameScene.sks** files.

Build and run with the simulator, or better yet, an actual device.

Basic gameplay

Zombie Piranhas is a simple fishing game. Tap on the fisherman to drop the hook. This will cast out your line into a deep blue lake filled with Yum Fish — and Zombie Piranhas! Tap anywhere on the screen to stop the hook and start fishing.

The goal is to catch as many Yum Fish as possible while avoiding the Piranhas. If you catch a Piranha you'll get infected, become a zombie and lose a fisherman. After losing three fishermen (lives), the game is over.

If you catch a Piranha, you can try to knock the fish off the hook by tapping frantically on it — but hurry! You don't want to become a zombie, do you?

Creating a new target

Getting your game to run on macOS is as easy as creating a new target — well, almost. :] You'll have to make a few adjustments as well.

From Xcode, select **Zombie Piranhas** from the top of the project navigator. Then choose **File > New > Target...**

From the template panel, choose **macOS/Application/Game** and click **Next**. Enter **Zombie Piranhas macOS** for the Product Name and verify the Language is set to **Swift** and the Game Technology is **SpriteKit**, then click **Finish**.

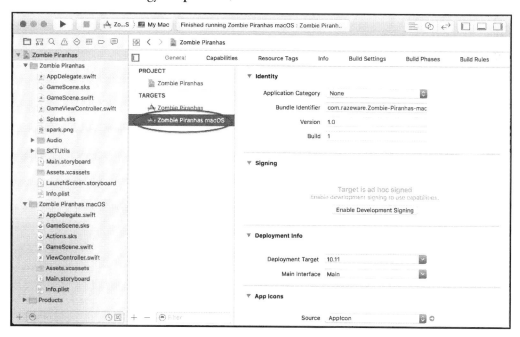

You now have a shiny new macOS target! To see what you've accomplished, set the active scheme to **Zombie Piranhas macOS > My Mac**, then build and run.

Wait, what? Where's the fish? OK, so you still have some work to do.

Whenever you add a new game target to an existing project, Xcode also creates new resource files. You won't be using these, so you're going to turn off their **Target Membership** flags.

Open the **Zombie Piranhas macOS** group from the project navigator, then select **GameScene.sks**, **Actions.sks** and **GameScene.swift**.

From the Utilities pane on the right side of the Xcode window, choose the **File Inspector**. In the Target Membership section, disable **Zombie Piranhas macOS**.

Fortunately, you don't have to reinvent the wheel every time you add a new platform. You can share files and resources between targets by setting their Target Membership flags.

From the iOS **Zombie Piranhas** group, select **GameScene.sks** and **GameScene.swift**. This time you're going to enable **Zombie Piranhas macOS**.

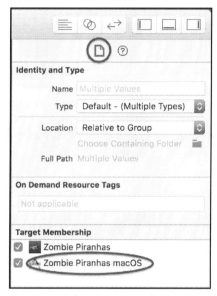

You'll also need to set the Target Membership to include **Zombie Piranhas macOS** on the following files:

- **Splash.sks**

- Everything within the **Audio** group.

- Everything within the **SKUtils** group.

- **Assets.xcassets**

To avoid naming conflicts, rename the Assets.xcassets file located in the **Zombie Piranhas macOS** group to **Assets/_macos.xcassets**. Next, open **Assets/_macos.xcassets** and rename AppIcon to **AppIcon_macOS**.

Then, select the **Zombie Piranhas** project from the top of the project navigator. Choose the **Zombie Piranhas macOS** target, select the **General** tab, then set **App Icons > Source** to **AppIcon_macOS**.

Now, open **Zombie Piranhas/GameScene.swift** and add this line just before `touchesBegan(_:with:)`:

```
#if os(iOS)
```

And this line just after `touchesBegan(_:with:)`:

```
#endif
```

`UITouch` and `UIEvent` aren't supported by macOS, so you want the compiler to skip this code unless the target is iOS. Don't worry, there are counterparts for this code in macOS that you'll learn about in the next section.

> **Note:** These are **preprocessor directives** and are used to include or discard code depending on which platform Xcode is compiling for. You'll use these often to separate incompatible code between targets.

One more thing before you're ready to run. Open **Zombie Piranhas macOS/ViewController.swift**, and change `view.ignoresSiblingOrder` to the following:

```
view.ignoresSiblingOrder = false
```

This will make sure that overlapping sprites sharing the same `zPosition` will render properly. It's already set like this in the iOS target, but you need to do the equivalent for macOS.

Build and run to see all your hard work!

Nice! However, clicking on the fisherman doesn't do anything. That's because the preprocessor logic you added skipped the incompatible iOS `touchesBegan(_:with:)`. Time to fix that.

Events

One of the biggest differences between iOS and macOS is the lack of a touchscreen. In macOS, navigation is generally handled by using a mouse or trackpad to control the cursor.

Mouse events

SpriteKit provides several functions for handling mouse events, including:

- **mouseDown(with:)**: Similar to `touchesBegan(_:with:)`. Called when the user clicks the left mouse button or presses down on the trackpad.

- **mouseUp(with:)**: Similar to `touchesEnded(with:)`. Called when the user releases the mouse button or lifts up from the trackpad.

- **mouseDragged(with:)**: Similar to `touchesMoved(with:)`. Called when the user moves the mouse while depressing the button or dragging a finger across the trackpad.

> **Note:** For more information about responding to mouse events have a look at the `NSResponder` docs: https://developer.apple.com/reference/appkit/nsresponder

For the purposes of this game you only need `mouseDown(with:)`. Open **Zombie Piranhas/GameScene.swift** and add the following extension to the `GameScene` class, at the very bottom of the file, after the closing }:

```
#if os(OSX)
  // macOS Events
  extension GameScene {
    override func mouseDown(with event: NSEvent) {
      let location = event.location(in: self)
      handlePlayerAction(at: location)
    }
  }
#endif
```

By creating an extension within the `#if os(OSX)` directive, you keep all your macOS specific methods separate from the main class. This is where you'll put your macOS specific event methods to keep your code clean and organized.

Build and run, and click on the fisherman:

Now you're fishing! Just watch out for those darn Zombie Piranha!

Key events

Many macOS games also provide keyboard shortcuts for navigation, or to toggle modes or features. Adding support for key events is easy!

Still within **Zombie Piranhas/GameScene.swift**, add the following method to your extension, just below `mouseDown(with:)`:

```
override func keyDown(with event: NSEvent) {
  guard !event.isARepeat else { return }
  let keyCode: UInt16 = event.keyCode
  print("keyCode = \(keyCode)")
}
```

Build and run, then press some keys on your keyboard. You'll notice that every time you press a key, the `keyCode` is printed to the console. Be sure to press the **Spacebar** and **B** keys and take note of their corresponding `keyCodes`.

Also, note the `isARepeat` check — if you hold a key down, it will continually fire key-down events, but you only want to handle the key press once. `isARepeat` tells you that the event was a result of the key being held down.

```
keyCode = 53
keyCode = 36
keyCode = 49
keyCode = 11



All Output ◇          ⊙ Filter                    🗑 ⬜⬜
```

Now that you know what the `keyCodes` are for the Spacebar and B key, replace the print statement within `keyDown(with:)` with these lines:

```swift
if keyCode == 49 { // Spacebar
  if gameState == .readyToCast {
    castLine()
  } else if gameState == .casting {
    stopHook()
  }
} else if keyCode == 11 { // 'B' key
  bashFish()
} else {
  super.keyDown(with: event)
}
```

This code first checks if the spacebar was pressed, then either casts the line or stops the hook depending on the state of the game. You also listen for the B key to give the user an alternate way to bash Zombie Piranhas off the hook. If a different key was pressed, fall back to the default implementation of `keyDown(with:)`.

Build and run the game. Press the spacebar to cast and stop, and press B repeatedly to bash that pesky Piranha!

Scaling

Everything is looking pretty good so far. However, you may have noticed that everything looks quite large and your label nodes seem to be missing. That's because the scene was originally built for iOS devices: **GameScene.sks** was designed with portrait orientation in mind.

SpriteKit auto-magically takes care of scaling the scene according to the scene's `scaleMode`. Since the `scaleMode` of GameScene is set to `aspectFill`, the landscape orientation of the macOS app results in everything being scaled up to fit the large screen width. It also means there's extra cropping on the top and bottom of the scene.

You'll need to tweak things a bit to get everything to look just right on macOS.

Positioning the labels

Your labels are floating somewhere offscreen. Start by bringing them back into view.

Within **Zombie Piranhas/GameScene.swift**, add these lines to `setupScene()`, just below the comment that reads `// macOS Stuff`:

```
#if os(OSX)
  let labelYScaleFactor: CGFloat = 0.87
  statusLabel!.position.y =
    statusLabel!.position.y * labelYScaleFactor
  scoreLabel!.position.y =
    scoreLabel!.position.y * labelYScaleFactor
  livesLabel!.position.y =
    livesLabel!.position.y * labelYScaleFactor
#endif
```

Again, you use preprocessor directives to tell the compiler that you want to only use this code for the macOS target. The label nodes' y positions are scaled by 87%, bringing them back into view.

> **Note:** In case you are wondering how I came up with 0.87 for `labelYScaleFactor`, it was purely trial and error. I was looking for a position that looked good both in windowed mode and in full screen.

Build and run to verify that your labels are displaying correctly.

Shrinking the fish

Now that you have the labels positioning correctly, it's time to scale down the game objects.

Start by adding this variable to the class properties:

```
var sceneContentsScale: CGFloat = 1.0
```

You'll use this property to scale your game objects depending on the platform target. The default for the iOS target is `1.0`.

Next, scroll back to `setupScene()` and add the following line within the `#if os(OSX)` directive, just after the code to scale the label positions:

```
sceneContentsScale = 0.5
```

Now, add theses lines to `setupScene()` just below `#endif`:

```
boatSprite!.setScale(sceneContentsScale)
line!.setScale(sceneContentsScale)
scoreLabel!.setScale(sceneContentsScale)
livesLabel!.setScale(sceneContentsScale)
```

You change the `sceneContentsScale` value for the macOS target only. You also make the code that applies `sceneContentsScale` global to all targets, in case you want to tweak this for other targets in the future.

Now, you can scale back the fish as well. Find the `spawnFish(type:amount)` method and replace this line:

```
fishSprite.setScale(CGFloat.random(min: 0.40, max: 1.0))
```

With the following lines:

```
let fishScale = CGFloat.random(min: 0.40, max: 1.0)
fishSprite.userData?["fishScale"] = fishScale
fishSprite.setScale(fishScale * sceneContentsScale)
```

Here, you create a random scale to determine the size of the fish and save it to the sprite's userData for later use. Then, you adjust the size again according to sceneContentsScale.

Next, replace the line that reads:

```
fishSprite.userData?["life"] = fishLife * fishSprite.yScale
```

With:

```
fishSprite.userData?["life"] = fishLife * fishScale
```

The "life" of a fish determines how many times you need to bash it before it drops from the hook. Smaller fish should have a shorter life that's independent of sceneContentsScale.

Go to catchFish(fish:) and insert the following code after fish.removeFromParent():

```
fishCaught?.setScale(fish.userData?["fishScale"] as! CGFloat)
```

Child nodes inherit the parent's scale. fishCaught will be a child of hook, which is a child of line — and line's scale is set to sceneContentsScale. The original fish node (where you copied fishCaught from) was a direct child of the scene.

Here, you remove the sceneContentsScale factor so it won't be applied twice. Without this tweak, the fish sprite will appear to shrink as it's caught.

Build and run to see what's happened to those fish:

All of your sprites appear to scale properly now. But what about those bubbles? They seem a bit large as well.

Making bubbles tiny

Still in **Zombie Piranhas/GameScene.swift**, scroll to `setupScene()` and replace this line:

```
(childNode(withName: "bubbles") as? SKEmitterNode)?
  .advanceSimulationTime(60.0)
```

With the following:

```
let bubbles = childNode(withName: "bubbles") as! SKEmitterNode
bubbles.particleScale =
  bubbles.particleScale * sceneContentsScale
bubbles.particleScaleRange =
  bubbles.particleScaleRange * sceneContentsScale
bubbles.particleScaleSpeed =
  bubbles.particleScaleSpeed * sceneContentsScale
bubbles.advanceSimulationTime(60.0)
```

Here, you capture a reference to the bubbles' `SKEmitterNode` and scale the particles before you advance the simulation time.

Now, go to `catchFish(fish:)` and add these lines after the point where you create `splash`:

```
splash!.particleScale =
  splash!.particleScale * sceneContentsScale
splash!.particleScaleRange =
  splash!.particleScaleRange * sceneContentsScale
splash!.particleScaleSpeed =
  splash!.particleScaleSpeed * sceneContentsScale
```

Just like you did with the bubbles, you scale the particles according to `sceneContentsScale`.

While you're here, tone down the screen-shaking effect that happens when a fish nabs the hook.

Change this line:

```
let shakeAmount = CGPoint(x: 0,
  y: -(150.0 * fishCaught!.yScale))
```

To read:

```
let shakeAmount = CGPoint(x: 0,
  y: -(150.0 * fishCaught!.yScale) * sceneContentsScale)
```

Before you do another build and run, there's one more scaling issue to address — the hook!

Go to `updateFish(fish:)`, and at the top, change `hookRadius` to:

```
let hookRadius:CGFloat = 100.0 * sceneContentsScale
```

Build and run to see all your hard work in action!

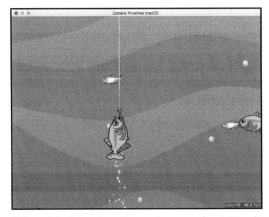

Your macOS version of Zombie Piranhas is nearly complete! But have you noticed something odd about the distance the hook travels?

It appears you have a little bit more work to do.

Going deep

GameScene.sks was built for iOS, which supports portrait orientation. Because Macs are inherently in landscape orientation, you'll need to rework a little more of the code. Start by fixing the depth of the cast.

Go to `castLine()` and replace this line:

```
let hookDepth = CGFloat(3600.0)
```

With this preprocessor logic:

```
#if os(iOS)
```

```
    let hookDepth = CGFloat(3600.0)
  #elseif os(OSX)
    let hookDepth = CGFloat(7000.0)
  #endif
```

This adjustment accounts for the new, smaller scales of `boatSprite` and `line`. Note that simply dividing `hookDepth` by `sceneContentsScale` doesn't quite work, since the positions of the line and hook need to be adjusted due to the smaller scale of the boat.

Next, modify `update(_:)` by replacing the code that updates the camera with the following:

```
// Update Camera
let hookPosition = convert((hook?.position)!, from: line!)
#if os(iOS)
  let maxCameraDepth: CGFloat = -1545.0
#elseif os(OSX)
  let maxCameraDepth: CGFloat = -1800.0
#endif
if hookPosition.y < boatSprite!.position.y &&
   hookPosition.y > maxCameraDepth {
  camera?.position = CGPoint(x: 0.0, y: hookPosition.y)
}
```

The camera will now go to a further depth so that the shorter landscape view shows the ocean bottom.

Finishing touches

There's a few finishing touches left — starting with the app icon.

Crafting an icon for a macOS app isn't much different than making an iOS app icon. Open **Zombie Piranhas macOS/Assets_macos.xcassets/AppIcon_macOS**, then drag the corresponding art from **projects/starter/Icon Art** into their respective slots.

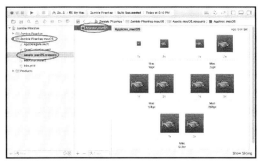

Build and run, then look at your shiny new icon down in the dock.

> **Note:** If the icon doesn't display, try a **Product > Clean** from Xcode's menu then build and run again.

Now that you have your icon taken care of, you have to take care of the app name. If you submitted it as is sits now, Apple would reject "Zombie Piranhas macOS" as it's against Apple policy to include a reference to the intended platform in an app's name.

The app takes the target name as its default name. It's good practice to name your targets to describe it's platform, but not so good for the Mac App Store. Fortunately, it's an easy fix.

Select **Zombie Piranhas** from the top of the project navigator, then choose the **Zombie Piranhas macOS** target.

Next, select the **Build Settings** tab and type **Product Name** in the search box.

From the **Product Name** heading, double-click on **Zombie Piranhas macOS**. Then replace $(TARGET_NAME) with **Zombie Piranhas**.

Now to clean up your menu. Open **Zombie Piranhas macOS/Main.storyboard**. First, rename the application menu to **Zombie Piranhas** by double-clicking the item right in the storyboard, or by selecting the item and then editing Title in the Attributes Inspector.

Then, rename any menu item that references **GameTemplate** to **Zombie Piranhas**. Finally, change the title of the window to **Zombie Piranhas**.

Playing in a sandbox

If you plan on submitting your game to the Mac App Store, you're required to enable **application sandboxing**. When your app is running in a sandbox, it's isolated to its own space in memory and has access to *only* the system resources it needs. This provides a more secure environment for both your app and the user.

To enable the sandbox, select **Zombie Piranhas** from the top of the project navigator, then choose the **Zombie Piranhas macOS** target. Next, choose the **Capabilities** tab. In the **App Sandbox** group, click the **OFF** button to toggle it to **ON**. Notice that this adds a new file — **Zombie Piranhas.entitlements** — to the macOS group in the project navigator.

For your game, that's all it takes!

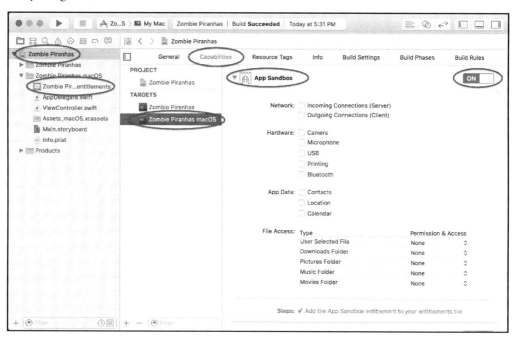

> **Note:** Other more complicated games may require additional entitlements. For more information about App Sandboxing check out https://developer.apple.com/library/mac/documentation/Security/Conceptual/AppSandboxDesignGuide

Build and run, then kick back, relax and enjoy some nice fishing. Just watch out for those Piranhas!

> **Note:** While you're fishing, try playing the game full screen for an even more immersive experience! Just click the little green circle at the top left of the window.

Congratulations — you learned how to take an existing Xcode project for an iOS app and create a new platform target for macOS. This was one of many approaches you can take when building a new target. Depending on your game's requirements, you might also need separate artwork, scenes and Swift files to make the transition.

In the next chapter, you'll take your cross-platform skills to the next level by creating a target for tvOS. I bet you can't wait to see Zombie Piranhas on the big screen!

Challenge

Now that Zombie Piranha is running in landscape on your Mac, try making use of that extra real estate. Wouldn't it be great if your fisherman could drift back and forth from one scene edge to the other?

Here are a few hints:

- Create a new method named `updateBoat()` to update the boat's position. Take a look at `updateFish(fish:)` for inspiration. Make sure the boat only moves while the fishing line is pulled up (`gameState == .readyToCast`).

- Flip the boat horizontally at the scene bounds. Leave a little buffer room so that the hook doesn't cross the scene edges.

- Call your method from `update(_:)`.

- Don't forget to use preprocessor directives; you only want this code to run on macOS.

Be sure to try this challenge on your own. But remember, if you get stuck, you can find the solution at **projects/challenge/Zombie Piranhas**.

Chapter 19: tvOS Games

By Michael Briscoe

When Apple released the fourth generation Apple TV with tvOS, a new opportunity opened up for developers. Not only can you create XML-based template apps, but also native apps that share many of the same APIs and frameworks that you're already familiar with — including SpriteKit!

You can now create amazing games, or port existing ones, to your big-screen TV. There are some tremendous opportunities ahead as the Apple TV evolves to approach the power of traditional gaming consoles.

Design considerations

The user interacts differently with their Apple TV than with other devices. There is no touch screen to touch, or cursor to move with a mouse. Instead, the user sits across the living room equipped with a remote. Similar to a trackpad, the remote has a touch surface that can detect gestures. Instead of a cursor, navigation is achieved by *focus*, either with a parallax effect or by highlighting an object.

Keep in mind that your player may be a fair distance away from the screen. Game content and text should be large, clear, and readable. HDTV screens can vary in size and resolution, so try to avoid placing important content close to the edges.

> **Note:** To learn more about tvOS app design see "tvOS Human Interface Guidelines": https://developer.apple.com/tvos/human-interface-guidelines/

In this chapter, you'll add a tvOS target to the Zombie Piranhas game. Along the way, you'll learn some important concepts for creating games for the tvOS platform.

Review

> **Note:** We begin where we left off with the challenge from the last chapter. If you didn't complete the challenge, or are skipping ahead, no worries — just open the starter project for this chapter.

So far you've taken the existing iOS game Zombie Piranhas and created a macOS target that runs landscape in a window on your Mac.

Click on the fisherman or press the spacebar to drop the hook. This will cast out your line into a lake filled with fish. Click anywhere, or press the spacebar, to stop the hook and start fishing. The idea is to catch as many Yum Fish as possible while avoiding the Piranhas.

Now it's time to take your cross-platform skills to the next level by adding support for the big screen! Be warned — zombie fish appear larger and scarier on your TV!

Adding a tvOS target

The first step in getting your game to run on Apple TV is to create a new platform target. You'll practice what you learned in the previous chapter. Select **Zombie Piranhas** from the top of the project navigator. Then, from the Xcode menu bar choose **File > New > Target...**

This time from the template panel, choose **tvOS/Application/Game** and click **Next**. Enter **Zombie Piranhas tvOS** for the Product Name and verify the Language is set to **Swift** and the Game Technology is **SpriteKit**, then click **Finish**.

Just to make sure everything went according to plan, set the active scheme to **Zombie Piranhas tvOS > tvOS Simulator > Apple TV 1080p**, then build and run.

If all went well, you'll see the familiar message: "Hello, World!". Perfect! Time to move on.

> **Note:** Do you want to test your apps on your Apple TV device instead of the simulator? You'll need a USB-A to USB-C (male to male) cable, available from Apple and other online retailers. Plug the cable into the small USB-C port just above the HDMI port on the Apple TV. Once connected to your Mac, choose the Apple TV listed under the available schemes in Xcode.

Open the **Zombie Piranhas tvOS** group from the project navigator, then delete **GameScene.sks**, **Actions.sks**, **Game.xcassets** and **GameScene.swift**.

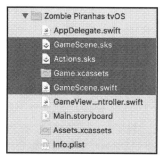

Just as you did in the previous chapter, from the iOS **Zombie Piranhas** group, set the Target Membership to include **Zombie Piranhas tvOS** on the following files:

- **GameScene.sks**
- **GameScene.swift**

- **Splash.sks**

- Everything within the **Audio** group.

- Everything within the **SKUtils** group.

- **Assets.xcassets**

To avoid naming conflicts, rename the Assets.xcassets file located in the Zombie Piranhas tvOS group to **Assets_tvos.xcassets**.

Now, open **Zombie Piranhas/GameScene.swift** and scroll to `castLine()`. Change the line that reads `#elseif os(OSX)` to the following:

```
#elseif os(OSX) || os(tvOS)
```

Then, go to `update(_:)` and again, change the line that reads `#elseif os(OSX)` as shown below:

```
#elseif os(OSX) || os(tvOS)
```

This tells the compiler to include the code inside this directive for macOS *or* tvOS. Because the Apple TV has a landscape orientation like your Mac, you don't need to change these values.

Next, just below the `#endif` directive in `setupScene()`, add the following lines:

```
// tvOS Stuff
#if os(tvOS)
  let labelYScaleFactor: CGFloat = 0.85
  let labelXScaleFactor: CGFloat = 0.92

  statusLabel!.position.y =
    statusLabel!.position.y * labelYScaleFactor
  scoreLabel!.position.y =
    scoreLabel!.position.y * labelYScaleFactor
```

```
    livesLabel!.position.y =
      livesLabel!.position.y * labelYScaleFactor

    scoreLabel!.position.x =
      scoreLabel!.position.x * labelXScaleFactor
    livesLabel!.position.x =
      livesLabel!.position.x * labelXScaleFactor

    sceneContentsScale = 0.5
  #endif
```

Again, use preprocessor directives to tell the compiler you only want to use this code for the tvOS target. You scale the label nodes' y positions by 85% to bring them back into view. Because you want to give a bit of a margin from the edges of the screen, you also scale back the x position of `scoreLabel` and `livesLabel`.

OK, time to include the challenge from last chapter. Find `updateBoat()` and modify the preprocessor directive just above it to the following:

```
#if os(OSX) || os(tvOS)
```

Next, go to the end of `update(_:)` and change the directive just above the call to `updateBoat()` to do the same:

```
#if os(OSX) || os(tvOS)
```

You're probably starting to get real comfortable using preprocessor directives to branch your code for different platforms.

Before you're ready to run, remember — there was something you had to modify in each of the view controllers. Open **Zombie Piranhas tvOS/GameViewController.swift**, and change `view.ignoresSiblingOrder` to:

```
view.ignoresSiblingOrder = false
```

Now, build and run to see Zombie Piranhas on the big screen!

So far, everything you've done up until this point has been a review on adding a new target and using preprocessor directives. It's time to start diving a bit deeper into tvOS!

The remote

At the moment, your happy fisherman is just drifting about aimlessly. But he's there to go fishing and catch some fish! Open **Zombie Piranhas/GameScene.swift** and implement this platform-specific extension to the end of the file:

```
#if os(tvOS)
  // tvOS Events
  extension GameScene {
    func remoteTapped(_ recognizer: UITapGestureRecognizer) {
      goFish()
    }

    func goFish() {
      if gameState == .readyToCast {
        castLine()
      } else if gameState == .casting {
        stopHook()
      } else if gameState == .gameOver {
        resetGame()
      }
    }
  }
#endif
```

remoteTapped(_:) is called when the touch surface on the remote has been tapped, which in turn calls goFish() to check the game state and continue accordingly. Now you need to add a UITapGestureRecognizer to call remoteTapped(_:).

Go to setupScene(). Add these lines to the // tvOS Stuff preprocessor logic:

```
let tapRecognizer = UITapGestureRecognizer(target: self, action:
  #selector(remoteTapped(_:)))
tapRecognizer.allowedPressTypes = [NSNumber(value:
UIPressType.select.rawValue)]
view!.addGestureRecognizer(tapRecognizer)
```

Using UITapGestureRecognizer is the recommended way to handle button taps and presses for the remote. Here, you only need to recognize UIPressType.select. This is when the user physically clicks the touchpad.

Available UIPressTypes are:

• upArrow: top edge of the touchpad was tapped.

- `downArrow`: bottom edge of the touchpad was tapped.

- `leftArrow`: left edge of the touchpad was tapped.

- `rightArrow`: right edge of the touchpad was tapped.

- `select`: touchpad was pressed.

- `menu`: menu button was pressed.

- `playPause`: play/pause button was pressed.

Build and run, click the touchpad to cast the line, and click it again to stop the hook.

> **Note:** If you're using the simulator, you can use a simulated remote by going to **Hardware > Show Apple TV Remote**.

Oh no! A Zombie Piranha! Your fisherman won't be happy for long.

Now that you can drop the hook and start fishing, it's time to add the code to knock those Piranhas off the hook.

Add this method just below `remoteTapped(_:)`:

```
override func touchesBegan(_ touches: Set<UITouch>,
    with event: UIEvent?) {
  bashFish()
}
```

Yes, you're seeing right. That's the same `touchesBegan(_:with:)` that you would use for an iOS app. It's great if you want to detect simple taps on the touchpad. However, it behaves a bit differently on tvOS. If you check the touch location it always returns the center of the screen, or in this case the camera's location. So the touch location is not very useful.

Build and run again. Now, tapping on the touchpad will bash those pesky Piranhas off the hook!

> **Note:** If you're using the simulator remote, simply pressing the Option key will be treated as a tap.

Capturing motion data

Wouldn't it be great if you could physically use a casting motion with your arm to drop the hook? After all, the Apple TV Remote *does* have an accelerometer. This type of gesture would make it feel more like you're actually fishing in a virtual lake.

It's a bit tricky, but you can access motion data from the remote's accelerometer.

Go to **Zombie Piranhas tvOS/AppDelegate.swift**. At the top of the file, just below `import UIKit`, add these lines:

```
import GameController

protocol ReactToMotionEvents {
  func motionUpdate(_ motion: GCMotion) -> Void
}
```

This delegate protocol will be used to allow `GameScene` to react to motion events, which you'll get to a little later. Next, add this property just below `var window: UIWindow?`:

```
var motionDelegate: ReactToMotionEvents? = nil
```

Now, add this method:

```
func setupControllers(_ notification: NSNotification) {
  let controllers = GCController.controllers()
  for controller in controllers {
    controller.motion?.valueChangedHandler =
        { (motion: GCMotion)->() in
      self.motionDelegate?.motionUpdate(motion)
    }
  }
}
```

Finally, add the following code to `application(_:didFinishLaunchingWithOptions:)` above `return true`:

```
NotificationCenter.default.addObserver(self,
    selector: #selector(setupControllers(_:)),
    name: NSNotification.Name.GCControllerDidConnect, object: nil)

NotificationCenter.default.addObserver(self,
    selector: #selector(setupControllers(_:)),
```

```
   name: NSNotification.Name.GCControllerDidDisconnect,
   object: nil)

 GCController.startWirelessControllerDiscovery(
   completionHandler: nil)
```

To receive motion data from the remote, you must treat it as a `GCController`. When the app finishes launching, you register `AppDelegate` as an observer for `GCControllerDidConnect` and `GCControllerDidDisconnect` notifications, then begin looking for wireless controllers — in this case, the Apple TV Remote.

Once the remote is discovered, the `GCControllerDidConnect` notification is sent, which fires `setupControllers(_:)` to add value observer that updates the delegate with motion data.

Time to implement the delegate. Go back to **Zombie Piranhas/GameScene.swift** and add the following to the top of the file, just below the `import` statements:

```
#if os(tvOS)
   import GameController
#endif
```

This code will only compile for the tvOS version and imports the `GameController` framework.

Next, go to `setupScene()` and add the following to the `// tvOS Stuff` logic:

```
let appDelegate = UIApplication.shared.delegate as! AppDelegate
appDelegate.motionDelegate = self
```

This sets `GameScene` as the app delegate's `motionDelegate`. There will be a compile error; you'll fix that momentarily. First, implement the `motionUpdate(_:)` method just below `remoteTapped(_:)`:

```
func motionUpdate(_ motion: GCMotion) {
  if motion.userAcceleration.y > 8.0 {
    if gameState == .reelingIn {
      bashFish()
    } else {
      goFish()
    }
  }
}
```

Whenever the value of the accelerometer changes, `motionUpdate(_:)` checks the `userAcceleration.y` to see if it exceeds a threshold of `8.0`. You'll hit this threshold if you abruptly move the remote up or down or shake it. If the motion exceeds the threshold, fishing begins.

Lastly, change the tvOS extension declaration to adopt the `ReactToMotionEvents` protocol:

```
// tvOS Events
extension GameScene: ReactToMotionEvents {
```

Build and run to give it a go. Try casting as if you were holding a real fishing pole. You can stop the hook as it's descending by pulling up on the remote. If you catch a Piranha, shake the remote furiously to get that bad boy off!

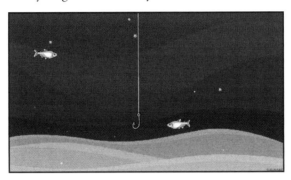

Now that's fishing!

> **Note:** You must use an actual Apple TV Remote to capture motion data. There is no accelerometer support with the simulator remote.

More gestures

Next, you'll add another `GestureRecognizer` to change the direction of the boat. Add this method just below `remoteTapped(_:)`:

```
func handlePanFrom(_ recognizer: UIPanGestureRecognizer) {
  if gameState == .readyToCast {
    if recognizer.state == UIGestureRecognizerState.ended {
      let distance = recognizer.translation(in: view)
      let tolerance: CGFloat = 900.0

      if distance.x > tolerance { // Swipe Right
        if boatSprite!.xScale < 0.0 {
          // Flip Boat
          boatSprite?.run(SKAction.scaleX(
            to: sceneContentsScale,
            duration: 0.5))
        }
      } else if distance.x < -tolerance { // Swipe Left
        if boatSprite!.xScale > 0.0 {
```

```
          // Flip Boat
          boatSprite?.run(SKAction.scaleX(
            to: -sceneContentsScale,
            duration: 0.5))
        }
      }
    }
  }
}
```

When a `UIPanGesture` is recognized, this method will be called. If the recognizer state has ended, the horizontal distance of the swipe is checked and compared with a tolerance to filter out unintended touches. If the distance is positive, the swipe is right; if it's negative, left. Then the `boatSprite` is flipped accordingly.

Scroll to `setupScene()` and add these lines just below the code for adding the `tapRecognizer`:

```
let panRecognizer = UIPanGestureRecognizer(target: self,
  action: #selector(handlePanFrom(_:)))
view!.addGestureRecognizer(panRecognizer)
```

This code adds the `UIPanGestureRecognizer` to the view so the `handlePanFrom(_:)` method will fire.

Build and run, then swipe left and right to change the boat's direction.

Now, instead of waiting for the boat to reach the edge of the screen to flip, you're in control of its direction.

> **Note:** If you're using the simulator remote, hold down the Option key while swiping across the simulated touchpad to create a pan gesture.

Finishing touches

Now that you have Zombie Piranhas running beautifully on tvOS, you can add its icon and top shelf image.

Parallax icons

The icon for a tvOS app is a bit different than those on other platforms. That's because tvOS makes use of a parallax effect and requires icons to have between two to five layers. When the icon is rendered, each layer moves independently at slightly different increments, creating a sense of depth.

Open **Zombie Piranhas tvOS/Assets_tvos.xcassets**, then open the **App Icon & Top Shelf Image** group.

Notice there are two App Icons: **App Icon - Large** and **App Icon - Small**. The large icon is used by the App Store and is sized at 1280px by 768px. The small icon is used on the Apple TV Home screen when your app is installed. Its size is 400px by 240px.

From the **projects/starter/resources/tvOS Icons/Large** folder, drag **ZP_tvOS_large_back.png** to the **App Icon - Large/Back** slot in Xcode. Now, drag the remaining icon art into their respective slots to complete the large icon.

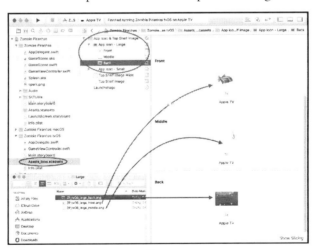

Repeat this process for the **App Icon - Small**.

The top shelf

If the user has placed your game in the top row of the home screen, a static image displays when the game is in focus on the top shelf to entice the user to play.

From the **projects/starter/resources** folder, drag the **ZP_tvOS_top_shelf.png** file into the slot for **Top Shelf Image**.

One more thing: Select **Zombie Piranhas** from the top of the project navigator, then choose the **Zombie Piranhas tvOS** target. Next, select the **Build Settings** tab and type **Product Name** in the search box. From the **Product Name** heading, double-click on **Zombie Piranhas tvOS**. Then replace **$(TARGET_NAME)** with **Zombie Piranhas**.

Like in the previous chapter, you want the app name to appear as Zombie Piranhas and not as the target name. Build and run, and press the **MENU** button to return to the Apple TV home screen.

There's your beautiful top shelf image and icon! Notice that when your icon is in *focus* and you move your finger around slowly, the icon has shine and depth. That's the parallax effect!

> **Note:** If you're not seeing the top shelf image, remember that your app needs to be in the top row.

Congratulations — you've just added another platform to your game! In the next chapter, you'll learn how to make Zombie Piranhas run in watchOS...because we all need biting zombie fish on our wrists! For now, kick back on the couch with a bowl of popcorn and your virtual fishing pole.

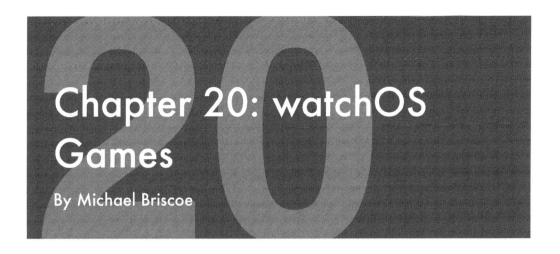

Chapter 20: watchOS Games

By Michael Briscoe

One of the best announcements at WWDC 2016 was the addition of SpriteKit to watchOS. This has the potential to enhance any Apple Watch app by providing rich media support and animation. Most importantly, you now have the ability to port existing iOS games and create compelling new ones.

Designing games for your wrist

The Apple Watch may be small, but there's a big heart behind that tiny screen. Your users will interact with your game using several input and feedback technologies:

- **Gesture recognizers**: Use touch gestures such as tap, pan, swipe and long press for scrolling, movement and navigation.

- **Digital Crown**: The crown can be used as a simple analog control for selection, scrolling or even a *Pong*-like game paddle.

- **Accelerometer**: This can be used to enhance game interactions, such as intuitively changing the direction of a ball.

- **Haptic feedback**: A combination of vibration and tone that adds realism to your game by providing tactile feedback at key moments.

SpriteKit platform differences

With watchOS 3, you get most of the powerful nodes and features you've grown to know and love with SpriteKit. However, there are some differences and limitations.

- **WKInterfaceSKScene:** Instead of `SKView`, your `SKScene` file is presented by an instance of `WKInterfaceSKScene`.

- **No CIFilter:** There is no support for core image filters, but you can achieve most of the same effects with `SKShader`.

- **SKAudioNode:** There is no support for positional audio on the watch, but you can play sounds with `SKAudioNode` and `SKAction.playSoundFileNamed(_:waitForCompletion:)`.

- **No SKVideoNode:** If your game needs to play video clips, use `WKInterfaceMovie`.

> **Note:** To learn more about creating apps for watchOS see, App Programming Guide for watchOS

Review

> **Note:** We begin where we left off from the last chapter. If you're skipping ahead, no worries — just open the starter project for this chapter.

You've taken Zombie Piranhas from the iPhone, to your Mac's screen, to your Apple TV. In this chapter, you'll take the last step and create a platform target for your Apple Watch. Beware! Zombie Piranhas can bite off your hand — and turn you into a zombie!

Adding a watchOS target

You know the drill by now. The first step to getting your game on watchOS is to create a new target. As you've done in the last two chapters, select **Zombie Piranhas** from the top of the project navigator. Then choose **File > New > Target...**

From the template panel, choose **watchOS/Application/Game App** and click **Next**. Enter **Zombie Piranhas watchOS** for the Product Name and verify that the Language is set to **Swift**, the Game Technology is **SpriteKit**, and **Include Notification Scene** is not checked, then click **Finish**. Then, if prompted, **Activate** the Zombie Piranhas watchOS scheme.

This time you'll notice the template creates two groups of files and two targets:

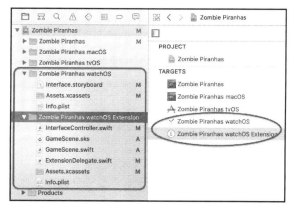

- **Zombie Piranhas watchOS** is where the storyboard, icon and **Info.plist** files will be stored.

- **Zombie Piranhas watchOS Extension** is where the meat of your app will reside. Here you'll find the controller, delegate, scene and other class files.

To make sure everything went according to plan, do a build and run:

Yup, it's "Hello, World!" again!

> **Note:** If you have an Apple Watch, you can run directly on your device by connecting your iPhone to your Mac. Then, choose your paired and connected watch from the scheme menu at **Zombie Piranhas watchOS > Device > (your iPhone + Apple Watch)**.

Open the **Zombie Piranhas watchOS Extension** group from the project navigator, then delete **GameScene.sks** and **GameScene.swift**.

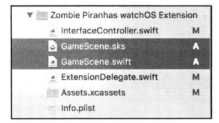

Just as before, from the iOS **Zombie Piranhas** group, set the Target Membership to include **Zombie Piranhas watchOS Extension** on the following files:

- **GameScene.swift**

- **Splash.sks**

- Everything within the **Audio** group.

- Everything within the **SKUtils** group *except* **SKTAudio.swift**.

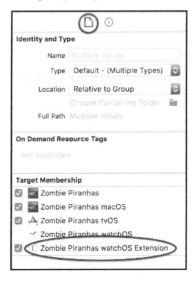

Adding optimized artwork

In the previous two chapters, you shared the same artwork across all platforms. With the Apple Watch, there is limited space and processor resources so it's important to optimize where you can. You'll add new versions of the artwork and scene file that have been scaled down to better fit the dimensions of the watch.

Open **Zombie Piranhas watchOS Extension/Assets.xcassets**, then drag the **Artwork** folder from **projects/starter** into **Assets.xcassets**.

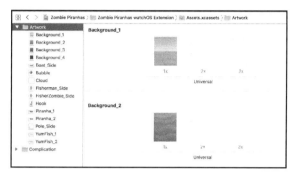

Next, drag **GameScene.sks** from **projects/starter** to **Zombie Piranhas watchOS Extension**. Make sure **Copy items if needed** is checked, then click **Finish**.

> **Note:** To save time, the new **GameScene.sks** file was created for you. If you would like know how it was put together and what's different, feel free to open it and take a look.

Diving into code

Open **Zombie Piranhas/GameScene.swift** and add the following lines to the top of the file, just below `import SpriteKit`:

```
#if os(watchOS)
   import WatchKit
#endif
```

This imports the **WatchKit** framework you'll use later to access some platform-specific classes.

Next, insert this preprocessor directive just above `didMove(to:)`:

```
#if !os(watchOS)
```

Then, close the directive just after `didMove(to:)`:

```
#endif
```

Because watchOS doesn't use `SKView`, `didMove(to:)` will not compile, so you've included a directive to skip this method. Next, you'll create a new extension and start adding some platform-specific code. Implement this at the end of **GameScene.swift**:

```
#if os(watchOS)
  // watchOS
  extension GameScene {
    override func sceneDidLoad() {
      setupScene()
    }
  }
#endif
```

Before you can get things running on watchOS, you have to add a few more directives. Start by scrolling to `castLine()` and insert this code just above `#endif`:

```
#elseif os(watchOS)
  let hookDepth = CGFloat(1350.0)
```

Next, find `resetHook()` and replace the `let targetDepth` line with this:

```
#if os(watchOS)
  let targetDepth = CGFloat(50.0)
#else
  let targetDepth = CGFloat(100.0)
#endif
```

Go to `spawnFish(type:amount:)` and replace the line that defines `fishY` with:

```
#if os(watchOS)
  let fishY = CGFloat.random(min: -700.0, max: 515.0)
#else
  let fishY = CGFloat.random(min: -1900.0, max: 1450.0)
#endif
```

Next up, find `updateFish(fish:)` and swap out the definition of `hookRadius` to:

```
#if os(watchOS)
  let hookRadius:CGFloat = 50.0
  let offset = CGPoint(x: 6.0, y: 30.0)
#else
  let hookRadius:CGFloat = 100.0 * sceneContentsScale
  let offset = CGPoint(x: 12.0, y: 60.0)
#endif
```

Then change the `let convertedHookPosition` line to:

```
let convertedHookPosition = CGPoint(
  x: hookPosition.x - offset.x,
  y: hookPosition.y - offset.y)
```

Now go to `catchFish(fish:)` and replace the `fishCaught!.position` line with the following:

```
#if os(watchOS)
  fishCaught!.position = CGPoint(x: -6.0, y: -30.0)
#else
  fishCaught!.position = CGPoint(x: -12.0, y: -60.0)
#endif
```

And finally, add this to `update(_:)` within the `// Update Camera` section just above `#endif`:

```
#elseif os(watchOS)
  let maxCameraDepth: CGFloat = -600.0
```

All these changes simply modify some hard coded values to compensate for the different node sizes and positions on the smaller screen.

Now update `resetGame()` to the following:

```
func resetGame() {
  #if os(watchOS)
    NotificationCenter.default.post(
      name: NSNotification.Name("Reload"), object: self)
  #else
    let newScene = GameScene(fileNamed:"GameScene")
    newScene!.scaleMode = .aspectFill
    let reveal = SKTransition.flipHorizontal(withDuration: 0.5)
    view?.presentScene(newScene!, transition: reveal)
  #endif
}
```

As stated earlier, watchOS doesn't use an `SKView`. Since `GameScene` doesn't have access to the `WKInterfaceSKScene` instance, you'll post a notification to tell `InterfaceController` to reload the game.

Now you'll add the notification observer.

From the **Zombie Piranhas watchOS Extension** group, open **InterfaceController.swift** and add the following to the top of the file:

```
import SpriteKit
```

Then, add the following property just below @IBOutlet var skInterface:

```
var gameScene: GameScene!
```

This will hold an instance of GameScene so that you can call methods on it from InterfaceController. This will come in handy later when you start adding gestures.

Implement this method below awake(withContext:):

```
func loadScene() {
  gameScene = GameScene(fileNamed:"GameScene")
  gameScene.scaleMode = .aspectFill
  let reveal = SKTransition.flipHorizontal(withDuration: 0.5)
  skInterface.presentScene(gameScene, transition: reveal)
  skInterface.preferredFramesPerSecond = 30
}
```

Now, replace awake(withContext:) with this updated version:

```
override func awake(withContext context: Any?) {
  super.awake(withContext: context)

  NotificationCenter.default.addObserver(self,
    selector: #selector(loadScene),
    name: NSNotification.Name("Reload"), object: nil)

  loadScene()
}
```

When the game is over and resetGame() is called, a notification is posted and observed by InterfaceController, which in turn calls loadScene() to restart the game.

Build and run to see what you've accomplished!

Now that you've got Zombie Piranhas running on watchOS, it's time to start delving into some platform-specific interactions.

Gesture recognizers

The Apple Watch handles gesture recognizers a bit differently than other platforms. Instead of using `UIGestureRecognizer` there is `WKGestureRecognizer`, and the gestures are added to the storyboard rather than in code. Start by adding a simple tap recognizer to get the fisherman fishin'.

Adding a tap gesture

Open **Zombie Piranhas watchOS/Interface.storyboard**.

From the Object Library, drag a **Tap Gesture Recognizer** to the **SpriteKit Scene**:

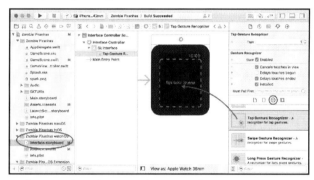

Show the **assistant editor** and make sure that **InterfaceController.swift** is open. Then from the storyboard outline view, **Control-drag** from **Tap Gesture Recognizer** to the **InterfaceController.swift** file in the assistant editor. When the connection pop-up appears, select **Action** for Connection and name it **didTap**, then click **Connect**.

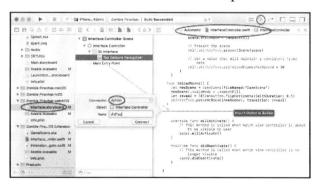

Switch back to the **standard editor** and open **Zombie Piranhas/GameScene.swift**. Implement this method in the watchOS extension, right after sceneDidLoad():

```
func didTap(_ recognizer: WKTapGestureRecognizer) {
  switch gameState {
  case .readyToCast:
    castLine()
  case .casting:
    stopHook()
  case .reelingIn:
    bashFish()
  case .gameOver:
    resetGame()
  default:
    break
  }
}
```

Next, open **Zombie Piranhas watchOS Extension/InterfaceController.swift**. Implement didTap(_:) by adding the following code:

```
// forward to the gameScene
gameScene.didTap(sender as! WKTapGestureRecognizer)
```

Build and run, then tap on the watch. The WKTapGestureRecognizer you added to the storyboard calls the didTap(_:) method in InterfaceController, which in turn forwards the tap to gameScene.didTap(_:).

Now cast your line and enjoy some wrist fishing. If you catch a Piranha, tap furiously on the screen to bash it off!

Yikes! Not another Zombie Piranha!

Adding a swipe gesture

What if the player doesn't like where their cast ended up? Like any good fisherman, you should be able to reel in your line when you don't like your spot. You'll add this new functionality just for the watchOS platform.

Using a `WKSwipeGestureRecognizer` you can determine if the player swipes up on the watch screen. An upwards swipe will reset the hook, ready for a new cast.

Open **Zombie Piranhas watchOS/Interface.storyboard**.

This time, drag a **Swipe Gesture Recognizer** to the **SpriteKit Scene**. Then, show the assistant editor and make sure that **InterfaceController.swift** is open. From the storyboard outline view, Control-drag from **Swipe Gesture Recognizer** to the **InterfaceController.swift** file in the assistant editor.

When the connection pop-up appears, select **Action** for Connection and name it **didSwipe**, then click **Connect**. Switch back to the **standard editor**.

Make sure that the **Swipe Gesture Recognizer** is selected and that the **Attributes Inspector** is showing. Set the swipe direction by choosing **Swipe Gesture Recognizer > Swipe > Up** from the drop-down menu:

Open **Zombie Piranhas/GameScene.swift**. Add the following method to the watchOS extension, right after `didTap(_:)`:

```swift
func didSwipe(_ recognizer: WKSwipeGestureRecognizer) {
  if gameState == .fishing {
    resetHook()
  }
}
```

Go back to **Zombie Piranhas watchOS Extension/InterfaceController.swift**. Implement the didSwipe(_:) method like so:

```
// forward to the gameScene
gameScene.didSwipe(sender as! WKSwipeGestureRecognizer)
```

Build and run. The next time your cast is in a bad spot, just swipe up to yank it out of there!

Quick — swipe up!

Working with the Digital Crown

The little rotating dial on the side of your watch – the **Digital Crown** — lets you scroll content without obstructing it with your fingers. This behavior comes free for developers who use interface elements such as tables, but there was no direct way to access the crown's data — until now!

With watchOS 3 it's easy to adopt the Digital Crown and read data directly using your interface controller.

For a game developer, this opens up some interesting possibilities, such as using the crown as an analog control.

You'll give your fisherman further control of their cast by using the Digital Crown as a "reel". This will allow the player to decide exactly where they want the hook, and provide another way to avoid catching those pesky Piranhas!

Start by opening **Zombie Piranhas/GameScene.swift**. Add these variables to the properties at the top of the file:

```
#if os(watchOS)
var hookDeltaPerFrame: CGFloat = 0.0
var reelDecelerateFactor: CGFloat = 0.0
#endif
```

Next, scroll to the bottom of **GameScene.swift** and add the following method to the watchOS extension, right after `didSwipe(_:)`:

```
func updateReel() {
  let hookDepthDelta =
    hookDeltaPerFrame * reelDecelerateFactor
  line!.size.height = line!.size.height - hookDepthDelta
  hook!.position.y = hook!.position.y + hookDepthDelta

  if hook!.position.y >= -50.0 {
    hook!.position.y = -50.0
    line!.size.height = 50.0
    reelDecelerateFactor = 0.0
    removeAction(forKey: "ReelSound")
    gameState = .readyToCast
    return
  }

  if hook!.position.y <= -1350.0 {
    hook!.position.y = -1350.0
    line!.size.height = 1350.0
    reelDecelerateFactor = 0.0
    removeAction(forKey: "ReelSound")
  }

  reelDecelerateFactor = reelDecelerateFactor * 0.95

  if reelDecelerateFactor < 0.02 {
    reelDecelerateFactor = 0.0
    gameState = .fishing
    fishingTimer = CFAbsoluteTimeGetCurrent()
  }
}
```

Then, add these lines to the end of `update(_:)`:

```
#if os(watchOS)
  if reelDecelerateFactor > 0.0 {
    updateReel()
  }
#endif
```

When the scene calls `update(_:)`, you check to see if `reelDecelerateFactor` is greater than `0.0`, and if so, call `updateReel()`. This means the reel is spinning and hasn't come to a stop yet. This method is what actually moves the hook, according to the `hookDeltaPerFrame` multiplied by `reelDecelerateFactor`. It also checks the hook's boundaries and incrementally scales `reelDecelerateFactor` down so that the hook will slow before stopping.

> **Note:** The reel will be slowed down each frame by the `reelDecelerateFactor`. 0.95^77 is just under 0.02, so if the game runs near 30 frames per second and `reelDecelerateFactor` has an initial value of 1.0, the hook will come to a stop 2-3 seconds after a Digital Crown rotation.

Next, implement this method just below `updateReel()`:

```
func reelTurn(rotateSpeed: CGFloat) {
  // 1
  if fishCaught == nil && !hook!.hasActions() {
    gameState = .casting
    // 2
    var hookDeltaMagnitude = abs(rotateSpeed) * 10.0
    hookDeltaMagnitude = min(hookDeltaMagnitude, 20.0)
    // 3
    if reelDecelerateFactor < 0.1 && hookDeltaMagnitude > 6.0 {
      run(reelStartSound, withKey: "ReelSound")
    }
    // 4
    hookDeltaPerFrame = hookDeltaMagnitude * rotateSpeed.sign()
    // 5
    reelDecelerateFactor = 1.0
    tickTimer = CFAbsoluteTimeGetCurrent()
  }
}
```

This is the method you'll call when the Digital Crown rotates. Going over each part:

1. First, check to make sure there is no fish on the line and that the hook is not animating due to a regular cast or reel-in. Then, set the game state to `casting`.

2. Calculate an appropriate `hookDeltaMagnitude` and prevent it from exceeding `20.0`. This keeps the reeling at a visually realistic speed.

3. Set some limits on when to play the `reelStartSound` so it's not always playing.

4. Set `hookDeltaPerFrame` to the `hookDeltaMagnitude` multiplied by the appropriate sign. A negative number means that the crown is rotating towards the wearer and the hook will drop down.

When this number is positive, the crown is rotating away from the user and the hook moves up.

5. Finally, set `reelDecelerateFactor` to `1.0` to get the hook moving.

Now that your done setting everything up in the scene, it's time to see how to directly access Digital Crown data!

Accessing Digital Crown data

Adopting the crown for use in your game is really easy. The main interface controller has the `crownSequencer` property that you can access directly to query the crown's current state. You can get the crown's `rotationsPerSecond`, and check whether it's idle or not. You can also define a delegate which is notified as crown data is changed. This is the approach you'll take for Zombie Piranhas.

Open **Zombie Piranhas watchOS Extension/InterfaceController.swift**. At the top of the file, change the class declaration to read as follows:

```
class InterfaceController: WKInterfaceController,
  WKCrownDelegate {
```

This redefines the class to adopt the `WKCrownDelegate` protocol.

Now, add this delegate method just below `didSwipe(_:)`:

```
func crownDidRotate(_ crownSequencer: WKCrownSequencer?,
                    rotationalDelta: Double) {
  let rotateSpeed = CGFloat(
    crownSequencer!.rotationsPerSecond)
  if rotateSpeed != 0.0 {
    gameScene.reelTurn(rotateSpeed: rotateSpeed)
  }
}
```

When the crown is turned, the delegate will be notified and call `crownDidRotate(_:rotationalDelta:)`. Here, you're setting `rotateSpeed` based on the `crownSequencer!.rotationsPerSecond` property. If it's not `0.0`, pass the `rotateSpeed` to GameScene's `reelTurn(rotateSpeed:)`.

Before you can access the crown's data, you have to set its delegate and focus. Add the following code to `willActivate()` just below the call to `super`:

```
crownSequencer.delegate = self
crownSequencer.focus()
```

That's all there is to start reeling with the Digital Crown. Build and run, then turn the crown to cast your line!

> **Note:** To simulate the turning of the Digital Crown within the simulator, make sure the cursor is hovering over the screen, then use a scrolling gesture with your mouse or trackpad.

The accelerometer

The Apple Watch also has an accelerometer similar to that of the iPhone; you access the accelerometer through `CMMotionManager`. Note that the watch uses the accelerometer to detect when the watch is raised and lowered and will blank the screen accordingly. Keep this in mind when when planning your use of the accelerometer — subtlety is what you're shooting for.

In Zombie Piranhas you'll use the accelerometer to add a little drift to your fisherman's boat.

Begin by opening **Zombie Piranhas/GameScene.swift**, then add this `import` statement to the top of the file right below `import WatchKit`:

```
import CoreMotion
```

Implement this method at the end of the watchOS extension, right after `reelTurn(rotateSpeed:)`:

```
// MARK: - Accelerometer
func accelerometerUpdate(
    accelerometerData: CMAccelerometerData) {
  if gameState == .readyToCast {
    let screenEdgeBuffer: CGFloat = 67.0
    let xDelta: CGFloat = (size.width * 0.5)
      - boatSprite!.size.width/2 - screenEdgeBuffer
    let acceleration = accelerometerData.acceleration
```

```
    let currentXPosition = boatSprite!.position.x
    var positionX = currentXPosition
      + (5.0 * CGFloat(acceleration.x))

    // Check boundaries
    if positionX > xDelta {
      positionX = xDelta
    } else if positionX < -xDelta {
      positionX = -xDelta
    }

    // Flip boat
    if acceleration.x > 0.1 && boatSprite!.xScale < 0.0 {
      boatSprite?.run(SKAction.scaleX(to: 1.0, duration: 0.5))
    }
    if acceleration.x < -0.1 && boatSprite!.xScale > 0.0 {
      boatSprite?.run(SKAction.scaleX(to: -1.0, duration: 0.5))
    }

    boatSprite!.position.x = positionX
  }
}
```

When this method is called, it reads the accelerometer data and moves the boat right or left, flipping the sprite horizontally depending on its direction. It also checks the boat's boundary so that it doesn't drift offscreen.

Now, switch back to **Zombie Piranhas watchOS Extension/InterfaceController.swift**. Add the following import statement to the top of the file:

```
import CoreMotion
```

Then, add this constant to the class properties:

```
let motionManager = CMMotionManager()
```

This creates an instance of `CMMotionManager` so you can access the accelerometer. Next, go to `awake(withContext:)` and add this line just above `loadScene()`:

```
motionManager.accelerometerUpdateInterval = 1.0/30.0
```

Your accelerometer will update its data approximately 30 times per second. Go to `willActivate()` and add the following code:

```
if motionManager.isAccelerometerAvailable {
  motionManager.startAccelerometerUpdates(
      to: OperationQueue.current!,
      withHandler: { data, error in
    guard let data = data else { return }
```

```
    self.gameScene.accelerometerUpdate(accelerometerData: data)
  })
}
```

This bit of code checks to make sure that the accelerometer is available. It then sets up the handler to call on every update, which in turn passes that data to your `accelerometerUpdate(accelerometerData:)` method in `gameScene`.

Finally, add this line to `didDeactivate()`, right after the call to `super`:

```
motionManager.stopAccelerometerUpdates()
```

This prevents the accelerometer from updating when your app is in the background, conserving battery power.

Build and run; as you slightly rock your hand back and forth, the boat will drift from side to side.

> **Note:** You'll need an actual Apple Watch to see the effects of the accelerometer, as it's not supported in the simulator.

Haptic feedback

Another great feature of the Apple Watch is its **Taptic Engine**. This technology provides a vibration and a brief audio tone to get the wearer's attention. As a game developer you can use this to your advantage to create an immersive experience with touch and sound.

There are nine specific haptic patterns you can use in your games:

- **Notification:** Use this to alert the user that something important has happened, like when you catch a fish.

- **Up/Down:** These haptics alert when a certain value has increased or decreased significantly. For instance you could use the up haptic when you gain a life, or the down when your health is low.

- **Success:** A goal has been completed successfully. You caught a big fish!

- **Failure:** An action has failed. This could be used when you've caught a Zombie Piranha, or lost all your fisherman.

- **Retry:** An action has failed but may be retried. This could be used when your hook comes up without any fish.

- **Start/Stop:** This should be used when the user is starting or stopping an action, like when you first start fishing.

- **Click:** This subtle click haptic could be used when turning the fishing reel.

These are a few examples; you won't actually implement them all in Zombie Piranhas. They are meant to draw attention to important events. Overuse can diminish their effectiveness, so consider your use of haptics with care. Again, subtlety is key.

> **Note:** The Taptic Engine is different than standard audio in that you can only play one haptic pattern at a time.

Using haptics in your game is ridiculously easy. All it requires is one line of code!

Open **Zombie Piranhas/GameScene.swift** and go to `castLine()`. Add the following line to the `watchOS` directive just below `let hookDepth`:

```
WKInterfaceDevice.current().play(.start)
```

Still within `castLine()`, add these lines to the `castAndReel` completion block after setting `self.fishingTimer`:

```
#if os(watchOS)
  WKInterfaceDevice.current().play(.stop)
#endif
```

Next, go to stopHook() and add similar lines to above, again just after setting
fishingTimer:

```
#if os(watchOS)
  reelDecelerateFactor = 0.0
  WKInterfaceDevice.current().play(.stop)
#endif
```

In addition to playing the stop haptic feedback, you fix a bug that prevented you from
stopping the hook after moving it with the Digital Crown.

Lastly, go to checkForFish() and add these lines inside the last } else { branch at
the bottom of the method:

```
#if os(watchOS)
  WKInterfaceDevice.current().play(.retry)
#endif
```

Build and run your game; you will now hear (and feel, if you're running on an actual
watch) a brief chime when you start and stop your cast. The retry haptic will play when
the hook comes back without a fish.

Finishing touches

If you've been testing your game on an actual Apple Watch you may have noticed some lag. That's because the watch doesn't have the same processing power or memory as an iPhone. This should be an important consideration when designing your game for watchOS.

One of the best things you can do to help boost the performance of Zombie Piranhas is to reduce the complexity of the scene. Still in **Zombie Piranhas/GameScene.swift**, go to `setupScene()` and replace the lines that spawn the fish:

```
spawnFish(type: yumFish!, amount: 10)
spawnFish(type: piranha!, amount: 20)
```

...with the following code:

```
#if os(watchOS)
  spawnFish(type: yumFish!, amount: 5)
  spawnFish(type: piranha!, amount: 10)
#else
  spawnFish(type: yumFish!, amount: 10)
  spawnFish(type: piranha!, amount: 20)
#endif
```

Because of the smaller screen on the watch, you really don't need as many fish anyway, so you reduce the number by half to improve performance. Build and run on an actual Apple Watch, and you should see a significant boost in performance without taking anything away from the game experience.

Adding an icon

All that's left to do is add your icon art. Open **Zombie Piranhas watchOS/Assets.xcassets/AppIcon**, then drag the corresponding art from **projects/starter/Icon Art** into their respective slots.

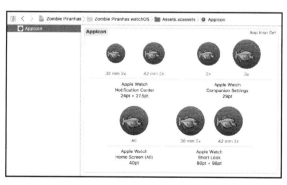

Build and run, then press the crown to go to the Home screen to view your new icon.

> Note: As mentioned before, don't forget to change the **Packaging Product Name** for **Zombie Piranhas watchOS** to just **Zombie Piranhas**.

Congratulations! You've just finished adding a watchOS target for Zombie Piranhas!

Where to go from here?

In these last three chapters, you've taken a compete iOS game and learned how to make it cross-platform by adding targets for macOS, tvOS and watchOS. You learned about **preprocessor directives** and how to use them to isolate platform-specific code, as well as the differences between each platform.

You now have the knowledge and the tools to create compelling content across all Apple devices. I encourage you to learn as much as you can about all four Apple platforms. Planning to release your game on multiple platforms gives you a a wider audience and lets you take advantage of the unique features of each platform.

Section VI: Advanced Topics

In this section, you'll learn some APIs other than SpriteKit that are good to know when making games for the Apple platforms. In particular, you'll learn how to add Game Center leaderboards and achievements into your game. You'll also learn how to use the ReplayKit API.

In the process, you'll integrate these APIs into a top-down racing game named Circuit Racer, where you take the role of an elite race car driver out to set a world record — which wouldn't be a problem if there wasn't all this debris on the track!

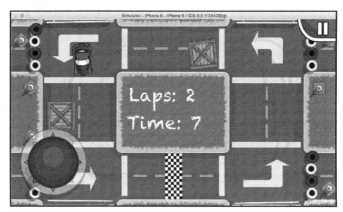

Chapter 21: Game Center Achievements

Chapter 22: Game Center Leaderboards

Chapter 23: ReplayKit

Chapter 21: Game Center Achievements

By Ali Hafizji

So far, all of the minigames you've created for this book have been single-player. Personally, I prefer a little friendly competition!

Luckily, adding head-to-head action to your games is easy to do in iOS thanks to Apple's Game Center APIs.

Over the next two chapters, you'll learn all about Game Center and how to integrate it into a SpriteKit game. In this chapter, you'll learn about Game Center and take a quick tour of its features. Along the way, you'll learn how to authenticate the local player, enable achievements and add support for them to your game. In the next chapter, you'll continue your exploration of Game Center by adding support for leaderboards.

Let the competition begin!

Getting started

You are going to integrate Game Center into a car racing came called **Circuit Racer**.

Circuit Racer is an exciting game, but it's also quite simple. The player has to complete laps around a track within a fixed period of time. For a little extra fun, the player has the option of choosing a vehicle type and a track with a difficulty level of easy, medium or hard.

By this point in the book, you've already learned enough about SpriteKit to make this game on your own, so to save you some time we've built a starter project for you with the gameplay implemented. This way, you can stay focused on the main theme of this chapter — Game Center.

This starter project is a great review of what you've learned so far in this book. Before you begin, you should open the project in the **starter** folder and take a tour of the existing code.

A good place to start would be **Main.storyboard** in the **CircuitRacer** group. This will give you an understanding of how the game is structured and what view controllers are present in the game.

Now select the **CircuitRacer** target, build and run the game and get behind the wheel for a few laps. You can race to beat the clock, but that's about it. It's your job to turn on Game Center, integrate it into the app and add specific achievements that the player can accomplish, like completing the hardest level.

If you're ready to learn how to add a new level of interactivity to your game, then buckle up, pull on your racing gloves and rev up your coding engine! It's time to begin.

Introducing Game Center

If you're an iOS gamer, you've no doubt come across Game Center already. Game Center provides a set of APIs you can integrate into your game to support achievements, leaderboards, challenges, turn-based gaming, real-time multiplayer gaming and more.

Why should you add Game Center support to your game? Well, not only can it significantly up your game's fun quotient — it can also increase your downloads.

Using Game Center, players can challenge friends to beat their high scores or — if your game has multiplayer support — invite them to play. In either case, Game Center will present the new player with the option to download or buy your app, providing a viral growth mechanism.

Now that you've seen the benefits of supporting Game Center, read on to explore the API — specifically, its two most popular features: achievements and leaderboards.

Configuring your app to use Game Center

To do anything with Game Center, you first have to configure your app to use it. This involves three steps:

1. Turn on your app's Game Center capability.

2. Register your app on iTunes Connect.

3. Enable Game Center features such as achievements and leaderboards.

In this section, you'll perform these steps one at a time.

> **Note:** If you've used Game Center before, this process may be routine for you by now. In that case, feel free to complete these steps yourself and skip to the "Authenticating local players" section.

Turning on Game Center

Open Circuit Racer in Xcode and select the **CircuitRacer** target. In the **General** tab, you'll see the **Bundle Identifier** property in the **Identity** section.

Change the bundle identifier to a unique name.

> **Note:** Each bundle ID must be globally unique. Since *com.razeware.CircuitRacer* and *com.razeware.CircuitRacer-Swift* have already been used, along with a selection of other variations, you'll need to think up another unique ID.

Then, set the **Team** drop-down to **your developer profile**.

Next, select the **Capabilities** tab. In the **Game Center** section, switch the selector to the **On** position.

> **Note:** If you receive an error with a **Fix Issue** button, click the button to fix the issue. Usually, this is related to adding entitlements to your App ID or that you need to come up with a unique bundle identifier.

Registering your app on iTunes Connect

The next step is to register your app on Apple's iTunes Connect site.

Log in to iTunes Connect. Then, go to **My Apps** and click the + button in the top-left corner. Choose **New App** to add a new app.

On the first screen, select **iOS** as the platform and enter a unique value in the **App Name** field; this is the name that appears in the App Store, which is why it must be unique. I used "CircuitRacer-Swift"; you'll need to put on your racing-helmet thinking cap and come up with your own app name.

> **Note:** Because this is only a test app, you can use something like **[Your Name] Circuit Racer**, using your actual name in place of the words "Your Name".

Select **English** as the **Primary Language**.

Next, enter **100** as the **SKU Number**. This can be any number or word, so if you want, you can set it to something else.

Finally, select the **Bundle ID** you created in the previous step.

> **Note:** If your bundle ID is not present in the drop-down, first verify that it exists in the Apple Developer Member Center. If not, then create it manually. Xcode is sometimes not able to create and register the bundle ID automatically.

When you're done entering all the values, click **Create**.

You should see the following, but with different values in the fields:

Hooray! You've registered your app with iTunes Connect, and there are only a few more steps remaining to activate Game Center.

Configuring Game Center achievements

Circuit Racer will have four achievements that players can unlock:

1. **Destruction Hero**: A player will earn this achievement whenever they hit the crates more than 20 times during a single race. You'll hide the achievement initially, meaning this achievement won't be visible in Game Center until the player has earned it. A player will be able to achieve this multiple times.

2. **Amateur Racer**: A player will earn this when they complete the easy level.

3. **Intermediate Racer**: A player will earn this they complete the medium level.

4. **Professional Racer**: A player will earn this when they complete the hard level.

It's time to create your game's achievements. In iTunes Connect, select the **Features** button and select **Game Center** from the left panel.

Ready to add the first achievement?

Click the + button in the **Achievements** section. iTunes Connect will present you with a screen on which you can enter the details about the achievement.

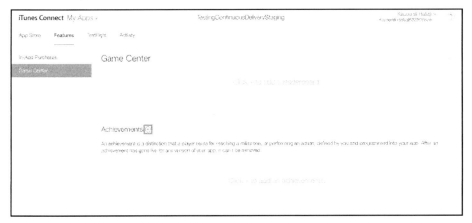

In the **Achievement** subsection, perform the following actions:

- Enter **DestructionHero** for the **Achievement Reference Name**. This is an internal name you can use to search for the achievement on iTunes Connect.

- Enter **[Your app Bundle ID].destructionhero** for the **Achievement ID**. This is a string that uniquely identifies each achievement. It's generally good practice to use the bundle ID as a prefix while setting up the achievement ID, as it ensures the ID will be globally unique.

- Enter **100** for the **Point Value**. This refers to the number of points the achievement is worth. Each achievement can have a maximum of 100 points, and all achievements combined can be worth a maximum of 1000 points.

- Select **Yes** for **Hidden**. This property keeps the achievement hidden until the player achieves it (or a percentage of it) for the first time.

- Select **Yes** for **Achievable More Than Once**. As the name suggests, this property allows the player to earn this achievement more than once. Moreover, when you set this property to **Yes**, players will be able to receive achievement challenges from their friends even for achievements they've already earned.

Next, select **Add Language** in the **Achievement Localization** section and do the following:

- Select **English** for the **Language**.

- Enter **Destruction Hero** for the **Title**. This is the achievement's title as it will appear in Game Center.

- Enter **Bang into an obstacle more than 20 times** for the **Pre-earned Description**. This is the description for the achievement in Game Center before the player has earned it. Although this achievement is hidden, it will become visible if the player completes even a portion of the achievement.

- Enter **Banged into an obstacle more than 20 times** for the **Earned Description**. This is the description in Game Center after the player has earned the achievement.

- From the resources for this chapter, select **achievement-destruction.png** for the **Image**. You'll need to add an image for each language you support, which in this case is just one. The image is in the language-specific section because there's a chance your image might include text. In this case, it doesn't, so you could reuse it for multiple languages.

Click **Save** to save the localization. Then, click **Save** on the achievement screen, which will take you back to the main Game Center screen. There, you'll see your new achievement in the Achievements section — Destruction Hero!

Now that you know what you're doing, create the other three achievements yourself by following the same process.

Here's a table showing the values you'll use, but be sure to replace [**Your app Bundle ID**] with your own bundle ID:

Achievement reference name	Achievement ID
AmateurRacer	[Your app Bundle ID].amateurracer
IntermediateRacer	[Your app Bundle ID].intermediateracer
ProfessionalRacer	[Your app Bundle ID].professionalracer

For each achievement, set **Point Value** to **100**, **Hidden** to **No** and **Achievable More Than Once** to **Yes**. Also add English localizations for all three achievements. You may enter whatever you like for the title and descriptions. The **Resources** folder contains an appropriate icon for each of the three achievements.

Sweet! Now that you've set up everything, it's time to crack your knuckles and write some code.

Authenticating local players

To get started, you're going to write code to authenticate the player. Without an authenticated player, you can't use any of Game Center's features.

In Xcode, right-click on the **CircuitRacer** group and select **New Group**. Name the group **GameKit**.

Next, right-click on the new group and select **New File…**. Choose the **iOS/Source/ Cocoa Touch Class** template and click **Next**. Name the class **GameKitHelper** and make it a subclass of **NSObject**. Verify the **Language** is set to **Swift** and click **Next**. Select **Create** and save the file.

This GameKitHelper class is where you're going to put all of your Game Center code. As an added benefit, you'll be able to use this same class in your own games — without having to rewrite anything. Now, *that's* pretty awesome!

Open **GameKitHelper.swift** and replace the contents of the file with the following:

```
import UIKit
import Foundation
import GameKit

class GameKitHelper: NSObject {

  static let sharedInstance = GameKitHelper()

  var authenticationViewController: UIViewController?
  var gameCenterEnabled = false
}
```

GameKit is the name of the framework that includes all the classes you need to access Game Center, so you import it along with Foundation and UIKit.

The GameKitHelper class will behave as a singleton, meaning it's a shared instance of GameKitHelper that you can access from anywhere in the app. The sharedInstance static property returns this instance.

Within the class, you declared an optional property called authenticationViewController — more on this in the next section. The gameCenterEnabled property stores a Bool that, as the property's name suggests, tells you whether or not Game Center is enabled for the player.

Authentication callbacks

Since Game Center authentication happens asynchronously, the callback can be triggered at any point, even when the player is racing around your tracks! To handle this, you're going to use NSNotificationCenter, so the first thing you need to do is define a name for this notification.

Add the following to the top of **GameKitHelper.swift**, just after where sharedInstance is declared:

```
static let PresentAuthenticationViewController =
  "PresentAuthenticationViewController"
```

Now, add the authentication code to the class by adding the following method:

```
func authenticateLocalPlayer() {
  // 1
  GKLocalPlayer.localPlayer().authenticateHandler =
    { (viewController, error) in
    // 2
    self.gameCenterEnabled = false
    if viewController != nil {
      // 3
      self.authenticationViewController = viewController

      NotificationCenter.default.post(name: NSNotification.Name(
        GameKitHelper.PresentAuthenticationViewController),
        object: self)
    } else if GKLocalPlayer.localPlayer().isAuthenticated {
      // 4
      self.gameCenterEnabled = true
    }
  }
}
```

This method authenticates the player with Game Center. Here's a step-by-step explanation:

1. First, you set the authenticateHandler of the GKLocalPlayer object. The Game Kit framework may call this handler multiple times.

2. The player authentication status can change each time the handler is called, so ensure that gameCenterEnabled is reset to false before determining if authenticated.

3. If the player is not logged into Game Center, the Game Kit framework will pass a view controller to the authenticateHandler closure. It's your duty, as the game's developer, to present this view controller to the user, when appropriate. Ideally, you should do this as soon as possible. You'll store this view controller in the authenticationViewController variable. The code also raises your notification.

4. If the player is successfully authenticated, you enable all Game Center features by setting the `enableGameCenter` Boolean to `true`.

> **Note:** The `error` object is primarily for debugging purposes, so it's not necessary to display this to the user. Game Kit will handle displaying important errors for you.

The code is now in place to authenticate with Game Center — all you need to do is call it.

Integrating authentication into your game

Pause for a moment to think about the architecture of the game. Each screen in Circuit Racer is a separate view controller and is controlled by a navigation view controller. Therefore, you're going to implement authentication by creating a subclass of `UINavigationViewController`.

Right-click on the **/CircuitRacer/ViewControllers** group, select **New File…** and choose the **Cocoa Touch Class** template. Name your class **CircuitRacerNavigationController** and make it a subclass of **UINavigationController**. Verify the **Language** selected is **Swift**, click **Next** and **Create**.

Now you need to set the class of your game's navigation controller to your new class. Open **/CircuitRacer/Main.storyboard** and select the navigation controller.

In the Identity Inspector, inside **Custom Class**, set the **Class** property to
`CircuitRacerNavigationController`.

Great! Just a few more steps.

Open **CircuitRacerNavigationController.swift** and add the following method:

```
func showAuthenticationViewController() {
  let gameKitHelper = GameKitHelper.sharedInstance

  if let authenticationViewController =
      gameKitHelper.authenticationViewController {
    topViewController?.present(
      authenticationViewController,
      animated: true, completion: nil)
  }
}
```

This will present the authentication view controller over the top view in the navigation
stack.

Next, override `viewDidLoad()`, as follows:

```
override func viewDidLoad() {
  super.viewDidLoad()

  NotificationCenter.default.addObserver(self,
    selector: #selector(showAuthenticationViewController),
    name: NSNotification.Name(
      GameKitHelper.PresentAuthenticationViewController),
    object: nil)

  GameKitHelper.sharedInstance.authenticateLocalPlayer()
}
```

You simply register for the `PresentAuthenticationViewController` notification and
make a call to `authenticateLocalPlayer()` of the `GameKitHelper` class.

> **Note:** As a general rule, you should always authenticate the local player as soon as
> the game starts.

And add this to deregister for notifications when the object is deallocated:

```
deinit {
  NotificationCenter.default.removeObserver(self)
}
```

Build and run. If everything goes well, when the game launches, the system will present you with the Game Center authentication view if you are not signed in to Game Center:

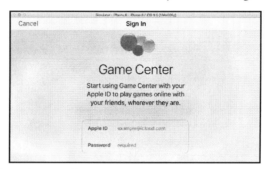

Enter your credentials and press **Go**.

As you may already know, you only need to authenticate with Game Center once. If you are already authenticated, Game Center will present a banner similar to the one shown below:

Adding achievements

You have already set up four achievements in iTunes Connect, so now you can go straight to writing code within Circuit Racer to award the achievements at the appropriate times.

Open **GameKitHelper.swift** and add the following method:

```
func reportAchievements(achievements: [GKAchievement],
  errorHandler: ((Error?)->Void)? = nil) {

  guard gameCenterEnabled else {
    return
  }

  GKAchievement.report(achievements,
    withCompletionHandler: errorHandler)
}
```

To report an achievement, you first need to create a `GKAchievement` object that stores the achievement's identifier and its completion percentage. You'll create those objects later, but for now, assume you have an array of `GKAchievement` objects that you want to report to Game Center.

The good news is, once you have this array, there's only a single line of code required when you want to send it: simply call `report(_:withCompletionHandler:)` from `GKAchievement`. This method automatically handles network errors for you and will resend the data to Game Center until it arrives successfully.

It's time to integrate this into Circuit Racer for its specific achievements.

Creating a helper class for achievements

To handle Circuit Racer's achievements, you're going to create a helper class. This will ensure that all the code that is specific to how CircuitRacer's achievements are created is in one place. Also, not having this in the `GameKitHelper` class ensures that you can use that in your games without having anything related to CircuitRacer.

Right-click on the **GameKit** group, select **New File…**, choose the **Swift File** template and click **Next**. Name the file **AchievementsHelper.swift** and click **Create**.

Open **AchievementsHelper.swift** and replace its contents with the following:

```
import Foundation
import GameKit

class AchievementsHelper {

  static let MaxCollisions = 20.0
  static let DestructionHeroAchievementId =
    "com.razeware.CircuitRacer.destructionhero"
  static let AmateurAchievementId =
    "com.razeware.CircuitRacer.amateurracer"
  static let IntermediateAchievementId =
    "com.razeware.CircuitRacer.intermediateracer"
```

```
    static let ProfessionalHeroAchievementId =
      "com.razeware.CircuitRacer.professionalracer"
}
```

Next, change the achievement IDs to exactly match the ones you created in iTunes Connect, replacing com.razeware.CircuitRacer with [Your app Bundle ID]. Remember — capitalization matters!

Next, add the following class method:

```
class func collisionAchievement(noOfCollisions: Int)
  -> GKAchievement {

  //1
  let percent =
    Double(noOfCollisions)/AchievementsHelper.MaxCollisions
      * 100

  //2
  let collisionAchievement = GKAchievement(
    identifier: AchievementsHelper.DestructionHeroAchievementId)

  //3
  collisionAchievement.percentComplete = percent
  collisionAchievement.showsCompletionBanner = true
  return collisionAchievement

}
```

This is a static helper method that makes it easy for you to report progress for the Destruction Hero achievement. Remember, you're going to grant this achievement once a user has collided with 20 crates in a single race.

collisionAchievement(noOfCollisions:) takes a parameter specifying the number of collisions that have occurred so far. It returns a GKAchievement that you can send to the reportAchievements(achievements:errorHandler:) method you just wrote.

Here's a quick breakdown of the method:

1. You can report achievement progress even if it's only partially complete. This calculates the percent completed based on the number of boxes the player has hit so far, compared to the value of 20 set in the MaxCollisions static variable.

2. You create a GKAchievement object using the Destruction Hero achievement identifier.

3. You set the percentComplete property of the GKAchievement object to the value calculated in the first step.

Now that you have a helper method to create the Destruction Hero achievement, it's time to do the same for the achievements corresponding to each difficulty level. Remember, you'll unlock these achievements only when the player has completed the corresponding levels.

Add the following method:

```
class func achievementForLevel(levelType: LevelType) ->
    GKAchievement {
  var achievementId = AchievementsHelper.AmateurAchievementId
  if levelType == .medium {
    achievementId = AchievementsHelper.IntermediateAchievementId
  } else if levelType == .hard {
    achievementId =
      AchievementsHelper.ProfessionalHeroAchievementId
  }

  let levelAchievement =
    GKAchievement(identifier: achievementId)

  levelAchievement.percentComplete = 100
  levelAchievement.showsCompletionBanner = true

  return levelAchievement
}
```

This method is similar to `collisionAchievement(noOfCollisions:)` and creates an achievement depending upon the game level.

Now that you have these helper methods in place, you need to make use of them in the game.

Integrating achievements into your game

Open **GameScene.swift** and import the `GameKit` framework:

```
import GameKit
```

Add a variable to the class to track the number of collisions between the car and boxes:

```
var noOfCollisions = 0
```

You also need to define constants for the physics categories: one for the car and one for the boxes. You'll use these physics categories to determine whether the objects colliding are the car and a box. You aren't interested in boxes colliding with other boxes!

Declare the categories as follows:

```
static let CarCategoryMask: UInt32 = 1
static let BoxCategoryMask: UInt32 = 2
```

Note: You dealt with collision categories in previous chapters of this book, so they probably look familiar to you by now. That's a good sign!

Add this line to `didMove(to:)` to set `contactTestBitMask` to the appropriate category mask for the car node:

```
childNode(withName: "car")?.physicsBody?.contactTestBitMask =
    GameScene.BoxCategoryMask
```

Next, you need to tell the scene about physics collisions. Create an extension that implements `SKPhysicsContactDelegate`, and then, within that extension, implement `didBegin(_:)` to test for collisions between the car and a box:

```
extension GameScene: SKPhysicsContactDelegate {
  func didBegin(_ contact: SKPhysicsContact) {
    if contact.bodyA.categoryBitMask != UInt32.max
        && contact.bodyB.categoryBitMask != UInt32.max
        && (contact.bodyA.categoryBitMask +
          contact.bodyB.categoryBitMask
          == GameScene.CarCategoryMask +
          GameScene.BoxCategoryMask) {

      noOfCollisions += 1
      run(boxSoundAction)
    }
  }
}
```

`didBeginContact(contact:)` is called every time two physics bodies in the game collide. If the collision is between the car and a box, you increment the collision counter you declared earlier by 1 and, just for fun, play a collision sound.

Finally, add this line at the end of `didMove(to:)` to set the `GameScene` object as the physics contact delegate:

```
physicsWorld.contactDelegate = self
```

All that's left to do is report achievements. Add the following new method:

```
func reportAllAchievementsForGameState(hasWon: Bool) {

  var achievements = [GKAchievement]()

  achievements.append(AchievementsHelper.collisionAchievement(
    noOfCollisions: noOfCollisions))

  if hasWon {
    achievements.append(AchievementsHelper.achievementForLevel(
      levelType: levelType))
  }

  GameKitHelper.sharedInstance
    .reportAchievements(achievements: achievements)
}
```

In this method, you pass in a `Bool` that describes if the player won or lost the game. If the player won, you create an achievement for that level and report it to Game Center. Either way, you report the collision achievement.

Lastly, you need to call that method from within your game. Switch to **GameActiveState.swift** and in `update(deltaTime:)`, modify the code at the bottom that checks for the "game over" state to the following:

```
if timeInSeconds < 0 || numberOfLaps == 0 {
  if numberOfLaps == 0 {
    stateMachine?.enter(GameSuccessState.self)
    gameScene.reportAllAchievementsForGameState(hasWon: true)
  } else {
    stateMachine?.enter(GameFailureState.self)
    gameScene.reportAllAchievementsForGameState(hasWon: false)
  }
}
```

In the code above, you call the new function, `reportAllAchievementsForGameState(hasWon:)`, and pass in a `Bool` value for the win/lose state.

It's time to run some tests — on your mark, get set, go!

Build and run the program, and try to win on each of the tracks. I know it might be difficult to finish all three levels, but if you want those achievements, you better complete those laps before time's up! Every time you earn an achievement, Game Center will show a banner showing which achievement you've earned.

Achievement completed. You've successfully added achievements to your game!

Initializing the built-in user interface

You have achievements in your game, but what if your players want to see what achievements they've unlocked so far?

The Game Kit framework provides a class called `GKGameCenterViewController` that allows your players to view their achievements, leaderboards and challenges from within your game. You're going to add this to Circuit Racer.

To present the Game Center view controller, your `GameKitHelper` class will need to conform to the `GKGameCenterControllerDelegate` protocol.

Open **GameKitHelper.swift** and create an extension that implements the appropriate protocol and dismisses the `gameCenterViewController`:

```
extension GameKitHelper: GKGameCenterControllerDelegate {
  func gameCenterViewControllerDidFinish(
    _ gameCenterViewController: GKGameCenterViewController) {

    gameCenterViewController
      .dismiss(animated: true, completion: nil)

  }
}
```

To show the Game Center view controller, add the following method to the class:

```
func showGKGameCenterViewController(viewController:
    UIViewController) {
  guard gameCenterEnabled else {
    return
  }
```

```
//1
let gameCenterViewController = GKGameCenterViewController()

//2
gameCenterViewController.gameCenterDelegate = self

//3
viewController.present(gameCenterViewController,
    animated: true, completion: nil)
}
```

The above method is responsible for creating and displaying the
GKGameCenterViewController. The steps involved in doing so are:

1. First, you initialize a GKGameCenterViewController object.

2. Next, you set the delegate of the GKGameCenterViewController. Game Center
    informs the delegate when the user finishes interacting with this view controller.

3. Finally, you present the view controller.

That's all it takes to present the GKGameCenterViewController — now you need to
integrate it into Circuit Racer.

Integrating the UI within your game

Open **/CircuitRacer/Main.storyboard** and navigate to the **HomeScreenViewController**.

Select the **View as...** button on the bar below the design canvas. Choose **iPhone 6s** for
Device and **Landscape** for Orientation:

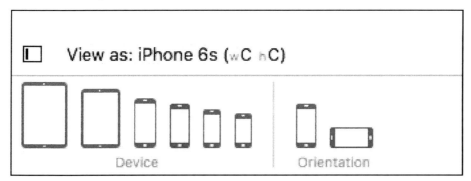

Drag a **Button** from the **Object Library** into the view controller. Set its **Type** to **Custom**,
delete its title and set the **Image** as **btn_gamecenter**.

At this point, your view controller will look like this:

To make the button appear correctly, go to the Size Inspector and set the **width** to **300** and the **height** to **54**, set the **x-position** to **149** and the **y-position** to **288**, and then apply the following constraints:

- **Constraint 1**: Control-drag from Game Center button to **Game Center button** and select **Aspect Ratio**.

- **Constraint 2**: Control-drag from Game Center button to **Play button** and select **Center Horizontally**.

- **Constraint 3**: Control-drag from Game Center button to **Background image** and select **Center Vertically**.

- **Constraint 4**: Control-drag from Game Center button to **Play button** and select **Equal Widths**.

Next, select the **Play button** and look at the constraints in the Size Inspector. Double-click on the **Align Center Y** constraint. Verify **Button.Center Y** is on top and set the **Constant** to **0** and the **Multiplier** to **1.29**.

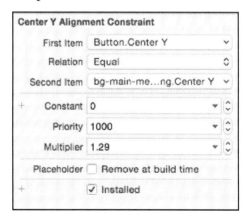

Similarly, select the Game Center button and look at the **Size Inspector** to see the button's constraints. Double-click on the **Align Center Y** constraint. Verify that **Button.Center Y** is the first item and set the **Constant** to **0** and the **Multiplier** to **1.75**.

Your buttons will now appear centered and in a suitable position on all devices. If there are warnings to update the frames, go to **Editor > Resolve Auto Layout Issues > Update Frames**.

Finally, you need to add an action for the Game Center button.

Select the **HomeScreenViewController** and make sure the assistant editor is open with **HomeScreenViewController.swift** showing. Control-drag from the Game Center button to **HomeScreenViewController.swift** and enter **gameCenter** for the name.

For **Connection**, select **Action**; for **Type**, select **UIButton**. Finally, click **Connect**.

Now within **HomeScreenViewController.swift**, implement the new method as follows:

```
@IBAction func gameCenter(_ sender: UIButton) {
  SKTAudio.sharedInstance().playSoundEffect("button_press.wav")
  GameKitHelper.sharedInstance
    .showGKGameCenterViewController(viewController: self)
}
```

Build and run the program and wait for Game Center to authenticate the player. Once that happens, press the Game Center button. This will open `GKGameCenterViewController`:

That's it! You've added Game Center, achievements and a Game Center view controller to Circuit Racer. Remember, every time a player earns an achievement it will be visible in her profile on the Game Center app. More achievement, more virality. Yay!

In the following chapter, you'll learn all about the latest Game Center leaderboard features — but first, a quick challenge for you.

Challenges

This challenge will ensure you've understood the majority of this chapter. If you get stuck, you can find the solutions in the resources for this chapter, but give it your best shot first!

Challenge 1: Racing Addict achievement

Create a new achievement in iTunes Connect named **Racing Addict**. Hide it initially and award it if the player completes a race 10 times without closing the app.

Here are a few hints:

• Create a variable to track the number of times the local player has played the game.

• Every time the game completes, report the achievement with the appropriate `percentComplete`.

• You can use an image already in use by the other achievements to create this achievement.

Chapter 22: Game Center Leaderboards

By Ali Hafizji

In the previous chapter, you learned the steps required to set up your game to use Game Center, authenticate the local player and enhance the player's experience with achievements. You also implemented Game Center's built-in user interface.

In this chapter, you'll focus on another awesome Game Center feature: leaderboards. Think of a leaderboard as a database of the scores of all players in your game, which makes it possible for a player to see how her scores match up with those of other players. It's a great way to get players to play your game "just one more time" to see if they can increase their scores and move up the leaderboard.

Traditionally, implementing leaderboards meant developing performant server-side components and configuring load-balanced, server-side infrastructure. Game Center provides all of this for you, making it easy to add leaderboards to your game — with just a few lines of code, you're set.

It's time to try this out by adding some leaderboards to Circuit Racer!

> **Note:** This chapter begins where the previous chapter's challenge left off. If you were unable to complete the challenge, don't worry; simply open CircuitRacer from the **starter** folder of this chapter's resources to begin in the right place. Don't forget to update the app's bundle identifier to your own, and update the achievement IDs in **AchievementsHelper.swift** appropriately.
>
> If you skipped the last chapter, then you'll need to set up Circuit Racer in iTunes Connect and register a number of achievements. For instructions on how to perform these steps, see the previous chapter.

Getting started

There are five steps to add leaderboards to your game. Here's a quick overview.

1. **Authenticate the local player**: Remember, to use any Game Center feature, you first need to authenticate the local player.

2. **Create a strategy for using leaderboards in the game**: Decide how many leaderboards the game is going to have and what scores will drive each leaderboard.

3. **Configure leaderboards in iTunes Connect**: Add each leaderboard and set its name and formatting, such as the score range. Optionally, add an image for each leaderboard.

4. **Add code to report scores to Game Center**: In the same way you added code to send an array of GKAchievement objects to Game Center, you need to add code to send an array of GKScore objects.

5. **Add code to display the leaderboards to the player**: As you did for achievements, you'll use the GKGameCenterViewController. Optionally, you can also retrieve the score data and display the leaderboard in a custom user interface.

The rest of this section will take you through these steps one by one.

Authenticating the local player

You added support for player authentication to Circuit Racer in the previous chapter, so you can skip this step. If you'd like to go over the process one more time, have a look at authenticateLocalPlayer() in the GameKitHelper class.

Creating a leaderboard strategy

To support leaderboards, your game needs scoring criteria that will let it calculate a score every time the player finishes a race. The only restriction Game Center puts on this score is that it must be a 64-bit integer.

Since Circuit Racer is a race against time, there is a single scoring criterion: the amount of time it took for the local player to complete each track. The players who finished the track in the shortest amount of time will be at the top of the leaderboard.

Sounds like a plan!

Before moving on to the next step, you also need to determine the number of leaderboards your game will support. How many you have depends on the kind of game you are making, but having multiple leaderboards can give the player a more detailed view of the position she holds among all the game's players.

Having multiple leaderboards also gives players the opportunity to do well on certain leaderboards when they might not be able to push for the top positions on others.

In Circuit Racer, the player chooses a car and then selects a difficulty level. You're going to create a leaderboard for each of the possible car/difficulty level combinations so that players have the chance to climb the leaderboard with their favorite cars and tracks.

To account for all possible car/difficulty combinations, you're going to create a total of nine leaderboards. For example, the first leaderboard will be titled "Yellow Car Easy Level Fastest Time." Later in the chapter, you'll use these nine leaderboards to create leaderboard sets.

Configuring leaderboards in iTunes Connect

Log in to iTunes Connect using your credentials and select the **My Apps** option. Then, choose your Circuit Racer app — the exact name is unique and will be whatever you called it when going through the last chapter. Go to **Features > Game Center**.

Select the + button under the Leaderboards section.

Click **Choose** under the **Single Leaderboard** option.

Note: The other option, Combined Leaderboard, allows you to create a new "virtual leaderboard" that combines the results of several leaderboards.

For example, you could create a leaderboard for Circuit Racer named "Any Car Easy Level Fastest Time" that combines the results of "Yellow Car Easy Level Fastest Time," "Blue Car Easy Level Fastest Time" and "Red Car Easy Level Fastest Time".

You would still report your players' scores to each individual leaderboard — this just provides an easy way to aggregate the results for players across several leaderboards that share the same score format type and sort order.

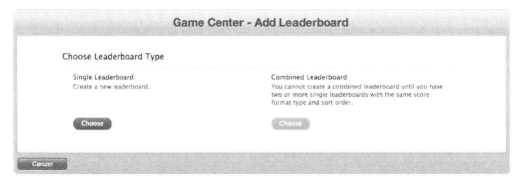

If you're wondering what each field means, don't fret! Enter the following values:

- **Yellow Car Easy Level Fastest Time** for the **Leaderboard Reference Name**. This is a string that represents the internal name for the leaderboard. You can use this string to search for leaderboards within iTunes Connect.

- **[Your app Bundle ID].yellowcar_easylevel_fastest_time** for the **Leaderboard ID**. This string uniquely identifies the leaderboard; you'll use it to report scores to Game Center. It's generally good practice to use your app's bundle ID as a prefix.

- **Elapsed Time - To the Second** as the **Score Format Type**. This field specifies the format of the scores you'll use to submit this particular leaderboard. Your game's scoring criterion is based on time, so this is an appropriate format.

- **Best Score** as the **Score Submission Type**. This field specifies which score the leaderboard will display: the best one or the most recent one.

- **Low to High** as the **Sort Order**. This field dictates how the scores are arranged in the leaderboard. In the case of Circuit Racer, the lowest time refers to the fastest time.

- **1 To 15** for the **Score Range**. Even though this field is optional, I recommend you add a value here. You'll learn more about this field in the sections to come, so stay tuned.

For now, enter **1** and **15**. There's no way a player can get a faster time than 1 second, and 15 seconds is the maximum time allowed to complete the easy level as defined in the game's **LevelDetails.plist** file.

Single Leaderboard

Leaderboard Reference Name	Yellow Car Easy Level Fastest Time
Leaderboard ID	com.razeware.CircuitRacer.yellowcar_easylevel_fastest_time
Score Format Type	Elapsed Time - To the Second
Score Submission Type	⦿ Best Score ☐ Most Recent Score
Sort Order	⦿ Low to High ☐ High to Low
Score Range (Optional)	1 To 15
	0:00:01 0:00:15

The next step is to add a language. Select the **Add Language** button in the **Leaderboard Localization** section. Keep in mind that these are the settings that affect what your users will see, so choose wisely.

Fill in the following details:

- **English** for the **Language**

- **Yellow Car Easy Level Fastest Time** for the **Name**. This is the name of the leaderboard that players will see.

- **Elapsed Time (hours, minutes, seconds, ex. 5:01:18)** for the **Score Format**. This is the format Game Center will use to display the scores in the leaderboard.

- **seconds** for the **Score Format Suffix**. This is an optional suffix that Game Center adds when displaying the score. Circuit Racer measures a player's score in seconds.

- **Image**. You can optionally upload an image for each language. In this chapter, you won't be adding any images to leaderboards, though I highly recommend that you do so in your own games.

> **Note:** You can add multiple languages to each leaderboard, and Game Center will display the correct language according to the locale set on the phone.

Click the **Save** button when you're done entering all the details. This will create a new leaderboard, as shown below.

Now, you need to create the other eight leaderboards for the game. Since you already know how to create a single leaderboard, the rest should be easy. Make sure you follow the table below while entering the data required for each leaderboard.

Yes, this may be a bit repetitive, but think of it this way: by the time you're done, you'll be an old pro at setting up leaderboards in iTunes Connect! :]

Reference Name	Leaderboard ID	Score Range
Yellow Car Medium Level Fastest Time	[Your app Bundle ID].yellowcar_mediumlevel_fastest_time	1 To 25
Yellow Car Hard Level Fastest Time	[Your app Bundle ID].yellowcar_hardlevel_fastest_time	1 To 35
Blue Car Easy Level Fastest Time	[Your app Bundle ID].bluecar_easylevel_fastest_time	1 To 15
Blue Car Medium Level Fastest Time	[Your app Bundle ID].bluecar_mediumlevel_fastest_time	1 To 25
Blue Car Hard Level Fastest Time	[Your app Bundle ID].bluecar_hardlevel_fastest_time	1 To 35
Red Car Easy Level Fastest Time	[Your app Bundle ID].redcar_easylevel_fastest_time	1 To 15
Red Car Medium Level Fastest Time	[Your app Bundle ID].redcar_mediumlevel_fastest_time	1 To 25
Red Car Hard Level Fastest Time	[Your app Bundle ID].redcar_hardlevel_fastest_time	1 To 35

Enter whatever you like for the English localization for each, based on the previous example.

After you're done entering all the details, your leaderboards table in iTunes Connect should look like the one below:

Leaderboards (9)

Leaderboards allow users to view the top scores of all your app's Game Center players. Leaderboards that are live for any app version can't be removed.

Reference Name	Leaderboard ID	Type	Default	Status
Yellow Car Easy Level Fastest Time	com.razeware.Circui...	Single	Default	Not Live
Yellow Car Medium Level Fastest Time	com.razeware.Circui...	Single		Not Live
Yellow Car Hard Level Fastest Time	com.razeware.Circui...	Single		Not Live
Blue Car Easy Level Fastest Time	com.razeware.Circui...	Single		Not Live
Blue Car Medium Level Fastest Time	com.razeware.Circui...	Single		Not Live
Blue Car Hard Level Fastest Time	com.razeware.Circui..	Single		Not Live
Red Car Easy Level Fastest Time	com.razeware.Circui...	Single		Not Live
Red Car Medium Level Fastest Time	com.razeware.Circui...	Single		Not Live
Red Car Hard Level Fastest Time	com.razeware.Circui...	Single		Not Live

Reporting scores to Game Center

With your leaderboards set up in iTunes Connect, it's time to write some code. To keep things simple, you're going to add a method to the `GameKitHelper` class that will report a score to a leaderboard identified by its leaderboard ID.

Make sure Circuit Racer is open in Xcode, open **GameKitHelper.swift** and add the following method:

```
func reportScore(score: Int64, forLeaderboardID leaderboardID:
    String, errorHandler: ((Error?)->Void)? = nil) {
  guard gameCenterEnabled else {
    return
  }

  //1
  let gkScore = GKScore(leaderboardIdentifier: leaderboardID)
  gkScore.value = score

  //2
  GKScore.report([gkScore], withCompletionHandler: errorHandler)
}
```

The code you just wrote creates and sends a score to Game Center. Here's a step-by-step explanation:

- First, the method creates an object of type `GKScore` to hold information about the player's score. Game Center expects you to send scores using this object. Game Center also returns objects of type `GKScore` when you retrieve scores. As you can see, a

GKScore simply stores a value: the number to send to the leaderboard, which in this case is the number of seconds.

- Next, the method reports the score using report(_:withCompletionHandler:) from GKScore. You pass in the optional errorHandler as the completion handler. Note that these errors are mainly for debugging purposes though and generally you don't have to worry about adding logic to handle them. report(_:withCompletionHandler:) will take care of auto-resending scores on network failures.

Great work! You have all the code in place to send scores to Game Center. Open **GameScene.swift** and add the following property:

```
let leaderboardIDMap =
  ["\(CarType.yellow.rawValue)_\(LevelType.easy.rawValue)":
 "com.razeware.CircuitRacer.yellowcar_easylevel_fastest_time",
    "\(CarType.yellow.rawValue)_\(LevelType.medium.rawValue)":
 "com.razeware.CircuitRacer.yellowcar_mediumlevel_fastest_time",
    "\(CarType.yellow.rawValue)_\(LevelType.hard.rawValue)":
 "com.razeware.CircuitRacer.yellowcar_hardlevel_fastest_time",
    "\(CarType.blue.rawValue)_\(LevelType.easy.rawValue)":
 "com.razeware.CircuitRacer.bluecar_easylevel_fastest_time",
    "\(CarType.blue.rawValue)_\(LevelType.medium.rawValue)":
 "com.razeware.CircuitRacer.bluecar_mediumlevel_fastest_time",
    "\(CarType.blue.rawValue)_\(LevelType.hard.rawValue)":
 "com.razeware.CircuitRacer.bluecar_hardlevel_fastest_time",
    "\(CarType.red.rawValue)_\(LevelType.easy.rawValue)":
 "com.razeware.CircuitRacer.redcar_easylevel_fastest_time",
    "\(CarType.red.rawValue)_\(LevelType.medium.rawValue)":
 "com.razeware.CircuitRacer.redcar_mediumlevel_fastest_time",
    "\(CarType.red.rawValue)_\(LevelType.hard.rawValue)":
 "com.razeware.CircuitRacer.redcar_hardlevel_fastest_time"]
```

This property is a dictionary, where the key is a string with format CarType_LevelType and the value is its corresponding leaderboard ID. For example, the key 0_0 would have a leaderboard ID of com.razeware.CircuitRacer.yellowcar_easylevel_fastest_time.

Make sure you change the leaderboard IDs to exactly match the ones you entered into iTunes Connect — and remember, capitalization matters.

Switch to **GameActiveState.swift** and add the following variable:

```
private var maxTime = 0
```

This stores the total amount of time the player has to complete the current level. You'll use it to calculate the amount of time it took the player to complete the current track.

Next, add the following line at the bottom of `loadLevel()`:

```
maxTime = timeInSeconds
```

This stores the maximum time for the current level.

Now, open **GameScene.swift** and add the following method:

```
func reportScoreToGameCenter(score: Int64) {
  GameKitHelper.sharedInstance.reportScore(score: score,
    forLeaderboardID:
    leaderboardIDMap[
    "\(carType.rawValue)_\(levelType.rawValue)"]!)
}
```

This reports a new score simply by calling the method you added to `GameKitHelper`.

Back in **GameActiveState.swift**, inside `update(deltaTime:)`, modify the block of code that detects the "game over" state as follows:

```
if timeInSeconds < 0 || numberOfLaps == 0 {
  if numberOfLaps == 0 {
    stateMachine?.enter(GameSuccessState.self)
    gameScene.reportAllAchievementsForGameState(true)
    //New code
    gameScene.reportScoreToGameCenter(score: Int64(maxTime
      - timeInSeconds))
  } else {
    stateMachine?.enter(GameFailureState.self)
    gameScene.reportAllAchievementsForGameState(false)
  }
}
```

Here, you're simply adding a line to report the score when the player completes the level.

Finally, it's time to test everything. Build and run the project.

After you successfully complete a track, the game automatically reports your score to Game Center. Check the debug console to see if anything went wrong. If you don't see any error logs, and you used the right leaderboard IDs, then Game Center should be successfully receiving your score.

YAY!!!!

Displaying leaderboards

Conveniently, Game Center provides helper methods that retrieve the scores in each leaderboard using the GKLeaderboard object. Once you have the scores, you can present the leaderboards to the player in any view.

However, there's a much easier way to display leaderboards if you don't want to create your own custom user interface: GKGameCenterViewController. You added support for this view controller in the last chapter, so the leaderboards are actually available to the player in your app right now!

All you have to do is launch the GKGameCenterViewController by selecting the **GAME CENTER** button on the home screen of the game. Build and run the app and give it a shot.

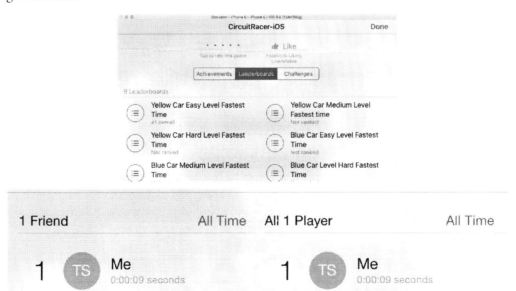

Congratulations — your app has leaderboards!

If you only wanted to learn how to add basic leaderboards to your app, you could stop reading now and skip ahead to the next chapter. But if you want to learn a few advanced things about leaderboards, read on!

Leaderboard sets

Now that you're familiar with leaderboards, you should take a look at leaderboard sets. This feature was introduced in Game Center under iOS 7.

Leaderboard sets give developers the ability to combine several leaderboards into a single group. Think of a leaderboard set as a tagging framework. Each leaderboard can belong to one or several groups/sets. This allows you to organize your leaderboards into a structured hierarchy, rather than a long list like the nine leaderboards you currently have, which could feel overwhelming to a player.

To add support for leaderboard sets in Circuit Racer, you need an organizing strategy. You're going to group your leaderboards according to car type. Thus, all the leaderboards for the yellow car will belong to the "Yellow car" group, and so forth.

To visualize this, take a look at the table below:

Yellow car	Blue car	Red car
yellowcar_easylevel_fastest_time	bluecar_easylevel_fastest_time	redcar_easylevel_fastest_time
yellowcar_mediumlevel_fastest_time	bluecar_mediumlevel_fastest_time	redcar_mediumlevel_fastest_time
yellowcar_hardlevel_fastest_time	bluecar_hardlevel_fastest_time	redcar_hardlevel_fastest_time

> **Note:** You could also organize the leaderboards according to their difficulty level. Since leaderboard sets provide the capability to tag leaderboards multiple times, it would be easy to do it both ways.

Log in to iTunes Connect and open the **Features > Game Center** page for Circuit Racer just as you've done before.

Under the leaderboards section, you'll find a button titled **More**. Click that button and select the **Move All Leaderboards into Leaderboard Sets** option to create your first leaderboard set.

Leaderboards allow users to view the top scores of all your app's Game Center players. Leaderboards that are live for any app version can't be   Mor ⌄
removed.

Move All Leaderboards into Leaderboard Sets

Reference Name   Leaderboard ID   Delete Test Data

On the next screen, enter **Yellow car** for the **Leaderboard Set Reference Name** and [**Your app Bundle ID**].**yellowcar** for the **Leaderboard Set ID**.

Click the **Continue** button when you're done entering the data.

Now you need to add leaderboards to this set. On the next screen, under the section **Leaderboards in This Set**, select the **Add to Leaderboard Set** button. Since this is the Yellow Car group, all the leaderboards pertaining to the first car should be a part of this group.

As the image above depicts, you first select the leaderboard you want to add to the set. Start with **Yellow Car Easy Level Fastest Time** Next, you enter a display name for the leaderboard within the set. Since the set is named "Yellow car", it makes sense to label this leaderboard as **Easy level**. After you've done that, click **Save**.

In the same fashion, add the other two leaderboards pertaining to the yellow car to this set, naming them **Medium level** and **Hard level**.

Now, you need to name the leaderboard set. Under the **Leaderboard Set Localization** section, select the **Add Language** button. Select **English** as the language and enter **Yellow car** for the display name. Choose the leaderboard image **leaderboard-yellow.png** located in **/starter/Resources** and click **Save**.

Using the **Add Leaderboard Set** button in the first section of the page, repeat the above procedure for the blue and red cars. Make sure you give them ID values of [**Your app Bundle ID**].**bluecar** and [**Your app Bundle ID**].**redcar** to remain consistent with the yellow car leaderboard set, replacing [**Your app Bundle ID**] with your own bundle ID, of course.

> **Note:** If you decide to support leaderboard sets, you need to ensure that every leaderboard is part of at least one set.

Finally, once you've organized all of the leaderboards into their respective sets, select the **Save** button at the bottom right. You will now see three display sets under the **Leaderboard Sets** section:

Notice the link to **View Leaderboards in Leaderboard Sets.** This can be quite useful to visualize your leaderboard sets — click it, and you'll see a list of all your leaderboard sets in a table.

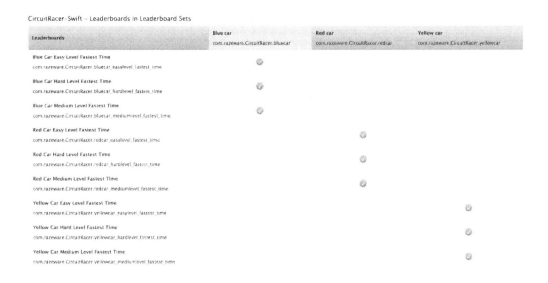

> **Note:** Don't worry if the ordering of the columns and rows differ. This chart is simply generated to view which leaderboards belong to which sets.

That's it! Everything in iTunes Connect is ready. The next step is to show the leaderboard sets to the player. Once again, the easiest way to do that is to use the `GKGameCenterViewController`.

But you don't need to add any code! Simply build and run.

When you tap the **GAME CENTER** button on the home screen, the `GKGameCenterViewController` opens and displays the leaderboard sets you created in iTunes Connect. Note that it might take a bit of time for your leaderboards to show up in your app — if they don't appear right away, wait a few minutes and try again.

Ah, sweet simplicity! Now instead of nine leaderboards, you see only three, and it's a lot easier to navigate between them thanks to the hierarchical organization.

Security in Game Center

You should be quite familiar with Game Center's features now. To keep gameplay fair, you'll next take a look at security in Game Center. This is important to understand because you don't want players cheating and submitting false scores!

How does submission work?

First, let's consider how the system handles submissions.

When your game sends a score to Game Center, it doesn't send it directly to the Game Center servers. Instead, it sends the score to the **gamed daemon**, which in turn sends it to the servers.

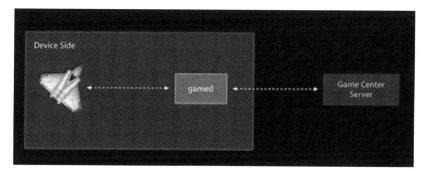

Why does the system manage communication this way? To answer that question, imagine that the device sending out the score has an Internet connectivity problem. In such a situation, the gamed daemon stores the scores and will send them to the Game Center servers when the Internet connection is back.

This means you don't have to worry in case the Internet connection is wonky. Game Center takes care of all the heavy lifting for you.

Limit cheating

Believe it or not, there are people out there who are going to try to cheat by submitting unearned scores — even scores that aren't humanly possible to achieve! Game Center provides three ways to combat cheating within your game:

1. **Signed submissions**: This feature is totally free and you don't need to make any changes to your game to use it. When your game submits scores or achievements to the gamed daemon, it automatically attaches a cryptographic signature to the submission. Game Center rejects any submission that doesn't have this signature.

2. **Score range**: Another way to limit cheating is to use the score range property on a leaderboard. The score range specifies minimum and maximum values that you think a player could possibly achieve for a particular leaderboard. Any score that's outside the specified range is deleted. You set up score ranges when you created your leaderboards earlier.

3. **Score/player management**: To view this console, log in to iTunes Connect and select any leaderboard. You'll see a list of the top 100 players in that leaderboard. This helps you, the developer, to view scores submitted on behalf of players. You can choose to remove a score from a leaderboard and you can even choose to remove a player, thereby preventing that player from posting scores to that leaderboard again. This is an extremely powerful tool, and as the saying goes, "With great power comes great responsibility." Make sure you use this power appropriately and only when needed.

That's a wrap for leaderboards — except for one final challenge!

Challenges

This chapter has only one challenge, designed to give you a bit more practice with leaderboard sets.

Challenge 1: More leaderboard sets

Make three new leaderboard sets, organized by difficulty, from the nine leaderboards you created in this chapter. Remember, you only have to make the changes in iTunes Connect, and the `GKGameCenterViewController` will automatically show them in the leaderboards section.

You don't need to make any changes to your project to complete this challenge, so there is no solution project for this chapter.

Chapter 23: ReplayKit

By Ali Hafizji

In the previous two chapters, you increased Circuit Racer's oomph factor by adding basic support for Game Center. In this chapter, you're going to add support for ReplayKit using the APIs introduced in iOS 9.

Imagine beating your friend at a game — one the two of you have been glued to for months. A moment like this must go down in history forever! ReplayKit lets you record these awesome gaming moments; the cherry on top is that you can also share these moments with others.

ReplayKit records the audio and visuals of the running app. Along with that, it records the audio from the device's microphone. The output from this recording is a full HD video that looks amazing on the TV, phone and the Web. ReplayKit also lets users trim, preview and share the final video on any social network.

Your friend will no longer be able to deny that time you crushed him like a bug on a rock — a pixelated rock, of course!

> **Note:** This chapter begins where the previous chapter's challenge left off. If you were unable to complete the challenge or skipped ahead from an earlier chapter, don't worry — simply open the starter project from this chapter's resources to pick up in the right place. Don't forget to update the app's bundle identifier to your own, update the achievement IDs in **AchievementsHelper.swift** and update the leaderboardIDMap in **GameScene.swift** appropriately.

Getting started

ReplayKit is extremely easy to integrate into your app. As a developer, you only have to work with two APIs: RPScreenRecorder and RPPreviewViewController.

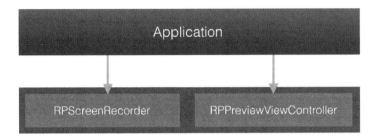

RPScreenRecorder, as the name suggests, is used to start and stop recording. It's a singleton, and every app has access to its own shared instance of this class.

RPPreviewViewController, similarly well-named, is a view controller that can be presented once recording is complete. This view controller lets users trim, preview and share their recordings.

Although you're only working with two simple APIs, under the hood, the architecture is a bit more complicated:

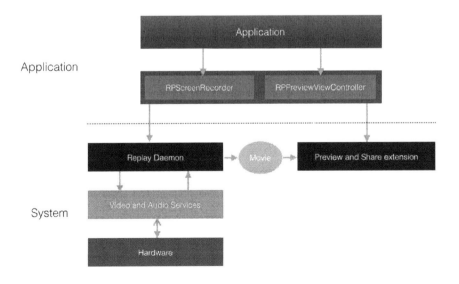

The `RPScreenRecorder` communicates with the replay daemon, which in turn communicates with the lower-level video and audio services. While doing this, it encodes the data in real time and writes it to a movie file in a secure location.

This file is accessible only to ReplayKit's internal services. You may be wondering how it's possible to access a secure file. Luckily, the API is designed in such a way that when you stop recording, `RPScreenRecorder` will create an instance of `RPPreviewViewController`. This instance already knows the location of that secure file. From there, all you need to do is present `RPPreviewViewController` when recording is complete. Simple enough!

Integrating ReplayKit

To add support for ReplayKit, you need to perform these steps:

1. **Create a recording strategy**: Decide when the game will start and stop recording gameplay.

2. **Modify the user interface**: Add visual elements to let the user know that recording is in progress, as well as an interface to let the user stop and preview a recording.

3. **Check for availability**: Since ReplayKit is only available on devices incorporating the A7 processor or higher, you'll need to hide all of the ReplayKit user interface elements when it's not supported.

4. **Start and stop recording**: You'll use an auto-record strategy so your player won't miss a minute of her game.

5. **Preview and share the recording**: This uses the built-in `RPPreviewViewController` to make reviewing and sharing the game a breeze.

The rest of this chapter will take you through these steps one by one. As you can see, the actual API is easy and straightforward; most of your time will be spent on integrating it nicely into the game.

Creating a recording strategy

Before adding ReplayKit, it's best to create a plan for your recording strategy. Take a look at the scene flow in Circuit Racer:

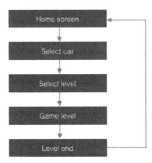

This scene flow is quite common in games. Almost every game has a menu, followed by the game scene, which ultimately transitions to the end scene. From there, you can either replay the level or start over.

Since the gameplay sessions are short in Circuit Racer, you're going to opt for an automatic recording strategy. This means that you're going to tell ReplayKit to start recording immediately as the level starts, and then stop when the level ends.

You also want the user to preview the recording and share it; however, instead of showing the preview controller as soon as the level ends, you're going to defer this until you present the level "end scene", after all of the action has died down.

Here's how the scene flow will look when you're done Integrating ReplayKit:

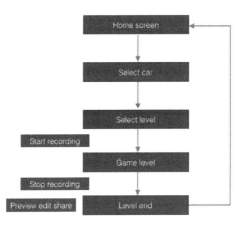

> **Note:** Every game is different, and the above strategy may not work for all games. You should always choose what's best for your game. For example, an RPG has longer game sessions, so it doesn't make sense to record the entire game session. In this case, you may want to give the player the option to start or stop recording, rather than handling it automatically.

Modifying the user interface

With that strategy in mind, open your CircuitRacer project (or the starter project) in Xcode. Drag and drop all of the resources from the **/starter/Resources** folder into the asset catalog (**CircuitRacerAssets.xcassets**) of the project.

Open **Main.storyboard** and select the **View as...** button on the bar below the design canvas. Choose **iPhone 6s** for Device and **Landscape** for Orientation.

Navigate to the **HomeScreenViewController** and drag and drop a **Button** from the Object Library onto the view controller; set its Type to **Custom**, **delete** "Button" so the Default Title is empty and set the Image as **btn_autorecord_off**.

Before you add the required constraints, use the **State Config** drop-down and set both the **Highlighted** and **Selected** Image to **btn_autorecord_on**.

At this point, your view controller will look like this:

To make the button appear correctly, go to the Size inspector and set its X position to **527** and its Y position to **28**. Also, set its Width to **120** and its Height to **36**.

Finally, set the following constraints:

- **Constraint 1**: Control-drag from Auto record button to **Root view**, and select **Trailing space to container margin**.

- **Constraint 2**: Control-drag from Auto record button to **Auto record button**, and select **Aspect ratio**.

- **Constraint 3**: Control-drag from Auto record button to **Top Layout Guide**, and select **Vertical spacing**.

- **Constraint 4**: Control-drag from Auto record button to **Background image**, and select **Equal Widths**.

Now, select the **auto-record button** and look at the constraints in the Size inspector. Double-click on the **Trailing Space** constraint and set the Constant to **0**. Similarly, set the Constant for the **Top Space** constraint to **10**.

Next, double-click the **Equal Width** constraint and set the Multiplier to **0.2**.

The auto-record button should now appear in a suitable position on all devices.

Since your strategy is to automatically record gameplay, this button will let the player toggle this feature on and off.

Build and run your game. You'll see the auto-record button on the home screen.

Next, you're going to change the **SuccessScene.sks** and **FailureScene.sks** files. Since you present them when the user finishes a game, you're going to add a few sprites to let the user preview the recorded video.

Open **/CircuitRacer/Scenes/SuccessScene/SuccessScene.sks**. Select the **CircuitRacer** sprite and the ones named **replay** and **cancel**, and set their X positions to **-220**. This will create some room on the right.

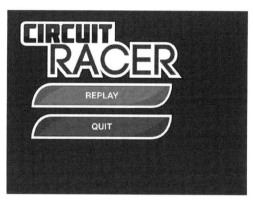

Now, open the Media Library and drag and drop the **btn_autorecord_small_off**, **level_1_preview_frame** and **play_icon** sprites to the canvas. Set the following properties for each of the sprites you added:

- **auto_record_small_off**: Set Name to **screen_recording_toggle**, Parent to **Overlay**, X position to **800** and Y position to **640**.

- **level_1_preview_frame**: Set Name to **view_recorded_content**, Parent to **Overlay**, X position to **800** and Y position to **306**.

- **play_icon**: Set Parent to **view_recorded_content**, X position to **0**, Y position to **0**, Z position to **1** and leave Name **empty**.

All the sprites will now be in suitable positions, and your final canvas will look like the one below:

Before you proceed to the next section, make the same changes to **/CircuitRacer/Scenes/ FailureScene/FailureScene.sks**.

Build and run your game. You should see the sprites on the **Failure** and **Success** scenes.

The sprites you just added don't function as buttons — at least not yet. You'll take care of that now.

Open **/CircuitRacer/InputSources/ButtonNode.swift**. This is a helper class that turns `SKSpriteNode` nodes into buttons.

Then replace the `ButtonIdentifier` enum with the following:

```
enum ButtonIdentifier: String {
  case resume = "resume"
  case cancel = "cancel"
  case replay = "replay"
  case pause  = "pause"
  //New Code
  case screenRecordingToggle = "screen_recording_toggle"
  case viewRecordedContent = "view_recorded_content"

  static let allIdentifiers: [ButtonIdentifier] =
    [.resume, .cancel, .replay, .pause,
     .screenRecordingToggle, .viewRecordedContent]

  var selectedTextureName: String? {
    switch self {
    // New Code
    case .screenRecordingToggle:
      return "btn_autorecord_small_on"
    default:
      return nil
    }
  }
}
```

Here, you add two new cases to the enum: `screenRecordingToggle` and `viewRecordedContent`. The first one represents the auto-record sprite and the second represents the preview video sprite.

Now, open **/CircuitRacer/Scenes/GameScene/GameScene+Buttons.swift** and add the following cases to `buttonPressed(button:)`:

```
case .screenRecordingToggle:
  print("Screen recording toggle tapped")
case .viewRecordedContent:
  print("View recorded content button tapped")
```

This is where you will add logic to handle when these buttons are tapped. Build and run your game.

Notice how when you tap the **auto record** and **preview recorded content** buttons on the Success/Failure scenes, you see one of the following log statements in the console, depending on which button you pressed:

```
Screen recording toggle pressed
View recorded content button pressed
```

Awesome! You're almost done making the UI changes required to integrate ReplayKit. The last thing to add is a tiny recording indicator to show that recording is in progress; you'll add this to the game scene.

Open **GameScene.sks** and add **indicator_rec** from the Media Library to the canvas. Set its Name to **record_indicator**, its X position to **1657** and its Y position to **1275**. It will look like this:

You have to look closely! You will only display this when gameplay is being recorded.

Checking for availability

As mentioned earlier, screen recording may not be available due to unsupported hardware. It may also be unavailable because the device is displaying video over AirPlay or TV Out, or because another app is using the recorder.

If recording isn't available for one of those reasons, you're going to hide all of the UI elements you added in the previous steps.

Right-click on the **CircuitRacer** group and select **New File...**. Choose the **Swift File** template and click **Next**. Name the file **AutoRecordProtocol.swift** and click **Create**.

Replace the contents of the file with the following:

```
import Foundation
import ReplayKit
```

```
protocol ScreenRecordingAvailable: class {
  var screenRecordingAvailable: Bool { get }
}

extension ScreenRecordingAvailable {

  var screenRecordingAvailable: Bool {
    return RPScreenRecorder.shared().isAvailable
  }
}
```

The `ScreenRecordingAvailable` protocol defines a computed `Bool` property that tells you whether or not screen recording is available. Using the power of protocol extensions, you've defined the getter to return the `RPScreenRecorder.shared().isAvailable` value. As the name suggests, this tells you whether or not recording is available.

With the protocol implementation in place, it's time to switch to the home screen. Although you have the auto-record button showing, tapping it doesn't really do anything. You'll take care of this now.

Add a **Swift File** to the **ViewControllers** group and name it **UIViewController+AutoRecord.swift**. Then, replace the contents of the file with the following:

```
import Foundation
import UIKit

extension UIViewController {

  @IBAction func toggleScreenRecording(_ button: UIButton) {
    SKTAudio.sharedInstance()
      .playSoundEffect("button_press.wav")
    button.isSelected = !button.isSelected
  }
}
```

The above code simply plays a noise and changes the `isSelected` property of the button when the `IBAction` is invoked. You're using an `extension` because it gives you the ability to move the auto-record button to any other view controller and still reuse this code. Pretty sweet, eh?

Open **Main.storyboard** and navigate to the **HomeScreenViewController**. Then open the assistant editor and navigate it to **UIViewController+AutoRecord.swift**. Control-drag from the `IBAction` in UIViewController+AutoRecord.swift to the **auto-record button** in Main.storyboard. This should connect the Touch Up Inside event for the button to the `toggleScreenRecording(_:)` method. Verify by looking at the **Connections Inspector** with the **auto-record button** selected.

Build and run your game.

Now, when you tap the auto-record button, it stays in its selected state.

Next, open **/CircuitRacer/ViewControllers/HomeScreenViewController.swift** and add an IBOutlet for the auto-record button:

```
@IBOutlet weak var autoRecordButton: UIButton!
```

Before you forget, switch back to **Main.storyboard** and connect the button to this outlet.

Create a new group under **CircuitRacer** and name it **ScreenRecording**. In it, create a new **Swift File** and name it **HomeScreenViewController+ScreenRecording.swift**.

Replace the contents of the new file with the following:

```
extension HomeScreenViewController: ScreenRecordingAvailable {

  override func viewWillAppear(_ animated: Bool) {
    super.viewWillAppear(animated)
    autoRecordButton.isHidden = !screenRecordingAvailable
  }
}
```

This code simply hides the `autoRecordButton` when screen recording isn't available. Of course, you'll need to connect the `autoRecordButton` to the new `IBOutlet` within the storyboard before that can happen.

Build and run your game again.

> **Note:** To see this working, you'll need to run the program on an older device — any device older than the iPhone 5s will do, since ReplayKit is not supported on those devices. Or you can temporarily modify the `screenRecordingAvailable` getter in **AutoRecordProtocol.swift** to test it. When you do, you'll notice the auto-record button is now hidden.

Awesome! Now you're going to add similar changes to the `GameScene`.

Under the **ScreenRecording** group, create a new **Swift File** named **GameScene+ScreenRecording.swift**.

Replace the contents of the file with the following code:

```
import Foundation
import UIKit
import ReplayKit

extension GameScene: ScreenRecordingAvailable {

}
```

You're making sure the `GameScene` conforms to the `ScreenRecordingAvailable` protocol. You'll add more methods to this momentarily.

Next, open **/CircuitRacer/Scenes/GameScene/GameScene.swift** and add the following code to `didMove(to:)`.

```
let recordIndicator = childNode(withName: "record_indicator")
    as! SKSpriteNode
recordIndicator.position = CGPoint(x: pauseButton.position.x
    - pauseButton.size.width/2,
  y: pauseButton.position.y + pauseButton.size.height/2)
```

The code first locates the `recordIndicator` sprite by name, and then positions the `recordIndicator` next to the `pauseButton`.

Finally, you need to change the **FailureScene** and **SuccessScene**. Since both `GameFailureState` and `GameSuccessState` extend `GameOverlayState`, you'll make the changes there.

Open **/CircuitRacer/Scenes/GameStates/GameOverlayState.swift** and add the following helper method:

```
func buttonWithIdentifier(identifier: ButtonIdentifier)
    -> ButtonNode? {
  return overlay.contentNode.childNode(
    withName: "//\(identifier.rawValue)") as? ButtonNode
}
```

The above method looks for a `ButtonNode` with the supplied identifier and returns it.

Next, add the following code to `didEnter(from:)`:

```
buttonWithIdentifier(identifier: .screenRecordingToggle)?
    .isHidden = !gameScene.screenRecordingAvailable
buttonWithIdentifier(identifier: .viewRecordedContent)?
    .isHidden = !gameScene.screenRecordingAvailable
```

This toggles the visibility of the buttons based on whether screen recording is available.

Build and run your game. Just like before, to see this working, you'll have to run the program on an older device or do some temporary testing modifications. When you do, you won't see the UI elements you created in the previous steps — which is a good thing.

Starting and stopping recordings

Since you're following an auto-record strategy, you need to store a `Bool` in order to know when the user has disabled or enabled automatic recording. You can use `UserDefaults` for this so that the value will be saved when the app is closed and opened again.

Open **AutoRecordProtocol.swift** and add the following code at the end:

```swift
// 1
let screenRecorderEnabledKey = "screenRecorderEnabledKey"

// 2
protocol AutoRecordProtocol: class {
  func toggleAutoRecord()
  var screenRecordingToggleEnabled: Bool { get }
}

// 3
extension AutoRecordProtocol {

  var screenRecordingToggleEnabled: Bool {
    return UserDefaults.standard.bool(
      forKey: screenRecorderEnabledKey)
  }

  func toggleAutoRecord() {
    let autoRecord = UserDefaults.standard.bool(
      forKey: screenRecorderEnabledKey)
    UserDefaults.standard.set(!autoRecord,
      forKey: screenRecorderEnabledKey)
  }
}
```

Here's what you're doing in the above code:

1. First, you define a `String` variable to use as a key to access the auto-record property in `UserDefaults`.

2. The `AutoRecordProtocol` defines a method to toggle auto-recording, as well as a computed property that tells you whether or not auto-recording is enabled.

3. You create a protocol extension to implement `toggleAutoRecord()` and the computed property.

Open **UIViewController+AutoRecord.swift** and conform to the `AutoRecordProtocol` by modifying the `extension` declaration:

```swift
extension UIViewController: AutoRecordProtocol {
```

Now, when the user selects the auto-record button, you'll call `toggleAutoRecord()`. To do this, add the following line of code to the end of `toggleScreenRecording(_:)`:

```swift
toggleAutoRecord()
```

By default, auto-record should be enabled, so you'll need to set the default value in `UserDefaults`.

Open **AppDelegate.swift** and add the following line to
`application(_:didFinishLaunchingWithOptions:)`, just before the `return`
statement:

```
UserDefaults.standard.register(
  defaults: [screenRecorderEnabledKey : true])
```

Before you build and run your game, you need to set the default `isSelected` state for
the auto-record button.

Open **HomeScreenViewController+ScreenRecording.swift** and add the following line
to `viewWillAppear(_:)`:

```
autoRecordButton.isSelected = screenRecordingToggleEnabled
```

Build and run your game; notice how the auto-record button is selected by default. Also,
if you turn off auto-recording, and then kill the app and start it again, the auto-record
button will remain off, thus remembering its selected state.

With that in place, open **GameScene+ScreenRecording.swift** and conform to the
`AutoRecordProtocol`:

```
extension GameScene: AutoRecordProtocol,
  ScreenRecordingAvailable {
```

Now, add the following method to the extension:

```
func startScreenRecording() {
  // 1
  guard screenRecordingToggleEnabled
    && screenRecordingAvailable else { return }

  // 2
  let sharedRecorder = RPScreenRecorder.shared()

  sharedRecorder.delegate = self
```

```
    // 3
    sharedRecorder.startRecording { error in
      if let error = error {
        self.showScreenRecordingAlert(message:
          error.localizedDescription)
      }
    }
  }
```

Note: The code you just added will generate Xcode compile errors. Don't worry — you'll fix those next.

As the name suggests, the new method will start the recording process. Here's a brief explanation of how it works:

1. The method first checks to see if screen recording is available and enabled.

2. Next, it gets access to the `RPScreenRecorder` singleton and sets the `delegate`.

3. Finally, the method calls the `startRecording(handler:)` method of the `RPScreenRecorder`. This method will ask the user for permission to record gameplay. If the user doesn't give the required permission, or if there's an issue with recording, it calls the error block.

It's time to fix those Xcode errors.

Add the following helper method to the class:

```
func showScreenRecordingAlert(message: String) {
  isPaused = true

  let alertController = UIAlertController(title: nil,
    message: message, preferredStyle: .alert)

  let alertAction = UIAlertAction(title: "OK", style: .default)
    { _ in
      self.isPaused = false
    }
  alertController.addAction(alertAction)

  DispatchQueue.main.async {
    self.view?.window?.rootViewController?
      .present(alertController, animated: false,
        completion: nil)
  }
}
```

The new helper method simply pauses the game and displays a message using a UIAlertController.

Next, you need to conform to the RPScreenRecorderDelegate protocol. To do so, add the following extension to the same file:

```
extension GameScene: RPScreenRecorderDelegate {
  func screenRecorder(_ screenRecorder: RPScreenRecorder,
      didStopRecordingWithError error: Error,
      previewViewController: RPPreviewViewController?) {
    self.previewViewController = previewViewController
  }
}
```

ReplayKit will call screenRecorder(_:didStopRecordingWithError:previewViewController:) if recording was stopped without you explicitly telling it to stop — for example, if the user declines to allow recording. Notice that it has an optional argument of type RPPreviewViewController. This represents the view controller that has the ability to preview, trim and share the recording.

Now to fix those pesky compile errors. Open **GameScene.swift** and add the following variable to the GameScene class:

```
var previewViewController: RPPreviewViewController?
```

At this point, build, **but do not run**, the project. You won't have any compile errors.

Since you have a method to start recording, it's time to add a method to stop it. Open **GameScene+ScreenRecording.swift** and add the following method to it:

```
func stopScreenRecording(with
    @escaping completionHandler: ((Void) -> Void)) {
  // 1
  let sharedRecorder = RPScreenRecorder.shared()

  // 2
  sharedRecorder.stopRecording {
      (previewViewController, error) in
    if let error = error {
      // 3
      self.showScreenRecordingAlert(
        message: error.localizedDescription)
      return
    }

    if let previewViewController = previewViewController {
      // 4
      previewViewController.previewControllerDelegate = self
```

```
        self.previewViewController = previewViewController
    }
    // 5
    completionHandler()
  }
}
```

> **Note:** Just like before, you'll have compile errors, but you'll fix those momentarily.

Here's the method breakdown:

1. First, you get a reference to the `RPScreenRecoder` singleton.

2. Then, you call the `stopRecording(handler:)` method of `RPScreenRecoder`.

3. In case of an error, the method displays it onscreen using the `showScreenRecordingAlert` helper method.

4. If a valid instance of `RPPreviewViewController` is present, the method stores it for later use. This is where you will normally get a reference to the preview view controller.

5. Finally, you call the completion handler.

Next, you need to implement the `RPPreviewViewControllerDelegate`. To do so, add the following extension to the same file:

```
extension GameScene: RPPreviewViewControllerDelegate {
  func previewController(
      _ previewController: RPPreviewViewController,
      didFinishWithActivityTypes activityTypes: Set<String>) {
    previewViewController?.dismiss(
      animated: true, completion: nil)
    SKTAudio.sharedInstance().resumeBackgroundMusic()
  }
}
```

ReplayKit will call `previewController(_:didFinishWithActivityTypes:)` when the user has completed interacting with the preview controller. All you're doing here is dismissing the view controller and resuming background music — and fixing the compile error!

Next, add the following three helper methods after `stopScreenRecording(with:)`:

```
func discardRecording() {
  RPScreenRecorder.shared().discardRecording {
    self.previewViewController = nil
```

```
    }
  }

  func stopAndDiscardRecording() {
    let sharedRecorder = RPScreenRecorder.shared()
    if sharedRecorder.isRecording {
      sharedRecorder.stopRecording {
          (previewViewController, error) in
        self.discardRecording()
      }
    } else {
      discardRecording()
    }
  }

  func displayRecordedContent() {
    guard let previewViewController = previewViewController else {
      fatalError("The user requested playback, but a valid preview
controller does not exist.")
    }
    guard let rootViewController =
      view?.window?.rootViewController else {
        fatalError("The scene must be contained in a window with a
root view controller.")
      }

    previewViewController.modalPresentationStyle = .fullScreen

    SKTAudio.sharedInstance().pauseBackgroundMusic()
    rootViewController.present(previewViewController,
      animated: true, completion:nil)
  }
```

discardRecording() discards the recorded video. You should call this method once you no longer need the recorded video. stopAndDiscardRecording will stop any in-progress recording if needed and then discard it.

displayRecordedContent() displays the RPPreviewViewController instance.

Phew! That was a lot of code. But don't worry, you're done with the bulk of the code you need to set up recording. All you need to do now is call these methods in the appropriate places.

Open **GameScene.swift** and after didMove(to:), add this method:

```
  func showOrHideRecordingIndicator() {
    let recordIndicator = childNode(withName: "record_indicator")
      as! SKSpriteNode
    recordIndicator.isHidden =
      !screenRecordingToggleEnabled || !screenRecordingAvailable
  }
```

And add the following to the end of `didMove(to:)`:

```
showOrHideRecordingIndicator()
startScreenRecording()
```

This will hide or show the `recordIndicator` depending on if recording is enabled, and attempt to start screen recording when gameplay starts.

Next, open **GameOverlayState.swift** and replace `didEnter(from:)` with the following:

```
override func didEnter(from
    previousState: GKState?) {
  super.didEnter(withPreviousState: previousState)
  gameScene.isPaused = true
  gameScene.overlay = overlay

  // 1
  if self is GameSuccessState || self is GameFailureState {
    // 2
    if let autoRecordToggleButton = buttonWithIdentifier(
        identifier: .screenRecordingToggle) {
      autoRecordToggleButton.isHidden =
        !gameScene.screenRecordingAvailable
      autoRecordToggleButton.isSelected =
        gameScene.screenRecordingToggleEnabled
    }

    if let viewRecordedContentButton =
        buttonWithIdentifier(identifier: .viewRecordedContent) {
      // 3
      viewRecordedContentButton.isHidden = true

      // 4
      gameScene.stopScreenRecording {
        // 5
        if self.gameScene.levelType == .easy {
          viewRecordedContentButton.texture =
            SKTexture(imageNamed: "level_1_preview_frame")
        } else if self.gameScene.levelType == .medium {
          viewRecordedContentButton.texture =
            SKTexture(imageNamed: "level_2_preview_frame")
        } else {
          viewRecordedContentButton.texture =
            SKTexture(imageNamed: "level_3_preview_frame")
        }
        // 6
        let recordingEnabledAndPreviewAvailable =
          self.gameScene.screenRecordingToggleEnabled
          && self.gameScene.previewViewController != nil
        viewRecordedContentButton.isHidden =
          !recordingEnabledAndPreviewAvailable
      }
```

```
      }
    }
  }
```

The best way to go over this code is to break it down into smaller pieces:

1. First, you check to see if the overlay is of type `GameSuccessState` or `GameFailureState`.

2. Then, you set the `isSelected` and `isHidden` states for the auto-record button.

3. Next, you hide the `viewRecordedContentButton` before attempting to stop the screen recording.

4. Then, you call the `stopScreenRecording` method of `GameScene`.

5. This step updates the texture of `viewRecordedContentButton` depending on the level being played.

6. Finally, if recording is enabled and the preview view controller is available, you set the `isHidden` property of `viewRecordedContentButton`.

Build and run your game on a physical device. Now, recording will start and stop when the game starts and ends.

Of course, you can't preview the recording yet, because you haven't written the code to do so. You'll do that next.

> **Note:** At the time of writing, ReplayKit doesn't work with the simulator; you must run all of your tests on an actual device.

Previewing and sharing recordings

You already have everything in place to preview the recording, so this section will be a breeze — I promise. :]

Open **GameScene+Buttons.swift** and add the following line to the `viewRecordedContent` switch case:

```
displayRecordedContent()
```

This line of code displays the `RPPreviewViewController` when the user taps the preview recording button.

While you're at it, add the following to the `screenRecordingToggle` switch case:

```
toggleAutoRecord()
button.isSelected = screenRecordingToggleEnabled
```

Now the auto-record button in the Success/Failure scenes can toggle auto-recording.

Finally, modify the `cancel` and `replay` cases to be:

```
case .cancel:
  stopAndDiscardRecording()
  gameSceneDelegate?.didSelectCancelButton(gameScene: self)
case .replay:
  discardRecording()
  stateMachine.enter(GameActiveState.self)
  showOrHideRecordingIndicator()
  startScreenRecording()
```

This way, you clean up any previous recording:

• When the player quits to the home screen (`cancel`), a recording may currently be in progress, so call `stopAndDiscardRecording()`.

• When the player replays a level after completing it, simply call `discardRecording()`.

You don't have to worry about in-progress recordings here since the player can only replay a level after completing it and any recording has already been stopped.

Build and run your game. When you finish playing, tap the preview recording button. This will pop open the `RPPreviewViewController`, as shown below:

You can use the scrubber on the bottom to trim the recording, and you can use the share button in the top-right to share the video with your friends.

Where to go from here?

As you've learned, adding ReplayKit is quite easy and only requires working with two classes: RPScreenRecorder and RPPreviewViewController.

To summarize, here's a quick round-up of the steps you need to follow to integrate ReplayKit:

1. Create a strategy to start and stop recording.

2. Modify your game's user interface to fit the recording strategy.

3. Check if screen recording is available

4. Start and stop recording using ReplayKit's APIs.

5. Preview and share the recording.

Armed with all of this knowledge, you can add ReplayKit to your own games.

Challenges

You're off the hook for this one; this chapter has no challenges. w00t! :]

Section VII: Bonus Section

In this bonus section, you'll learn how to properly request game assets from a professional artist, which includes where to find one and how to hire one!

Want to create your own 2D assets? No problem. This bonus chapter also includes step-by-step instructions for recreating the main character of Cat Nap.

Chapter 24: 2D Art for Programmers

Chapter 24: 2D Art for Programmers

By Mike Berg

In this book, you've created some great mini-games, but they've all used pre-made art. You may wonder how you can get art like that in your own games — and that's what this chapter is all about!

These days, to succeed in the App Store, your game not only needs to be fun and innovative; it needs to look attractive. This is a problem for many aspiring game developers — because although you may be great at programming and game design, you might not be so great at making your game look the way it does in your daydreams. There's a reason many games feature doodle or stick man art!

The good news is that you have two solid options as a game developer: You can either hire an artist to help out, or you can make the art yourself. After all, making art is a skill you can practice and improve, just like any other skill.

In this chapter, I'll first help you decide whether you'd prefer to hire a game artist or make your own art. In the event you choose to do it yourself, I'll show you how to create cartoon artwork for your video game in a style that's similar to the art you've used in this book:

I'll also provide tips for how you can continue to develop your skills as a game artist. By the end of this chapter, you'll have a solid starting point and a map for making your games look as great as they play!

Choose your path: Hire or DIY?

When deciding how to acquire art for your game, you have two basic choices: You can hire an artist or make the art yourself.

Hire an artist

There are advantages to hiring an artist:

- **Work with a pro.** If you hire an artist, you can get someone who's already great at her craft, and likely has been practicing for years. She can focus on what she's good at, leaving you free to focus on your own specialty — which is likely programming!

- **Choose your style.** Different artists have different styles — and your game might benefit from a certain type of style. By hiring an artist, you can look around and find someone whose style is the perfect fit for your game.

- **Rapid development.** If you have to make the art as well as program the game, you've just doubled your development time. Obviously, splitting up the work can save a lot of time, letting you get your game to market faster.

- **Collaboration.** Sometimes working with an artist can help you improve your game, as you share ideas and feed off each other's energy and passion. Think of the best games you've seen — I bet most of them were made by a team of at least two!

Think this option is for you? If so, feel free to skip ahead to "How to find and hire an artist". But first, you may want to consider your other option...

Do it yourself

Doing it yourself has advantages, as well:

- **Save money.** Sadly, most artists won't be willing to make art for your game out of the kindness of their hearts or for promises of future money — they'll want cold, hard cash. And often, that's the very thing that indie game developers lack. If saving money is on your mind, doing it yourself might be the only option.

- **Build skills.** Many indie developers find the process of making a game exciting, and want to learn the skills involved in every step. If this sounds like you, maybe you want to make art simply for the experience and skills you'll pick up along the way.

- **Lack of dependencies.** Working with an artist requires considering someone else's schedule. If you need a piece of art right away, you'll need to wait until the artist is available to work on it. If you make the art yourself, or at least know enough basics to make some placeholders, you can keep moving at the rapid speed that game development often entails.

- **Glory and honor.** The final benefit of doing it yourself is the pure bragging rights you'll earn. "See that game? Yeah, I programmed it *and* made all the art myself. Booyah." Just be prepared for a long development cycle! :]

Think this option is for you? If so, you can skip ahead to "Getting started".

How to find and hire an artist

Many game developers struggle with finding an artist. Here are some tips to get you in touch with a suitable artist as quickly as possible.

Conferences and meet-ups

As with looking for work, one of the best ways to find an artist is through networking: You meet one in person at an event in your field, or have one recommended to you by a friend or colleague. How to network? In a nutshell, get yourself out to conferences, local meet-ups and user groups.

I can recommend these conferences:

- **Game Developers Conference (GDC):** http://www.gdconf.com/
- **Apple's Worldwide Developers Conference (WWDC):** https://developer.apple.com/wwdc/
- **Unite:** https://unite.unity.com/
- **IndieCade:** http://www.indiecade.com/
- **RWDevCon:** https://www.rwdevcon.com/

As for meet-up groups, search **meetup.com** for your local area. The best meet-ups are game developer, artist, or iOS hangouts. You can also check game developer forums like https://forums.tigsource.com/ or http://www.gamedev.net/ to see if there are any local meet-ups or game jams in your area.

Twitter

Many game developers hang out on Twitter. While you won't necessarily get to know someone personally on Twitter, it's a great way to expand your list of developer contacts around the world, and connect with people who you may eventually meet at a conference or event.

Be an active Twitter user and get to know the work of those you follow and those who follow you. The larger your network of developers, the easier it will be for you to find someone with the skills you need when the time comes.

Search for portfolios

Do a web search for portfolios of the style you require: "pixel art portfolio" or "fantasy cartoon art portfolio". You know what you're looking for and you'll quickly see the range of quality available. This will help you make a choice even if you'd rather go with a personal recommendation.

Here are some additional online resources for portfolios:

- A lot of artists post their work on **Deviant Art** — it's often a great way to find up-and-coming artists: http://www.deviantart.com/

- If you're into pixel art, look no further than **Pixel Joint**, a community of pixel artists who regularly post their work and portfolios: http://www.pixeljoint.com/

- **3D Total** has a terrific gallery that's organized into categories like Character, Sci-Fi, Fantasy and Cartoon. The site also has very active forums: http://www.3dtotal.com/galleries/Scenes

- The **Polycount** forum has portfolios specific to game art: http://www.polycount.com/forum/

- **Cartrdge** is an excellent game-specific portfolio site: https://cartrdge.com

Call for applications

Post your project needs on your website and on job boards. Here are a few sites and boards where you can post jobs:

- **Concept Art** has a job board with a lot of game illustrators: http://www.conceptart.org/forums/

- **Gamasutra** has a job board: http://jobs.gamasutra.com/

- **3D Total, Polycount, Pixel Joint, GameDev.net** and **TIGSource**, all mentioned above, also have job boards.

Of the applications you receive, discard those without good portfolios, regardless of their experience. A portfolio should demonstrate the artist's ability to do the job in the style you want it done.

Does this really work?

Yes! As an example, Ray and I first got to know each other via Twitter. He looked at my online portfolio a few times, so he was familiar with my work. A few years ago, we met in person at a conference. Over the years, we stayed in touch, and that's how I came to work on this book!

The moral of the story is this: Get to know artists you admire, preferably in person, and make connections — you never know when you might want to work together on a project!

Paying your artist

As I mentioned earlier in this chapter, most artists aren't willing to work for free — you'll need to find some way to compensate them for their time and effort. This section will cover what to expect, as well as my personal recommendations.

Revenue share contracts

With a revenue share contract, you promise an artist a percentage of the income from your game, but little or no money up front.

These types of contracts are often appealing to indie game developers with little money to spend, but it's very hard to find an experienced artist who is willing to take this kind of deal. Many an artist has been burned by promises of a revenue share that fails to deliver in the end!

These types of deals only seem to work if you have a strong, preexisting relationship with the artist. For example, if your good friend or significant other is an artist, you might be in business. Also, the artist will probably need to be passionate about the project for it to work out — otherwise, she might lose motivation and interest.

If you don't have an artist on hand who trusts you and believes in your project, you'll probably have to pay an artist up front. This can be a good thing — if your game does well, you'll get to keep the profits for yourself!

Fixed-quote contracts vs. hourly contracts

If you're going to pay the artist up front, you have a choice: You can either pay her a fixed amount, or you can pay her by the hour.

The principal advantage of a fixed-quote contract is that you know how much you're going to spend.

However, I personally recommend against fixed-quote contracts. Game dev projects are constantly evolving; at the beginning of a project, it's impossible to know how much art the project will eventually require. As soon as the artist's time goes over what was expected for the fixed quote because of evolving to-do lists, her interest, motivation and passion for the project are likely to drop like a stone.

Here's what works for my clients and me. My own method is to provide an **estimate** based on the initial asset request list. I will then send an invoice for a percentage of that estimate (usually 50%, or a smaller percentage if the project is larger), to be paid up front.

As I work on the project, I keep very detailed track of my time and provide the client with **regular updates** that show how I've used my time. I send an **interim invoice** every time the total owing reaches a certain agreed-upon amount. For example, the client and I might have an agreement that I send an interim invoice for every $2,000 of work.

This method gives both the client and the artist the freedom to change the to-do list on the fly, which is always necessary while a game is in development. Potential disagreements over cost-value can be headed off before they develop. The client knows exactly what she's getting for her money, and the artist stays motivated and involved in the process.

Price expectations

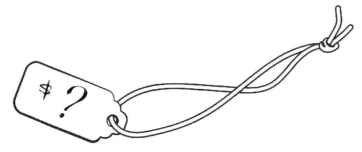

People often ask me, "How much do artists charge to make art for a game?" If you're hiring an experienced artist, you can expect to pay anywhere from $30-$90 per hour. At the time of writing, my own rate is $70 per hour.

Generally, the more skilled the artist, the more you can expect to pay. You might find an artist who is willing to take less, but expect her experience and the overall result to be commensurate. "You get what you pay for" is an old adage for a reason.

There's also great value in finding an artist with **experience making video game art** — iOS-specific experience is especially helpful. There are many ways an artist can make your life as a developer easier (or harder!), and her level of game development experience is a large factor.

For example, an artist who knows about object coordinates, anchor points, texture atlases and overdraw will be able to provide you with graphic files that are ready to use in your tools of choice, requiring as little extra processing on your end as possible.

Knowledge of games and how they work will help an artist create assets that are efficient and extensible, for long-term reuse and adaptability in the event of future updates. Occasionally, changes to one art asset can require updates to several others; good game artists will know how to keep these sorts of snowball effects to a minimum.

That's it for my advice when it comes to hiring an artist. If this is the route you've decided to take, stop reading here and go find yourself an awesome artist.

But if you're eager to learn how to make art yourself, read on!

Getting started

The rest of this chapter will show you how to create a cat sprite in a style similar to that of the sprites you've used in your mini-games throughout this book:

You'll create the artwork in Adobe Illustrator using vector shapes. This will let you use the artwork at any resolution or size without degrading the quality of the image.

If you don't already have access to Adobe Illustrator, you can download a free trial here: https://creative.adobe.com/products/download/illustrator

This will install an interface to Adobe's Creative Cloud, which lets you try many different Adobe products for a short period of time.

Once you have Illustrator installed and ready to go, pull out a pencil and paper and get ready to sketch.

Begin with a sketch

You're first going to make a rough sketch to give yourself a general idea of the shape of the art, so you can trace it in Illustrator later.

The type of paper you use for this kind of sketch doesn't matter — use whatever you have on hand, as long as it's clear of other markings. To draw, use a pencil.

The cat you'll be sketching is made up of four main shapes: **head**, **body**, **front legs** and **tail**. Here's a quick preview of the four main shapes:

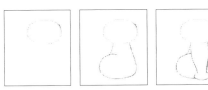

Now follow the instructions below to draw the cat, consulting the images as you go.

The shapes shown here are just guides; if you're comfortable with adapting as you go, please put your own spin on them!

1. First, draw an oval for the head.

2. Then draw the pear-shaped bottom of the body a bit larger than the head, with the upper body/neck stretching up to meet the head.

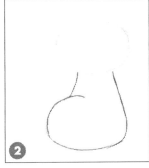

3. Near the head and close to the edges of the body, draw two smooth lines that converge a bit at the bottom for the legs.

4. At the bottom of the legs, add an open half-circle for the tops of the feet.

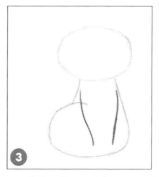 

5. For the bottoms of the feet, add an arc that's a bit flatter than the tops of the feet.

6. Define the shape of the tail, starting with the leftmost curve. Add a second curve to give it thickness. Cartoon tails can be a lot thicker than real tails!

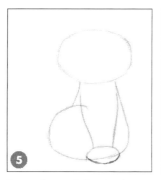 

7. Now that you have the cat's basic shape, add some detail. Cartoon cats can have pointy cheeks. Don't ask why!

8. Look at each arc of the ear separately. Start near the middle of the head and draw an arc slightly up, but mostly out. Then curve down and slightly inward to finish.

9. Round out the sides a bit, where the ears meet the head, and add a bit of height to the top of the head.

10. Think of the eyes as egg shapes, tilted inward a bit. The nose is a flat oval.

11. Add a short, vertical line under the nose with a wide "W" shape underneath for the mouth. A wide arc over the nose defines the cat's snout.

12. Add large arcs for the irises, some straight whiskers pointing slightly upward, and don't forget those eyelashes for extra loveability.

13. Moving on to the legs, draw a straight line down the middle, not quite as high as the outer lines for the legs.

14. Cut a small wide triangle out of the bottom center of the feet to make them point slightly outward. Add two short lines on each foot to make toes.

15. Smooth out the arc for the back a bit. Add a line for the top of the back leg.

16. One at a time, add curved points to make up the fur at the end of the tail. Make them varied in size, with the middle one the biggest.

17. Add a curve near the end of the tail, and curves over the top edge of each paw. These will define areas with white fur.

18. **Optional**: Erase unnecessary lines. You only need to do this if your drawing is very "sketchy" (which is OK!) and it's hard to see the final lines, which are the ones you'll be going over in Illustrator.

Getting the sketch into Illustrator

Don't worry if you don't have a scanner — the camera on your iPhone or iPad works just as well for this purpose. Lay your sketch flat in a well-lit area and hold your iPhone directly over it. Try to get the angle as square as possible. Line up the edges of your page with the edges of the screen to help with this.

Email yourself the photo, using the **Large** setting when asked how you want to resize the image. Save the image to your computer.

Open Illustrator and select **File > New...** (shortcut: **Command-N**) to create a new document named **cat**. Choose **Devices** (or Mobile, depending on your version of Illustrator) from the **Profile** drop-down, and choose **iPhone 5/5s** from the **Size** drop-down. This will give you an image that is 640x1136 pixels, which is the resolution of an iPhone 5 screen. Click **OK**.

> **Note:** If you have an older version of Illustrator, you won't see the **iPhone 5/5s** option in the **Size** drop-down. Just set the pixel dimensions manually; it works out to be the same thing.

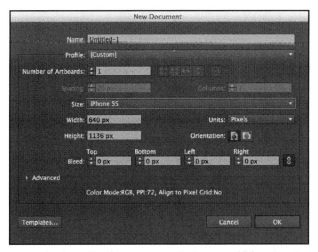

Select **File > Place...** and select the file you emailed yourself for the sketch. Leave the checkbox options as they are by default, with only **Link** selected. Click **Place** to add your sketch to the Illustrator file.

You'll see the "Place" cursor, along with an icon of your image.

 1/1

Click and **drag** to draw a box that mostly fills the canvas. This sets the size and position of your placed file.

Note: Again, older versions of Illustrator may look a little different here.

Many of the controls you'll use to modify your artwork are organized into what Illustrator calls **palettes**. You can find them on the right side of the screen. It's a good idea to make sure the ones you'll use most often are visible.

Select **Window > Workspace > Essentials**. If all you see are buttons, click the tiny **Expand Panels** button at the top right of each panel:

You'll see an arrangement of palettes that looks something like this — don't worry if it's not exactly the same:

In the **Layers palette** (select **Window > Layers** if you don't see it), click the **empty square next to the "eye" icon** on the layer for the cat. This will lock the layer, preventing you from selecting it or moving it accidentally.

Now, click the **Create New Layer** button to add a layer; you'll use the new layer to hold your vector tracing.

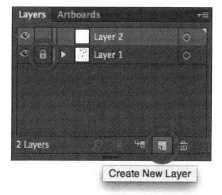

Tracing the sketch with vector lines

Before you begin tracing the sketch, you should set your default colors.

At the bottom of the **Tools palette**, there are swatches for the current fill color (the solid box) and the stroke color (the box with the thick outline). Illustrator will use these fill and stroke colors for any object you create.

Press **D** to set the default colors for stroke and fill: white fill, black stroke. Click the **fill** swatch, which is a white square:

Press the **forward slash key** (/) to clear the fill swatch and make it transparent — a red line will appear through the swatch. Now the Pen tool will draw black lines with no fill, which is ideal for creating outlines.

Next, select the **Pen tool** (shortcut: **P**). With the Pen tool, every click creates an anchor point for the curve, and dragging lets you define the direction and "strength" of the curve for that point. You may be familiar with the concept of a Bézier curve from programming — that is what you can create with this tool!

Click to draw straight lines with sharp corners; click-and-drag to create curves. A curved point has "handles" that define the direction and strength of the curve. Each handle is a dot at the end of the line coming out of the point:

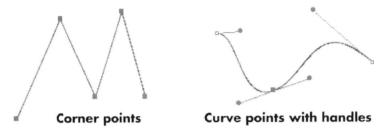

Corner points   **Curve points with handles**

Follow the instructions below to use the Pen tool to trace the ears of the cat, which will be simple 3-point curves. Your first point will be a curve, so start by clicking and dragging, as shown below. And yes, you can edit a line after you've drawn it — more on that soon.

1. Click at the start of the line and drag toward the upper-left.

2. Click at the tip of the ear and drag out shorter handles, roughly perpendicular to the first set of handles.

3. Click at the end of the line and drag a handle out until the line looks right.

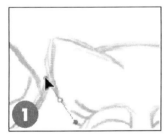 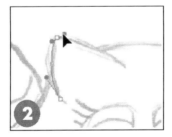 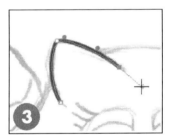

Hold the **Command key** and click anywhere else on the canvas to finish creating that line. Use the **Selection tool** (shortcut: **V**) and click on the line you just created:

At the top of the screen, increase the stroke width to something more substantial, such as 4px.

Continue creating paths for the top of the head and the other ear. The Pen tool remembers the settings for the last line you selected, so new lines will have the same stroke thickness.

Great work! It can take some time to get used to the Pen tool, but with a little practice, you'll create your lines with minimal fuss.

Editing a path

Your line won't always look exactly the way you want it to on the first try, and that's OK! It's easy to adjust the shape of a line.

To change a line after you've created it, use the **Direct Selection tool** (shortcut: **A**) to click on the line:

This will highlight the points. Click on a single point to show its handles. Drag the point to move it, or drag the handles to adjust the angle and strength of the curve.

> **Note:** Illustrator has a feature called **Smart Guides**. If it's turned on, it will attempt to snap points, paths and even 90-degree angles automatically. It's often easier to edit your lines with Smart Guides turned off. Select **View > Smart Guides** (shortcut: **Command-U**) to toggle this feature.

Creating complex lines

Lines with a mix of curves and sharp corners, like the cat's pointy cheeks, require one extra step during their creation. Rather than creating curved lines and then editing each sharp corner afterward, you can create these corners while drawing the path. The key is to **Option-drag** a handle immediately after you create it. Try it yourself by following these instructions:

1. Click and drag the first point's handle downward.

2. Click and drag to create the second point.

3. With the Pen tool still active, **Option-drag** the handle so it points roughly toward the next corner.

  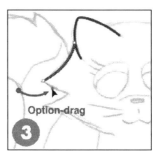

This method lets you create almost any shape of line with a single series of mouse gestures, all without having to change tools. Remember, once you've created a line, you can always refine its shape with the **Direct Selection tool**.

 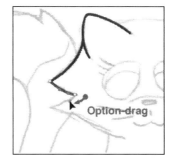

Use this method to create the rest of corners for this line, as shown here:

Rounding the ends of the lines

By now, you may have noticed that each line is squared off at the ends. This stands out and looks bad if your lines don't meet exactly. Rounding the ends can help make your lines more visually pleasing.

Press **Command-A** to select all. In the **Stroke palette** (select **Window > Stroke** if you don't see it), set the **Cap** and **Corner** buttons to **Round**. If you don't see the Cap and Corner buttons, click the palette menu button at the top right and select **Show Options**.

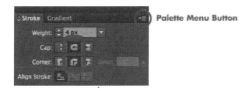

Finishing the outlines

Using the skills you've learned so far, create the rest of the outlines for the cat, until all of your lines are vector paths.

> **Note:** Press **Command-S** to save. If you want to have a look at the lines I've created at this point, go to the resources for this chapter and open **final/cat-01-outlines.ai**.

Custom stroke widths

Now that all of your lines are done, your drawing looks much cleaner! You're well on your way to creating beautiful, game-ready art. It does look a little mechanical, though, since all the lines are exactly the same width.

You can use the **Width tool** (shortcut: **Shift-W**) to give your art a more hand-drawn look.

> **Note:** The Width tool is only available in Illustrator CS5 and up.

1. With the **Width tool**, **hover** your cursor over the tip of the ear. The tool shows a little white circle that indicates it will add a new width point here.

2. **Click and drag** to make the line slightly wider at that point.

3. Illustrator makes the line thicker, with a smooth transition to the end points.

Create a default width profile for illustration

That was easy, but there's a way to speed this up even further!

Use the **Selection tool** (**V**) to click on the line you just edited. At the top of the screen, you'll see some options for the current path, including a drop-down that shows the **Width Profile** you just created.

Click this drop-down and click **Add to Profiles**:

Name it **Thick in the middle**. This creates a reusable width profile that you can apply to any path. Press **Command-A** to select all the paths in your drawing, and then select your new profile from the **Width Profiles** drop-down.

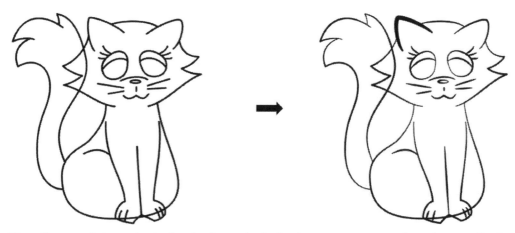

The effect is subtle, so look closely if you don't think you see it. Now those lines really do look more like they were hand-drawn. And originally, they were!

Notice how in the picture above, the path on the left ear (the first one you made) is thicker than the others. If this happened to you, select the thicker path with the **Selection tool (V)** and change its stroke width back to **4px** in the bar at the top of the screen:

Using other width profiles for different line shapes

In certain places, your stroke widths may still not look exactly as you'd like. Select all of the eyelashes by **Shift-clicking** them with the **Selection tool**. Click the **Width Profile** pop-up and select the triangular profile:

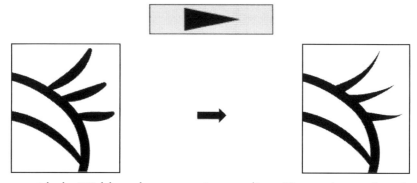

Experiment with the Width tool to customize your lines. Keep going until you're happy with how they look.

The Width tool is powerful, with several features not covered here. For a more detailed look, watch this video: https://helpx.adobe.com/illustrator/atv/cs5-tutorials/using-variablewidth-strokes.html

> **Note:** Press **Command-S** to save your file. My version of the file at this point is in the **final** folder and is called **cat-02-width-tool.ai**.

Coloring your artwork

After you've finished tweaking the widths of your lines, add some color. Start by using the **Selection tool (V)** to select the outline of the head:

Select **Edit > Copy** (shortcut: **Command-C**), then **Edit > Paste in Back** (shortcut: **Command-B**) to create a copy of the paths in exactly the same position, layered behind the current paths. This will be the starting point for creating a colored shape that fits precisely behind the lines that already exist.

Press **Shift-X** to reverse the fill and stroke colors. Your fill was transparent before, so now your strokes are transparent and your fills are black. It looks a little strange, but you're about to fix that:

You need to edit these points, but since they're behind and completely covered by the outline paths, it's impossible to be sure you're editing the points for the fill and not the paths for the stroke.

To solve this, select **Object > Group** (shortcut: **Command-G**) to group the new set of paths, and double-click the group to enter **Isolation Mode**. This lets you work on the contents of the group without any other objects getting in the way.

In Isolation Mode, Illustrator has faded the rest of your art a bit, showing you that it can't be selected.

You need to join all these separate paths together to make one solid shape that you can color. Use the **Direct Selection tool (A)** to draw a marquee around the bottom two points to select them:

Select **Object > Path > Join** (shortcut: **Command-J**) to join the two points. This joins the left and right paths, creating a filled path that's almost the size of the cat's head, but still open at the top:

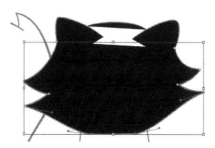

Use the **Direct Selection tool** (**A**) to select the point of the path just below the cat's left ear. **Shift-click** the left point of the curve that forms the top of the cat's head:

Press **Command-J** to join the points. Your cat's head should now be completely filled. The path is still open at the top right, under the ear, but that's OK. You're going to merge it with the ear shapes next.

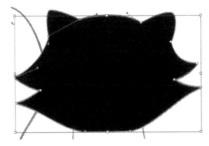

Using the Pathfinder to combine shapes

The **Pathfinder** is a very powerful set of tools that lets you combine multiple shapes in interesting ways. You'll start by using the simplest function, **Unite**, to combine all three color fills into a single shape.

Switch to the **Selection tool** (**V**) and **Shift-click** each of the ears to add them to the current selection. In the **Pathfinder palette** (select **Window > Pathfinder** if you don't see it), click the **Unite** button. This merges all three paths into a single shape.

With the fill shape selected, it's time to give it a better color. In the **Swatches palette** (select **Window > Swatches** if you don't see it), select a color for your cat:

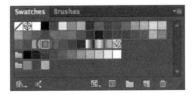

Note: If the stroke color changes instead of the fill, press **Command-Z** to undo, press **X** to make the fill color the active swatch, and then select your color again.

Double-click outside of your shape to exit Isolation Mode. You've finished your first filled shape!

Why have you colored the head separately? It's best to create a separate fill for each basic shape so that when you get to the shading stage, you can layer shading objects behind objects in front.

For example, you'll layer the shading for the body behind the shape of the legs. If the fill for the body and legs were the same object, it wouldn't be possible to layer them without doing some extra trimming of the shaded area — this will become clear shortly.

Use the same method to create filled shapes for the legs, body and tail. Remember the basic steps:

1. Use the **Selection tool (V)** to select the paths that create the outline of the area you're trying to fill.

2. Select **Edit > Copy (Command-C)**, then **Edit > Paste in Back (Command-B)** to create a copy of the paths in exactly the same position.

3. Press **Shift-X** to reverse the fill and stroke colors.

4. Select **Object > Group (Command-G)** to group the new set of paths.

5. Double-click the group to enter **Isolation Mode**.

6. As necessary, combine the paths with the **Direct Selection tool (A)** and **Command-J**, or via the **Unite** button in **Pathfinder**.

Once you're done, use the **Selection tool** (**V**) to select the lines and fill for the tail and send them to the back by pressing **Command-Shift-[**.

Note: Press **Command-S** to save. Refer to **cat-03-basic-fill.ai** in the **final** folder to start from here.

Coloring the eyes

Next, add some color to the eyes.

Select the outer, egg-shaped ovals for both eyes with the **Selection tool** (**V**). Copy the paths (**Command-C**) and paste behind (**Command-B**). Swap the stroke and fill colors (**Shift-X**) to create a filled path with no stroke. Click the white swatch in the **Swatches palette** to change the fill color to **white**.

1. With the **Selection tool** (**V**), click the top arc of the iris. Press **Command-C** to copy it, then **Command-B** to paste behind.

2. Press **Shift-X** to swap the fill and stroke colors.

3. Double-click the new black shape to enter **Isolation Mode.**

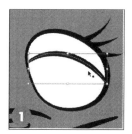 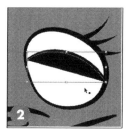 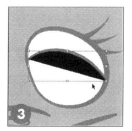

4. This shape isn't big enough for the iris. To make it the right shape, use the **Pen tool** (**P**) and click the end point of the path.

5. Then click once for each point shown here, covering the lower part of the eye with the new shape. Double-click outside the shape to leave Isolation Mode.

6. You need a duplicate of the white eye shape to use for the Pathfinder operation. Use the **Selection tool** (**V**) to click it. Press **Command-C** to copy and **Command-F** to paste in front.

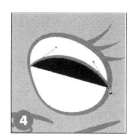 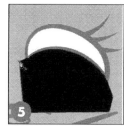 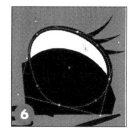

7. Still using the **Selection tool**, hold **Shift** and click the shape you just created for the iris.

8. In the **Pathfinder palette**, click the **Intersect** button.

9. The shapes are combined, leaving just the shape of the iris.

10. With the iris shape still selected, click a **green** color in the **Colors palette**.

11. Click on empty space on your document to deselect the iris shape. Click the **black swatch** in the **Swatches palette**. Then use the **Ellipse tool** (shortcut: **L**) to draw a black circle for the pupil.

12. Now you need a duplicate of the iris shape to use for the Pathfinder operation. Use the **Selection tool (V)** to select it. Press **Command-C** and then **Command-F** to create the duplicate.

 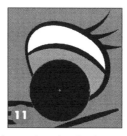 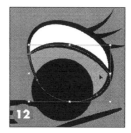

13. Hold **Shift** and click the pupil to select both shapes. In the Pathfinder palette, click the **Intersect** button.

14. You're left with the iris and pupil looking very nice.

15. Using the **Ellipse tool (L)**, draw a white circle to use for a highlight on the eye. Repeat this entire process for the other eye.

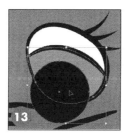  

16. Select the curves for the tops of the irises and change them to a dark green.

Note: Press **Command-S** to save. Refer to **cat-04-eyes.ai** in the **final** folder to start from here.

Coloring certain areas

You'll start adding extra color to your cat by making the end of the tail and the two front paws white.

You need a shape that's white with no stroke. Press **D** to set the default fill (white) and stroke (black). Make sure the stroke swatch is on top of the fill swatch, as shown here:

If it isn't, press **X** to switch them, bringing the stroke to the front. Press the **forward slash key** (/) to remove the stroke:

1. Using the **Pen tool**, draw a curved line across the tail, near the top. The curve should extend out past the edges of the tail, as shown. You'll trim it down later.

2. Continue the path around the end of the tail by clicking once for each point. Make sure you cover the end of the tail completely. The shape doesn't need to be closed — the Pathfinder tools work just as well on open paths.

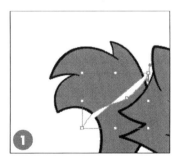
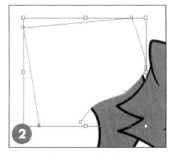

3. Use the **Selection tool** (V) to select the tail, press **Command-C** to copy it, then press **Command-F** to paste in front. You'll now use this copy of the tail shape with the Pathfinder to make the white path match the shape of the tail.

4. Hold the **Shift** key and click the white path so it's also selected. For the Pathfinder to work, it's important that *both the tail shape and the white shape you just created are selected*, that they are the *only shapes selected*, and that they are *overlapping*.

 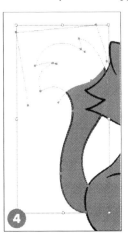

5. In the **Pathfinder** palette, click the **Intersect** button.

6. Illustrator trims away the parts of each shape that are *not* overlapping. What remains is a single shape for the white end of the tail.

A word about layers

I've spoken a bit about layers and the layering of objects. Here's a closer look at how this works.

Look at your **Layers palette**. Currently, there are two layers: one for your sketch, Layer 1, and one for your vector artwork, Layer 2. Click the disclosure triangle next to **Layer 2**:

This reveals all the **objects** that are within that layer:

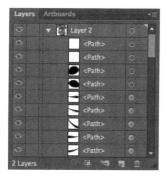

An object is a single path or shape. A single layer can hold any number of objects. As you can see, you've created a lot of objects in Layer 2 already! The Layers palette shows the objects in order of their **layering**. Objects at the top of the list appear onscreen *in front of* objects farther down the list.

Reordering object layers

You can change object layering by dragging an object's name up or down in the Layers palette, or you can use **Object > Arrange > Send Backward (Command-[)** or **Object > Arrange > Send Forward (Command-])**. From now on, when I refer to object layers, I mean the layering of objects *inside* Layer 2. You don't need to create new primary layers, or change the order of the two primary layers you have.

Getting back to your cat's tail, the white shape at the tip of the tail is currently sitting in front of the black outlines for the tail. You could press **Command-[** until it's behind the outlines, but that could get tedious in a document with many objects.

Instead, use the **Selection tool (V)** to select the white shape for the end of the tail, press **Command-X** to cut it, and then select **the object you want it to appear in front of** — in this case, the color fill shape for the entire tail — and press **Command-F** to paste in front. This is the fastest way to get an object *exactly* where you want it in the layer stack.

The white tip of the tail should now show up behind the stroke:

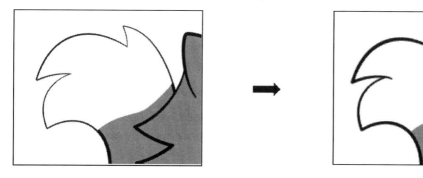

Follow the same steps to create a white fill for the front paws. As a reminder, here are the basic steps:

1. Use the **Pen tool (P)** to draw a shape that colors the area in the paws you want filled, overlapping the area outside the paws.

2. Use the **Selection tool (V)** to select the paws, press **Command-C** to copy them, then press **Command-F** to paste in front.

3. Hold the **Shift** key and click the white path so it's also selected.

4. In the Pathfinder palette, click the **Intersect** button.

5. Use the **Cut, select, paste in front** method, or use **Object > Arrange > Send Backward (Command-[)**, until the white shape is properly behind the black strokes, as you can see below:

The last piece to add is an oval around the cat's mouth and nose. Use the **Ellipse tool (L)** to create one:

To get the ellipse into the right place in the layer stack, use the paste-in-front technique to cut the white ellipse and paste it in front of the color fill for the head. This will place it behind all the strokes for the face.

> **Checkpoint!** Press **Command-S** to save. If you wish, you can start from here using the file **cat-05-tail-and-toes.ai** in the **final** folder.

A bit about shadow and light

Typically, in-game lighting comes from the top right. This is because many games have a general progression from left to right, so lighting from the top right highlights the hero's face as they progress.

With the light shining from the top right, shadows will fall on the lower-left areas of any given object:

To create shadows like this in Illustrator, you'll use almost the same Pathfinder technique you used to create the white areas for the tail and paws.

Start by using the **Selection tool (V)** to select the fill for the body. Then, follow these instructions:

1. Recall that two shapes are required for a Pathfinder operation. Press **Command-C** to copy the fill for the body. Then press **Command-F** *twice*.

2. Drag the currently selected shape (the topmost one) up and to the right a bit, shown here in black so it's easier to see. I also dragged the bottom-right resize handle up and to the left a bit to make it smaller.

3. Hold **Shift** and click the first copy you made of the body shape, so that they're both selected.

4. In the **Pathfinder** palette, click the **Subtract** button. Illustrator subtracts the front shape from the back shape.

5. What remains will work well for a shadow on the body. If you haven't already changed the color to black, click the **Fill** box in the toolbar on the left to bring it forward, then click the black swatch in the **Swatches palette**.

6. In the **Transparency palette** (select **Window > Transparency** if you don't see it), change the opacity to **30%**.

7. Remember to rearrange the layers. **Cut** the shadow shape, select the body fill shape, and then **paste in front (Command-F)**, as described earlier.

Use these steps to create shaded areas for the front legs, head and tail. Here are reminders of the steps to follow:

1. Select the area you want to shade with the **Selection tool (V)**.

2. Create two copies of the shape. Press **Command-C** to copy it, then press **Command-F** *twice*.

3. Move one of the copies up and to the right a bit, optionally resizing it.

4. **Shift-click** to select the original shape as well, and use **Pathfinder > Subtract** to create a new shadow area.

5. Set the color of the shadow area to **black** and set the transparency to **30%**.

Remember: Copy the base shape, paste twice, drag the top shape up and to the right and use the Pathfinder to subtract it from the first copy. Then, change the opacity and make sure it's layered correctly.

Extra shadow details for more depth

Extra shadows can help define some of the shapes in your art, providing a sense of depth even where there are no outlines. For example, in the image below, you can see shark-fin-like shapes used to show some fur sticking up in front of the ears, with the shaded area forming the inner ears themselves.

Create these by drawing a black path with the **Pen tool** (**P**) and then setting its transparency to **30%**. Here are the abbreviated steps:

1. Click and drag.

2. Click and drag.

3. Option-drag the handle.

 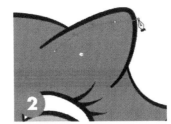 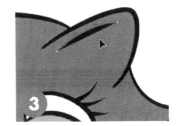

4. Click and drag.

5. Option-drag the handle.

6. Click and drag.

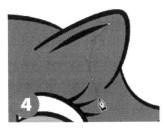  

7. Option-drag the handle.

8. Click once for a sharp corner with no handles.

9. Click and drag.

10. Option-drag the handle.

11. Click once on the first point to close the shape.

New set that shape to 30% transparency.

In the same way, add depth to the tufts of hair at the end of the tail. Imagine extending the inner line down further into the tail, then curving back up to the tip, and you have the shape for your tail shadows:

Save! Press **Command-S** to save your progress. A version of the file at this point is in the **final** folder and is called **cat-06-shaded.ai**.

Coloring the outlines

The final step is to color the outlines. Some game art will look great with black outlines, but usually, coloring the outlines brings out the color of the object and gives it even more depth.

Start by using the **Selection tool** (**V**) to select any one of the black outlines. In the menu bar, choose **Select > Same > Stroke Color**. This will select all of the black lines in the document.

Have a look at the swatches and make sure the stroke swatch is on top of the fill:

If it's not, click on it to bring it forward or press **X** to swap them. Click on a slightly darker version of your fill color in the **Swatches palette** to change your stroke color.

Some of your strokes can stay black (the nose) or be dark grey (the whiskers and mouth). Use the **Selection tool** (**V**) to select the strokes you want to change and then click the color in the **Swatches palette** that you want to use. This is mostly a matter of preference, so play around with the outlines until they look just the way you want.

You've finished your cat! Don't forget to save. Press **Command-S** to do so now.

> **Note:** A finished version of the Illustrator file is in the **final** folder as **cat-07-finished.ai.**

Exporting PNG files

In Illustrator, the **Artboard** refers to the dimensions of the document in which you are working. At the beginning of the chapter, you set the artboard to 640x1136 to match an iPhone 5 screen. If you were to export a PNG of the cat now, it would have a lot of unnecessary transparent space around the edges of the cat image.

Before you export the cat image, you need to shrink down the Artboard to match the size of the cat itself.

Select **Object > Artboards > Fit to Artwork Bounds** to make the Artboard match the size of the art.

That was easy! Select **File > Export > Export for Screens…**

Click the folder icon on the right side to choose a destination to save the files.

iOS games currently require three versions of your graphics to support all devices: non-Retina, Retina (2x), and iPhone 6 Plus (3x). You created your Illustrator document at Retina resolution for iPhone 5/5s (640x1136), so set up your export settings like this:

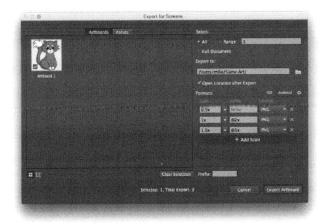

Congratulations! You've taken a blank piece of paper and turned it into a resolution-independent piece of game art, ready to use in your next project.

Challenges

Want to polish your artistic skills even more? Here are two more characters you can use as guides to practice the techniques you've learned in this chapter.

As always, if you get stuck, you can find the solutions in the resources for this chapter — but give it your best shot first!

Challenge 1: Squeak!

Your first challenge is to draw one of the simplest possible characters: a lowly mouse. The shape is nice and simple, so you can quickly practice going through the steps you've learned in this chapter, all on your own.

Challenge 2: Woof!

For a greater challenge, how about making a dog? This one involves more complicated shapes and more shadows to match.

If you've made both of these characters, a huge congratulations — you now have some solid tools on your tool belt to make excellent 2D game art!

Be sure to keep experimenting and most importantly, have fun. The key to developing your skills as an artist and a programmer is to practice, practice, practice.

If you'd like to share any of the artwork you create after following this chapter, we'd love to see it. Please stop by the book forums for show and tell!

Conclusion

We hope you enjoyed your 2D game-making adventure. If you worked through the entire book, you ended up with six complete games — built entirely from scratch using SpriteKit and Swift. Huzzah!

You now have all the knowledge it takes to make a hit game — so why not go for it?

Come up with a great idea, prototype a game, get people to play it, watch them for feedback and keep iterating and polishing your game based on all you have learned. Be sure to set aside time in your schedule to add juice to your game, and make sure you have killer art and sound effects, following the advice in the book.

We can't wait to see what you come up with! Be sure to stop by our forums and share your progress at www.raywenderlich.com/forums.

Want us to review your completed game? We have a monthly blog post where we review games written by fellow readers like you. If you'd like to be considered for this column, please visit this page after you release your game: www.raywenderlich.com/reviews

We have one final question for you: Did we succeed in our goal to write the best book on 2D game programming you've ever read? Please email us at ray@raywenderlich.com to let us know how we did — good or bad.

Thank you again for purchasing this book. Your continued support is what makes the tutorials, books, videos and other things we do at raywenderlich.com possible. We truly appreciate it.

Best of luck in all your game-making adventures,

— Caroline, Mike, Michael, Ali, Marin, Ray, Vinnie, Vicki, Chris and Tammy.

The *2D Apple Games by Tutorials* Team

Made in the USA
Middletown, DE
14 February 2017